Palgrave Studies in the History of Finance

The study of the history of financial institutions, markets, instruments and concepts is vital if we are to understand the role played by finance today. At the same time, the methodologies developed by finance academics can provide a new perspective for historical studies. Palgrave Studies in the History of Finance is a multi-disciplinary effort to emphasise the role played by finance in the past, and what lessons historical experiences have for us. It presents original research, in both authored monographs and edited collections, from historians, finance academics and economists, as well as financial practitioners.

Elise M. Dermineur · Matteo Pompermaier
Editors

Credit Networks in The Preindustrial World

A Social Network Analysis Approach

palgrave
macmillan

Editors
Elise M. Dermineur
Department of Economic History and International Relations
Stockholm University
Stockholm, Sweden

Matteo Pompermaier
Dipartimento di economia e management
Università degli studi di Brescia
Brescia, Italy

ISSN 2662-5164 ISSN 2662-5172 (electronic)
Palgrave Studies in the History of Finance
ISBN 978-3-031-67116-6 ISBN 978-3-031-67117-3 (eBook)
https://doi.org/10.1007/978-3-031-67117-3

Cover illustration: Alicia Llop

This Palgrave Macmillan imprint is published by the registered company Springer Nature Switzerland AG
The registered company address is: Gewerbestrasse 11, 6330 Cham, Switzerland

Contents

List of Contributors

Louis Bissières Université Paris 1-Panthéon Sorbonne, IDHES, Paris, France

David Carvajal University of Valladolid, Valladolid, Spain

Giuseppe De Luca Università degli Studi di Milano, Milan, Italy

Elise M. Dermineur Stockholm University, Stockholm, Sweden

Alberto Feenstra Leiden University, Leiden, The Netherlands

Laurence Fontaine Centre Maurice Halbwachs/PSL (Paris Sciences & Lettres), Paris, France

Marcella Lorenzini Università degli Studi di Milano, Milan, Italy

Stephan Nicolussi-Köhler University of Innsbruck, Innsbruck, Austria

Ruben Peeters University of Antwerp, Antwerp, Belgium

Matteo Pompermaier Università Degli Studi Di Brescia, Brescia, Italy

Hannah Robb University of Exeter, Exeter, UK

Rogier van Kooten University of Antwerp, Antwerp, Belgium; Utrecht University, Utrecht, The Netherlands

Martín L. E. Wasserman CONICET-UBA, Buenos Aires, Argentina

List of Figures

Chapter 2

Chapter 5

Chapter 6

Chapter 7

Chapter 8

Chapter 9

Chapter 10

Chapter 11

Chapter 12

List of Tables

CHAPTER 1

Introduction

Matteo Pompermaier

In recent years,[1] there has been a significant expansion in scientific literature devoted to the study of social networks. The very use of the term "network" has become increasingly common across a wide range of contexts.[2] This trend reflects the rising interest of the scholarly community in these structures, which "permeate our social and economic lives".[3]

As emphasized by Matthew Jackson in his comprehensive volume on social network analysis (henceforth SNA), networks are vehicles for human interaction. They affect the dissemination of information,

[1] The author would like to acknowledge the generous funding of the Library of Lund University, which supported us in publishing this book in open access.

[2] Florian Kerschbaumer, Linda von Keyserlingk-Rehbein, Martin Stark and Marten Düring, 'Introduction' in: Florian Kerschbaumer, Linda von Keyserlingk-Rehbein, Martin Stark and Marten Düring (eds.), *The Power of Networks. Prospects of Historical Network Research* (London and New York, 2020), 1–10, there p. 3; About the growing use of term "networks", see Claire Lemercier, 'Analyse de reseaux et histoire', in: *Revue d'histoire modern & contemporaine*, 52:2 (2005), 88–112.

[3] Matthew O. Jackson *Social and economic networks* (Princeton, 2008), there 17.

M. Pompermaier (✉)
Università Degli Studi Di Brescia, Brescia, Italy
e-mail: matteo.pompermaier@unibs.it

E. M. Dermineur and M. Pompermaier (eds.), *Credit Networks in The Preindustrial World*, Palgrave Studies in the History of Finance,
https://doi.org/10.1007/978-3-031-67117-3_1

and influence individuals' choices.[4] Despite evolving and growing more complex over time, human networks are governed by basic rules that are stable and predictable. For this reason, adopting a network perspective proves crucial in studying and thoroughly comprehending a variety of human actions.

This volume is the result of insightful discussions among the authors during a workshop organized by the editors at Stockholm University in October 2022, titled "Networks, Behavior, and Strategies in Early Financial Markets" (Stockholm, October 27 & 28 October 2022).[5] Overall, this volume aims to stress the significance of networks, as well as the importance of adopting a network perspective to investigate historical facts. In particular, its various chapters deal with a specific sub-group of networks based on credit transactions. Indeed, the book involves several authors who are experts in financial history. Their research delves into various periods and contexts, from fifteenth-century Europe to eighteenth-century North and South America, examining different forms of credit, intermediated and non-intermediated.

To develop a common framework, we asked the authors who participated in this volume to observe interpersonal credit transactions in the past through the lens of networks, using the approach they believed was the most suited according to their data and research questions. The result is characterized by a variety—which involves topics, contexts, periods, and methodologies—that can be considered as one of the most compelling aspects of the book. But it also poses a challenge. On the one hand, such a variety strengthens the whole discussion on historical SNA by offering an overview of the different kinds of possible explorations, from purely qualitative to a data-driven approach to networks based on large datasets. On the other, it also represents a challenge because it possibly endangers our effort to build a shared methodological framework. Overall, we believe it confirms the flexibility of SNA and its adaptability to different sources, periods, and research questions.

In editing this volume, we share Scott and Carrington's approach to social network analysis. They employ it as a structural paradigm, a means of conceptualizing and analyzing social interactions, shaping the lens

[4] From "the movies they see, which products they purchase, ... whether they protest, and so forth", Jackson, *Social and Economic Networks*,there 17.

[5] The editors would like to acknowledge the generous funding of the Marcus & Amalia Wallenberg Foundation (2020–2023), MAW2018.0015.

through which we observe historical facts and address historical questions, as well as the way data is collected and analyzed.[6] The abovementioned variety originated from the different answers each author gave to the questions "What is SNA?" and "How can it help you in your research?". The aim was to address two main discussions: the first one concerns the functioning of credit markets; the second one relates instead to the use of social network analysis and, more generally, digital humanities methodologies in historical research.[7]

Eventually, this volume poses more questions than it answers. It represents a first attempt to coordinate the work of different scholars working on credit networks and promote a series of original studies on the topic. The book emphasizes topics such as economic behavior and network interaction that have not yet received sufficient attention, especially in the pre-industrial period. Finally, it highlights gaps in the literature that still need to be addressed, stimulating new research in the field.

This brief introduction wants to highlight a few important points. The next section provides the reader with some basic notions about social network analysis and its origins as a field of study. The following part focuses more specifically on pre-industrial credit networks. Overall, the introduction highlights key references that could be beneficial for those who are approaching the theme of SNA for the first time, but it does not focus on the theory of such a method, which is extensively treated in Elise Dermineur's chapter. Finally, the last section introduces the various chapters, explains how they relate to each other, and points out the main ideas behind the whole book project.

1 A World of Networks

Studying the dynamics of human networks helps us to address many issues related to the mechanisms regulating our world. For instance, the specific position of an individual in their social network tells a lot about their influence and power. Additionally, the structure of a network allows us to foresee the dynamics underlying the spread of information,

[6] Peter J. Carrington and Scott John., 'Introduction', in: John Scott and Peter J. Carrington (eds), *The SAGE Handbook of Social Network Analysis*, (Los Angeles, 2011), 1–9, there pp. 5–6.

[7] The issue is discussed in Kerschbaumer et al., 'Introduction', there p. 4.

ideas, and even diseases—exemplified in the case of the recent COVID-19 pandemic.[8] Overall, adopting a network perspective is crucial to better comprehend a variety of social and economic phenomena, as well as natural ones. Indeed, as stated by Alexandra Marin and Barry Wellman, "causation is not located in the individual but in the social structure".[9] Individuals are embedded in social networks, they influence and in turn are influenced by one another's actions.

The ideas of networks and the acknowledgment of the importance of relationships between separated individuals have ancient roots. The analysis of social networks, however, especially visualized through a series of lines and dots, is more recent.[10] The first example of the use of graph theory, as we know it today, is considered to be Euler's attempt to solve the renowned problem of the seven bridges of Königsberg (1736). The city of Königsberg (now Kaliningrad) was formed by two large islands connected to each other and to both banks of the river by seven bridges. The challenge was to walk through the entire city, crossing each of those bridges exactly once. Euler approached the problem from a graph theory perspective and represented the various areas that composed the city and the bridges connecting them as vertices and edges. In so doing, he demonstrated that the graph had more than two vertices with an odd number of edges, proving that there was no possible solution to the problem.[11]

The fascination for the nature of the relations that link individuals to each other crossed the boundaries of academia. For instance, Frigyes Karinthy's short story titled "Chain-links" (1929) was able to captivate the imaginations of future generations of sociologists and mathematicians.[12] The play introduces the core idea that lies behind the theory of

[8] Matthew O. Jackson, *The human network: how we're connected and why it matters* (London, 2019), there p. 4.

[9] Alexandra Marin and Wellman Barry, 'Social Network analysis: an introduction', in John Scott and Peter J. Carrington (eds), *The SAGE Handbook of Social Network Analysis* (Los Angeles, 2011), 11–26, there 13. See also Niall Ferguson, *The Square and the Tower: Networks and Power, from the Freemasons to Facebook* (New York, 2018).

[10] For a detailed analysis of the development of SNA see Carrington and Scott, 'Introduction', 1–9.

[11] Carrington and Scott, 'Introduction', there 4.

[12] Frigyes Karinthy, 'Chain-links', in: Mark Newman, Albert-László Barabási, and Duncan J. Watts (eds), The structure and dynamics of networks (Princeton, 2011), 21–26; Jackson, *The human network*, there 54.

the "six degrees of separation", later further explored in John Guare's play of the same name.[13] The basic idea is that "nobody ... [needs] more than five links in the chain to reach, just by using the method of acquaintance, any inhabitant of our planet".[14] "Chain-links" suggests that the world is shrinking because of technological advancements, and all individuals are now connected through short chains of acquaintances.

This theory was then tested by the famous social psychologist Stanley Milgram with his "small-world experiment". He demonstrated that random people in the United States are typically only five or six steps away from each other.[15] The small-world theory was later developed by Duncan Watts, who highlighted that such structures describe the most common type of human network, in which most nodes are not directly connected but can reach any other node within a limited number of steps, facilitated by intermediary nodes.[16]

Overall, SNA as a branch of knowledge is comparatively recent and developed gradually over time. The discipline expanded and spread across various fields of research, ranging from psychology and sociology, to mathematics, and physics. For a long time, however, it remained largely unnoticed by historians. Still, in the late 1990s, Charles Wetherell highlighted the persisting unfamiliarity of historians with such a method, and wanted to contribute to its diffusion. He provided both a theoretical explanation of SNA and a practical demonstration of its application. On the theoretical side, Wetherell focused on the interdependency of actors in the past, and its importance in the dissemination of information. On the empirical one, he applied SNA to investigate the relationship between kinship and communities in a nineteenth-century village situated in modern Latvia. He highlighted the structured nature of networks,

[13] John Guare, *Six Degrees of Separation: A Play* (Random House, 1990).

[14] Karinthy, 'Chain-links', there 25.

[15] For a detailed description of the experiment see Jackson, *Social and Economic Networks*, there 86.

[16] Duncan J. Watts, 'Networks, dynamics, and the small-world phenomenon', in: *American Journal of sociology*, 105:2 (1999), 493–527; Duncan J. Watts, and Strogatz Steven H., 'Collective dynamics of 'small-world' networks', in: *Nature*, 393 (1998), 440–442. See also Albert Reka and Albert-Laszlo Barabasi, 'Statistical mechanics of complex networks', in: *Review of modern physics*, 74 (2002), 48–85, there 48.

which enables scholars to identify and study patterns, crucial in defining the economic, political, and social structure.[17]

The work that probably contributed the most to the spread of SNA in the historical field was authored by the sociologist John Padgett and the political scientist Christopher Ansell. They managed to bring attention to the analysis of social network and boost enthusiasm around the methodology. Their seminal paper "Robust Action and the Rise of the Medici, 1400–1434" had a relevant influence on historical research and stands as one of the earliest—and one of the best-known—applications of social network analysis to historical sources.[18]

The study delves into the intricate marriage, economic, and patronage network built by Cosimo de' Medici, and the critical role it had in his rise to power in fifteenth-century Florence. The authors highlight the concept of "robust action" referring to Cosimo's distinctive style of control. They show that the Medici network comprised two distinct components: individuals with whom the Medici established exclusively economic relations, and other individuals with whom the Medici established marriage alliances. Cosimo's network was strongly affected by residential patterns and resulted in a highly centralized structure capable of assuring top-down control and enforcing discipline. Relying on SNA, the paper describes the mechanism explaining Cosimo's influence within Florence, illuminating the complex power dynamics among the Renaissance elite.[19]

Moving alongside the same trajectory, John Padgett studied (alone and in collaboration with other colleagues) late-medieval Florentine society from different perspectives, focusing both on economic and social relationships. In a well-known paper, he joined the debate with Richard Goldthwaite and Anthony Molo regarding the "openness" of the Florentine elites.[20] Using SNA, Padgett examines marriage patterns, family structures, and social mobility in Florence between 1282 and 1494,

[17] Charles Wetherell, 'Historical social network analysis', in: *International review of social history*, 43 (1998), 125–144, there 126.

[18] John F. Padgett and Christopher K. Ansell, 'Robust Action and the Rise of the Medici, 1400–1434', in: *American journal of sociology*, 98:6 (1993), 1259–1319.

[19] Not by chance, this study is often used as one of the classic examples for the role and relevance of social networks; see, for instance, Jackson, *Social and Economic Networks*, there 18–21.

[20] See John F. Padgett, 'Open Elite? Social Mobility, Marriage, and Family in Florence, 1282–1494', in: *Renaissance Quarterly*, 63:2 (2010), 357–411, there 357.

showing both lineage fluidity and alternative phases of strong upward mobility with the admission of new men into the old Florentine elites through weddings.

As mentioned earlier, over the past two decades the use of SNA in historical research has expanded significantly. Recently, the volume by Kerschbaumer et al. has presented the "best practices of HNR (Historical Network Research)" and explored the diverse approaches developing from the application of network analysis to historical data. The excellent book by Kerschbaumer and his co-authors, highly inspirational for this volume, stresses that there is no consensus on the appropriate application of SNA. Historians have adapted the theoretical principles of SNA to their research, to the available sources, and to the specific questions they seek to address.[21] This diversity of approaches (and possibilities) in the context of an always-evolving methodology is well exemplified in this volume.

2 Pre-industrial (Credit) Networks

Pre-industrial Europe offers fertile ground for the analysis of social networks. Social scientist Karl Polanyi coined the concept of embeddedness to describe the typical economy of pre-industrial society.[22] He claimed that human action is not driven solely by the pursuit of self-interest, but rather embedded in social relations and motivated by a desire for a system of institutions that embodies cultural values. This embeddedness was replaced during the industrial development by the rise of a new "market society", based on self-regulating markets, and opportunistic behavior by economic agents.[23]

The importance of embeddedness in the pre-industrial world and the role of trust in different aspects of economic and social life are often

[21] Kerschbaumer et al., *The power of networks*; see particularly the introduction for the description of the general approach of the book. The citation is at p. 4.

[22] Karl Polanyi, *The great transformation: the political and economic origins of our time* (Boston, 2001).

[23] Granovetter argues that the transition between an embedded and dis-embedded world has to be reconsidered. As claimed by Granovetter, "Actors do not behave or decide as atoms outside a social context, nor do they adhere slavishly to a script written for them", their actions "are instead embedded in concrete ongoing system of social relations". Mark Granovetter, 'Economic action and social structure: The problem of embeddedness', in: *American Journal of Sociology,* 91:3 (1985), 481–510, there 487.

acknowledged in the literature. Abundant research focuses on international finance and global commerce, describing the specific social norms and hierarchies that fostered cooperation in these large networks. This clearly appears in Ana Sofia Ribeiro's recent study on the trading network revolving around the Spanish merchant Simon Ruiz, or the analysis of the Armenian merchant network by Alexandr Osipian. Both authors analyze in detail the mechanisms implemented to establish and maintain trust between the members of a network, and possible punishment for misconduct—usually the exclusion from the network itself.[24]

The abovementioned concept of embeddedness explains well the social mechanisms that sustained peer-to-peer credit transactions in pre-industrial Europe. Indeed, in premodern societies, before the establishment and diffusion of banks and the so-called "institutionalization of trust", the networks of credit involving family, friends, and neighbors held significant importance.[25] They acted as a safety net for individuals and allowed them to mitigate risks and uncertainty, offering a partial solution to problems that are now addressed by the welfare state.[26]

[24] Ana S. Ribeiro, 'The evolution of norms of trade and financial networks in the first global age: the case of the Simon Ruiz's network', in: Catia Antunes and Amelia Polonia (eds), Beyond Empires. Global, Self-Organizing, Cross-Imperial Networks, 1500–1800 (Leiden-Boston, 2016), 12–40; Alexandr Osipian, 'Debt, Trust and Reputation in Early Modern Armenian Merchant Networks', in: Laura Kolb and George Oppitz-Trotman, Early Modern Debts. 1550–1700 (London, 2020), 153–180.

[25] Quote D'Maris Coffman, Cinzia Lorandini and Marcella Lorenzini, 'Introduction', in: D'Maris Coffman, Cinzia Lorandini and Marcella Lorenzini (eds), Financing in Europe. Evolution, Coexistence and Complementarity of Lending Practices from the Middle Ages to Modern Time (Cham, 2018), 1-19, there p 3. See for instance Elise Dermineur, 'Rethinking debt: The evolution of private credit markets in pre-industrial France', in: *Social Science History*, 42:2, (2018), 317–342; Elise Dermineur, 'The evolution of credit networks in pre-industrial Finland'; in: *Scandinavian economic history review*, 70:1 (2022), 57-86; Craig Muldrew, *The Economy of Obligation: The Culture of Credit and Social Relations in Early Modern England* (New York, 1998); Elise Dermineur and Matteo Pompermaier, 'Credit Networks in renaissance Florence: revisiting the catasto of 1427', in: *Rises – Ricerche di storia economica e sociale*, 8:1-2 (2022), 89-110. Elise Dermineur, 'Trust, norms of cooperation, and the rural credit market in eighteenth-century France', *Journal of Interdisciplinary History*, 45:4 (2015), 485-506.

[26] Green and Owens propose a broader definition of welfare that includes direct or indirect support from kin and family and is not only intended as a provision for the poor that comes from the state. David R. Green and Alastair Owens (eds.), *Family welfare: gender property, and inheritance since the seventeenth century* (Westport, 2004).

Craig Muldrew and Laurence Fontaine highlight the relevance of trustworthiness based on personal knowledge to support and promote credit transactions. Both scholars investigated the social relationships that linked individuals involved in credit transactions. They assessed the underlying mechanisms of a loan, stressing the role of trust and reciprocity.[27] Drawing from E.P. Thompson's notion of "The Moral Economy of the English Crowd", Craig Muldrew significantly advanced the discourse on credit networks. He focuses on the moral dimension of credit and argues that "the culture of the early modern market was inherently moral".[28] His central thesis challenges the notion of self-interest, as described by Adam Smith, and supports the idea that individuals do not perceive their actions through such a lens. Muldrew asserts that while profit and success were important, they could only be attained through cooperation within a framework of social relationships sustained by trust. The market relations were "based on moral knowledge about others", strong connections that bound communities together.[29] Despite not relying on graph theory per se, the network discourse is critical in such an interpretation of human relations.

In her book "The Moral Economy", Laurence Fontaine, who also contributes a chapter to this volume, partly delves into the lower strata and their credit behavior. She focuses on informal credit, which formed the backbone of the everyday economy; credit serves as a social bond grounded in personal relationships, where reputation and trust hold significant importance. Fontaine highlights the widespread indebtedness that characterized pre-industrial societies, where the terms of the transaction and the expectations of borrowers and lenders were usually agreed upon by the parties involved.[30] Echoing Muldrew's analysis, she considers credit an obligation that strengthens social bonds, even when the prospects of repayment are slim. From this perspective, credit not only serves an economic function but also plays a crucial role in shaping social relationships.

[27] Laurence Fontaine, *The Moral Economy. Poverty, credit and Trust in Early Modern Europe* (Cambridge, 2014); Muldrew, *The Economy of Obligation*.

[28] Craig Muldrew, 'Interpreting the market: the ethics of credit and community relations in early modern England', in: *Social History*, 18:2 (1993), 163–183, there 169.

[29] Muldrew, 'Interpreting the market', there 169, citation at p. 178.

[30] Dermineur, 'The evolution of credit networks in pre-industrial Finland'.

"The Moral Economy" emphasizes the existence of concentric circles of potential lenders, which encompass family, friends, neighbors, and local elites. These circles mirror the findings of Padgett and McLean's research on the dynamics of interpersonal credit in Renaissance Florence.[31] Using SNA, the authors show that commercial credit among Florentine companies was strictly linked to non-economic social connections, particularly familial and neighborhood ties. They emphasize that merchant banks operated in a collaborative network and that economic relations were influenced by family dynamics (international banking) and residential patterns (domestic banking). On the same lines, Mclean and Gondal examined the circulation of interpersonal credit, further expanding the approach developed by Padgett and McLean.[32] Relying once again on SNA, the authors argue that credit was considered an obligation, very much in line with Muldrew and Fontaine's findings, and posed challenges in the context of a society based on social connections. The Florentine study emphasizes once again the importance of homophily in credit relations, especially linked to residential patterns.[33]

Graph theory offered a way to measure mathematically the different roles played by individuals in the context of these networks. In fact, some nodes are clearly in a better position to acquire and share information, are able to influence other nodes, and contribute to keeping the whole network connected. An excellent example of these mechanisms comes from a recent study by Abhijit Banerjee et al. on the diffusion of microfinance in Indian villages, which investigates how decisions taken from households—in the specific case, to switch or not to microfinance—are influenced by their social networks.[34] Before Banerjee et al., Mark Granovetter's paper on "The strength of weak ties" demonstrated how

[31] John F. Padgett and Paul D. McLean, 'Economic credit in renaissance Florence', in: *The Journal of Modern History*, 83:1 (2011), 1–47.

[32] Paul D. McLean and Neha Gondal. 'The circulation of interpersonal credit in Renaissance Florence' in: *European Journal of Sociology/Archives Européennes de Sociologie*, 55:2, (2014), 135–176.

[33] See also Dermineur and Pompermaier, "Credit Networks in Renaissance Florence"; this topic is treated in several chapters in this volume (among others, Dermineur, Pompermaier, Wasserman, Nicolussi-Köhler).

[34] Abhijit Banerjee, Arun G. Chandrasekhar, Ester Duflo, and Matthew O. Jackson, 'The diffusion of micro finance', in: *Science*, 341:6144 (2013), 1,236,498.

different nodes and connections in a network facilitate the spread of information. Granovetter argues that acquaintances are more influential than close friends in spreading information, because of the structure of their connections: rumors or information diffused through strong ties are likely to be confined, while those transmitted through weak ties cover more extensive social ground. Relevant in the field is also Ronald Burt's analysis of "structural holes", which shows the negative effects arising from the disappearance of certain nodes.[35] These holes are gaps between individuals who possess complementary sources of information: intermediaries represent those pivotal nodes within the network whose absence would significantly damage overall interconnectivity.

In the specific case of credit networks, intermediaries serve as connectors between the supply and demand of credit. They solve issues of asymmetric information by gathering pertinent data on prospective lenders and assessing borrowers' creditworthiness, and their collaterals. Research on intermediaries flourished after the study of Hoffman et al. on notarial intermediation in France between the seventeenth and nineteenth centuries. They shed light on the complex network of information that revolved around notaries, facilitating credit exchanges. Notaries not only connect demand and offer, but they actively share surplus borrowers or lenders among their peers, resulting in borrowers and lenders moving from one location to the other following the orchestrated intermediation of notaries. From this point of view, French notaries provide us with a clear demonstration of how credit intermediation worked and show the networks that linked borrowers, lenders, and intermediaries.[36]

[35] Ronald S. Burt, *Brokerage and Closure: An Introduction to Social Capital* (Oxford, 2005); Ronald S. Burt, 'Structural holes versus network closure as social capital', in: Nan Lin, Karen Cook, Ronald S. Burt (eds.) Social capital (New York, 2017), 31–56.

[36] See Philip T. Hoffman, Gilles Postel-Vinay, and Jean-Laurent Rosenthal, 'What Do Notaries Do? Overcoming Asymmetric Information in Financial Markets: The Case of Paris, 1751', in: *Journal of Institutional and Theoretical Economics (JITE) / Zeitschrift Für Die Gesamte Staatswissenschaft* 154:3 (1998), 499–530; about the notarial intermediation in Paris, see Philip T Hoffman, Gilles Postel-Vinay, and Jean-Laurent Rosenthal, *Priceless markets: the political economy of credit in Paris, 1660–1870* (Chicago, 2000); Philip T. Hoffman, Gilles Postel-Vinay, and Jean-Laurent Rosenthal, *Dark Matter Credit: The Development of Peer-to-Peer Lending and Banking in France* (Princeton, 2019). For a broader perspective on France and a discussion about a "Network of Knowledge", see Hoffman et al., *Dark Matter Credit*, chapter 4. Also, see in this book Giuseppe De Luca and Marcella Lorenzini, 'Notary lending networks in northern Italy in the eighteenth and

This brief summary highlights one important feature that characterized pre-industrial credit markets, their variety. It concerns the actors involved, the context (urban and rural), the tools used to supply loans, the intermediated or non-intermediated nature of transactions, and so forth. This volume reflects well such a variety. We believe that all authors successfully highlight several relevant aspects of pre-industrial credit markets, shedding light on the basic mechanisms that regulated them.

It is now clearer why the earlier mentioned diversity is one of the strengths of this volume: it allows us to explore and compare both rural and urban contexts, peer-to-peer and intermediated transactions, stressing the role of several professional categories, such as notaries, merchants, and moneychangers. A diversity that proves fundamental to describe what was an articulated human action. Overall, SNA appears for what it is: a useful method to simplify the complexity and uncover the mechanisms that lie behind human action. The diverse use of such methodology, be it more qualitative or quantitative, appears as the result of the prevalence of historical questions and material over the research method.[37]

3 Overview and Aims of the Book

This volume has several objectives. First, as stated above it represents a first attempt to coordinate the work of different scholars working on credit networks in past societies and promote a series of original studies on the topic. The different chapters offer a broad overview of the topic, emphasizing international and long-term comparisons. The various authors center their studies on specific actors (professional or social groups), in both urban and rural contexts, stressing the relevance of these networks in allocating financial resources. As in all first attempts, the volume aims to open the path for further research on the same line. Second, despite a growing literature, the emphasis on economic behavior and network interaction has not received sufficient attention, especially regarding the pre-industrial period. The book aims to tackle this issue and explore the possibilities offered by SNA for the study of past financial markets and networks. Third, we hope this volume will also encourage the

nineteenth centuries'; Ruben Peeters and Rogier van Kooten, 'Looking for dark matter credit: exploring notarial credit markets in Antwerp and its surroundings ca. 1835'.

[37] The issue is discussed in Kerschbaumer et al., 'Introduction'.

further diffusion of SNA among historians. We believe it offers a valuable guide for a broad audience of historians, who can assess how the same methodology is employed using source material.

At the same time, the book also problematizes the methodology and highlights its shortcomings. Indeed, visualization and statistical analysis allow us to draw a picture of social relations and social life. Yet, as we will see, social network analysis is ill-equipped to grasp and analyze the subtleties and complexities of human relations. For example, power relations, a typical feature of credit relations, are difficult to perceive even with the help of a visual interface. Edges and nodes do not render the depth, complexity, and essence of interpersonal relationships. The qualitative aspect of these relationships needs to be found through other (more traditional?) methods of inquiry and archival evidence.[38]

The volume contributes to offering different interpretations regarding how a network perspective can facilitate the study of credit networks. Is SNA a strictly mathematical approach? Or rather, a lens through which to observe, from a more qualitative perspective, historical and economic phenomena? Historians may face constraints due to the nature of the sources they have access to, which can significantly impact their analytical method.[39] In some cases, they are fortunate to work with exceptionally detailed sources, enabling the application of quantitative and mathematical methodologies. For instance, in this volume, we can highlight Ruben Peeters and Rogier van Kooten's study of Belgian notaries, Louis Bissières' examination of the network of an American merchant, and Matteo Pompermaier's work on the Florentine *catasto*. In other cases, authors are limited by their sources to employing more qualitative methods but still focus on individuals' interdependencies. This is exemplified in the work of Laurence Fontaine, Hannah Robb, and Stephan Nicolussi-Köhler. Additionally, some authors adopt a middle-ground approach, utilizing SNA to a limited extent as a tool to address specific aspects of their research and to address their research questions.

The volume starts with Elise Dermineur's piece, which focuses on the SNA methodology and its two main approaches: network visualization

[38] Dermineur and Pompermaier, 'Credit Networks in renaissance Florence', there 175–176.

[39] Social Networks as a perspective, the sociogram is only visual representation that is not always possible nor always needed. Discussion on the method, use of sociogram see Lemercier, 'Analyse de reseaux et histoire', especially pp. 90–91.

and graph theory. The chapter aims to guide historians taking their first steps with SNA: it offers an overview of network analysis at the macro, meso, and micro levels. The author highlights the advantages of graph theory, describes the meaning of several indexes, and the use of different measures. Dermineur emphasizes the advantages of graph theory, explains various indexes' meanings, and discusses centrality measures. Yet, she also addresses three key challenges in SNA: the complex nature of ties between individuals, the dynamic nature of relationships, and the transitivity assumption. This chapter serves as a comprehensive methodological introduction, even though not all papers in the book utilize graph theory and mathematical approaches.

The volume follows with three different chapters that adopt a network perspective without developing any quantitative analysis. Laurence Fontaine's piece offers a comprehensive qualitative examination of the mechanisms underlying the formation and maintenance of networks. The chapter builds upon her research on the moral economy, and focuses on how individuals and communities perceive, explain, and enforce economic practices according to moral principles and societal norms.[40] Fontaine explores how individuals form networks to cope with uncertain futures, and discusses the importance of trust and reputation in establishing interpersonal networks, with a specific focus on merchants over a long period.

The chapters of Hannah Robb and Stephan Nicolussi-Köhler share limitations in the source material that does not allow them to employ a quantitative approach. Still, they develop a fascinating network analysis in two different contexts. Robb's chapter delves into the involvement of women in peer-to-peer credit networks in early modern England. It sheds light on how married women played a significant role in everyday credit transactions, particularly in rural areas. Through depositions, Robb examines the presence of women in these networks, both as lenders and borrowers. An intriguing hypothesis explored is the impact of women's marital status: the author demonstrates that marriage provided women with greater movable domestic wealth and a crucial "tactile knowledge" essential for accessing the credit market. Drawing from various sources, Robb conducts a qualitative analysis of credit networks, emphasizing

[40] Fontaine, *The Moral Economy*.

gendered practices and the connections between local and broader credit networks.

Stephan Nicolussi-Köhler studies instead the credit network of the village of Laas, situated in modern South Tyrol, in the late fourteenth century. Drawing from notarial records, the author examines in detail the network of credit transactions within the village, and its connections to the larger markets in the nearby cities, particularly those revolving around the merchants residing in Merano. Nicolussi-Köhler highlights the role of notaries as intermediaries in resolving information asymmetries and provides insights into the mechanisms governing local credit markets, emphasizing key nodes in the village's credit network.

The two following chapters have in common their focus on ego-networks, i.e., networks centered around a particular individual. Alberto Feenstra studies the capital market in the Netherlands of the eighteenth century and highlights how the province of Friesland, a province located in the country's northern part, accessed the Amsterdam capital market for borrowing. The chapter delves into the relationships between the financial organization of provinces and the evolution of payment methods, emphasizing the significance of local brokers as informal financial intermediaries. Louis Bissières investigates instead the network of Levi Hollingsworth, an important merchant who operated in Philadelphia in the 1780s. Analyzing Hollingsworth's account book, Bissières reveals an intense circulation of goods and credit across the Atlantic Ocean. Through social network analysis, Bissières delves into Hollingsworth's role within his merchant network, discerning varied uses of credit among his associates. The author uncovers a complex structure built on trust, manifested in diverse relationships between Hollingsworth and his associates. Social network analysis proves instrumental in highlighting nodes' positions and the implications of specific roles within the merchant network.

The next three papers focus on the role of specific groups or actors in a network. Moving alongside the path traced by Bissières' study, David Carvajal and Matteo Pompermaier employ a rather quantitative approach to SNA. Their chapters share an interest in the same professional category—the moneychangers—despite focusing on two different periods and contexts. Carvajal investigates the Castilian credit market during the sixteenth century, focusing on relevant regional fairs. Using notarial sources, he traces credit networks among different moneychanger communities attending fairs, examining the influence of homophily in financial transactions, especially the impact of family and geographical networks on credit networks. Matteo Pompermaier focuses instead on the interpersonal credit market in fifteenth-century Florence, with a particular emphasis on the role of the moneychangers. Relying on the Florentine Catasto of 1427, he maps the credit market within a specific area of Florence (the *gonfalone* Nicchio). Through social network analysis, Pompermaier illustrates how moneychangers served as crucial connectors in the credit network, enhancing market efficiency by bridging various communities and overcoming information asymmetries.

Afterward, Martin Wasserman's contribution shifts to nineteenth-century Argentina and explores the diffusion of checks as a means of payment in Buenos Aires between 1823 and 1826. Through both qualitative and network perspectives, Wasserman investigates the reasons behind the diffusion and acceptance of checks as a means of payment and stresses the key role of specific nodes involved in this network of transactions. The chapter illustrates how influential actors within a network can drive significant institutional changes in the financial landscape.

The last two chapters study the intermediary function of the same actors, the notaries. Giuseppe De Luca and Marcella Lorenzini examine notarial credit in the Northern part of Italy. They focus on the Milanese notaries, who were central figures in large credit networks, linking various locations and facilitating transactions between creditors and borrowers. Similar to their French counterparts, Milanese notaries acted as matchmakers between creditors and debtors, a critical function in the context of markets where the banking sector was not yet developed. Through an extensive database, the authors also retrace the ego-networks of some notaries to show how their brokerage activity worked in detail. They investigate the credit activity, focusing on collateral and interest rates, and show how and why the notaries were able to play this intermediary role.

Finally, Ruben Peeters and Rogier van Kooten look for "dark matter credit" in Belgium in the nineteenth century. To this end, the authors employ geographical mapping and social network analysis to examine the notarial credit market in Antwerp and the surrounding areas. They are particularly interested in investigating notarial intermediation and measuring the transactions established between actors residing in the city and its periphery. As was the case of De Luca and Lorenzini's chapter, this paper takes inspiration from Hoffman et al. research on French notaries, and adds to the exploration of notarial credit intermediation, expanding beyond the French context. Not by chance, the chapter recalls the title of a book by Hoffman et al., which highlights the existence of a "big debt" that despite its size remained unnoticed.[41] Peeters and van Kooten's findings underscore the dynamic nature of Antwerp's credit market and its connections, not only with surrounding regions but also within Belgium and internationally.

References

Secondary Sources

Banerjee, Abhijit, Arun G. Chandrasekhar, Ester Duflo., and Matthew O. Jackson. 2013. The diffusion of micro finance. *Science* 341 (6144): 1236498.

Burt, Ronald S. 2001. Structural holes versus network closure as social capital. In *Social Capital*, edited by Nan Lin, Karen Cook, Ronald S. Burt, 31–56. New York: Aldine de Gruyter.

Burt, Ronald S. 2005. *Brokerage and Closure: An Introduction to Social Capital.* Oxford: Oxford University Press.

Carrington, Peter J., and Scott John. 2011. Introduction. In *The SAGE Handbook of Social Network Analysis*, edited by John Scott and Peter J. Carrington, 1–9. Los Angeles: Sage.

Coffman, D'Maris, Cinzia Lorandini and Marcella Lorenzini. 2018. Introduction. In *Financing in Europe. Evolution, Coexistence and Complementarity of Lending Practices from the Middle Ages to Modern Time*, D'Maris Coffman, Cinzia Lorandini and Marcella Lorenzini, 1–19. Cham: Palgrave.

Dermineur, Elise. 2015. Trust, norms of cooperation, and the rural credit market in eighteenth-century France. *Journal of Interdisciplinary History* 45 (4): 485–506.

Dermineur, Elise. 2018. Rethinking debt: The evolution of private credit markets in pre-industrial France. *Social Science History* 42 (2): 317–342.

Dermineur, Elise. 2022. The evolution of credit networks in pre-industrial Finland. *Scandinavian Economic History Review* 70 (1): 57–86.

Dermineur, Elise, and Matteo Pompermaier. 2022. Credit Networks in renaissance Florence: revisiting the catasto of 1427. *Rises – Ricerche di storia economica e sociale* 8 (1–2): 89–110.

Ferguson, Niall. 2018. *The Square and the Tower: Networks and Power, from the Freemasons to Facebook.* New York: Penguin books.

Fontaine, Laurence. 2014. *The Moral Economy. Poverty, Credit and Trust in Early Modern Europe.* Cambridge: Cambridge University Press.

[41] "It is like the dark matter that makes up some eighty-five percent of the universe but cannot be directly observed", Hoffman et al., *Dark Matter Credit*, there 1.

Granovetter, Mark. 1985. Economic action and social structure: The problem of embeddedness. *American Journal of Sociology* 91 (3): 481–510.

Green, David R., and Alastair Owens, eds. 2004. *Family Welfare: Gender Property, and Inheritance Since the Seventeenth Century*. Westport: Praeger.

Guare, John. 1990. *Six Degrees of Separation: A Play*. Random House.

Hoffman, Philip T., Gilles Postel-Vinay, and Jean-Laurent. Rosenthal. 1998. What do notaries do? Overcoming asymmetric information in financial markets: The case of Paris, 1751. *Journal of Institutional and Theoretical Economics (JITE)/Zeitschrift Für Die Gesamte Staatswissenschaft* 154 (3): 499–530.

Hoffman, Philip T., Gilles Postel-Vinay, and Jean-Laurent Rosenthal. 2000. *Priceless Markets: The Political Economy of Credit in Paris, 1660–1870*. Chicago and London: The University of Chicago Press.

Hoffman, Philip T., Gilles Postel-Vinay, and Jean-Laurent Rosenthal. 2019. *Dark Matter Credit: The Development of Peer-to-Peer Lending and Banking in France*. Princeton: Princeton University Press.

Jackson, Matthew O. 2008. *Social and Economic Networks*. Princeton: Princeton University Press.

Jackson, Matthew O. 2019. *The Human Network: How We're Connected and Why It Matters*. London: Atlantic Books.

Karinthy, Frigyes. 2011. Chain-links. In *The Structure and Dynamics of Networks*, edited by Mark Newman, Albert-László Barabási, and Duncan J. Watts, 21–26. Princeton: Princeton University Press.

Kerschbaumer, Florian, Linda von Keyserlingk-Rehbein, Martin Stark and Marten Düring. 2020. Introduction. In *The Power of Networks. Prospects of Historical Network Research*, edited by Florian Kerschbaumer, Linda von Keyserlingk-Rehbein, Martin Stark and Marten Düring, 1–10. London and New York: Routledge.

Lemercier, Claire. 2005. Analyse de réseaux et histoire. *Revue d'histoire moderne & contemporaine* 52 (2): 88–112.

Marin, Alexandra and Wellman Barry. 2011. Social network analysis: An introduction. In *The SAGE Handbook of Social Network Analysis*, edited by John Scott and Peter J. Carrington, 11–26. Los Angeles: Sage.

McLean, Paul D., and Neha Gondal. 2014. The circulation of interpersonal credit in Renaissance Florence. *European Journal of Sociology/Archives Européennes de Sociologie* 55 (2): 135–176.

Muldrew, Craig. 1993. Interpreting the market: The ethics of credit and community relations in early modern England. *Social History* 18 (2): 163–183.

Muldrew, Craig. 1998. *The Economy of Obligation: The Culture of Credit and Social Relations in Early Modern England*. New York: St. Martin's Press.

Osipian, Alexandr. 2020. Debt, trust and reputation in early modern Armenian merchant networks. In *Early Modern Debts. 1550–1700*, edited by Laura Kolb and George Oppitz-Trotman, 153–180. London: Palgrave.

Padgett, John F., and Christopher K. Ansell. 1993. Robust action and the rise of the Medici, 1400–1434. *American Journal of Sociology* 98 (6): 1259–1319.

Padgett, John F. 2010. Open elite? Social mobility, marriage, and family in florence, 1282–1494. *Renaissance Quarterly*, 63 (2): 357–411, there 357.

Padgett, John F., and Paul D. McLean. 2011. Economic credit in renaissance Florence. *The Journal of Modern History* 83 (1): 1–47.

Polanyi, Karl. 2001. *The Great Transformation: The Political and Economic Origins of Our Time*. Boston: Beacon Press.

Reka, Albert, and Albert-Laszlo. Barabasi. 2002. Statistical mechanics of complex networks. *Review of Modern Physics* 74: 48–85.

Ribeiro, Ana S. 2016. The evolution of norms of trade and financial networks in the first global age: The case of the Simon Ruiz's network. In: *Beyond Empires. Global, Self-Organizing, Cross-Imperial Networks, 1500–1800*, edited by Catia Antunes and Amelia Polonia, 12–40. Leiden-Boston: Brill.

Watts, Duncan J. 1999. Networks, dynamics, and the small-world phenomenon. *American Journal of Sociology* 105 (2): 493–527.

Watts, Duncan J., and Steven H. Strogatz. 1998. Collective dynamics of 'small-world' networks. *Nature* 393: 440–442.

Wetherell, Charles. 1998. Historical social network analysis. *International Review of Social History* 43: 125–144.

CHAPTER 2

Historical Social Network Analysis and Early Financial Exchanges

Elise M. Dermineur

1 Introduction

The recent use of Social Network Analysis (SNA thereafter) has brought a new impulse to social and economic history, contributing to our understanding of how societies and economies function. Perhaps, more importantly, it has given a new significance to social structures. Yet, its adoption by historians is still in its infancy.[1] Following in the footsteps of political scientist John Padgett and sociologist Paul McLean and their

[1] See the excellent Florian Kerschbaumer, Linda von Keyserlingk-Rehbein, Martin Stark, Marten Düring (eds.), The Power of Networks (London, 2020).

E. M. Dermineur (✉)
Stockholm University, Stockholm, Sweden
e-mail: elise.dermineur@ekohist.su.se

E. M. Dermineur and M. Pompermaier (eds.), *Credit Networks in The Preindustrial World*, Palgrave Studies in the History of Finance,
https://doi.org/10.1007/978-3-031-67117-3_2

work on credit in Renaissance Florence, economic historians have delved into the SNA approach with encouraging results.[2]

How can historians of early financial markets use SNA? The aim of this chapter is to introduce the reader to the use of social network analysis, giving particular attention to its application in the study of early and preindustrial financial markets. Credit networks featuring peer-to-peer lending are privileged. This chapter explores the opportunities offered by this approach but also its pitfalls.

There has been much debate to determine the scientific nature of SNA. Is it a method, a theory, a paradigm, or something looser like an approach?[3] This chapter considers SNA as an approach, a useful tool of visualisation and analysis that can unveil interesting features otherwise not available to the researcher. As an approach, SNA has advantages but also limitations.

The first part of this contribution highlights the basic principles of SNA with reference to early financial markets. Readers familiar to SNA might want to jump to the next section. The second part focuses on the benefits of using SNA while studying preindustrial credit. It also points to the possible methodological issues one may encounter. And finally, the last part proposes a tentative outline for a future research agenda in this area.

[2] John F. Padgett and Paul D. McLean, 'Economic Credit in Renaissance Florence' in: *The Journal of Modern History* 83:1 (2011), 1–47. Andreas Gestrich and Martin Stark, *Debtors, Creditors, and Their Networks: Social Dimensions of Monetary Dependence from the Seventeenth to the Twentieth Century*, 1st edition (London, 2015); Elise M. Dermineur, 'The Evolution of Credit Networks in Pre-Industrial Finland,' in *Scandinavian Economic History Review* 70:1 (2021), 1–30. Francesca Odella, 'A Network Perspective of Economic Relations and Markets,' in: *Österreichische Zeitschrift Für Geschichtswissenschaften* 23:1 (2012), 42–71; Cinzia Lorandini and Francesca Odella, 'Private Lending in an Alpine Region during the Eighteenth Century: A Family of Merchant-Bankers and Their Credit Network,' in: *Enterprise & Society* 24:3 (2022), 1–28. Odella, Francesca, and Cinzia Lorandini. 'Testing historical theories with SNA. Structure and evolution of a credit network' in: *Computational Social Science* 2 (2021), 181-200.

[3] Claire Lemercier, 'Formal Network Methods in History: Why and How?', in: Georg Fertig (ed.), Social Networks, Political Institutions, and Rural Societies (Turnhout, 2015), 281–304.

2 Social Network Analysis: A Basic Introduction to Visual and Mathematical Representations

The reader might be well acquainted in the use of SNA, but it is perhaps worth recalling that SNA consists of two complementary approaches. One is the visual representation and the second is the mathematical analysis of networks and its agents. We will deal with the former in the first section and discuss the latter in the part that follows.

2.1 The Power of Visualisation

The adage "a picture is worth a thousand words" certainly finds resonance in various languages. It certainly holds a vital role in network studies. Visual representation of connections (ties) between nodes (or vertices) is useful for conducting insightful analyses. Networks, especially those comprising numerous actors and complex relationships, can be daunting to decipher. Using graphical representations as a lens (or a working interface) to visually represent these networks facilitates the identification of patterns and structures. This visual interface serves a dual purpose: it unveils insights into the network's own structure but also reveals positions of individual nodes within it. The general structure of the network, for example, gives a mesoscopic overview of the peer-to-peer lending market at instant *t* (see Fig. 1).

In examining the network's structure, a graphic representation enables the researcher to identify central and peripheral elements, providing a "scalable" perspective, which means that relationships can be seen from multiple levels.[4] Consider Fig. 1, representing the credit exchanges within the rural parish of Lycksele in Northern Sweden in 1930.[5] The data extracted from probate inventories for that year reveals 787 nodes and 866 edges, featuring a prominent central component, often called giant component, surrounded by smaller star networks and isolated nodes. In this case, the large clustering in the middle means that people living in

[4] See, for example, John Haggerty and Sheryllynne Haggerty, 'Visual Analytics of an Eighteenth-Century Business Network' in: *Enterprise & Society* 11:1 (2010), 1–25.

[5] Riksarkivet, Lycksele tingslags häradsrätt AIId:3 and 4.

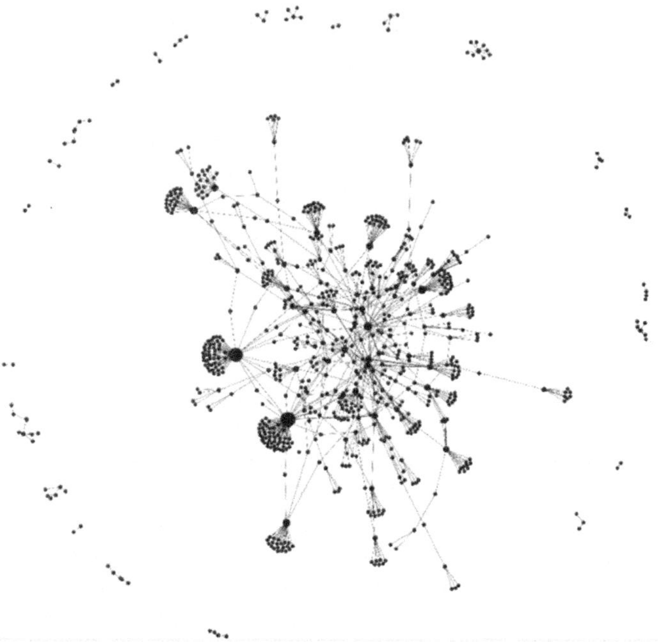

Fig. 1 Network of financial transactions in the parish of Lycksele in 1930 based on probate inventories (created in Gephi by the author)

the parish often resorted to peer-to-peer lending. It suggests cooperative and prosocial behaviours, features that made lending smoother.[6] Yet, such clustering also underscores the interdependency of the actors in the network. In the context of peer-to-peer lending, a network with such high clustering implies that defaults may propagate rapidly within the cluster. This is reinforced by visible long chains of credit, a trail of connected single nodes.

The visual identification of cliques or cohesive groups within subgroups is of critical value. A clique, in mathematical terms, constitutes a "maximal

[6] Matthew O. Jackson, 'Networks in the Understanding of Economic Behaviors', in: *Journal of Economic Perspectives*, 28:4 (2014), 3-22, there 17.

subgraph of three or more nodes", where all members share connections with each other.[7] These cliques signify intensified interactions, reinforced solidarity, social control, potential repeated exchanges, or information redundancy among their members. Identifying cliques in extensive networks can be a complicated task. In this respect, the interface provides a useful tool for visual identification. We will see in the next part that it is possible to mathematically identify both cliques and communities.

Apart from cliques, visualising connections can unveil concealed features. For instance, Fig. 2 emerges from the data in Fig. 1, concentrating solely on the relationships between banks and their clients.[8] This visualisation unveils a surprise; the shared pool of clients among banks in the context of banking institutions emergence.[9] In the centre stands Handelsbanken, surrounded by other banking institutions. These banks shared a substantial portion of their clientele, a detail that might have evaded the researcher's notice without the visual representation of a graph.

Similarly, visualisation facilitates the detection of isolated islands, representing less connected members. These could encompass various groups, outsiders, less integrated members of the community such as immigrants, ethnic minorities, or even women, depending on the context. In Fig. 1, for example, nodes on the margin and isolated nodes are often members of the Sámi community living in northern Sweden. Finally, it is important to stress that visualisation also gives us information about what we do not see in the graph (if we know what to look for).[10]

Overall, using a visual graphic representation of credit relations within a group or a community as an interface for analysis can enable the researcher to identify patterns, structures, and more easily detect interesting connections. But it should be used with a critical eye. A graph can

[7] Charles Kadushin, *Understanding Social Networks: Theories, Concepts, and Findings* (Oxford, 2012), there 47.

[8] Riksarkivet, Lycksele tingslags häradsrätt AIId:3 and 4.

[9] See also Elise M. Dermineur, "The Evolution of Credit Networks in Pre-Industrial Finland," *Scandinavian Economic History Review* 70:1 (2022), 57–86.

[10] Lemercier, 'Formal Network Methods in History: Why and How?'.

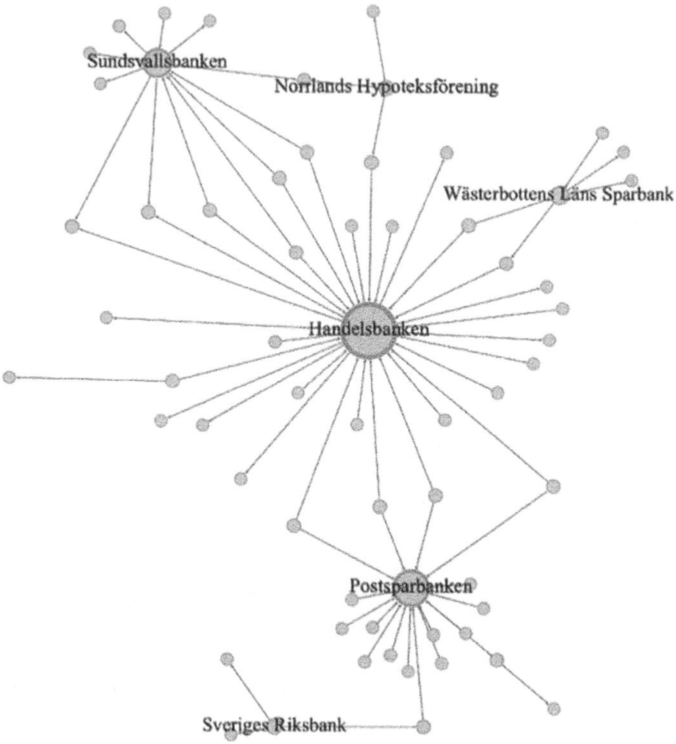

Fig. 2 Banking institutions and their clients in Lycksele in 1930 based on probate inventories (excerpt from the main component)

produce more often than not an "illusion of certainty".[11] Both the structure of the overall network itself and the positions of certain nodes can be further analysed with mathematical tools.

[11] Robert Gramsch-Stehfest, "Community Detection and Structural Balance: Network Analytical Modelling of Political Structures and Actions in the Middle Ages," in *The Power of Networks* (Routledge, 2020), 37–55. 37.

2.2 *Mathematical Representation*

The second and complementary approach is the measuring or mathematical analysis of the network and its agents. It can help us to interpret the different forms of social dynamics and aggregation. Relational characteristics, in particular the position of the nodes in the network and their interactions with each other, can be translated into useful measures. One can distinguish, for example, homophilic patterns, spheres of influence and diffusion, potential scopes of action, information access, and capital and information flows. This part introduces the reader to the basic approaches. More advanced measures do exist and can be explored further.[12]

2.2.1 Network as a Whole

Connections in a network can be seen from different levels, often referred to as "scalable reading". One can consider the network as a whole, discussed here, or one can focus on the nodes themselves and their relationships with one another within the said network, discussed in the next sub-section.[13]

The size of a network is of considerable importance. A peer-to-peer lending network of 25 households for example has a different meaning than a notarial credit network of 2,000 lenders and borrowers who might not know each other. With 25 nodes in a directed network, there are 600 possible ties. With 2,000 nodes, there are almost 4 million possible ties.[14] The dynamics of interaction, the depth, and the meaning of these relationships in those two different networks are de facto diametrically different.

One useful measure in this respect is the density measure, which relates to the cohesion of the network. It generally depends on the size of the graph and therefore the number of nodes. This is why the density of different graphs is difficult to compare. This measure runs between 0 and 1. In a directed network of 25 households, where 200 ties are realised

[12] Robert Gramsch-Stehfest, 'Community Detection and Structural Balance: Network Analytical Modelling of Political Structures and Actions in the Middle Ages', in: Florian Kerschbaumer, Linda von Keyserlingk-Rehbein, Martin Stark, Marten Düring (eds.), The Power of Networks (London, 2020), 37–55, there 37.

[13] For application see, for instance, Emily Erikson, *Between Monopoly and Free Trade: The English East India Company, 1600-1757* (Princeton, 2014).

[14] In an undirected network, these figures would be divided by two.

among the 600 possible ones, the density is 0.33, i.e. a third of all possible ties are made. Depending on the type of community and the type of credit exchange we examine, density might be necessarily low; not all ties can be realised. Density affects the ease of the flux of exchange between the nodes. But it also says something about how much members of the same community can monitor and sanction deviant behaviour. For example, a high density may allow reputations to travel fast. It is generally understood that high density brings people closer and exhibits features of solidarity.

In the same vein, measures pertaining to the whole network can reveal features about social organisation. The diameter, for example, is a measure of the network as a whole. It is the longest distance between any two nodes in a network. For a large network, the diameter is often calculated for the giant component. It is an indication of reachability.

This is connected to clustering. If my friends are friends with one another, we talk about clustering.[15] We can use several measures, such as a clustering coefficient. High clustering, or closure, a common feature of peer-to-peer lending networks, plays a critical role in the enforcement of social norms.[16] Coleman argues that closure allows the monitoring of behaviour, the spread of information and reputation, and helps prescribe behaviour.[17] In small communities, for example, closure often meant that debtors who struggled with repayment might be barred from future loans or forced to pay additional compensation to seal future contracts.

Yet, on the other hand, limited connections might be beneficial in another way. Weak ties are those connections with nodes with whom one has limited links.[18] Associated with weak ties are structural holes, which relate to the intermediaries, the nodes that connect the others. Weak ties are the critical bridges between disparate clusters, removing them would remove any connection between those clusters. Structural holes are gaps between those clusters, where weak ties are lacking. Brokers have the capacity to bridge the gap or the hole.

[15] See Jackson, *Social and Economic Networks*, there 34.

[16] James S. Coleman, 'Social Capital in the Creation of Human Capital', *American Journal of Sociology* 94 (1988), 95-120.

[17] Coleman, 'Social Capital in the Creation of Human Capital'.

[18] Mark Granovetter, 'The Strength of Weak Ties', in: Peter V. Marsden and Nan Lin (eds.) *Social Structure and Network Analysis* (Beverly Hills and London and New Delhi, 1982), 105–130.

To go further, one can also study blockmodeling in a network. Blockmodeling enables the detection of structural patterns in a network and insists on the positions of nodes. As such, network relations are studied among positions rather than actors. Network structure can also be studied in terms of reciprocity (nodes and dyadic relationships where two nodes are both lenders and borrowers), transitivity ("the friends of my friends are my friends"), and network position (blockmodeling). These measures are usually helpful with specific research questions.

We can also detect community structure and clusters, known as community detection.[19] It can be a useful approach to understand, for example, certain patterns of credit circulation and distribution. A community is defined as a group of nodes that interact tightly with each other, more than with outsiders.[20] It is especially interesting to examine how a particular community interacts with and affects the rest of the network. Several methods of community detection exist, using algorithms such as CONCOR is one example.

2.2.2 Homophily

In a similar fashion, considering the relationships existing between different nodes, homophily is often brought up.[21] It is perhaps the most discussed aspect of networks. Homophily is the principle that "birds of a feather flock together".[22] It recognises that agents in a network share common attributes. If two nodes are connected, it is expected they share a certain number of characteristics. In the case of preindustrial financial networks, for example, lenders and borrowers are often from the same community or/and from the same trade.

There are at least two types of homophily: status homophily and value homophily. The first can be ascribed characteristics (i.e. sex, age, race,

[19] For best practice see, for example, Silvio. R. Dahmen, Ana L. C. Bazzan, and Robert. Gramsch, 'Community Detection in the Network of German Princes in 1225: A Case Study', in: Bruno Gonçalves et al. (eds.) Complex Networks (Cham, 2017), 193–200.

[20] We must remain careful with the definition of a community. See especially Jackson, *Social and Economic Networks*, there 446.

[21] Paul Lazarsfeld and Robert K. Merton, 'Friendship as a Social Process: A Substantive and Methodological Analysis', in: Berger, M., Abel, T. and Charles, H. (eds.), *Freedom and Control in Modern Society* (New York 1954), 18-66.

[22] Neha Gondal and Paul D. McLean, 'Linking Tie-Meaning with Network Structure: Variable Connotations of Personal Lending in a Multiple-Network Ecology', in: *Poetics* 41:2 (2013), 122–50.

etc.) or acquired (marital status, occupation, etc.). The second, value homophily, refers to attitudes and preferences. This term has often been labelled homogeneity.[23]

Homophily can often but not always explain why two nodes are connected to each other. A lot of studies have now shown that the same kind of people come together. And because they share certain attributes, it is assumed that they can influence each other. It is no surprise then that members of the same family or neighbours did lend money to each other in the early modern world. In 1427 Florence, about a third of all recorded credits in the famous catasto analysed by McLean and Gondal occurred between residents of the same neighbourhoods.[24] In the neighbourhood of Santo Spirito, half of the transactions were among neighbours living there.[25] Considering the embeddedness of economic transactions in social relations, this is hardly surprising.

Figure 3 exemplifies propinquity, a common homophilic attribute. In a collection of villages located in the south of Alsace in the seigneurie of Florimont, one notes that villagers preferred to deal with their fellow villagers rather than neighbours living in the next village.[26]

One of the dangers of networks with similar people is that they tend to prevent innovation and preserve traditional practices. The following example illustrates this point. In eighteenth century Alsace peasants with little gap in their bargaining power and wealth, lent and borrowed money in close circles. Almost no outsider to the community (i.e. seigneurie) was part of their lending network. Peasants were from the same area, if not from the same village (see Fig. 3). The high degree of homophily in this network meant that capital flow was constrained and limited. Practices of credit were often perpetuated year after year. High levels of

[23] Kadushin, *Understanding Social Networks,* there 19.

[24] Paul D. McLean and Neha Gondal, 'The Circulation of Interpersonal Credit in Renaissance Florence' in: *European Journal of Sociology / Archives Européennes de Sociologie* 55:2 (2014), 135–176, there 158.

[25] Elise Dermineur and Matteo Pompermaier, "Credit Networks in Renaissance Florence: Revisiting the Catasto of 1427" *Rivista Di Storia Economica e Sociale*, -2 (2022), 147-165.

[26] Elise Dermineur and Matteo Pompermaier, 'Credit Networks in Renaissance Florence: Revisiting the Catasto of 1427', in: *Rivista Di Storia Economica e Sociale,* 1-2 (2022), 147-165.

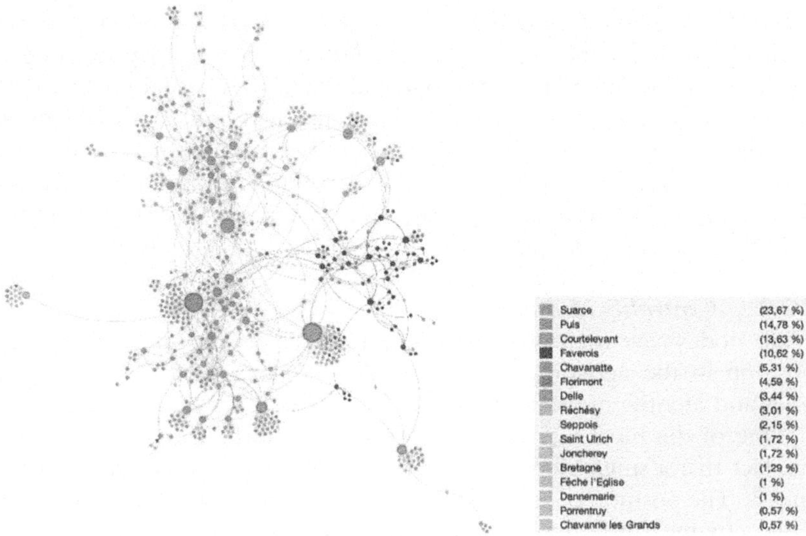

Fig. 3 Non-intermediated credit market by nodes' place of residency, seigneurie de Florimont, 1770–1790. The nodes are weighted according to their degree (grey nodes: other villages, less than 1% each)[27]

local clustering and tightly-knit neighbourhoods often hindered diffusion processes.[28] Yet, towards the end of the eighteenth century, local bourgeois from neighbouring growing towns started to enter this credit market, extending money to peasants. Because the new entrants did not share the same attributes as the peasants (not living in their villages and not being farmers themselves), they brought new rules to the game. While repayment had been flexible and negotiable among peasants before, the new actors demanded prompt repayment and did not hesitate to take their debtors to court in case of default. Only because new actors entered the network did innovation and change occur.[29] The new entrants influenced

[27] Adapted from Elise M. Dermineur, 'Peer-to-Peer Lending in Pre-Industrial France', in: *Financial History Review* 26:3 (2019), 359–88.

[28] Damon Centola, 'The Spread of Behavior in an Online Social Network Experiment', in: *Science* 329:5996 (2010), 1194–1197.

[29] Elise M. Dermineur, *Before Banks: The Making of Credit and Debt in Pre-Industrial France* (Cambridge, forthcoming), see chapter 6.

practices and erased former ones.[30] They also changed the structure of the network. This is something researchers noted in present-day India upon the diffusion of microcredit. Not only did the introduction of micro loans change the structure of local networks, it also had critical consequences. In extending loans, microfinance companies contributed to the deterioration of the quality of existing networks in Indian communities because they stopped the socialisation process. A network can be destroyed under the influence of external factors.[31]

2.2.3 Centrality Measures

While nodes have their own properties, they can also be analysed via their position in the network. Different measures allow us to examine their roles and identify meaningful actors.

One of the most interesting features of network analysis comes from the fact that a single node benefits (or suffers) from an indirect relationship.[32] The position of an individual in a given network is thus of interest. Centrality measures can give information on lenders and borrowers' roles and activities and point to those who sustained or influenced credit. Four main centrality measures can help us to explore the position of individual nodes in a network: degree centrality, closeness centrality, betweenness centrality, and eigenvector centrality measures.[33]

Degree centrality is the simplest measure of the four; it is the number of connections that a node has, a popularity measure, meaning the number of connections a person has the potential to influence in a network. Nodes with high degree centrality, for example, may impose new trends and norms. In directed networks, the degree centrality measure can be divided into two: in-degree and out-degree. For example, it is a helpful

[30] See also Abhijit Banerjee et al., 'The Diffusion of Microfinance', *Science* 341:6144 (2013): 1236498.

[31] Banerjee et al., 'The Diffusion of Microfinance'.

[32] Jackson, *Social and Economic Networks,* there 23. See also Stephen P. Borgatti, "Centrality and Network Flow", in: *Social Networks,* 27:1 (2005): 55–71.

[33] For a more specific approach see especially Borgatti, 'Centrality and Network Flow'; Stephen P. Borgatti, Kathleen M. Carley, and David Krackhardt, 'On the Robustness of Centrality Measures under Conditions of Imperfect Data', in: *Social Networks*, 28:2 (2006): 124–136; Sébastien de Valeriola, 'Can Historians Trust Centrality?', in: *Journal of Historical Network Research*, 6:1 (2021), 85-125; Francis Bloch, Matthew O. Jackson, and Pietro Tebaldi, 'Centrality Measures in Networks', in: *Social Choice and Welfare* 61:2 (2023), 413–453.

distinction to differentiate claims and liabilities. In a visual network, it is often helpful to locate the biggest lenders or borrowers and see where in the network they are placed. Yet, the biggest players are not always central and well connected to the rest of their community. Similarly, the "Matthew effect" in network sciences describes the preferential attachment process. Nodes with more connections than others tend to increase their connectivity at a higher rate and therefore maintain their popularity.

Closeness centrality can help to clarify how well connected a node is. A high score means that a node can easily reach any other node. This measure allows to determine how well information can flow between particular agents. It is a "reachability" measure.

Betweenness centrality indicates how well a node is situated in a network. A node with a high score is defined as a "hub" or sometimes as a broker. This is perhaps one of the most important measures. Consider the graph below (Fig. 4), the node in the middle, node 2, has a high betweenness centrality score, both receiving credit (from 1, 3, and 4) and passing on credit (to 5, 6, 7, and 8), acting therefore potentially as a broker. Betweenness centrality is a measure often associated with influence. It is helpful to determine who has the most interpersonal influence on others. Considering the embeddedness of economic relations in the social tissues of communities, betweenness centrality can be used to determine influence and power within the network and perhaps more largely within the community. In a ground-breaking article, Padgett and Ansell show that the Medici family in Renaissance Florence became the most powerful not because of its wealth—the Strozzi were wealthier—but because of the family's higher betweenness centrality. In other words, the Medici often lie on the shortest path between Florentine elite families thanks to their relationships through marriage. Their central position granted them access to information, business deals, and political influence. Padgett and Ansell conclude, "Medicean political control was produced by network disjunctures within the elite, which the Medici alone spanned".[34] This is perhaps one of the most useful centrality measures while considering a large network of credit transactions. Brokers are not always easily detectable in a dataset.

[34] John F. Padgett and Christopher K. Ansell, 'Robust Action and the Rise of the Medici, 1400-1434', in: *American Journal of Sociology*, 98:6 (1993), 1259–1319, there 1259.

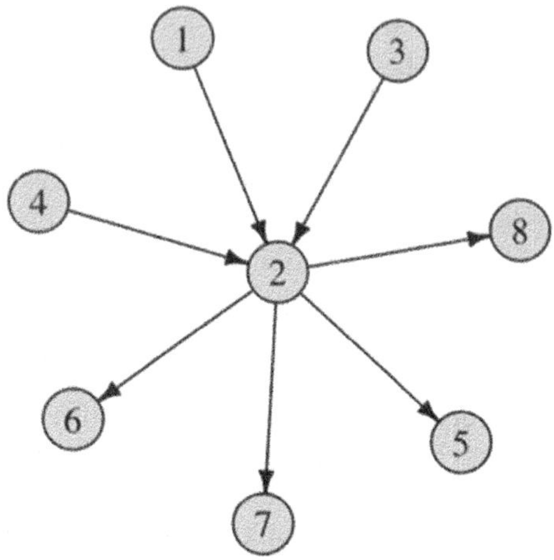

Fig. 4 Betweenness centrality: the node in the middle has the highest score (created in R by the author)

To be really influential, though, brokers need to be located at the core of the network, not on its periphery. In fact, one can use the Bonacich centrality measure, similar to betweenness centrality, which measures the embeddedness of a certain node. If a node is connected to agents that are not so well connected, or isolated, then its role is theoretically more important because others tend to be more dependent on that node. Contrary to this, a node connected to well-connected nodes might be more dependent on them.[35]

The last measure is eigenvector centrality ("it's who you know"), which indicates the importance of a node determined by the importance of its neighbours.[36] It is often referred to as a "popularity" measure. An individual with a small degree of popularity might have a high score of eigenvector centrality if his friends are popular.

Looking at Fig. 5, we can make the following observations.[37] Node 4, at the centre of the graph, has a degree of 2. As such, it is not the biggest player in the graph. Nodes 5 and 3 each have a degree of 3. Yet, node

[35] Phillip Bonacich, 'Power and Centrality: A Family of Measures', in: *American Journal of Sociology*, 92:5 (1987), 1170-1182.

[36] Matthew O. Jackson, *The Human Network: How Your Social Position Determines Your Power, Beliefs, and Behaviors* (New York, 2019), there 43.

[37] Illustration inspired by Jackson, *Social and Economic Networks,* there 38-43.

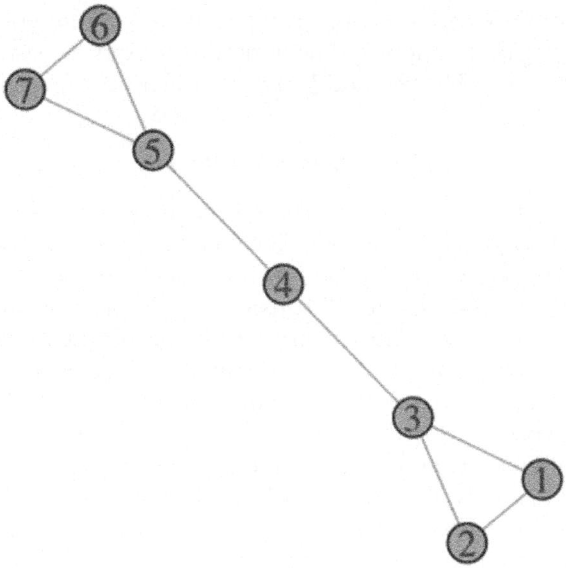

Fig. 5 Centrality illustration (created in R by the author)

4 is the most central node. It has a high betweenness centrality (0.60 compared to nodes 3 and 5 which each have 0.53). Removing node 4, for example, would alter the structure of the network and give a totally different result. Node 4 ranks second for eigenvector centrality (0.54) behind nodes 3 and 5 (each 0.63). Note: note that in a directed, the calculations to evaluate a node's prestige are different. Incoming links from nodes who have themselves a high number of incoming links matter.

3 The Limits of SNA Applied to Early Financial Networks

SNA therefore offers interesting tools of analysis for financial history. Yet, this approach is not without its challenges. This part disregards the traditional issues related to data limitations, such as missing data or problems related to the identification of individuals (homonymy for example). Instead, it focuses on three major problems that need to be considered while using SNA for the examination of credit relations. The first is the limitation of SNA regarding the complexity and meaning of ties. The second is the critical notion of time in networks. And the last, similar and related to the second, is the problem of transitivity assumption.

3.1 *Quality of the Ties*

In preindustrial Europe, relationships between lenders and borrowers went beyond simple economic ties. The literature has long pointed to the embeddedness of economic relations in the social tissue.[38] Peer-to-peer lending in the relative absence of banking institutions was often as much an economic matter as a social one. Credit ties formed among neighbours, acquaintances, and kin. Even intermediated credit, via a notary for example, was constituted by a degree of social relations.[39] As such, early financial networks operated on a logic of social interactions, which might have been different from the logic of the modern market precisely because of the embeddedness of these networks in the social tissue.[40] They often operated based on social norms and codes. As Kate Davison remarks "networks do not stand apart from culture, they are formed, maintained, and broken with reference to norms and expectations".[41]

Yet, to analyse the nature and depth of these social relations, social network analysis is ill-equipped.[42] It cannot grasp and analyse the subtleties and complexities of human relations. It does not say much

[38] Craig Muldrew, *Economy of Obligation: The Culture of Credit and Social Relations in Early Modern England* (New York, 1998); Laurence Fontaine, *The Moral Economy: Poverty, Credit, and Trust in Early Modern Europe* (New York, 2014). Recently, Dermineur, *Before Banks: The Making of Credit and Debt in Pre-Industrial France.*

[39] Dermineur, *Before Banks: The Making of Credit and Debt in Pre-Industrial France,* see chapter 3.

[40] Brian Uzzi, 'The Sources and Consequences of Embeddedness for the Economic Performance of Organizations: The Network Effect', in: *American Sociological Review* 61:4 (1996), 674–698. See also Tobias Gössling, 'Proximity, Trust and Morality in Networks', in: *European Planning Studies* 12:5 (2004): 675-689. See also Karen S. Cook and Richard M. Emerson, 'Power, Equity and Commitment in Exchange Networks', *American Sociological Review*, 43:5 (1978), 721-739.

[41] Kate Davison, 'Early Modern Social Networks: Antecedents, Opportunities, and Challenges', in: *The American Historical Review*, 124:2 (2019), 456-482.

[42] Something remarked by Barry W. Davison and Charles Wetherell, 'Social Network Analysis of Historical Communities: Some Questions from the Present for the Past', in: *The History of the Family* 1:1 (1996): 97-121,; Claire Lemercier, 'Analyse de réseaux et histoire', *Revue d'histoire moderne & contemporaine*, 52:2 (2005), 88–112.

about the quality and diversity of the ties, or of multiplexity. In any social network, there is a necessary asymmetry in the opportunities and expectations of people. Lenders and borrowers often agreed on transactions of a different intrinsic nature.[43] A loan could be profitable to both parties; reciprocal, echoing past dealings; predatory, emphasising the power of the lender over the borrower; charitable, in the sense the lender extended money knowing there was little hope of repayment; or granted, because of the strength of family obligations. The list could go on. As a result, ties in a network have different meanings and intrinsic value. Assuming that credit relations connecting nodes in a network were of a similar nature is a false assumption. Credit relations, especially personal ones, were not static, and their meaning evolved with time. They were also often complex and might have encompassed various categories at once and at the same time. Pierre Bourdieu reminds us that the lender could face a choice that was not entirely hers, in a framework where lenders and borrowers exchanged under "a collective self-deception".[44] The more socially legitimate a loan request, the greater the moral obligation to comply with it.[45] Bourdieu further refers to "the exercise of gentle violence".[46] He posits that credit is "an attack on the freedom of one who receives it (...) it creates obligations, it is a way to possess, by creating people obliged to reciprocate".[47] SNA often seems poorly equipped to analyse such complex ties.

There is thus a need to provide qualitative depth to the analysis. First, cross-analysis of various documents can contribute to a better understanding of the complexity of ties. To assess the quality of ties in a credit network, for example, judicial court proceedings, account books, letters, or diaries could help to establish a typology of ties.

[43] See also Neha Gondal and Paul D. McLean, 'Linking Tie-Meaning with Network Structure'.

[44] Pierre Bourdieu, *Pascalian Meditations* (Stanford, 2000), there 192.

[45] Frederick Wherry, Kristin Seefeldt, and Anthony S. Alvarez, 'To Lend or Not to Lend to Friends and Kin: Awkwardness, obfuscation, and negative reciprocity', in: *Social Forces* 98:2 (2019): 753-793, there 758.

[46] Pierre Bourdieu, *Outline of a Theory of Practice* (Cambridge, 1977), there 193.

[47] Pierre Bourdieu, *Practical Reason: On the Theory of Action* (Stanford, 1998), there 94.

Recently, several scholars have moved away from the mathematical aspect of relations to ascribe qualitative meaning to ties.[48] Harrison C. White posits that ties are a relation between two identities. These identities are "sources of action". And these identities, he argues, operate in a framework he labels ***netdoms***, which are made of networks of relations (net) and domains of meaning or cultural terms of perception (dom), characteristic of those relations.[49] Ties can have multiple meanings. It is precisely this multiplexity that is often difficult to sort out.[50] In effect, position in the network provides access to certain types of meanings for nodes. Part of this domain of meanings is the set of "stories". For example, in a peer-to-peer lending network, nodes interact based on their identities, their expectations, and their customs. A lender part of multiple networks across various communities may bring different practices. The ties become stories between actors and carry meanings through expectations. These stories or past dealings then have an impact on subsequent exchanges. According to Gondal and McLean, "acting across netdoms here implies that meanings of interactions in succeeding domains are likely to be influenced by the lingering content of the set of entanglements and relations between actors in previous domains". In network terms, they add, "this can be measured by the composition and degree of multiplexity of ties between actors".[51] To illustrate their point, they consider the circulation of personal loans in Renaissance Florence, concluding that it is possible to track the meaning of exchange via structure.

Ultimately, this approach forces us to rethink the meaning of ties. One should not assume that all ties carry the same meaning in a given network; only cross-analysis of various sources via a careful microdata approach can help to create a meaningful tie typology. Future research may refine this approach and help to develop these tools.

This netdom approach contrasts somehow with the "actor-oriented" approach, albeit they are not mutually exclusive. In the latter, nodes

[48] Harrison C. White, ***Identity and Control: How Social Formations Emerge*** (Princeton, 2008); Gondal and McLean, 'Linking Tie-Meaning with Network Structure '.

[49] See also Gondal and McLean, 'Linking Tie-Meaning with Network Structure', there 125.

[50] See, for instance, Nicolas Ruffini-Ronzani, Sébastien de Valeriola, and Etienne Cuvelier, 'Dealing with the Heterogeneity of Interpersonal Relationships in the Middle Ages: A Multi-Layer Network Approach', in: ***Digital Medievalist*** 15:1 (2022).

[51] Gondal and McLean, 'Linking Tie-Meaning with Network Structure ', there 126.

choose to create, maintain, and sever ties based on their own preferences and expectations. These preferences might be based on various attributes, pertaining to themselves and towards various partners. The "actor-oriented" approach allows to test homophily, reciprocity, and transitivity. It is not an approach that ascribes too much weight to the environment and the circumstances, yet it can be used to help establish a typology of tie meaning.

3.2 Time as an Issue

The second major issue surrounding SNA to take into consideration is the constraint of time.[52] The network in Fig. 1, for example, represents all the credit relations for the year 1930 in a static fashion. It gives a false sense of steady reality. Yet, networks are rarely frozen in time. Individuals may die, move, or disappear while some new entrants may join the network.

One of the biggest issues here is to have a clear definition of the length of a relationship. In the case of credit relationships, one straightforward solution is to consider that a credit relationship existed the moment a contract was signed. This ignores the probable negotiations *ex ante* and thus the existing relationship already in place, with other possible exchanges that took place previously. In the same vein, considering that a credit relationship ceased to exist the moment a debt is reimbursed is also a straightforward interpretation. It does not account for the eventual benefits or constraints existing after the contract has expired. Moreover, other factors can impact the stability of networks, such as death.[53]

The question of the duration of a credit-debt relationship is a tricky one. Visual representations of early financial networks often entailed a

[52] Claire Lemercier, 'Taking time seriously: How do we deal with change in historical networks?' in: Markus Gamper.

Markus Gamper, Linda Reschke and Marten Düring, Knoten und Kanten III. Soziale Netzwerkanalyse in Geschichts- und Politikforschung (Bielefeld, 2015), there 183; Louis Bissieres, "Taking Time Seriously': An Empirical Approach to an American Merchant Network at the End of the 18th Century', in: *Journal of Historical Network Research* 8 (2023): 56-90. Melanie Conroy, Kimmo Elo, Malte Rehbein, Linda von Keyserlingk, 'Visualizing the Evolution of Historical Networks Using Small Multiples in Grid Charts', in: *Journal of Historical Network Research*, 7:1 (2022), 86-113; For best practice see, for example, Christophe Verbruggen, Hans Blomme, and Thomas D'haeninck, 'Mobility and Movements in Intellectual History: A Social Network Approach', in: *The Power of Networks* (London, 2020), 125-150.

[53] Something noted in Davison, 'Early Modern Social Networks ', there 476.

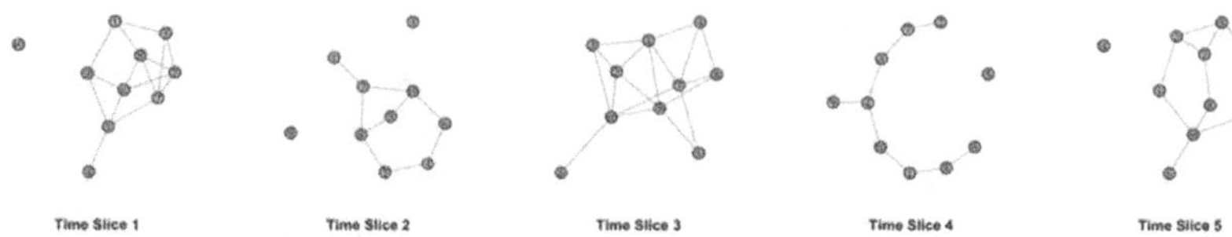

Fig. 6 Visual representation of random time slices (created in R by the author)

static representation. Yet, it is possible to represent the length of a credit relation by attributing several degrees of intensity based on the duration of the relation. It is also possible to create dynamic networks or multilayered networks.[54] Directional analysis can help to visualise the evolution of a network. A timeline network can be useful to identify a tipping point for example.[55] Most often, scholars use time slices to represent the evolution of networks in time (see Fig. 6).[56] It is much more difficult to examine temporal networks in depth with mathematical tools.[57]

3.3 Transitivity Assumption

A similar and complementary problematic issue is the transitivity assumption. Analysing aggregated networks without taking time into consideration means that we assume transitivity, i.e. the *friend of my friend is my friend* approach, regardless of the time frame.[58] In the following graph (Fig. 7), we assume that A and C are linked by B. But if we consider the date of the transaction between the parties, we notice that B had a

[54] Ingeborg van Vugt, 'Using Multi-Layered Networks to Disclose Books in the Republic of Letters, in: *Journal of Historical Network Research* 1 (2017): 25–51. See also the method proposed here (mainly for visualisation) Aris Xanthos et al., 'Visualising the Dynamics of Character Networks', in: *Digital Humanities* (Krakow, 2016), 417–419.

[55] See, for example, Naomi Rosenthal et al., 'Social Movements and Network Analysis: A Case Study of Nineteenth-Century Women's Reform in New York State', in: *American Journal of Sociology* 90-5 (1985): 1022–1054.

[56] See, for example, Martin Grandjean, 'Les Réseaux de La Coopération Intellectuelle. La Société Des Nations Comme Actrice Des Échanges Scientifiques et Culturels Dans l'entre-Deux-Guerres' PhD Thesis, Université de Lausanne, Faculté des lettres, 2018.

[57] To go further see Dane Taylor, Mason A. Porter, and Peter J. Mucha, 'Supracentrality Analysis of Temporal Networks with Directed Interlayer Coupling' arXiv (2019). For best practice using historical material see especially Bissieres, 'Taking Time Seriously'.

[58] Bissieres, 'Taking Time Seriously'; Lemercier, 'Taking Time Seriously'.

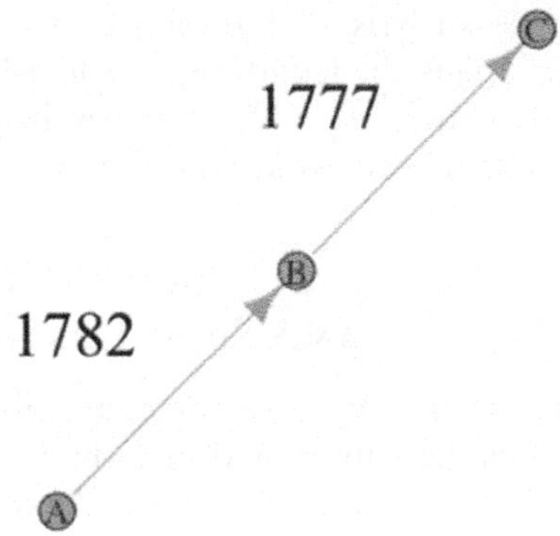

Fig. 7 - Example: time and betweenness centrality (created in R by the author)

connection with C before he did with A, affecting therefore the meaning of B's betweenness centrality.

One option to circumvent this problem and represent networks considering the constraints of time is to use paths (i.e. with dates of the actual credit transactions for example). Path refers to the sequence of nodes that are connected by time-consecutive edges. Paths, and de facto ties, are cut if temporal order is broken. As a result, we have different path lengths and a different kind of network. The benefit is to understand better how credit flowed within a specific group. To determine if this approach would be beneficial for researchers of early financial networks, one can compare aggregated betweenness and path betweenness to establish exactly how time affects network dynamics. Aggregated betweenness tends to overestimate connection and the importance of certain nodes. Path betweenness on the other hand is a useful tool to understand better the role of certain brokers in credit relations. Evidently, the relevance of such a method is highly dependent on the research questions asked. It is possible to analyse paths using packages such as pathpy2.[59]

Overall, SNA applied to early financial markets and networks is not without its challenges. First, the quality of ties differs within a network. The embeddedness of credit relations in the social tissue of communities calls for a refined typology of these ties. This can be established via

[59] Note that pathpy2 does not take into consideration dates before 1970. Yet, it is possible to circumvent this problem. See https://www.youtube.com/watch?v=TD0bBokSF6g See also Ingo Scholtes, 'IngoScholtes/Pathpy', Python, 2021, https://github.com/IngoScholtes/pathpy.

cross-analysis of archival material. Second, the representation of time and especially the length of a credit relationship is a complex issue. Therefore, researchers are advised to pay better attention to the sequence of credit exchanges to avoid representing a biased reality of flux and exchanges.

4 Early Financial Networks and SNA: Further Research Paths

There are at least three promising areas in which SNA could help researchers interested in early financial markets. The first pertains to the role of brokers and intermediaries. The second concerns the process of diffusion and contagion. And the third relates to the changes and evolution of credit markets, paying close attention to the vectors of change and the consequence of such development for the overall structure of the market.

4.1 *Brokerage and Intermediation*

The idea that certain nodes are assigned a significant function in the network has long been developed.[60] Structural holes and in particular "brokers", those who have exclusivity of access to other nodes, fill the most interesting roles to be examined in a network. The structural holes are the "occasional bridge relations between clusters".[61] And the brokers are the people who build the bridge. They are usually considered capable of passing information from one group to another, making the short path distance possible. Considering Fig. 8, node 25, for example, is a broker. She connects nodes 21, 22, 23, and 24 to the rest of the network. Without her, those nodes would be isolated. Brokers can be identified and assigned a broker score.[62]

[60] Ronald S. Burt, *Brokerage and Closure: An Introduction to Social Capital* (Oxford, 2005); Granovetter, 'The Strength of Weak Ties'. See as a good example of the use of brokerage measure in networks Henning Hillmann and Brandy L. Aven, 'Fragmented Networks and Entrepreneurship in Late Imperial Russia', *American Journal of Sociology* 117-2 (2011): 484-538.

[61] Burt, *Brokerage and Closure*, there 12.

[62] See in particular Roger V. Gould and Roberto M. Fernandez, 'Structures of Mediation: A Formal Approach to Brokerage in Transaction Networks', in: *Sociological Methodology* 19 (1989), 89–126, https://doi.org/10.2307/270949. And also Matthew

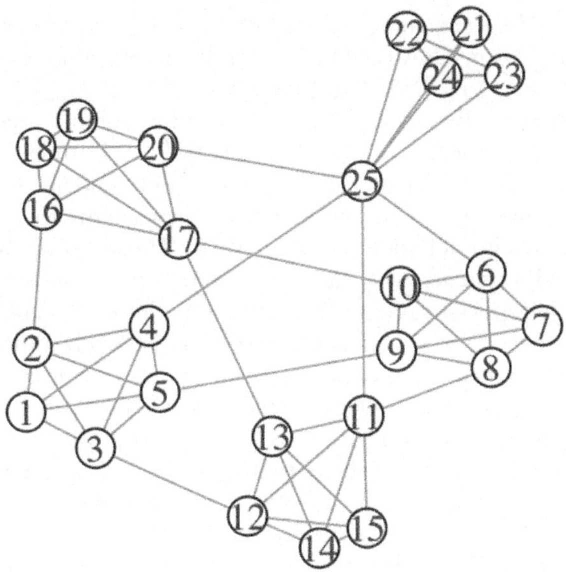

Fig. 8 - Structural holes and brokers (created in R by the author)

There has been an increasing interest in the role of intermediation in early financial markets since the pioneering publication of Hoffman, Postel-Vinay and Rosenthal, *Priceless Markets*. These authors argue that notaries in early modern France brokered a good deal of all the credit exchange in Paris. They based their argumentation on the enormous flows of notarial contracts available and therefore the amount of data notaries had access to. Notaries alone could resolve the problem of asymmetric information.[63] This idea that notaries acted as intermediaries has since been widely accepted.[64] Yet, their intermediary role could be tested

A. Peeples and W. Randall Haas Jr., 'Brokerage and Social Capital in the Prehispanic U.S. Southwest', in: *American Anthropologist* 115:2 (2013): 232-247. See their algorithm with Peeples and Randall.

[63] Philip T. Hoffman, Gilles Postel-Vinay, and Jean-Laurent Rosenthal, *Priceless Markets: The Political Economy of Credit in Paris, 1660-1870* (Chicago Press, 2001).

[64] Juliette Levy, 'Notaries and Credit Markets in Nineteenth-Century Mexico', in: *The Business History Review* 84:3 (2010): 459–78; Marcella Lorenzini, 'Borrowing and Lending Money in Alpine Areas During the Eighteenth Century: Trento and Rovereto

further with SNA to examine exactly how a notary brokered relationships and between whom. SNA could also help clarify whether a local notarial culture did exist, as recently suggested.[65]

As an example, Fig. 9 represents the entire notarial credit network of the city of Bordeaux in the year 1760.[66] It features the notaries (darker tone) and their clients (lighter tone, both lenders and borrowers regardless of their role). The notaries and their clients formed compact groups, almost ego-networks on their own. Those groups were linked by a few nodes, clients who dealt with more than one notary. Those nodes play an important role in the network because they linked different groups together. The use of SNA allows us to study different things here. First, the visual representation means we can identify those agents who turned to more than one notary for their deeds. Among them, one finds merchants, religious institutions, artisans, and noblemen. They are to be found in the middle of the network, connected to notaries with the biggest networks. Crossing information, it is possible to examine their roles further and the nature of the contracts they signed to find out more about their roles. Their identification could help with the difficult issue of notarial network formation. Did the notary broker relations between lenders and borrowers or did their clients pick them freely? Hoffman et alii. hypothesise that notaries shared their excess lenders and borrowers

Compared', in: D'Maris Coffman, Cinzia Lorandini, and Marcella Lorenzini (eds.) Financing in Europe: Evolution, Coexistence and Complementarity of Lending Practices from the Middle Ages to Modern Times, (Cham, 2018), 107–134; Lorenzini Marcella, 'Credit Market and Notaries in Verona in the Second Half of the Seventeenth Century', in: *The Journal of European Economic History* 44:1 (2015), 123-148; Laurie Nussdorfer, *Brokers of Public Trust: Notaries in Early Modern Rome* (Baltimore, 2009); Daniel Reupke and Gabriele B. Clemens, 'Der Notar Als Broker: Das Management Des Privaten Kreditmarkts', in: *Zeitschrift Für Verbraucher- Und Privatinsolvenzrecht* 8:12 (2009): 16–22.

[65] Claire Lemercier and Francesca Trivellato, '1751 and Thereabout: A Quantitative and Comparative Approach to Notarial Records', in: *Social Science History* 46:3 (2022): 555-583; Dermineur, "Peer-to-Peer Lending in Pre-Industrial France"; Dermineur, *Before Banks: The Making of Credit and Debt in Pre-Industrial France.*

[66] Based on the contrôle des actes, Archives Départementales de la Gironde 2C 157, 158, 159.

with each other.[67] SNA could further highlight this point and show how it happened.

There were other types of intermediaries in early financial markets, such as innkeepers, merchants, local shark lenders, pawnbrokers, and money changers. Visual representation of their networks can also lead to their identification and further clarifications of their role. SNA can help to

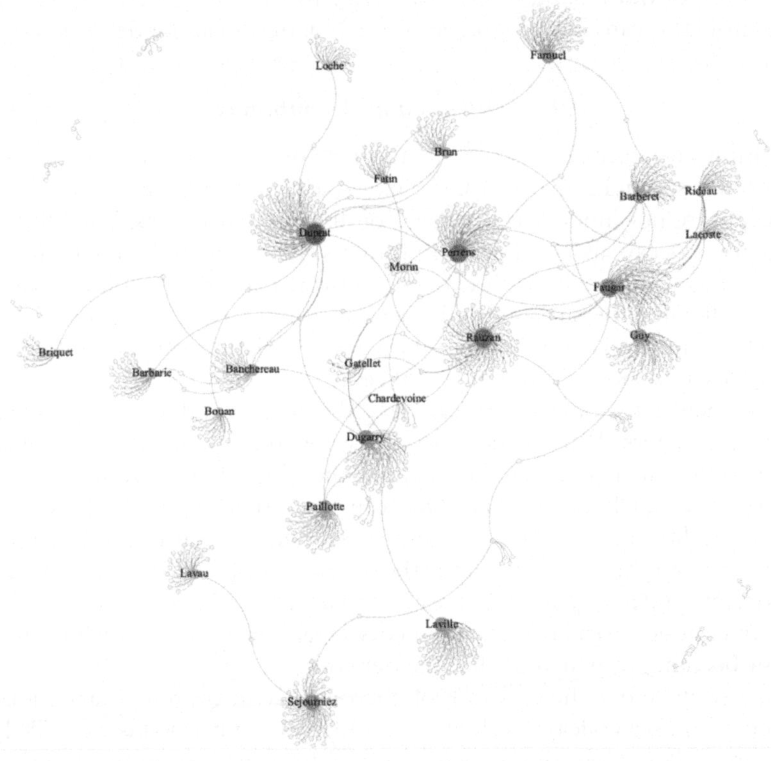

Fig. 9 Network of notaries, lenders, and borrowers in Bordeaux in 1760. (Nodes coloured after their degree centrality, the darker the higher) (created in Gephi by the author)

[67] Philip T. Hoffman, Gilles Postel-Vinay, and Jean-Laurent Rosenthal, *Dark Matter Credit: The Development of Peer-to-Peer Lending and Banking in France* (Princeton, 2019), there 108.

determine their function and how important they were thanks to a quantitative analysis of their networks and positions. Overall, SNA can bring answers to questions such as what did brokerage do in early financial networks? And what kind of information was passed on? What were the benefits of brokerage for all parties involved? How effective was it? Some of these questions can be answered by digging in notarial registers and judicial registers to get more information on the agents themselves and the nature of ties linking individuals. Years other than the one presented here on Fig. 8 can also be studied to see if patterns can be determined.

4.2 *Diffusion and Contagion*

Diffusion and contagion issues in the network have recently been put under the spotlight thanks to the Covid-19 pandemic. But these two concepts are not limited to the realm of diseases and viruses. Early financial networks can also exhibit these features. Diffusion and contagion are often studied in parallel with dynamic networks and their evolution over time. Influence, persuasion, and coercion can be traced between individuals (contagion). While innovation and emulation can take place in a network in a more diffuse way (diffusion).

In a network, some nodes can play the role of influential spreaders or early adopters. During the Covid-19 crisis, there were frequent references to the super spreaders for example, those people who contaminated others on a much larger scale. One can track them with the betweenness centrality measure and the degree centrality measure. High degree individuals might even accelerate the spread thanks to their reach. An important lender might be imposing certain practices, such as a certain type of contract, particular requirements (guarantees, etc.), which in turn might become normative within the network.

In a study about the diffusion of microfinance in contemporary India, Banerjee and his colleagues show how adopters of microloans were likely to share information about them. Thanks to a new measure, diffusion centrality, the authors could predict how widely and quickly others would be likely to adopt microfinance as well.[68]

The density and the cohesiveness of a network matter if we are to determine the degree of embeddedness of agents in the network and the

[68] Banerjee et al., 'The Diffusion of Microfinance'.

potential for contagion and diffusion. The overall average degree in a network thus matters for contagion. If nodes have more than one connection, the contagion spreads more easily. In a small credit network with high density, one could, for example, trace the spread of default.[69]

4.3 Changes Over Time

I have mentioned previously the challenge of accounting for time while using SNA. A related issue is to measure changes over time in a network structure. How can we track changes and evolution? What measures are useful? Visualisation of changes over time of sliced networks may indicate some paths to follow and develop further. But it is rarely enough for detecting forces of change. Instead, actor-driven models can be useful.[70]

As we have seen above, ties between agents occur often among people who share similar attributes, this is network autocorrelation, the "natural interdependence between network structure and the individual characteristics of the network actors".[71] The homophily principle is often invoked to explain this process. It is easier and more rewarding to interact with someone similar than dissimilar. In this kind of setting, actors may change their preferences and some of their attributes to match those of other people in the group, especially influential actors. The assimilation principle is well known, for example, among new entrants (new staff at work,

[69] Related to this issue see especially Timothy Besley and Stephen Coate, 'Group Lending, Repayment Incentives and Social Collateral', in: *Journal of Development Economics* 46:1 (1995), 1–18.

[70] The software SIENA (Simulation Investigation for Empirical Network Analysis) is often used to assess the strength of homophily and assimilation process. The reader may be well versed in the use of statistical models to use it. See further Christian Steglich, Tom A. B. Snijders, and Patrick West, 'Applying SIENA', in: *Methodology* 2:1 (2006), 48-56; William J. Burk, Christian EG Steglich, and Tom AB Snijders, 'Beyond Dyadic Interdependence: Actor-Oriented Models for Co-Evolving Social Networks and Individual Behaviors', in: *International Journal of Behavioral Development* 31,4 (2007), 397–404; Tom AB Snijders, Christian EG Steglich, and Michael Schweinberger, 'Modeling the Co-Evolution of Networks and Behavior', *Longitudinal Models in the Behavioral and Related Sciences* 31:4 (2007), 41–71; Tom A. B. Snijders, Gerhard G. van de Bunt, and Christian E. G. Steglich, 'Introduction to Stochastic Actor-Based Models for Network Dynamics', in: *Social Networks, Dynamics of Social Networks*, 32:1 (2010), 44–60; Emmanuel Lazega et al., 'Norms, Status and the Dynamics of Advice Networks: A Case Study', *Social Networks, Dynamics of Social Networks*, 34:3 (2012), 323–32.

[71] Steglich, Snijders, and West, 'Applying SIENA'.

new kids at school, or new neighbours or immigrants). Social interaction and social influence change how agents behave and choose to interact and with whom, in turn affecting the network structure. It becomes difficult then to determine how change occurs, especially when both nodes and network structure are dynamic. Evidently, this approach supposes social interactions[72]; it may be well suited for early financial networks featuring peer-to-peer lending.[73]

For example, SNA could highlight new paths in the study of the transition between traditional exchanges such as peer-to-peer lending and the lending of banking institutions. The transition from a peer-to-peer lending system in which personal connections prevailed to a much more impersonal system took more than a hundred years.[74] Indeed, despite the growing formalisation of the transactions, the personal lending market resisted the advent of banking institutions well.[75] In Sweden, for example, most people were not in contact with banks at all until World War I. In the town of Askersund, 70% of debts were still private in 1900. The same proportion can be found in Filipstad (63%), Rönö (71%), the rural parish of Askim (71%), and Östra Hising (82%), for example.[76] In the university town of Uppsala in 1910, 50% of debts were still contracted via peer-to-peer lending. Banks did not compete with the peer-to-peer credit market. Their market segment was different and responded to different needs.[77]

[72] For a detailed methodology, see especially Steglich, Snijders, and West, 'Applying SIENA'.

[73] See also Claire Lemercier and Paul-Andre Rosental, 'The Structure and Dynamics of Migration Patterns in 19th-Century Northern France' (2010), https://sciencespo.hal.science/hal-01063603; Burk, Steglich, and Snijders, 'Beyond Dyadic Interdependence'; See also Emily Buchnea, 'Transatlantic Transformations: Visualizing Change Over Time in the Liverpool–New York Trade Network, 1763–1833', in: *Enterprise & Society* 15:4 (2014), 687–721.

[74] See, for example, Håkan Lindgren, 'The Modernization of Swedish Credit Markets, 1840-1905: Evidence from Probate Records' in: *The Journal of Economic History* 62:3 (2002), 810-832.

[75] Håkan Lindgren, 'The Modernization of Swedish Credit Markets'.

[76] Axel Hagberg, 'Households Assets and Liabilities in Sweden 1800-1900', paper presented at the symposium Wealth and Debt Accumulation in Early Financial Markets, A Marcus Wallenberg Symposium, Stockholm, September 2018.

[77] Elise Dermineur, 'Peer to Peer Credit Networks in Sweden, 1810-1910', in: Juliette Levy and Christiaan van Bochove (eds.) (forthcoming) *Beyond Banks: A Comparative Framework for Understanding Credit Markets and Intermediation* (Cham, 2024).

People preferred thus to turn to their social networks to locate capital. And banks preferred a restricted circle of clients to deal with. For both, size mattered. Private individuals could use their social capital and local connections to locate the funds they needed within their own network. And banking institutions used the professional and intimate circles of their board members to monitor information and control the exchanges. Naomi Lamoureaux suggests that the establishment of banks in the nineteenth century in the United States owed much to social networks. The bank's board of directors funnelled much of the bank's capital to themselves, their families and others of their acquaintance. Personal guarantee was highly valued to secure a loan. Later, these successful establishments would open to the public to get deposits. Yet, there is much work to be done in uncovering the mechanisms behind such a transition and the various steps along the way. First, little is known regarding the impact of formalisation on traditional networks. How did traditional networks respond to such formalisation? Is there a loss of ability to borrow from traditional lenders after the adoption of formal means? How is the risk distributed after formalisation? It might be possible to observe a decrease in network density and closure. Second, how did banks choose their clients? A common assumption would be that banks accepted anyone who deposits funds. Yet, looking at the preliminary research available—such as the network of Fig. 2—it seems that client sharing between banks might be related to personal ties.[78] These personal ties might have facilitated information access about clients and reduced transaction costs. Clients were certainly not shared randomly. However, the importance of these personal ties might have excluded some potential customers who were newcomers and/or not well connected. As a result, these individuals might have continued to seek credit within their own personal and private network. It would be useful to study further people in the network who adopted formalisation, the so-called early adopters, and see if, because of their popularity, the trend spread further. Here, the actor-model cited above could be of some help.[79]

[78] See Dermineur, 'The Evolution of Credit Networks in Pre-Industrial Finland'.

[79] See also for instance Tim E. Crumplin, 'Opaque Networks: Business and Community in the Isle of Man, 1840–1900', in: *Business History* 49:6 (2007), 780–801.

5 Conclusion

Social network analysis as an approach can be a particularly useful tool of analysis for historians. As a visual interface, SNA can help the researcher to identify patterns and structures otherwise impossible to detect in a large dataset. As a mathematical tool, SNA can answer important questions about the role of nodes in a given network as well as the structure of a particular network.

Yet, SNA is an approach that is still to be perfected. Social and economic historians interested in adopting the tools of SNA need to be aware of its flaws. While considering credit transactions, the object of the present volume, SNA remains at the moment a limited tool in at least three areas. First, edges do not render well either the depth, complexity, or essence of interpersonal relationships. Some tools are available to create typologies of ties. Yet, depending on the research questions asked, they still remain limited. Second, SNA does not represent time effectively. The visual representation is often too static and does not account thoroughly for changes within the network. And finally, along the same lines, action and relationships need to be mapped properly to avoid an exaggerated representation of transitivity.

Despite these three major flaws, SNA can be a useful tool of analysis for historians interested in financial markets and networks. New forays can be realised in brokerage and intermediation activities. We know the significance of intermediaries in peer-to-peer credit market, SNA could further expand our knowledge about these actors. SNA could contribute to highlighting new patterns pertaining to contagion and diffusion, contributing especially to our knowledge of the adoption of new practices or the spread of default. Finally, SNA could be a useful tool to demonstrate the change over time of credit markets and map their evolution.

The field of historical network research is currently experiencing a leap forward. It is clear that historians of financial networks must come forward with their own tools and own adapted methods to make sense of past relations with their often incomplete material.

References

Primary sources

Archive départementales de la Gironde, 2C, 157–159.

Riksarkivet, Lycksele tingslags häradsrätt AIId:3 and 4

Secondary material

Banerjee, Abhijit, Arun G. Chandrasekhar, Esther Duflo, and Matthew O. Jackson. 2013. The Diffusion of Microfinance. *Science* 341 (6144): 1236498.

Besley, Timothy, and Stephen Coate. 1995. Group Lending, Repayment Incentives and Social Collateral. *Journal of Development Economics* 46 (1): 1–18.

Bissieres, Louis. 2023. 'Taking Time Seriously': An Empirical Approach to an American Merchant Network at the End of the 18th Century. *Journal of Historical Network Research* 8: 56–90.

Bloch, Francis, Matthew O. Jackson, and Pietro Tebaldi. 2023. Centrality Measures in Networks. *Social Choice and Welfare* 61 (2): 413–453.

Bonacich, Phillip. 1987. Power and Centrality: A Family of Measures. *American Journal of Sociology* 92 (5): 1170–1182.

Borgatti, Stephen P. 2005. Centrality and Network Flow. *Social Networks* 27 (1): 55–71.

Borgatti, Stephen P., Kathleen M. Carley, and David Krackhardt. 2006. On the Robustness of Centrality Measures Under Conditions of Imperfect Data. *Social Networks* 28 (2): 124–136.

Bourdieu, Pierre. 1998. *Practical Reason: On the Theory of Action*. Redwood City: Stanford University Press.

Bourdieu, Pierre. 1977. *Outline of a Theory of Practice*. Cambridge: Cambridge Core Cambridge University Press.

Buchnea, Emily. 2014. Transatlantic Transformations: Visualizing Change Over Time in the Liverpool-New York Trade Network, 1763–1833. *Enterprise & Society* 15 (4): 687–721.

Burk, William J., Christian EG. Steglich, and Tom AB. Snijders. 2007. Beyond Dyadic Interdependence: Actor-Oriented Models for Co-Evolving Social Networks and Individual Behaviors. *International Journal of Behavioral Development* 31 (4): 397–404.

Burt, Ronald S. 2005. *Brokerage and Closure: An Introduction to Social Capital*. New York: Oxford University Press.

Carrington, Peter J., John Scott, and Stanley Wasserman. 2005. *Models and Methods in Social Network Analysis*. Cambridge: Cambridge University Press.

Centola, Damon. 2010. The Spread of Behavior in an Online Social Network Experiment. *Science* 329 (5996): 1194–1197.

Coleman, James S. 1988. Social Capital in the Creation of Human Capital. *American Journal of Sociology* 94: 95–120.

Conroy, Melanie, Kimmo Elo, Malte Rehbein, and Linda von Keyserlingk-Rehbein. 2022. Visualizing the Evolution of Historical Networks Using Small

Multiples in Grid Charts. *Journal of Historical Network Research* 7 (1): 86–113.

Cook, Karen S., and Richard M. Emerson. 1978. Power, Equity and Commitment in Exchange Networks. *American Sociological Review* 43: 721–739.

Crumplin, Tim E. 2007. Opaque Networks: Business and Community in the Isle of Man, 1840–1900. *Business History* 49 (6): 780–801.

Dahmen, S. R., A. L. C. Bazzan, and R. Gramsch. 2017. Community Detection in the Network of German Princes in 1225: A Case Study. In *Complex Networks VIII*, edited by Bruno Gonçalves, Ronaldo Menezes, Roberta Sinatra, and Vinko Zlatic,193–200. Cham: Springer.

Davison, Kate. 2019. Early Modern Social Networks: Antecedents, Opportunities, and Challenges. *The American Historical Review* 124 (2): 456–482.

Dermineur, Elise M. 2025. *Before Banks: The Making of Credit and Debt in Preindustrial France*. Cambridge: Cambridge University Press.

Dermineur, Elise M. forthcoming. Peer to Peer Credit Networks in Sweden, 1810–1910. In *Beyond Banks: A Comparative Framework for Understanding Credit Markets and Intermediation*, edited by Juliette Levy and Christiaan van Bochove. Cham: Springer.

Dermineur, Elise M. 2019. Peer-to-Peer Lending in Pre-Industrial France. *Financial History Review* 26 (3): 359–388.

Dermineur, Elise M. 2021. The Evolution of Credit Networks in Pre-Industrial Finland. *Scandinavian Economic History Review* 70 (1): 57–86.

Dermineur, Elise M., and Matteo Pompermaier. 2022. Credit Networks in Renaissance Florence: Revisiting the Catasto of 1427 A Research Project in the Making. *Rivista Di Storia Economica e Sociale* 1 (2): 147–175.

Erikson, Emily. 2014. *Between Monopoly and Free Trade: The English East India Company, 1600–1757*. Princeton: Princeton University Press.

Fontaine, Laurence. 2014. *The Moral Economy: Poverty, Credit, and Trust in Early Modern Europe*. Cambridge: Cambridge University Press.

Gestrich, Andreas, and Martin Stark. 2015. *Debtors, Creditors, and Their Networks: Social Dimensions of Monetary Dependence from the Seventeenth to the Twentieth Century*. London: German Historical Institute.

Gondal, Neha, and Paul D. McLean. 2013. Linking Tie-Meaning with Network Structure: Variable Connotations of Personal Lending in a Multiple-Network Ecology. *Poetics* 41 (2): 122–150.

Gössling, Tobias. 2004. Proximity, Trust and Morality in Networks. *European Planning Studies* 12 (5): 675–689.

Gould, Roger V., and Roberto M. Fernandez. 1989. Structures of Mediation: A Formal Approach to Brokerage in Transaction Networks. *Sociological Methodology* 19: 89–126.

Gramsch-Stehfest, Robert. 2020. Community Detection and Structural Balance: Network Analytical Modelling of Political Structures and Actions in the

Middle Ages. In *The Power of Networks*, edited by Florian Kerschbaumer, Linda von Keyserlingk-Rehbein, Martin Stark, Marten Düring, 37–55. London: Routledge.

Grandjean, Martin. 2018. Les Réseaux de La Coopération Intellectuelle. La Société Des Nations Comme Actrice Des Échanges Scientifiques et Culturels Dans l'entre-Deux-Guerres. PhD Thesis, Université de Lausanne, Faculté des lettres.

Granovetter, Mark. 1982. The Strength of Weak Ties. In *Social Structure and Network Analysis*, edited by Peter V. Marsden and Nan Lin, 105–130. Beverly Hills and London and New Delhi: Sage.

Haggerty, John, and Sheryllynne Haggerty. 2010. Visual Analytics of an Eighteenth-Century Business Network. *Enterprise & Society* 11–1: 1–25.

Hillmann, Henning, and Brandy L. Aven. 2011. Fragmented Networks and Entrepreneurship in Late Imperial Russia. *American Journal of Sociology* 117–2: 484–538.

Hoffman, Philip T., Gilles Postel-Vinay, and Jean-Laurent Rosenthal. 2019. *Dark Matter Credit: The Development of Peer-to-Peer Lending and Banking in France*. Princeton: Princeton University Press.

Hoffman, Philip T., Gilles Postel-Vinay, and Jean-Laurent Rosenthal. 2001. *Priceless Markets: The Political Economy of Credit in Paris, 1660–1870*. Chicago: Chicago University Press.

Jackson, Matthew O. 2010. *Social and Economic Networks*. Princeton: Princeton University Press.

Jackson, Matthew O. 2019. *The Human Network: How Your Social Position Determines Your Power, Beliefs, and Behaviors*. New York: Pantheon.

Kadushin, Charles. 2012. *Understanding Social Networks: Theories, Concepts, and Findings*. Oxford: Oxford University Press.

Kerschbaumer, Florian, Linda von Keyserlingk-Rehbein, Martin Stark, Marten Düring, eds. 2020. *The Power of Networks*. London: Routledge.

Lazega, Emmanuel, Lise Mounier, Tom Snijders, and Paola Tubaro. 2012. Norms, Status and the Dynamics of Advice Networks: A Case Study. *Social Networks, Dynamics of Social Networks (2)* 34 (3): 323–332.

Lemercier, Claire. 2005. Analyse de réseaux et histoire. *Revue d'histoire moderne & contemporaine* 52 (2): 88–112.

Lemercier, Claire. 2015a. Formal Network Methods in History: Why and How? In *Social Networks, Political Institutions, and Rural Societies*, edited by Georg Fertig, 281–304. Turnhout: Brepols Publishers.

Lemercier, Claire. 2015b. Taking time seriously: How do we deal with change in historical networks? In *Knoten und Kanten III. Soziale Netzwerkanalyse in Geschichts- und Politikforschung*, edited by Markus Gamper, Linda Reschke and Marten Düring, 183–211. Bielefeld.

Lemercier, Claire, and Paul-Andre Rosental. 2010. The Structure and Dynamics of Migration Patterns in 19th-Century Northern France. HAL Id: hal-01063603. https://sciencespo.hal.science/hal-01063603.

Lemercier, Claire, and Francesca Trivellato. 2022. 1751 and Thereabout: A Quantitative and Comparative Approach to Notarial Records. *Social Science History* 46 (3): 555–583.

Levy, Juliette. 2010. Notaries and Credit Markets in Nineteenth-Century Mexico. *The Business History Review* 84 (3): 459–478.

Lindgren, Hakan. 2002. The Modernization of Swedish Credit Markets, 1840–1905: Evidence from Probate Records. *The Journal of Economic History* 62 (3): 810–832.

Lorandini, Cinzia, and Francesca Odella. 2022. Private Lending in an Alpine Region during the Eighteenth Century: A Family of Merchant-Bankers and Their Credit Network. *Enterprise & Society* 24 (3): 838–865.

Lorenzini, Marcella. 2018. Borrowing and Lending Money in Alpine Areas During the Eighteenth Century: Trento and Rovereto Compared. In *Financing in Europe: Evolution, Coexistence and Complementarity of Lending Practices from the Middle Ages to Modern Times*, edited by Coffman D'Maris, Cinzia Lorandini and Marcella Lorenzini, 107–34. Cham: Springer.

Lorenzini, Marcella. 2015. Credit Market and Notaries in Verona in the Second Half of the Seventeenth Century. *The Journal of European Economic History* 44 (1): 123–148.

McLean, Paul D., and Neha Gondal. 2014. The Circulation of Interpersonal Credit in Renaissance Florence. *European Journal of Sociology / Archives Européennes de Sociologie* 55 (2): 135–176.

Miller, McPherson, Lynn Smith-Lovin, and James M. Cook. 2001. Birds of a Feather: Homophily in Social Networks. *Annual Review of Sociology* 27 (1): 415–444.

Muldrew, Craig. 1998. *Economy of Obligation: The Culture of Credit and Social Relations in Early Modern England*. London: Palgrave.

Nussdorfer, Laurie. 2009. *Brokers of Public Trust: Notaries in Early Modern Rome*. Baltimore, MD: Johns Hopkins University Press.

Odella, Francesca. 2012. A Network Perspective of Economic Relations and Markets. *Österreichische Zeitschrift Für Geschichtswissenschaften* 23 (1): 42–71.

Padgett, John F., and Christopher K. Ansell. 1993. Robust Action and the Rise of the Medici, 1400–1434. *American Journal of Sociology* 98 (6): 1259–1319.

Padgett, John F., and Paul D. McLean. 2011. Economic Credit in Renaissance Florence. *The Journal of Modern History* 83 (1): 1–47.

Peeples, Matthew A., and W. Randall Haas Jr. 2013. Brokerage and Social Capital in the Prehispanic U.S. Southwest. *American Anthropologist* 115 (2): 232–247.

Reupke, Daniel, and Gabriele B. Clemens. 2009. Der Notar Als Broker: Das Management Des Privaten Kreditmarkts. *Zeitschrift Für Verbraucher- Und Privatinsolvenzrecht* 8 (12): 16–22.

Rosenthal, Naomi, Meryl Fingrutd, Michele Ethier, Roberta Karant, and David McDonald. 1985. Social Movements and Network Analysis: A Case Study of Nineteenth-Century Women's Reform in New York State. *American Journal of Sociology* 90 (5): 1022–1054.

Ruffini-Ronzani, Nicolas, Sébastien de Valeriola, and Etienne Cuvelier. 2022. Dealing with the Heterogeneity of Interpersonal Relationships in the Middle Ages: A Multi-Layer Network Approach. *Digital Medievalist*, 15 (1): 1–28.

Scholtes, Ingo. 2021. IngoScholtes/Pathpy. Python. https://github.com/IngoScholtes/pathpy.

Snijders, Tom A. B., Gerhard G. van de Bunt, and Christian E. G. Steglich. 2010. Introduction to Stochastic Actor-Based Models for Network Dynamics. *Social Networks, Dynamics of Social Networks* 32 (1): 44–60.

Snijders, Tom A. B., Christian E. G. Steglich, and Michael Schweinberger. 2007. Modeling the Co-Evolution of Networks and Behavior. *Longitudinal Models in the Behavioral and Related Sciences* 31 (4): 41–71.

Christian, Steglich, Tom A. B. Snijders, and Patrick West. 2006. Applying SIENA. *Methodology* 1: 48–56.

Taylor, Dane, Mason A. Porter, and Peter J. Mucha. 2019. Supracentrality Analysis of Temporal Networks with Directed Interlayer Coupling. arXiv https://doi.org/10.48550/arXiv.1906.06366.

Uzzi, Brian. 1996. The Sources and Consequences of Embeddedness for the Economic Performance of Organizations: The Network Effect. *American Sociological Review* 61 (4): 674–698.

de Valeriola, Sébastien. 2021. Can Historians Trust Centrality? *Journal of Historical Network Research*, 6(1).

Verbruggen, Christophe, Hans Blomme, and Thomas D'haeninck. 2020. Mobility and Movements in Intellectual History: A Social Network Approach. In *The Power of Networks*, edited by Kerschbaumer Florian, Linda von Keyserlingk-Rehbein, Martin Stark, Marten Düring, 125-150. London: Routledge.

van Vugt, Ingeborg. 2017. Using Multi-Layered Networks to Disclose Books in the Republic of Letters. *Journal of Historical Network Research* 1: 25–51.

Barry, Wellman, and Charles Wetherell. 1996. Social Network Analysis of Historical Communities: Some Questions from the Present for the Past. *The History of the Family* 1 (1): 97–121.

White, Harrison C. 2008. *Identity and Control: How Social Formations Emerge*. Princeton: Princeton University Press.

Xanthos Aris, Isaac Pante, Yannick Rochat, and Martin Grandjean. 2016. Visualising the Dynamics of Character Networks. *Digital Humanities*, 417–419, https://hal.science/hal-01525567.

CHAPTER 3

Formation and Sustainability of Financial Networks in Early Modern Europe

Laurence Fontaine

1 Introduction

In early modern Europe, uncertainty dominated all areas of life. Both men and women were constantly preoccupied either with countering the risks that threatened them or managing their effects. The fragile economic equilibrium that working-class families achieved by putting the whole family to work was undermined as soon as illness or unemployment struck one of its members. The need for money and capital was thus at the heart of family survival. It was also necessary to meet the multiple needs of craft and commercial businesses. Being able to rely on solid financial networks is indeed everyone's dream. But the rules governing finance in the aristocratic societies of the time were highly restrictive and, before going into the various types of strategies implemented to create reliable financial networks, it is important to present these rules.

Let me make it clear from the outset that for me there is no difference between the market economy and capitalism because, as soon as

L. Fontaine (✉)
Centre Maurice Halbwachs/PSL (Paris Sciences & Lettres), Paris, France
e-mail: laurence.fontaine@ehess.fr

E. M. Dermineur and M. Pompermaier (eds.), *Credit Networks in The Preindustrial World*, Palgrave Studies in the History of Finance,
https://doi.org/10.1007/978-3-031-67117-3_3

money circulates and as soon as its use can be sold or rented, there is the possibility of accumulation and constitution of capital and therefore the capacity for rapid enrichment of its holders. However, its development could be held back, as it was in Europe until the end of the political domination of the aristocracies. In fact, pre-industrial Europe had two systems of exchange that reflected different economic cultures and, more broadly, two opposing political economies.On the one hand, a gift economy still very much alive, based on the domination of aristocrats, and on the other, a capitalist economy which was very much in place and which was constantly growing, and whose development threatened to destroy the society based on orders and statutes.[1] At a time when religion was the basis of power, it was through religion that priests and warriors protected themselves from the foreseeable attacks on the roots of their domination that were threatened by the potential of the capitalist economy.

The prohibition of interest-bearing loans, which is the driving force of capitalism, was, together with the moral condemnation of avarice, i.e., saving, the weapons used to restrain the development of the market society. But because it is impossible to prohibit something that everyone needs, derogations to the prohibition soon appeared. The needs of commerce were the first to move the set of religious precepts by introducing the time of merchants with the notions of risk, or damage arising *damnum emergens* and *lucrum cessans*.[2]

In the eighteenth century, the State, because it needed money and because the burden of debt weighed too heavily on the social structures, and especially on the aristocracy, took up this issue with determination. It removed usury cases from the ecclesiastical power and protected most of the aristocratic property with the *fideicommis*. The definitions of the word "credit" express well, in English, French as well as Spanish dictionaries, the state of the balance of power: they first insist on the reputation, then on political and economic power that the reputation gives and, lastly, they speak of mutual loans between merchants. Furetière's dictionary,

[1] Laurence Fontaine, *The Moral Economy. Poverty, credit and Trust in Early Modern Europe* (Cambridge, 2014).

[2] In the case of *damnum emergens*, a loan offered without interest could be compensated if the lender suffered a loss as a result of having lent his money; the case of lucrum cessans could only be invoked when three criteria were met: the compensation requested had to be reasonable and never greater than the loss; proof of the loss had to be provided; and the loan had to be free from the outset.

printed in 1688 and 1689, adds a verbal expression: "on credit." And the only example that he gave is that of the merchants' financial ruin when they grant credit to the lords. Moreover, the meanings ascribed to the expression *à crédit* all evoke inanity, uselessness, involuntary wastage or baselessness.[3]

It was not until the Enlightenment that thinking about credit left the framework of the status society and became universal. Montesquieu, Véron de Forbonnais, Turgot, Adam Smith all conclude, quoting Montesquieu, that "the lender compensates himself for the peril of the contravention."[4] Moreover, the impossibility of institutionalizing the financial sector, since it is illegal, also raised the question of contract and trust between individuals.

In his *Mémoire sur les prêts d'argent*, Turgot starts his argumentation with a story about crooks who used the laws against usury and the different courts of justice to swindle merchants who had lent them money within the ordinary course of their business. The result was that the town of Angoulême itself was ground to a halt because the merchants had stopped the trade of money. From this example, he shows that the inapplicable laws only served to create crooks and smugglers, "that the shame and risk associated with loans bearing interest are added costs that the borrower always pays," and that much money remained in the coffers. In the interests and for the enrichment of all, he asked then that the law be brought in line with practice.[5]

In addition to this ever-present possibility of criminalizing credit, even if everyone does it, there is the fact, well known to all economic actors, that debt portfolios are all heavily loaded with bad debts. The main reason for this is that credit is more often a matter of obligation than of free choice, because everyone is inserted into horizontal and vertical networks of relations that are all crossed by debt. It is difficult to refuse credit to one's family, one's friends, one's dependents, and impossible for artisans and merchants to refuse credit to aristocrats.

The study of the merchants' debt portfolios shows that they all included family credits, merchant credits, and credits granted to "friends"

[3] Antoine Furetière, *Dictionnaire universel* (La Haye-Rotterdam, 1690).

[4] Laurence Fontaine, *The Moral Economy. Poverty, Credit, and Trust in Early Modern Europe* (Cambridge, 2014), chap. 7.

[5] Anne-Robert Jacques Turgot, *Mémoire sur les prêts d'argent* (Schelle, 1770).

and that they all depended on the good and bad fortunes of their family members. The analysis of about sixty bankruptcies in Lyon between 1763 and 1771 also shows the imbalance between the claims and the assets of the merchants and confirms the destabilizing role of the credit granted to the aristocracy.[6]

After this necessary reminder of the political framework governing finance, I turn my attention to merchants and describe the strategies implemented by a fifteenth-century merchant, Francesco di Marco Datini: because the archives he left behind provide an insight into all the risks faced by entrepreneurs at that time, knowing that finance was the lifeblood of any enterprise, and because he succeeded in building an industrial and commercial empire despite the many political and economic uncertainties he had to face. We then move on to the eighteenth century to study the practices of merchants and trade books to show that practices have hardly changed since the fifteenth century, and that trust is still rooted in morality and friendship. Finally, we will then understand why networks based on a shared religious or village affiliation, which I present in a third section, are the best adapted to last in such an environment. And I will show that these merchant and financial networks are still relevant today in many Asian and Latin American countries.

2 Datini and the Difficulties of Being a Merchant in the Fifteenth Century

In a society totally embedded in innumerable credit relationships with virtually no regulatory systems to control their excesses and in a largely unpredictable economic environment, the question of the sustainability of financial networks is particularly acute and the issue of trust is crucial. However, the question of trust was not the same for all social groups: for most social actors, it was above all a question of finding ways to avoid meeting their social obligations. Merchants, on the other hand, had no

[6] Maurice Garden, 'Aires du commerce lyonnais au XVIIIe siècle', in: Pierre Léon (ed.), *Aires et structures du commerce français au XVIIIe siècle* (Lyon, 1973), 265–299, there 270–272. See these groups' debt obligations in: David Biem, 'Les offices, les corps et le crédit d'État: l'utilisation des privilèges sous l'Ancien Régime', in: *Annales ESC*, 2 (1988), 379–404.

such choice: they had to navigate between their family and social obligations, the demands of the market and those of the aristocrats, who were difficult to refuse credit and who paid late and badly in any case.

Thanks to the 150,000 letters preserved by Francesco di Marco Datini in his palace of which 7,000 were written by his hand, we are able to understand how he succeeded in building a commercial empire worthy of the time. He sought to be informed about everything in order to make his way and succeed in the face of so many uncertainties and contrary winds.[7]

The first uncertainty had to do with men: managing the impossibility of trusting anyone was the crux of his strategy. Datini had few collaborators. He chose men he had mixed with at work or during his visits or then those with whom he had ties of kinship or friendship, and also took on relatives of friends and associates. The obligation to write regularly that he imposed on them helped keep up relationships; it compelled them to provide frequent accounts and gave him an understanding of the economic and political situation in the world. He was always fearful that his collaborators and associates would place their own interests or those of their family above their loyalty to him. Indeed, given the plurality of networks of which every individual was a part and to which he was considered obligated, and given the weak institutional mechanisms available to the merchant when faced with dishonest behavior, it is easy to see why Datini spent his time combing through the accounts and asking for precise regular business reports. His fears were not misplaced: one of his most faithful collaborators found it hard not to put his own interests and those of his relatives first.

In a world where commercial institutions were almost non-existent, knowing whom to trust was based on individual behavior: a man who lived with probity and moderation, who was not unfaithful to his wife, and who neither gambled nor blasphemed was more likely to behave well in business than one who allowed his passions to govern him. Besides, when in Barcelona, his Florence and Prato collaborator turned into an

[7] Laurence Fontaine, 'Un marchand du xve siècle face aux incertitudes du temps', communication made on april 20, 2010 about the book: Giampiero Nigro (ed.), *Francesco di Marco Datini: L'uomo e il mercante* (Florence 2010). Michele Cassandro, 'Aspetti della vita dell'uomo e del personaggio', in Nigro (ed.), *Francesco di Marco* Datini, 3–55, there 13–14; Carolyn James, 'Le lettere di Margherita Datini (1384–1410)', in Nigro (ed.), *Francesco di Marco Datini,* 57–77.

irascible man given to womanizing and gaming such that in spite of his great competence, his misconduct led to profits well below those earned by his counterparts in Valencia and Majorca.[8]

Therefore, the success of merchant enterprises came at a price: one's affiliations, interests, and even one's passions all had to be subjugated to the interests of the firm for which one worked. But all the care he took to build trust becomes derisory when death stroke, and it often prowled around, decapitating businesses and weakening the links patiently forged with other trading houses. When death stroke somewhere, a domino effect was activated and the men of trust had to move to fill the empty places in the network or liquidate the business. Death, Francesco di Marco's most formidable adversary, was also the big winner: it took the lives of Francesco's children and many of his associates; in the process, it took its toll on the business, forcing the merchant to curb his expansion, close branches and left no male heir to succeed him.

In addition to the uncertainty of men were the equally formidable political uncertainties. After the plague, the Datini enterprise had to contend with the warlike folly of men which brought plunder in its wake and paralyzed trade, even though it opened the war and arms market. The letters sought to anticipate the events: they described those in power and attempted to see through their political designs. Possible alternatives were always discussed to find ways and means of overcoming obstacles: How to get round this obstacle? How do we reach the promising markets of Catalonia if Genoa, an ideal position, cannot be maintained? Should we set up in Venice? Take the Alpine routes when the seas are too unsafe? Should we use nominees or flags of convenience? The links with politics were complex and ambivalent: the aim was both to avoid war—and even then, soldiers could sometimes be supplied—and to please the warrior elites, who were the best customers and could prohibit or facilitate trade. The intermingling of politics and economics was inextricable.

The third area of uncertainty was specific to the trading circuit, since we must not forget the difficulties of controlling all the parameters that could affect the production, circulation, and sale of goods, such as the lack of raw materials because the plague or war had mown down men, or because the climate had prevented harvests; the cargo hijacked by pirates and men who had to be bought back; the storm that sunk ships; the fire

[8] Angela Orlandi, 'La compagnia di Catalogna: un successo quasi inatteso', in Nigro (ed.), *Francesco di Marco Datini,* 357–396.

that destroyed towns; and always the war and plague that emptied purses and reduced the number of potential consumers. One also needed to be aware of the competition; keep track of price and currency trends, know the routes and alternative routes, etc. Datini devised solutions for every problem. He responded to the problem of supplies, which could cease if war broke out, if labor became scarce or even if rivals drove up the price of wool when an epizootic had reduced the herd, by signing exclusive agreements with the most sought-after workers, by providing credit to others in order to attract them, or by bringing in raw materials, as in 1402–1403 during periods of crisis in English supplies, when Datini found a way to supply the Flemish looms by bringing in wool from Catalonia or Scotland.[9]

Taken together, all this information made it possible to envisage alternatives in the face of all the unforeseen events that continually changed the best-laid plans. It was also the key to good deals, for those who have fresh money to invest without delay, or for those who know how to react to news and changing tastes. Of course, knowing the value of currencies and following the monetary reforms undertaken by kings to wipe out their debts were at the heart of speculation and profits on foreign exchange, and the slightest variations in the currency of a marketplace were immediately passed on to Datini.

To prosper in an aristocratic and religious world and accommodate the arbitrariness of politics, he had to know how local bodies functioned to get trade permits and buy favor with the customs and in strategic places so as to get preferential treatment for his goods. Money in the form of gift or credit was still the merchant's major weapon with which he could buy tax and commercial benefits from powerful aristocrats. Money was thus lent to them at high rates of interest to be repaid in the form of benefits given.

Limiting the arbitrariness of religious and aristocratic power required that one maintained good personal relationship with those in high positions in the Church and the State. An exchange of letters, invitations and gifts helped develop such relationships. This was backed by the exchange of gifts; Datini thus took on cardinal Baldassare Cossa who went on to become antipope John XXIII. All such relationships culminated in meetings and hospitality. With this grammar of social relationships in mind, it

[9] Francesco Guidi Bruscoli, 'I rapporti con il Nord-Europa', in Nigro (ed.), *Francesco di Marco Datini,* 407–428.

is not difficult to understand why Datini took so much care and spent so much time making his house worthy of the Great. He courted all levels of power, regularly received the governor of Prato where he was based, invited all his wealthy neighbors and any person of power who passed through Prato, wherever they came from, because one never know who one might need one day. The Venetian ambassador received in 1397 was consulted four years later in 1401, when Datini was thinking of moving to Venice. He even received Louis II of Anjou in 1409 and 1410, and the expense was such that to thank him, the king gave him the precious gift of the right to insert the golden lily of France in his arms and seals. A magnificent reward and a boost to his reputation, as we would say today, which attracted aristocratic clients to him.

Offering hospitality to such dignitaries required the presence of a wife capable of managing, entertaining and fitting into these networks of political sociability, so vital to the business of the merchant. Margherita, whom he married just before his return to Tuscany when she was only sixteen years old, had to assume all these responsibilities. She learnt to read, worked at calligraphy, dictated two hundred and fifty letters, and took charge of the household and all related work in the absence of her husband, as their fates were intertwined: in spite of having different aspirations, the family's success was their common asset. In a world where collaborators and friends had multiple loyalties, wives were faithful allies; so, despite all her protestations and moods, Margherita proved to be a staunch ally.[10]

With the palace he has built for himself, the contradiction between the values of the merchant and those of the aristocracy was vividly apparent, as it reflected the antagonistic cultures between which Datini had to live with. Francesco counted every penny and hated waste, while the aristocrat made a fault of the former and a virtue of the latter. Datini knew this, and to seduce the powerful he bought objects of great value and spent lavishly to honor them. But once his guests had left, the precious objects went back into the cupboards to await another great occasion, or were used to oblige a few relations by lending them to him. Moreover, the most beautiful room was reserved for them and was only opened to receive his

[10] Simonetta Cavaciocchi, 'Il mercante e il murare', in Nigro (ed.), *Francesco di Marco Datini,* 135–167, there 137–9 and 154–7.

distinguished guests; he himself was content with a much more modest room.[11]

3 Reputation and Friendship

Three centuries later, the fickleness of human nature remained unchanged and, like in the fifteenth century, reputation in the sense of fame, *fama*, was revealed through the same types of conduct: no bad manners (drinking, gambling, insults), no bad sexual conduct and no breaking of one's word.[12] It was therefore not only a question of honoring one's commitments; it was also a question of translating the internalization of moral values into one's behavior. These traits lasted throughout the early modern period. Still at the crossroads of the eighteenth and nineteenth centuries, the printed circulars that trading houses regularly sent to their correspondents in order to make themselves known contained an increasing amount of information about company members and their associates: deaths, marriages, family ties, career paths, etc. Information that would previously have been considered confidential was disseminated because it helped to build trust.[13]

An analysis of the violence trials in a Castilian village shows that a good half of them were the result of attacks on reputation. In each case, comments exchanged in front of witnesses, in the street, at the inn, or in a shop imply that the man or woman was not keeping his or her word or that he or she was unworthy of receiving credit. If no one was there to intervene, the aggressor did not hesitate to draw his weapons and take revenge,[14] because trust was always the *fama*, what was said in public.

Sexual insults which sullied the reputation of a merchant and which concerned as much the behavior of his wife as his own were devastating

[11] Simonetta Cavaciocchi, 'Il gusto dell'abitare", in Nigro (ed.), *Francesco di Marco Datini,* 201–215; Giampiero Nigro, 'Il mercante e la sua ricchezza', in Nigro (ed.), *Francesco di Marco Datini,* 81–104, there 99–100.

[12] Joseph Shatzmiller, *Shylock Reconsidered: Jews, Moneylending, and Medieval Society*, (Berkeley, 1990), there 41.

[13] Arnaud Bartolomei, 'La publication de l'information commerciale à Marseille et Cadix (1780–1820): la fin des réseaux marchands ?', in: *Rives nord-méditerranéennes*, 27 (2007), 85–105, there 93.

[14] Scott Taylor, 'Credit, Debt, and Honor in Castille, 1600–1650' in: *Journal of Early Modern History*, 7: 1–2 (2003), 8–27.

for his reputation. This tells us not just that the Europe of the time was steeped in Christian morality but also that this morality offered a financial guarantee. In the face of an uncertain economy and its crises, a debtor's being fearful of God and being faithful to one's spouse were two of the few elements creditors could cling to in the hope of recovering their money. It was one of the foundations of reputation and trust.

In the eighteenth century, a didactic literature flourished, striving to develop measurement techniques, calculation, and rational prediction. Although such counsel advocated the use of specific techniques, such as account books or shared systems of measurement, it was never really followed, for merchant techniques remained very rudimentary: despite the massive dissemination of business correspondence manuals, the eighteenth-century French trader was hardly more informed than his sixteenth-century counterpart, even if it was easier for him to be looked on as a man of quality.[15]

If a sort of precursor of *homo economicus* can be discerned in these new curiosities, the ceaselessly repeated insistence on forms of forecasting and calculation seems a little strange next to the commonly shared idea, also recognized in didactic literature, that even the most informed, calculating and responsible merchant found himself helpless, in most cases, in the face of money famines whose origins and evolution he could not control neither. Why, then, cultivate the powers of calculation when they offered no help in credit crises that could lead to ruin?

Here, a second antinomic aspect of building reputation comes into play, adding to economic rationality a sense of compassion and moral values. Other elements thus get included in the portrait of a man worthy of credit. Indeed, in addition to qualities we put in the category of economic rationality, a good trader must project a certain type of personality. Among many examples, here is *The Tradesman's Director*, published in 1756:

> Credit, that jewel of commerce, that fragile flower, cannot be cultivated with too much care, and as its precious possession depends on the goodwill of others, the conduct of the merchant in his entourage and towards his peers must be such that, in addition to a knowledge of the rules of calculation, he cultivates general goodwill and friendship in order to attract

[15] Pierre Jeannin, 'Distinction des compétences et niveau des qualifications', in Franco Angiolini and Daniel Roche (eds.), *Négoce et culture*, (Paris, 1995), 363–98.

> the respect and win the affection of others; on this good reputation will depend in many occasions the justice and courtesy that will be accorded to him.
> [...] [all] Men have more Reason to exercise this Virtue [Compassion], seeing they are certainly in a constant hazardous Situation, and though perfectly circumspect and parsimonious themselves, as their Effects are in so many different Hands, may chance to be hurried in an Instant to the most distressful Ebb, by the failure of a Customer or Correspondent; [...] he ought, by paying this Debt of Charity, to acknowledge the Mercy that has set him from above and protected him from Danger.[16]

It follows that helping an honest banker "might be proved to be the best and soundest Policy, and a Kindness done to himself.[17]"

William Stout, in his autobiography, boasted of never having prosecuted any of his debtors because "to lose all was of more satisfaction to me than getting all to the great cost of my debtor, and to the preservation of my reputation."[18]

These trade manuals viewed credit relations not so much as a rational economic choice of a partner but more as the knowledge of the partner's attitude and solidarity in times of a credit crisis. The purpose of all these recommendations was to instill a sense of generosity and Christian compassion, which would protect those who practiced it from the worst reverses of an unpredictable credit market.

Though the rhetoric appears, at first sight, to be intended to advance the techniques of economic rationality, in fact the object was to establish the merchant's "credit" so as to make it less likely that his goods would be seized by his creditors. Since the decision to act was in the hands of the creditors, the power to convince them that they should not act, or that they should act against others first, was essential. So this game delivered contradictory messages. On the one hand, the rhetoric of calculation and forecasting was part of the merchant's identity, something knowledge of which should help to build credit and suggested that an individual was a good risk when it came to lending money; on the other, the ethos of

[16] Charles Snell, *The Tradesman's Director, or the London and Country Shopkeeper's Companion* (London, 1756), there 9–10.

[17] Snell, *The Tradesman's Director*, there 9–13.

[18] John D. Marshall (ed.), *The autobiography of William Stout of Lancaster 1665–1752* (Manchester, 1967), there 120.

generosity was what ensured that the elasticity of the system worked in favor of those who championed it.

Accordingly, the study of bankruptcies teaches us a great deal about the cultural mechanisms of trust, as it brings out that they were not set off mechanically by an economic crisis, nor were they its direct indicator; on the contrary, they conveyed all the intricacies of the crises of trust. We learn that enterprises did not run the same risks in the face of legal bankruptcy and that the structures of the trading society were in the ultimate analysis determinant in choosing the bankrupt. Furthermore, the most affected were the recently established businessman, not very well-off, and who had just suffered a turn for the worse, and many houses well integrated in the city's social fabric were, on the other hand, spared even though their financial situation was as bad, if not critical. Thus, in their response to economic hazards, the trading society did not put all traders on an equal footing, because the ones the better established in the merchant society were by and large never declared bankrupt.[19]

The commercial world was remarkably unregulated, whether by institutions (such as banks) or by law. There was, of course, a whole series of laws concerning bankruptcy, particularly in England, where in the eighteenth-century people were far more likely to end up in prison for debt than for any other offense.[20] In France, since the sixteenth century, cases of non-payment have been settled before a consular court made up of merchants. In 1720, sixty-five towns in France had such a court. An analysis of the papers of these courts shows, however, that few cases of non-payment ended with a formal declaration of bankruptcy, and that compulsory execution was relatively rare in France compared with England; it nevertheless remained the last resort and a real possibility that haunted every bankrupt.[21] There were many debt suits everywhere, even though they were of little importance given the widespread use of

[19] Jean-Clément Martin, 'Le commerçant, la faillite et l'historien', in: *Annales ESC*, 6 (1980), 1251–1268.

[20] Johanna Innes, 'The King's Bench Prison in the later eighteenth century: law, authority and order in a debtors' prison', in John Brewer and John Styles (eds.) *An Ungovernable People. The English and their law in the seventeenth and eighteenth centuries* (London, 1980), 250–298.

[21] Serge Chassagne, 'Faillis en Anjou au XVIIIe siècle: contribution à l'histoire économique d'une province', in *Annales ESC*, 2 (1970), 477- 497; Pierre de Saint Jacob, 'Histoire économique et sociale dans les archives de la juridiction consulaire de Dijon, 1715–1789', in: *Bulletin de la Société d'histoire moderne*, 4 (1957), 2–10. Maurice

credit.[22] However, by focusing everyone's attention on the risk of being stigmatized if they lost the trust and support of other merchants, they acted as a moralizing and socializing force.

In this context of imposed credit, widespread overindebtedness and the unpredictability of financial crises that characterizes pre-industrial Europe, in which the economy was totally entangled in social relations, trust was not where we would expect it to be today. It was above all a question of ensuring the benevolent support of those with whom we shared business relationships.

William Stout's attitude faced with his relations' commercial debts illustrates this combination of social and moral obligations that affected even English merchants who could have been expected to manage to keep economic and private spheres apart. It also shows that, in order to uphold his reputation, a merchant must not restrict his generosity to his peers but extend it to the poorest. One of his former apprentices, John Thoughton, was jailed for debt, and a commission of bankruptcy was issued against him by a merchant from Liverpool to whom he owed 100 pounds. To avoid the expense of the commission, Stout took the trouble and time to sell his apprentice's shop goods at auction, because, he stated, "as he had been my apprintice, and the begining of his creddit by my recomendition, I thought my selfe obliged to use my endevours to make the most for the creditors." Later, his nephew, to whom he had sold his business, incurred debts of more than £900 in one year and Stout took it upon himself to pay off more than fifty creditors because many of them "were my best friends and close relatives of mine and I had recommended him." In fact, he claimed in his diary to have been "tender of oppressing poor people with law charges ... for the preservation of my reputation," because, he added, "losing everything was more satisfactory for me and my reputation than recovering everything at great expense for my debtor."[23]

Garden, 'Aires du commerce Lyonnais au XVIIIe siècle', in Pierre Léon (ed.,), *Aires et structures du commerce français au XVIIIe siècle*, (Lyon, 1975), 265–99.

[22] Yébenes, a town of 2,000 to 3,500 inhabitants south of Toledo has 550 debt-related cases out of 1,030 criminal cases; see Scott Taylor, 'Credit, Debt, and Honor', there 10.

[23] Marshall, *Autobiography*, there 120, 148-9, 208-9, and 225, quoted by Craig Muldrew, *The Economy of Obligation: The Culture of Credit and Social Relations in Early Modern England* (New York, 1998), there 257.

Thus, at every level of society, "credit" was according to the number of "friends" one could gather around one.[24] From the time of the curialisation of the aristocracies, credit was the nobleman's ability to make himself heard by the king, because it was at court that his largesse was dispensed. Friendship was understood as a moral relationship, one of aid and reciprocity. It cut across kinship as much as relationships chosen, principally among equals but politics could add an unequal dimension. It was composed of all kinds of economic and emotional exchanges. One lent money to one another when the need arose, introduced one's "friends" to influential people, entertained one another, and these relationships were stated in the language of affection. A few personal diaries provide an insight into the shape of friendship networks. In Thomas Turner's diary, in eighteenth-century England, he crossed paths with relatives and non-relatives and entered the sphere of politics; on the other hand, he systematically excluded from this circle of "friends" virtually all the neighbors and associates he met on a daily basis. On the other hand, he often spoke of his disappointment at the selfishness and coldness of his friends, and of the expectations, help, consideration, and warmth he would like to receive from them.[25]

The lessons of bankruptcies were shared by the actors of the time: they knew it was the lack of friends that led to the fall of new entrants. Thus, when a Swiss merchant went bankrupt in Lyon in the eighteenth century, his brother reproached him bitterly for being incapable of widening his circle of "friends": "had you made yourself known in Lyon, as I had always recommended to you, we would not have lacked for money."[26]

It was always a problem of information. Before the advent, in the nineteenth century, of businesses specializing in information on other businesses, each business developed an information network through correspondence. This consumed a great deal of time and energy, and

[24] Arlette Jouanna, *Le Devoir de révolte. La noblesse française et la gestation de l'État moderne (1559–1661)* (Paris, 1989), there 65.

[25] Naomi Tadmor, *Family and Friends in Eighteenth-century England Household, Kinship, and Patronage*, (Cambridge, 2001), there 212-215.

[26] Archives Départementales du Rhône, série B, papiers Cuentz, liasse XV, Paris 28 octobre 1721, quoted by Pierre Léon, Jacqueline Fayollet, and Maurice Garden, 'Recherche conjoncturelle et milieux économiques: hommes d'affaires suisses et mouvement économique lyonnais sous la Régence', in: *Publications de la Faculté des sciences économiques et sociales de l'université de Genève*, XX (1969), 101–19, there 113.

required a large staff.[27] The information was so unreliable and difficult to obtain that many opted finally for a very small number of regular business partners, although they did not give up the habit of using every exchange of letters to inform themselves about the state of affairs and reputation of men and women. Thus, Melchior Philibert, a prominent trader from Lyon in the first half of the eighteenth century, kept up a vast network of correspondents even though he did business with only a few of them: one or two large companies per area. There was a list of about ten names that always referred to the largest companies in each city. It was with them that he did at least 90 percent of his business. It was from them that he sought information about the many traders who wished to do business with him. To his correspondent from Carcassonne, Philibert wrote one day:

> "I am delighted to see what you have marked to me about him, for as you know, it is not gracious to run risks by pleasing one's friends."

Jean-Baptiste Bruny in Marseille was one such friend, and the two companies developed a loyal friendship. The exchange of business letters was thus coupled with an interest in private and family affairs. In return, these rare friends received preferential economic treatment:

> "There will always be money in the till for friends such as you, for whom I have genuine consideration, and complete trust."

wrote Melchior to Raymond Bruny on June 21, 1721. During the same year, when one of Bruny's nephews asked Philibert that he be given the same reduced provisioning rate as his uncle, he was explained the exceptional nature of this favor granted to Bruny "on account of our old association, and not wishing to look closely into their affairs, but they are the only friends with whom I have such dealings."[28] In this, he followed Savary's advice that wholesalers should avoid looking for funds on the

[27] A beautiful example in Robert Chamboredon, 'Toutes antennes déployées: les enseignements de la correspondance des frères Fornier entre Nîmes et Cadix (1748–1786)', *Rives nord-méditerranéennes*, 27 (2007), 65–84.

[28] Maurice Garden, 'Le grand négoce lyonnais au début du XVIIIe siècle. La maison Melchior Philibert: de l'apogée à la disparition', *Colloque franco-suisse d'histoire économique et sociale*, (Genève, 1969), 83–99, there 86–87.

marketplace and prefer instead the security of "special friends"[29]; and these ties of friendship and business between large trading houses were commonplace in Europe.[30]

Trust in the seventeenth and eighteenth centuries was therefore not where we would expect it to be today. It reflected both the deeply social nature of credit and its moral dimension. Reputation, based on values of generosity and benevolence, was required to mitigate the violence of the economy more than to help rationalize one's own economic commitments.

4 "Ethnic networks"

This approach to ordinary merchants helps us to understand the success of networks that we would call today "community networks" or "ethnic networks" because they are based, sometimes on the common belonging to the same group of villages and sometimes on a minority religion, as among the Protestants and especially the Mennonites. The case of the Jews, given their position as outcasts, is somewhat different.

The "ethnic" networks, whether they came from the Alps or Scotland, made the whole social spectrum of the villages work together, with, at the top, merchants, some of whom were among the richest inhabitants of the towns in which they settled, and, at the other end of the merchant chain, men who had little to offer in the way of collateral for the goods entrusted to them.

A series of mechanisms helped reduce the obligations and tensions that arose from the economic and cultural heterogeneity of these networks and the multiple belongings of each one.[31] Sharing the same kinship developed a commonality of interest, the main guarantee that business relations would be conducted in the interest of all. A family "banking" system was the basis for kin groups to expand their business by opening shops

[29] Jacques Savary, *Le Parfait négociant* (Paris, 1665), second part, there 6–7.

[30] Jean-Yves Grenier, *L'économie d'Ancien Régime. Un monde de l'échange et de l'incertitude* (Paris, 1996), there 129–130.

[31] Laurence Fontaine, *Histoire du colportage en Europe XVe-XIXe siècles* (Paris, 1993), chapter 1. Marina Romani, 'La tela del ragno: famiglie e banchi ebraici nell'Italia Centro – settentrionale (secc. XIV-XV)', in: *Cheiron*, 45–46 (2007), 89–111. Corine Maitte, les verriers d'Altare, HDR Lille 3, (2006). Corine Maitte, Les chemins de verre. Les migrations des verriers d'Altare et de Venise (XVIe-XIXe siècles) (Rennes, 2009).

and factories. Each partner invested most of his or her family's property in the company. Such family firms were extremely flexible and could be expanded or reduced to match the needs of trade, or of the enterprise, and the death, enrichment, or impoverishment of some member. In case the company is weakened by the death of one of its members, the contracts preserved show that measures were taken to tie up the capital invested until the end of the contract of association; the widow of the deceased merchant receiving fixed-term payments.

Endogamy was thus an essential part of the regulatory system to the extent that it aimed to protect the "banking" system and the attachment of each one to the merchant network. The exceptions to this rule can be attributed to the adjustments migrants had to make to enter the markets of the regions where they wished to trade. The ban on marrying outside the group was also applied by trading companies, because this made it possible to move men quickly according to the needs of the company and gave ample opportunity to keep an eye on them through the family that remained in the village.

Accordingly, analysis of merchant and migrant peddler networks shows that they were prisoners of multiple financial dependences and integrated into a system of social relations that helped them and watched over them. Association and guarantees were the two main obligatory forms of solidarity. But such solidarity was ambivalent and charged with tension because it implied that men were jointly responsible for both losses and profits. By linking together the property of one to the other, it caused the fall of one to weigh on the others, introducing yet another imbalance in the networks of relations.

For the moneylender, the extremely hierarchical organization of village migration and its rooting in the village elite, which played the role of both labor contractor and favored intermediary between city trading and street trading, provided the maximum security. Although surety in standing obliged one to show solidarity, it also led to informing: if a peddler tried to escape his or her creditors, his or her guarantors, those whose existence was threatened, would conspire with the merchants to find the peddler and compel him to pay. Such merchant solidarity secreted the elimination of black sheeps and forced peddlers to assume collectively the responsibility for the failure of some. This morality imposed on the group was backed up by the strategies of the village elite, who kept a sharp lookout for any change in property or reversal of fortune. For this purpose, the elite relied on their own family, village notables, and other peddlers who informed them about the state of each one's property and the changes in the composition of families likely to have an impact on the peddlers' solvency.

This example brings out the extreme rigidity of these networks as also the numerous constraints, which compelled, organized, regulated, and monitored trust.

4.1 Contemporary "business groups"

Although merchant networks have disappeared from Europe, they are still very much in evidence today in other parts of the world, and always with exceptional success. They intrigue economists who are also trying to explain the mechanisms at work in the success of these apparently archaic entrepreneurial forms. Mark Granovetter, who has worked in particular on Chinese entrepreneurial networks, places two elements at the heart of their success: the role of trust between members and the strength of the community. If trust is not lacking, explains the economist, it is because the community is so homogeneous that it is very difficult for its members to hide wrongdoings, or even to imagine them. It is also strong enough that there is no conflict over the delegation of authority.

Chinese enterprises are organized around credit, pooling of capital, and delegation of authority without fear of non-compliance. In addition to the strength of the communities, the researchers note that the position of individuals within the groups and kinship is clearly defined, which limits, compared to other looser kinship structures—where people belong to many overlapping interest groups—the claims that individuals may have on the firm, as one of the dangers is to have to distribute gratuities and favors beyond the financial capacity of the groups.[32] The danger is real because the fuzzier social systems suffer from the fact that when one of the many groups to which individuals belong is at the heart of a business, members of other groups can legitimately claim a share of the profits, and this multiplicity of possible claims creates a strong element of fragility, as Clifford Geertz's studies of Indonesian entrepreneurs also highlight.[33] We saw that this was one of Francesco Datini's major problems.

[32] Mark Granovetter, 'Les institutions économiques comme constructions sociales: un cadre d'analyse', in André Orléan (ed.) *Analyse économique des conventions* (Paris, 1994), 79–94.

[33] Clifford Geertz, *Peddlers and Princes* (Chicago, 1963), there 123.

Finally, the development of these companies is based on their ability to create "business groups" through alliances between families. This very common phenomenon has a specific name in each country: zaibatsu in Japan, chœbol in Korea, grupos economicos in Latin America. These groups vary in size, structure, and legal form. Some arise from a single family group which extends its domination through acquisition or alliance, as in Japan and Korea, whereas in Latin America it seems that the various groups arise independently and unite at a favorable time.[34]

Indeed, the organization of migrant merchant networks in pre-industrial Europe was very similar to the "ethnic business groups" that intrigue contemporary economists. Like them, they were based on the strength of kinship and on the strength of elites able to control the plural affiliations of the individuals working for the network.

Confidence was indeed, as economists have pointed out, at the heart of the success of these migrant networks, but it was not an element naturally produced by community membership: it was the result of continuous social control based on intelligence, surveillance, and the supervision of behavior, the limitation of individual choices and financial dependence with, for the richest, the obligation to invest their assets in common affairs and, for the poorest, the dependence of debt. Thus, social organization contributed to the strengthening of family and community solidarity to the detriment of individual choices. It was therefore easy to understand how the strength of the groups was built up and why there were so few conflicts of authority in the history of these business networks. These practices also explain why these networks are under-represented in the archives.

It is also necessary to insist, more than economists have done, on the mobility of members as the basis for the success of business networks. It allows for the best use of information by deploying and reorienting people to the needs of markets and by moving them around, without suffering the human and economic burdens of being rooted. Mobility has given business flexibility and adaptability.

However, the success of the large Asian groups is also based on their collusion with the administration to an extent that the networks of early modern Europe—even if they have used credit to princes to conquer market rights—have not experienced, probably because they have never

[34] Mark Granovetter, '*Les institutions économiques*', there 88.

been able to reach the dominant position that some have in their country thanks to the global market. In Korea, while the leaders of the largest chaebol, such as Samsung Electronics Co, have had to admit to irregularities in their management, they remain untouchable. Even the massive scandal in 2017 that saw President Park Geun-Hye impeached and the conglomerate's heir jailed for perjury and corruption, he did not stay in jail for long: too big to fail.[35]

5 Conclusion

We have seen how difficult it was to build sustainable financial networks in countries where aristocratic domination was prevalent because the risks faced by businesses in an unpredictable world were compounded by the rules of the financial and economic game created by Church-backed aristocracies to curb the development of capitalism and maintain their political supremacy.

Moreover, in addition to the uncertainty created by wars, endemic diseases, and the vagaries of the climate, families needed to be part of a variety of solidarities capable of supporting them in times of difficulty. These obligations of solidarity, which filled the portfolios with bad debts, also obliged everyone to defend the interests of the various members of the human networks in which they were involved. Hence the desire of entrepreneurs to gather as much information as possible on world events and on the people with whom they were likely to do business, and ultimately, as the surest strategy, their desire to work only with a limited number of reliable correspondents on whom they knew they could rely.

Adding a moral dimension to the quest for information about the state of affairs was another constant in the response of the commercial world to unforeseeable financial crises. It showed that people's moral reputation ultimately counted for more than the financial strength of their company, and that showing oneself charitable toward the victims of economic crises was the best insurance against the financial setbacks that could befall them despite the possible good management of their company.

[35] *Le Monde.fr*. "L'ex-présidente sud-coréenne Park Geun-hye placée en détention provisoire." March 31, 2017. https://www.lemonde.fr/asie-pacifique/article/2017/03/31/l-ex-presidente-sud-coreenne-park-geun-hye-placee-en-detention-provisoire_5103596_3216.html.

Studying the difficulties faced by ordinary merchants has highlighted, by contrast, the decisive advantages of merchant networks based on a shared religious or village affiliation, because they made it possible to reduce the most structural uncertainties of business: the control of the multiple affiliations of men, the capacity to develop effective surveillance systems and to move associates and employees according to the needs of the company. This type of organization is still successfully in place today.

References

Printed primary material

The Tradesman's Director, or the London and Country Shopkeeper's Companion (London, 1756).

Furetière Antoine, *Dictionnaire universel* (La Haye-Rotterdam, 1690).

Jouanna Arlette, *Le Devoir de révolte. La noblesse française et la gestation de l'État moderne (1559–1661),* (Paris, 1989).

Savary Jacques, *Le Parfait négociant,* (Paris, 1665).

Turgot, *Mémoire sur les prêts d'argent* (Schelle 1770).

Secondary material

Bartolomei, Arnaud. 2007. La publication de l'information commerciale à Marseille et Cadix (1780–1820): La fin des réseaux marchands? *Rives nord-méditerranéennes* 27: 85–105.

Biem, David. 1988. Les offices, les corps et le crédit d'État: l'utilisation des privilèges sous l'Ancien Régime. *Annales ESC* 2: 379–404.

Cassandro, Michele. 2010. Aspetti della vita dell'uomo e del personaggio. In *Francesco di Marco Datini: L'uomo e il mercante*, edited by Nigro Giampiero, 3–55. Florence: Firenze University Press.

Cavaciocchi, Simonetta. 2010a. Il mercante e il murare. In *Datini: L'uomo e il mercante*, edited by Nigro Giampiero, 135–167. Florence: Firenze University Press.

Cavaciocchi, Simonetta. 2010b. 'Il gusto dell'abitare. In *Datini: L'uomo e il mercante*, edited by Nigro Giampiero, 203–215. Florence: Firenze University Press.

Chamboredon, Robert. 2007. Toutes antennes déployées: Les enseignements de la correspondance des frères Fornier entre Nîmes et Cadix (1748–1786). *Rives nord-méditerranéennes* 27: 65–84.

Chassagne, Serge. 1970. 'Faillis en Anjou au XVIIIe siècle: Contribution à l'histoire économique d'une province. *Annales ESC* 2: 477–497.

Fontaine, Laurence. 2014. *The Moral Economy. Poverty, credit and Trust in Early Modern Europe*. Cambridge: Gallimard.

Fontaine, Laurence. (non-published). Un marchand du xve siècle face aux incertitudes du temps. Communication made on April 20, 2010.

Fontaine, Laurence. 1993. *Histoire du colportage en Europe XVe-XIXe siècles*. Paris. Albin Michel

Garden, Maurice. 1973. Aires du commerce lyonnais au XVIIIe siècle. In *Aires et structures du commerce français au XVIIIe siècle*, edited by Pierre Léon, 265–299. Lyon: Publication du Centre d'histoire économique et sociale de la région lyonnaise.

Garden, Maurice. 1969. Le grand négoce lyonnais au début du XVIIIe siècle. La maison Melchior Philibert: de l'apogée à la disparition. *Colloque franco-suisse d'histoire économique et sociale*, 83–99. Genève: Georg et Cie.

Geertz, Clifford. 1963. *Peddlers and Princes*. Chicago: University of Chicago Press.

Granovetter, Mark. 1994. Les institutions économiques comme constructions sociales: un cadre d'analyse. In *Analyse économique des conventions,* edited by André Orléan, 79–94. Paris.

Grenier, Jean-Yves. 1996. *L'économie d'Ancien Régime*. Paris: Un monde de l'échange et de l'incertitude.

Guidi, Bruscoli Francesco. 2010. I rapporti con il Nord-Europa. In *Francesco di Marco Datini: L'uomo e il mercante*, edited by Nigro Giampiero, 407–428. Florence: Firenze University Press.

Innes, Johanna. 1980. The King's Bench Prison in the later eighteenth century: Law, authority and order in a debtors' prison. In *An Ungovernable People. The English and their law in the seventeenth and eighteenth centuries,* edited by John Brewer and John Styles, 250–298. London: Rutgers University Press.

James, Carolyn. 2010. Le lettere di Margherita Datini (1384–1410). In *Francesco di Marco Datini: L'uomo e il mercante*, edited by Nigro Giampiero, 57–77. Florence: Firenze University Press.

Jeannin, Pierre. 1995. Distinction des compétences et niveau des qualifications. In *Négoce et culture*, edited by Franco Angiolini and Daniel Roche, 363–398. Paris: Éditions de l'EHESS.

Léon, Pierre, Jacqueline Fayollet, and Maurice Garden. 1969. Recherche conjoncturelle et milieux économiques: Hommes d'affaires suisses et mouvement économique lyonnais sous la Régence. *Publications de la Faculté des sciences économiques et sociales de l'université de Genève* 20: 101–119.

Maitte, Corine. 2009. Les chemins de verre. Les migrations des verriers d'Altare et de Venise (XVIe-XIXe siècles). Rennes.

Maitte, Corine. 2006. Les verriers d'Altare, HDR Lille 3.

Martin, Jean-Clément. 1980. Le commerçant, la faillite et l'historien. *Annales ESC* 6: 1251–1268.

Marshall, John D. (ed.). 1967. *The Autobiography of William Stout*, Third series, 14. Manchester: Chetham Society.

Muldrew, Craig. 1998. *The Economy of Obligation: The Culture of Credit and Social Relations in Early Modern England*. New York: Macmillan.

Nigro, Giampiero (ed.). 2010. *Francesco di Marco Datini: L'uomo e il mercante*. Florence: Firenze University Press.

Nigro, Giampiero. 2010. Il mercante e la sua ricchezza. In *Francesco di Marco Datini: L'uomo e il mercante*, edited by Nigro Giampiero, 81–104. Florence: Firenze University Press.

Orlandi, Angela. 2010. La compagnia di Catalogna: un successo quasi inatteso. In *Francesco di Marco Datini: L'uomo e il mercante*, edited by Nigro Giampiero, 357–396. Florence: Firenze University Press.

Romani, Marina. 2007. La tela del ragno: Famiglie e banchi ebraici nell'Italia Centro – settentrionale (secc. XIV-XV). *Cheiron* 45–46: 89–111.

de Saint, Jacob, and Pierre. 1957. Histoire économique et sociale dans les archives de la juridiction consulaire de Dijon, 1715–1789. *Bulletin de la Société d'histoire moderne* 4: 2–10.

Shatzmiller, Joseph. 1990. *Shylock Reconsidered: Jews, Moneylending, and Medieval Society*. Berkeley: University of California Press.

Taylor, Scott. 2003. Credit, Debt, and Honor in Castille, 1600–1650. *Journal of Early Modern History* 7 (1–2): 8–27.

Tadmor, Naomi. 2001. *Family and Friends in Eighteenth-century England Household, Kinship, and Patronage*. Cambridge: Cambridge University Press.

CHAPTER 4

Married Women in the Rural Credit Economy of Early Modern England, 1500–1700

Hannah Robb

1 Introduction

The study of early modern credit and its networks in rural society is fraught with challenges.[1] Unpaid debts were pursued predominantly in equity courts in urban centers. Though these urban courts served their rural hinterlands, the debts listed were predominantly those of

[1] Thanks to Prof Jane Whittle, Dr Mark Hailwood and Dr Taylor Auccoin who both provided useful feedback on this research and read drafts of the chapter. Also thanks to Amy Smith, PhD candidate at Bristol University, who provided guidance on the study of early modern alewives.

H. Robb (✉)
University of Exeter, Exeter, UK
e-mail: H.K.Robb@exeter.ac.uk

E. M. Dermineur and M. Pompermaier (eds.), *Credit Networks in The Preindustrial World*, Palgrave Studies in the History of Finance,
https://doi.org/10.1007/978-3-031-67117-3_4

men and contracted in and around commercial hubs.[2] Married women appear infrequently as litigants due to legal codes of coverture and our understanding of women's engagement in the credit economy is skewed towards the experience of widows and never-married single women.[3] This is compounded by those studies of probate records that exclude by their very nature married women and instead reveal the borrowing and lending patterns of more wealthy and legally independent women.[4] Yet, we know that married women were central to household economies. Alexandra Shepard has argued for married women to be reconsidered as 'asset managers' within their household with essential skills in valuing and judging the material worth of moveable domestic wares so often used for pawn or surety in credit contracts. Her work draws a broader definition of credit that considers consumption credit as part of the household economy managed by female heads of the household.[5] Rather than being 'pulled' into credit obligations through familial ties as suggested by Marjorie Keniston McIntosh, married women exerted authority in credit and retail as discerning consumers and asset managers.[6] This article explores the potential of depositional evidence for identifying married women in the credit economy. Depositions, taken from church courts, quarter session and coroner's reports from 1500–1700, are used to find incidental descriptions of women's commerce conducted on credit and their work associated with managing the credits and debts of their household. This approach to depositional evidence gives a broader view of

[2] Craig Muldrew, 'Credit and the Courts: Debt Litigation in a Seventeenth-Century Urban Community', in: *The Economic History Review* 46:1 (1993), 23–38; Craig Muldrew, 'Rural Credit, Market Area and Legal Institutions in the Countryside in England, 1550–1700', in: Christopher Brooks and Michael Lobban (eds.), *Commerce and Courts in Britain 1150–1900* (London, 1997), 155–178.

[3] Amy Erickson, 'Coverture and Capitalism', in: *History Workshop Journal* 59 (2005), 1–16; Craig Muldrew, '"A Mutual Assent of Her Mind"? Women, Debt, Litigation and Contract in Early Modern England', in: *History Workshop Journal* 55 (2003), 47–71.

[4] Amy M. Froide, *Never Married: Singlewomen in Early Modern England* (Oxford, 2005); Judith Spicksley, 'Never-Married Women and Credit in Early Modern England', in: Elise M. Dermineur (ed.), *Women and Credit in Pre-Industrial Europe* (Turnhout, 2018), 227–251; Cathryn Spence, *Women, Credit and Debt in Early Modern Scotland* (Manchester, 2016).

[5] Alexandra Shepard, 'Crediting Women in the Early Modern English Economy', in: *History Workshop Journal* 79 (2015), 1–23.

[6] Marjorie Keniston McIntosh, 'Women, Credit and Family Relationships in England, 1300–1620' in: *Journal of Family History* 30:2 (2005), 143–163, there 158.

women's involvement in rural credit networks. Women routinely engaged in the courts as witnesses and in their testimonies recalled incidental evidence to the case describing purchasing on credit, pawning goods or managing their household finances. These vignettes of quotidian credit, often for consumption, show women to have routinely engaged in the credit economy and show marriage to have been an important determinant that acted as an indicator of creditworthiness.

This study of credit networks uses a dataset of work tasks extracted from early modern depositions.[7] Evidence for work tasks following a verb oriented method, that is an individual actor performing a specific work task, have been collected from court depositions from the church courts, quarter sessions and coroners courts over the period 1500–1700. A sampling method has been used in the data collection. Depositions have been collected for one year in every 10 years from a broad geographical area covering the south west, east and north of England, capturing daily work and commerce in predominantly agrarian economies. The catalogue of work activities has produced a large dataset of 9,650 work tasks performed across the south west, north and east of England. Of these work tasks, 2,115 record commercial work, 331 record instances of financial management and 77 record instances of pawning. These three subcategories of the data all record exchanges paid either in coin, credit or kind and form the basis of this research. The methodology allows for both quantitative analysis of gendered patterns in the credit economy as well as qualitative accounts recalling the relationships behind credit agreements. There are some obvious challenges when recording women's work from court depositions. Women account for just 27.2% of witnesses in the court records used and both men and women were more likely to recall work activities performed by the same gender. To mitigate for this under-representation of women in the data, and given that the approach records all forms of work including care work and housework, a 50/50 multiplier of 2.59 has been applied that assumes half of all work tasks were performed by women.[8] When applied, broader trends in the data show

[7] The project has received funding from the European Research Council (grant agreement No 834385).

[8] Methodology outlined in Jane Whittle and Mark Hailwood, 'The gender division of labour in early modern England', in: *The Economic History Review* 73:1 (2020), 3–32; Details of the project and publications can be found at https://formsoflabour.exeter.ac.uk, (last accessed 19/10/22).

that women carried out over a third of all work tasks in the categories of agriculture and transport and just under half of work tasks in the category of commerce. Where the analysis in this article draws comparisons between the tasks performed by men and women, this multiplier has been used and clearly shown in the tables, indicated with an 'adjusted figure'.

This article considers the evidence we have in the dataset for financial networks in the rural economy of early modern England, with a particular focus on the gendered difference in patterns of borrowing and lending. Studies of credit networks in the early modern period are often determined by geographical boundaries reflected in the legal jurisdictions of manorial or borough courts or the accounts of individual notaries. Credit too is invariably accessed via studies of the litigation of debt. The data presented here offers an opportunity to analyze broader trends in the borrowing and lending habits of men and women in rural economies collected from depositions across a spectrum of legal institutions. In particular, we are able to capture evidence of the credit that bypassed civic and borough courts and credit deals that went smoothly without recourse to legal dispute. Few incidences relate directly to contested debts and instead the data reflects incidental evidence of quotidian credit mentioned in-passing by deponents when describing a transaction or the tangential movements of individuals in a case. As a result, the range of credit described in the data is broad and reflects the variety of credit utilized by households from the pewter drinking bowl borrowed by Ann Hawks from a maid to pawn for a shilling being 'in great want of relief for her children', to the boasts of Margaret Henshall in Cheshire, who claimed to have lent large sums on interest.[9] The project data offers an opportunity to explore the financial networks of rural early modern economies in England across a broad geographical area. Where credit is recorded as a work task in the data the biographical details of creditor and debtor are included (name, parish of residence, age and marital status) alongside additional categories that denote the value of the credit, the social relationships between creditor and debtor and the spatial descriptor where the credit was contracted.

The discussion begins with an analysis of the profile of creditors and debtors in the dataset, with a particular focus on the gender and marital status of borrowers and lenders, and the values of the credit

[9] Devon Record Office, QS/4/Box 55, 1650; Cheshire Record Office, EDC 5/1664/43, 1664.

extended. Much like the evidence found by Maria Ågren et al. in *Making a Living*, marital status appears to be the most important factor determining women's access to the credit economy.[10] Rather than marriage precluding women from borrowing and lending, it appears to have facilitated greater access to the ownership of moveable domestic wealth and a tactile knowledge obtained through the handling and valuing of objects essential to operating in the pawn industry and secondhand trade. The qualitative evidence of the depositions also points to the collaboration of husbands and wives to manage credit and debt. Analysis of mediation and management of debts shows that wives regularly handled coin to settle the debts of their husband. The rural credit economy prior to centralization and formalization through banking was 'not only limited, it was local'.[11] Our data captures this low level quotidian credit and highlights the role played by married women in localized credit economies. It presents a quantitative analysis of the profiles of creditors and debtors operating at the lowest levels of the credit economy where credit often functioned as an alternative currency. In doing so, it speaks to the works of Beverley Lemire who has highlighted the importance of credit as a household survival strategy in the urban plebeian commercial circuits of the seventeenth and eighteenth centuries.[12]

The article then considers the evidence for financial networks in the data. Aside from a handful of cases that recall the reckoning of accounts or that make reference to an established ongoing economic relationship, the depositions recount individual transactions between two actors without mention of any continued economic dependency. The data from the project does not lend itself to large quantitative modeling of credit networks. Individuals in the data rarely appear more than once and few

[10] Sofia Ling, Karin Hassan Jansson, Marie Lennersand, Christopher Pihl, Maria Ågren, 'Marriage and Work: Intertwined Sources of Agency and Authority', in: Maria Ågren (ed.) *Making a Living, Making a Difference: Gender and Work in Early Modern European Society* (Oxford, 2016), 80–102.

[11] Gilles Postel-Vinay, 'Change and Transformation of Premodern Credit Markets. The Importance of Small-Scale Credits', in: Stephan Nicolussi-Kohler (ed.), *Change and Transformation of Premodern Credit Markets; The Importance of Small-Scale Credits* (Heidelberg, 2021), 23–38, there 24.

[12] Beverly Lemire, *The Business of Everyday Life; Gender, Practice and Social Politics in England, c. 1600–1900*, (London, 2005); Beverly Lemire, *Petty Pawns and Informal Lending: Gender and the Transformation of Small-Scale Credit in England, c. 1600–1800* (Oxford, 1998).

deponents give descriptive clues as to the nature of their ongoing social and economic relationship. In a credit economy with limited access to intermediaries, depositional evidence provides the greatest insight into the undercurrent of credit networks. The analysis of networks here is principally qualitative and is centered on three key pieces of information recorded in the dataset: whether actors were known to one another, the distance between the parishes of creditor and debtor recorded as their place of residence and the spatial category where the credit was contracted. Through this analysis, we can see how far creditors and debtors travelled to contract credit and the key sites in local communities where financial business was conducted. The evidence presented in this article paints a picture of the rural economy in which credit was conducted between known individuals in relatively close proximity. The analysis supports the theory of a socially embedded credit economy in early modern England and draws out nuanced differences in men and women's credit networks. Despite accounting for nearly half of all recorded economic actors in the credit economy, women borrowed and lent sums of a lower value than their male counterparts. Women travelled shorter distances to obtain credit and, in most cases, sought credit within their home parish.

2 Creditors and Debtors

Throughout the depositions, deponents recall a range of credit in the rural economy, describing loans of money, payments in kind, deferred payments, reckonings, pawning of goods and exigent credit in the market. The evidence for credit and debt in the dataset thus reflects a broad range of credit agreements and is not limited to credit intended for investment but includes also credit as an alternative currency to facilitate commerce. Evidence for credit can be found in three principal categories in the dataset: commerce, financial management and pawning. As each transaction has been recorded in the dataset, the work activity of both buyer and seller has been recorded. Where the exchange has been recalled as having been conducted on credit, the actors have been ascribed a role as either 'creditor' or 'debtor'. In those few instances where deponents describe the reckoning of accounts, both parties have been recorded as debtor and creditor to reflect the dual roles in ongoing economic relations. The gender divisions with the multiplier applied for women's work can be seen in the Table 1.

Table 1 Creditors and Debtors, 1500–1700

	Creditor			*Debtor*		
	M	*F adj*	*F%*	*M*	*F adj*	*F %*
Commerce	44	10	18.5	50	13	20.6
Financial Management	76	54	41.2	73	13	15.1
Pawning	14	52	78.8	20	44	68.8
Totals	134	116	46.2	143	70	32.9

In the dataset, women make up nearly half of all creditors, 46.2% and 32.9% of all debtors. Yet, their involvement across the categories is uneven. Women make up just 15.1% of debtors in the category of financial management where the credit described was larger and related to the extension of coin, yet they comprised 41.2% of creditors in this category. The nature and value of this credit varied but notably includes instances of sums lent at interest for long-term investment. Joan Wever was recorded as a creditor to George Gatheredge in Sarum, Wiltshire, in 1601. George was bound for the sum of £40 'in his life time' to Joan after borrowing £22, which was 'part of her legacy for one year'.[13] The obligation was sealed by 'the help and interest' of William Carpenter, yeoman. When George Catheredge died, Joan Wever wielded the law to seek payment and George's wife and executor of his will, Agnes, was arrested and the goods to the value of £12 were seized from his estate and 8s 10d was paid for Joan's charges.

Lending on credit was not the preserve of men and women too appear as significant sources of finance in the early modern economy. Most notably from the table, women appear to dominate as both creditors and debtors in the pawn trade. The goods exchanged in pawn appear gendered. Women handled cloth, clothing, silverware, cooking pots and ribbons whilst men pawned alongside clothing, cloth and silverware, tools, building materials, livestock and animal skins. These are patterns mirrored in the goods bought and sold in the category of commerce. Women account for just 23.3% of buyers of livestock, using an adjusted figure, and rarely dealt with horses or building materials. They did however dominate in the exchange of smaller moveable domestic

[13] Hampshire Record Office, 21M65/C3/11, 1596.

wares, accounting for 77.5% of all buyers and 65.3% of all sellers in textiles, 70.2% of all buyers and 57.6% of all sellers of clothing and 66% of all buyers and 49.9% of all sellers of housewares. Women's predominance in the pawning trade reflects their commercial knowledge and their ability to judge the worth of the moveable domestic objects they encountered in the home and in the market. Alexandra Shepard has cautioned against oversimplifying women's tendency to deal in apparel and household goods in the credit economy at a time where the 'consumption of goods represented investment strategies rather than simply "spending"'.[14] Women's specialist knowledge in cloth and stitchery acquired through work placed them in an advantageous position to determine the value of these goods as stores of wealth. Their borrowing and lending against these objects in pawn 'became the sum and substance of plebeian budgeting, the source of liquidity for affluent and plebeian patrons throughout Europe'.[15] Credit in pawn was tied to the secondhand trade. Women accepting objects in pawn were not only valuing the goods as a store of wealth but they were also judging their potential for resale. The alewife Mary Page took a smock from Mary Murton in pawn for debts for ale but refused her husband's shoes.[16]

There is a large disparity in the average amounts contracted by men and women. There is less data available for the sums of credit lent and borrowed by women. When describing women's credit, deponents refer to 'some money', 'coins', 'amount' or describe a loan in kind. Deponents are more exact when describing men's credit, often recalling the sum borrowed and its intended purpose as well as the terms of its repayment. The average amount lent by men was £2 13s 6d, with a range of 4d–£40, whereas the average amount lent by women was just 3s 8d, with a range of 3d–£22. The average amount borrowed by men was £2 12s 4d, with a range of 4d–£40, whilst the average amount borrowed by women was 1s 9d, with a range of 3d–3s. For context, an average day laborer in the seventeenth century might earn between £10 and £15 per annum though this fluctuates according to region and gender with men

[14] Alexandra Shepard, 'Minding their own Business: Married Women and Credit in Early Eighteenth-Century London', in: *Transactions of the Royal Historical Society* 25 (2015), 53–74, there 56.

[15] Beverly Lemire, *The Business of Everyday Life*, 93.

[16] Cheshire Record Office, QJF/110/4/62, 1682.

commanding higher wages on average.[17] We can compare the amounts to the wider dataset and the prices recorded in commercial work tasks. The average sums for male creditors and debtors exceed the average value of goods bought and sold by men in the category of commerce in the work-task dataset, where the average value of goods recorded was £1 13s 1d. For women, the average value of recorded goods bought and sold in the category of commerce was 4s 2d, a sum slightly greater than the average sum they lent and significantly greater than the average amount they borrowed. Women borrowers sought smaller amounts from their creditors than male borrowers, sums that were relatively small when compared to the average value of goods bought and sold by women in the category of commerce.

Evidence for marital status was not consistently recorded for men in the depositions, though it was part of the legal formulae of the preamble in the depositions of women. The evidence we have for marital status is therefore limited to the women in the dataset. The Table 2 shows the importance of marital status for women's access to credit in rural credit economies.

The sample here is small but it does demonstrate some significant patterns in the marital status of women in the rural credit economy. Of all women listed as creditor or debtor in the dataset, 66.7% were married. Just 6.9% were recorded as widowed and 6.9% identified as never married. Married women appear more often in the dataset as creditors

Table 2 Marital status of female creditors and debtors, 1500–1700

Marital Status	*Creditor*	%	*Debtor*	%	*Total*	%
Married	32	72.7	16	57.1	48	66.7
Never Married	2	4.5	3	10.7	5	6.9
Widowed	3	6.8	2	7.1	5	6.9
Unknown	7	16	7	35	14	19.4
Total	44	100	28	100	72	100

[17] For notes on English currency and wages see Jane Whittle and Elizabeth Griffiths, *Consumption and Gender in the Early Seventeenth-Century Household: The World of Alice Le Strange* (Oxford, 2012), xiii. For a longer discussion of wages in the early modern English economy see Craig Muldrew, *Food, Energy and the Creation of Industriousness: Work and Material Culture in Agrarian England, 1550–1780* (Cambridge, 2011).

than they do debtors. This can be compared to women's marital status recorded across the project database. Marital status was an important indicator of reliability in the legal process and we therefore may expect married women to appear at a greater frequency in the legal records used here in the dataset. Married women make up 41% of all recorded actors, never-married 13%, widowed 9.4% and unknown 36.7%. Married women therefore make up a greater proportion of creditors and debtors compared to the larger sample whilst never-married and widowed women appear less frequently than we might expect. Women's engagement with the credit economy has long been linked to their marital status. Studies of probate accounts, wills, and inventories have shown widows and never-married single women to have been prolific lenders in the early modern credit economy. B A Holderness' original work in the 1980s, 'Widows in Pre-Industrial Society', stressed the importance of money lending on interest as a means for widowed women to ensure an ongoing economic independence; money lending was the 'most prominent economic function of the widow in English rural society'.[18] McIntosh's study of female sellers recorded in the equity courts across the period 1300–1620 again highlighted the scale of commerce conducted by widowed women who were able to exert economic freedom as their new marital status conferred greater legal independence.[19] More recently, Amy Froide's work on the role of never-married women in the credit economy has shown the single women of early modern Southampton to be significant investors in the urban economy. Wills from a broad spectrum of women, from those in service to those of substantial means, consistently show that women sought to invest their money be it for a future dowry or to sustain economic independence with over 40% of all women's wills listing debts outstanding.[20] Judith Spicksley's comparison between the single women of urban and rural communities in a series of localized studies of probate material across England has shown that never-married women became increasingly active as formal money lenders following the Act Against Usury in 1571. Putting money out to 'use' became increasingly common

[18] B. A. Holderness, 'Widows in pre-industrial society: an essay upon their economic functions', in: Richard Smith (ed.), *Land, Kinship and Life-Cycle* (Cambridge, 1984), 423–442, there 437.

[19] Marjorie Keniston McIntosh, *Working Women in English Society, 1300–1620* (Cambridge, 2005), 123–124.

[20] Froide, *Never Married*, 130–131.

as interest rates of 10% were widely accepted and women's access to legal restitution for the pursuit of unpaid rents increased.[21] Yet the study of married women in the credit economy has proven far more challenging to access. The creditworthiness of a married woman was bound to her household and her access to legal restitution granted by her husband.[22] Increasing dependency on written forms of proof at court again placed greater restrictions on women's lending and McIntosh has suggested that the increasing use of written instruments was concomitant with a decline in female creditors.[23] Yet for married women, engaging in the credit economy could form an important survival strategy for the management of the household economy either sustaining economic exchange to provide sustenance or providing a secondary income to the household budget, credit was 'a mechanism that enabled many to get by and a few to flourish'.[24]

Credit has been subsumed within studies of early modern households and economies of shift as a crucial factor in the survival strategies for poorer laboring households and buying, selling and financial management were all accepted components of housewifery.[25] The extent of a wife's authority over household finances was contested in some of the depositions presented at court. Margaret Henshall was presented by her husband at the church court in Chester in a suit of defamation in 1664. Aside from her deriding the sexual prowess of her husband, claiming 'she would rather kiss her dog's tail than her husband's lips', she had also boasted of her own financial success claiming to have lent significant sums of money for interest; 'she had 60s in Mr Trevett's hands, 40s in old Mr Wilroxon's hands, 6s in Mr Wilroxon's hands, 15s in one Smalworod's hands and 5s in Mr Lockett's hands and that she had interest for it'.[26] The dispute centered on Margaret's management of her husband's estate. Deponents in the case outlined the extent of her financial independence claiming she

[21] Spicksley, 'Never-Married Women'.

[22] McIntosh, 'Women, Credit, and Family Relationship'.

[23] McIntosh, *Working Women*, 85–98.

[24] Beverly Lemire, 'Introduction: Women, Credit and the Creation of Opportunity: A Historical Overview', in: Beverly Lemire, Ruth Pearson and Gail Campbell (eds.), *Women and Credit Researching the Past, Refiguring the Future* (Oxford, 2001), 3–14, there 4.

[25] Laurence Fontaine and Jürgen Schlumbohm, 'Household Strategies for Survival: An Introduction', in: *International Review of Social History* 45:S8 (2000), 1–17.

[26] Cheshire Record Office, EDC 5/1664/43, 1664.

had 'the profit of three or four cows constantly to dispose of' and what 'corn or malt her husband had he never kept locked from her but she might dispose of it as she pleased'. A deponent John Lowe, reflecting on her household management, claimed that her 'keeping and ordering of her husband's house was wary and thrifty enough' and that Margaret was of 'mild and sober character towards her neighbors'. Margaret herself mocked her husband's inability to maintain his household finances and his insatiable appetite, claiming that 'her husband had eaten or destroyed more than the whole family had done', tying his manhood to his financial inadequacy and insatiable greed. Clearly Margaret Henshall had some control over her household finances and was able to use her household surplus to generate a profitable income. Her thriftiness was praised by her neighbors though her husband took issue when she bragged of her financial independence coupled with her rejection of him in the marital bed after publicly, and apparently haughtily, refusing to 'submit and yield' herself to him following a court order.[27] Tensions in the household were fixed on Margaret's management of her husband's estate; whilst Margaret claimed to have lent money at interest her husband claimed she had, in fact, indebted the household.

The Henshall case demonstrates the extension of housewifery to financial management within and beyond the household, as Margaret engaged in the credit market for interest, and the deeply engrained language that associated financial management with gendered ideals around thrift, neighborliness, appetite and subservience. Deponents in the Henshall case attempted to apply important distinctions to the extent of Margaret's authority over assets in the household and the estate when they described her ownership of certain cows and corn. This tension is replicated in other cases captured in the dataset that attempted to draw a distinction between household finance and business. Husband and wife, Jarred and Janet, appeared in the church courts of Durham in a marital dispute in 1566. Deponents testified to 'much evil agreement' between the two with Jarred being a 'very straitman in his house keeping'.[28] He allowed his wife a small allowance and a portion of the cheese and butter she made but, after selling her produce at Newcastle market, he kept the takings of 40l which he reckoned with his father. Janet was allowed £5 to 'lay up' which she

[27] Record Office, EDC 5/1664/43, 1664.

[28] Durham Diocesan Records, DDR/EJ/CCD/1/2, f.122v-123r, 1565–1573.

saved for 3 years and spent just 4d on her childbed. Similar distinctions were drawn when mistress Wood, administering her husband's will in East Anstey, Devon in 1688, denied having any authority over the wider estate or knowledge of the value of livestock owned by her husband. Her neighbor claimed she had been 'little entrusted nor did concern herself with the management of her husband's estate or outdoor affairs only with the necessary affairs of housekeeping incumbent on a wife to look after as the taking care to provide meat and other necessaries for a family and the making of butter and cheese and such like'.[29] When handling her deceased husband's debts, she was unaware of what he owed and had owing. Women's authority over household finances was at times contested and important distinctions appear to have been drawn between household and business accounts, between credit within the home for consumption and credit intended for investment.

Although the depositions show that women's authority over business credits could be contested and negotiated, evidence also indicates that wives were entrusted to manage the debts of their husband and played an important role as mediators and managers of credit. When, in 1576, William Richards sought to repay Thomas Ballaman for 20 young sheep bought on credit, he found Thomas to be absent from his home and instead dined with Thomas's wife who took the payment of 25s owing to her husband. Joane Bailey approached Joane Hele in her home to demand money for ploughing owed to her husband.[30] In 1672, in the ale house of Richard Hatton in Sandbach Cheshire, appeared Ellen Rowlinson equipped to pay an outstanding debt of her husband to George Moore. Whilst stood in the alehouse, with her coin 'in the crown of her hat', she was approached by Thomas Gennis who handed her coin that he had borrowed from Raph Kennerly in order to pay an outstanding debt to George Moore. Thomas Gennis bid her to pay his borrowed coin to George Moore and to 'take a discharge from Master Moore when she had paid it' as proof of payment.[31] The widow Katherine Serls reflected on her time with her recently deceased husband and claimed that of an evening whilst her and her husband 'lay together in bed, he would remember and

[29] Devon Record Office, Chanter 8299, 1688–92.

[30] Devon Record Office, Chanter 880, Bayly v Hele.

[31] Cheshire Record Office, QJF/100/2/77, 1672.

talk of his debts'.[32] When taking an adjusted figure, women account for 43.4% of mediators to, and managers of, credit. Often they appear in the background of the depositional evidence as witnesses to credit. In a reckoning of accounts between William Browne and Richard Sound for the shoeing of a horse, it was Richard's maid, Ann Woodward, witness to the reckoning who persuaded her master to allow 5s in credit.[33] When Agnes Moore, at a clothier's in Norwich in 1580, bought kersey cloth on credit, the debt was recorded in the book of the clothier Richard Wright but was witnessed by Richard's wife.[34] Women not only facilitated the credit of their husbands but also other women. In 1691 in Tiverton, Devon, Juliana Keens along with John Hartnell accompanied Joanne Kerslake as she ventured to the home of Isabella Richards to demand an outstanding debt.[35] As onlookers and witnesses, women performed part of the communal memory attesting to credit and debt in their local economy and the creditworthiness of their wider networks and took note of their own household finances as their family members contracted debts. Rather than precluding women from the credit economy, marriage increased access to a knowledge of the value and worth of domestic goods and bestowed authority in the management of household finances.

3 Networks of Credit

Qualitative evidence for credit networks in the depositions is limited. A handful of cases describe longer chains of indebtedness. A single case in the church courts of York describes an explicit network of credit, facilitated by the roaming body of church courts officials. Thomas Emenson, a registrar to the Archdeacon of Cleveland north of York, was accused by the minister of Flexikirk, Thomas Bell, of being a knave, a liar, an adulterer and a usurer.[36] Bell was defiantly opposed to all lending on interest and in 1596 had published a short tract, *The Speculation of Usurie*, on the

[32] Hampshire Record Office, 21M65/C3/11, 1596.

[33] Northamptonshire Archives, QSR/1/59/41, 1669.

[34] Norfolk Record Office, DN/DEP/19/20/214–224, Collinson v Wright, 1581–1582.

[35] Devon Record Office, Chanter 8299, Richards v Kerslake, 1691.

[36] Borthwick Institute of York, CP.H.1171, Edmondson v Bell, 1614.

nature of usury and the religious justification for the abolition of the practice.[37] Subsequent depositions in the case reveal an organized network of formal credit within the legal infrastructure of the church. The officials within the church court of Cleveland formed a distinct credit network. Thomas Crawshawe, an 'advocate to the church court and others', mediated a credit contract between Thomas Rouche, described as 'kinsman', and Thomas Emenson, the accused usurer. Radolph Betson, ecclesiastical curate of Bagbie in the archdeaconry of Cleveland, facilitated a second loan between Rouche and Emenson, a sum of £20 or £30 charged at the rate of 10% for which Betson stood as surety. Emenson secured his loans via written credit instruments, bills and bonds, drawn up by the public notary situated within the city of York. Of those witnesses called in the case, three operated as public notaries. The credit operations of Emenson were secured through his personal networks established in the church courts of Cleveland but were secured and legitimated via the services of the public notary in York. Thomas Emenson and his network are rare in the court depositions. Few deponents gave extensive details about their credit networks. Where women recall ongoing economic relations, these are ordinarily familial. Joane Atkins reckoned an account with her daughter and son-in-law in her home in Castle Cary in 1612 and when Johan Nicholls sought credit, she pawned a blanket to her mother-in-law and sold another to her sister.[38] In capturing incidental details about creditors and debtors across the sample, we can draw some overarching trends that characterized this low level credit in the rural economy. The Table 3 categorizes the work tasks of creditors and debtors according to their relationship to one another, categorized as either 'known party' or 'unknown party' and, where this relationship cannot be ascertained from the depositions, this has been categorized as 'unknown'.

Unsurprisingly, the vast majority, 71.3%, of the creditors and debtors in the data were known to one another. Buying goods from unknown sellers was a common narrative used by deponents accused of being in possession of stolen goods. We can filter the results to consider only those credit relations considered incidental or related to the case. When we do, the percentage of creditors and debtors known to one another increases

[37] Thomas Bell, *The Speculation of Usurie*, (London, 1596).

[38] Somerset Record Office, D/D/Cd/55 1619–1621; Devon Record Office, QS/4/Box32/B/30–28, 1630.

Table 3 Relations between creditors and debtors, 1500–1700

Relations	*M*	*%*	*F*	*%*	*Total*	*%*
Known Party	187	67.5	62	86.1	249	71.3
Unknown Party	11	4	4	5.6	15	4.3
Unknown	79	28.5	6	8.3	85	24.3
Totals	277	100	72	100	349	100

further to 87%. Though women appear to have conducted a greater proportion of their credit with known parties than their male counterparts, this is a result of a larger category of 'unknown' relations in men's commerce conducted on credit. Comparisons can be made to commerce conducted using coin where just 53.9% of those commercial work activities conducted using coin were between known parties. As we might expect, credit was more commonly contracted between known individuals and coin between unknown parties. Evidence for credit between family members in the dataset is scarce. This is in part due to the nature of the depositions. Deponents named individuals but not always their relation to one another and so relations by marriage are harder to ascertain from the records. It is also possible that intra-familial credit relations were not recounted at court, that they were less likely to be disputed or were conducted away from crimogenic spaces where details of the credit might be recalled as incidental in the deposition. Broadly, credit was more likely to be contracted between known individuals with some suggestion of a pre-existing or ongoing social or economic relationship than the examples of buying and selling conducted using coin described in the dataset.

The formulaic preamble to each deposition does allow for some geographical mapping of the distances between creditors and debtors recorded in the dataset. Taking evidence from across the three categories of pawning, financial management and commerce in which creditors and debtors gave details of their parish, we can see the distances between creditor and debtor. It is not however always possible to ascertain the location in which the credit was contracted. Evidence of creditor/debtor relations is sometimes inferred from depositions recounting managing a debt, demanding payment or simply where deponents recall their finances in their account. Where details do recall this information, it suggests that where credits and debts were recalled at a marketplace both parties were likely to have travelled. For instance, in 1580, Lewis Hore and Anthony met at an alehouse in Newbury, Berkshire on market day to settle their debts. Lewis had travelled 28 miles and Anthony had travelled 13 miles.[39] The distances presented here are those between the home parishes of creditor and debtor and is not necessarily indicative of the distance travelled to contract credit. Where women are recorded extending credit to other women, both parties resided in the same parish in all but one case where a distance of 6 miles is recorded. The case in question detailed an instance of pawning between two women one of whom was described as an itinerant worker, a 'tinker', and therefore suggests that the female creditor was mobile.[40]

The patterns in the dataset enforce the long held assumption that women operating in informal rural credit networks for smaller sums were utilizing their existing local networks close to home. Where women extended credit to men, the average distance between creditor and debtor was 3 miles. Where men extended credit to women, the average distance between creditor and debtor was 3.4 miles. Women's credit thus appears highly localized. Where women appear in the dataset as debtor, this most frequently described commercial credit where women purchased household goods, raw material such as wool and cloth and consumables. The distance increases in instances where men gave credit to other men. Here the average distance was 5.5 miles with a range of 0–78 miles. Where the distance was greatest, there is an indication of a long-standing relationship. Robert Homer of Downton in Wiltshire travelled 40 miles to claim an outstanding debt from his old master and his master's brother in Bremhill.[41] John Grove travelled 78 miles from Maesbury to Exeter to collect an outstanding debt of £5 owed by his wife's brother-in-law.[42] The greater distances travelled by men in order to secure credit are usually tied to other work activities. 30% of the credit incurred by men was explicitly described as a form of deferred payment to facilitate the purchase of livestock. These large purchases not only inflate the average amount of credit contracted by men but also the distances travelled by men to secure credit as they travelled to and from markets droving livestock. Descriptions of these larger credit transactions for livestock suggest a wider credit network

[39] Hampshire Record Office, 21M65-C3-8, 1578–1582.

[40] Devon Record Office, QS/4/Box24/Ep26-27, 1620.

[41] Wiltshire and Swindon History Centre, A1-110-1683H/127–8, 1638.

[42] Suffolk Record Office, Q/SR/33/38, 1619.

in the marketplace, one in which credit could be contracted between 'unknown' individuals and facilitated by intermediaries. In an instance in the north west of England, Richard Buckley described how he attended the fair in his home town of Ashton-Under-Lyne, in Lancashire, at Martinmas in 1655. Here, he met for the first time William Handsley who had travelled 20 miles to the fair from his home parish in Cheshire. Buckley exchanged his white gelding mare for Handsley's grey mare with Handsley owing an additional £5 to be paid at the following Christmas again at the fair in Ashton-Under-Lyne. For security of the payment, Handsley entered a bond with Buckley for double the sum. When Christmas came and Handsley did not attend the fair or attempt to settle his debt, Buckley instructed the local bailiff to seize the horse and Handsley was made to pay the bond in full. Handsley and Buckley were unknown to one another when they entered the fair and details from the case suggest that the credit was arranged via an intermediary. When Buckley's kinsman Richard Hawarth asked why he had entered a bond without sureties from Handsley, 'being a mere stranger unto him', Richard Buckley replied that 'one William Allen informed [him] that the said Handsley was a sufficient man'.[43] Droving livestock was an almost exclusively male occupation, 93.5% of all droving work tasks in the work activities dataset were performed by men. In rural economies, men's near monopoly on droving and sales of livestock enabled them to access credit networks in the marketplace that had a reach beyond their immediate parish.

Applying spatial categories to the data, we can see the places in which credit was contracted and managed in rural economies. This data is taken from all work activities associated with contracting and managing credit. This includes instances such as reckoning household accounts or repaying debts over a drink. Many deponents did not give descriptive spatial information, particularly when recounting a long-standing debt, so when identifying these spaces, a large proportion remains unknown, 46.1%.

Where deponents do give details about where credit transactions took place, private homes appear most frequently, 27.2%. Women's credit was contracted predominantly in domestic spaces, and reflects in part the blurred boundaries between sites of domesticity and sites of commerce as homes performed a dual function as shop, alehouse and workshop.

[43] Lancashire Record Office, information of John Bruxton, QSB/1/1656.

Women's credit is almost entirely absent from markets and fairs, again linking male credit to larger-scale credit contracts associated with the buying and selling of livestock at more centralized markets. Alehouses appear as the second largest category in the data. Deponents frequently recall settling debts and accessing credit in the alehouse. Thomas Hole of Guildford recalled that he had an extant knowledge of the debts and accounts of his punter, James Cally, as he was 'drawer of the wine and beer' in the local inn the 'Full Moon' and that James had borrowed from him to 'help satisfy and pay those debts' in the inn.[44] When William Handsley and his property was seized by the bailiff in Lancashire, it was at the local alehouse where his creditor Richard Buckley awaited and the debt was repaid.[45] The prominence of the alehouse as site of financial management also reflects women's role in the pawning trade. Creditors accepting items for pawn in the dataset were often alewives and the predominance of alehouses in the Table 4 attests to the significance of alehouses not only as centers for commercial exchange, as in the case of Ellin Rowlinson carrying her coin in her hat to settle a debt or the case of Lewis Hore and Anthony who met an alehouse midway to settle an account, but also the multi-functional role of alewife as host and creditor.

Pawning was commonly associated with alewives in popular literature. In the ballad Joan's Ale, the tinker visiting Joan's alehouse settled his tab and pawned his kettle for more ale, the tailor pawned his cloak and the

Table 4 Spaces of credit, 1500–1700

Space	*M*	*%*	*F*	*%*	*Totals*	*%*
House	72	26	23	31.9	95	27.2
Alehouse	19	6.9	13	18.1	32	9.2
Market/fair	21	7.6	1	1.4	22	6.3
Shop/stall	14	5.1	7	9.7	21	6
Field	6	2.2	1	1.4	7	2
Church	1	0.4	0	0	1	0.3
Road	9	3.2	1	1.4	10	2.9
Unknown	135	48.7	26	36.1	161	46.1
Total	277	100	72	100	349	100

[44] Hampshire Record Office, 21M65/C3/11, 1596.

[45] Lancashire Record Office, information of John Bruxton, QSB/1/1656.

porter got drunk and 'lost his frock'.[46] Elenor Rumming, the alewife of the eponymous poem by John Skelton, accepted in pawn for ale: salt, a peck of rye, a spoon, hose, a hatchet, a spinning wheel, a thimble and a wedding ring amongst other personal goods of value and household consumables. Her customers made 'scant thryft, When they made such shift'. The protagonist in the ballad 'A goodfellowes complaint against strong beere' recalls his financial ruin in the alehouse. He bemoans 'my moneys spent my cloathes are pawnd: And tis strong beere that has undone mee'. He also recalls how he was able to access credit in the alehouse: 'When I had coine no tapster durst, Refuse to trust me shillings three'. Buying drink on credit with an ongoing account to be reckoned was commonplace and the alewife would have been responsible for the ongoing management of these debts.[47] The ballad 'A very pleasant new Ditty' is addressed to the 'Hostesse' of an alehouse. The author poses scenarios of various customers and highlights the duties of an alewife to run reckonings on credit drawn up in the alehouse:

> Suppose a young man spend,
> and then have no money to pay,
> He hath no credit, nor none youll lend,
> but you will his Castor stay.
> Yet still he will call for Beere,
> with a full couragious note:
> But when the reckoning he doth heare,
> now marry he hath never a grote.[48]

The alewives and landladies presented in early modern ballads were also comical figures who were the source of scorn. Upon being faced with a

[46] 'JOAN's Ale is New; OR: / A new merry Medly, shewing the power, the strength, the operation and the ver- / tue that remains in good Ale, which is accounted the Mother-drink of England, / All you that do this merry Ditty view, / Taste of Joan's Ale, for it is strong and new', printed for F. Coles, T. Vere, J. Wright / J. Clarke, W. Thackeray, & T. Passinger, 1678–1680, Crawford.EB.1130, National Library of Scotland. This discussion of alewives has been supported by fruitful conversations with Amy Smith, PhD candidate at Bristol University.

[47] 'A goodfellowes complaint against strong beere, / OR / Take heed goodfellowes for heere you may see / How it is strong beere that hath vndone me', Printed for F. Groue, 1630, 1.439 Pepys Ballads, Magadlene College.

[48] 'A very pleasant new Ditty', Printed at London for H. Gosson, 1625, Pepys Ballads 1.282–1.283.

series of lewd customers who sought to pawn their tools and clothing, the landlady in the ballad 'The Good Fellows Frolick' demanded 'do you your reckoning pay, and get you out of door; Of them she could no money get, which caused her to frown'. The landlady is pitched against the brawl of customers—the 'fool', 'puppy-dogg' and 'clown'—who mock her and 'call'd her nasty Whore', but her role as creditor in the alehouse is an accepted norm that underpins her character in the ballad.[49] Maintaining a tally for ale to be reckoned at a later date was customary for the alewife and explains the prominence of the alehouse or inn as a site of credit and commercial reckoning in the dataset. The alewife could be a useful source of credit for consumption and a source of small change when punters used the alehouse as a meeting point to settle their own finances.

Deponents describe giving objects in pawn for coin which they then went on to spend in the alehouse as well as paying for food, ale and bed and board in kind. In Bishop's Nympton, Devon, Hugh Mortymer came to a reckoning with the wife of one Sage, an alehouse keeper, after spending a night at the inn where he exchanged 3 handkerchiefs and a falling band in lieu of 7d owed for his stay and meal. The same Hugh Mortymer went on to stay for a night at an alehouse in neighboring South Molton and gave the alewife a calico band, a ruff and a handkerchief in lieu of his supper, bed and breakfast.[50] Mary Delling took a smock she had bought from a 'tinker's wife' on credit to exchange for bread and drink to the value of 9d to the alewife Pearse.[51] Alewives were routinely handling secondhand goods as payment in kind presumably with a view to its later use or resale. The widow Elizabeth Taylor travelled to the victualing house of John Winterbotham in Oldham Lancashire but requested to see his wife Susan in order to pawn a piece of linen cloth in lieu of payments owed for ale.[52] Even in instances where the running of an alehouse appears to have been a joint venture between husband and wife, it was the alewife who was sought to handle credit. Alewives appear in the data to be important nodes of exchange in the rural credit economy

[49] 'The Good Fellows Frolick', printed for I. Coniers in Duck-Lane, c.1682, Houghton library- Huth EBB65H; Eleanor Rumming's customers, who visited her upon a hill for ale, 'were fayne with a Chalke, To score on the balke, Or score on the tayle'.

[50] Devon Record Office, QS/4/Box32/EP33, 1630.

[51] Devon Record Office, QS/4/Box24/EP26-27, 1620.

[52] Lancashire Archive, QSB/1/1677.

and, though working in partnership with their husband, were experts in the value of the consumable goods given in pawn.

4 Conclusions

Reconstructing credit networks in the rural economy is fraught with challenges. The dataset generated from the project, 'Forms of Labour', has collected incidental descriptions of credit and debt in depositions, enabling a quantitative analysis of the qualitative accounts of early modern rural economies that negates some of these challenges. Collecting evidence from across jurisdictional boundaries in the church and secular courts, the data presents a study of credit and financial networks unbound by the geographical remits of a singular legal institution. The data presented here shows that women account for nearly half of all creditors and nearly a third of all debtors in the rural economy. The women recorded in the depositions were largely married women. Marriage for both men and women is more broadly linked to a period of greater financial autonomy and household consumption as husbands and wives established new familial households. Ågren and her team have found this trend to extend to other forms of work with married men and women exerting greater authority over others and commanding and paying others to perform work.[53] Being in a marital partnership also granted access to a wider social and economic network. Though, as in the case of Margaret Henshall, we find evidence of the breakdown of these marital obligations in an economic partnership, the depositions also routinely describe the work of wives managing the credit of their husbands. It is of no surprise that married women dominated the work activities associated with the management of credit in the work-task dataset compared to never-married and widowed women.

Patterns of consumption show a consistent gendered accumulation of goods bought, sold, borrowed, lent and pawned, that reflect wider trends in the gendered divisions of work and trade. Men's near monopoly on droving livestock to market brought men into wider credit networks in marketplaces further from home. It also allowed for chance encounters on the road where goods and livestock were sold but also credit obligations recounted and settled. Trade in livestock was a male-dominated trade and

[53] Ling, Hassan Jansson, Lennersand, Pihl, Ågren, 'Marriage and Work'.

encountered larger sums where credit was commonplace and livestock could be exchanged in long relations of indebtedness. Gendered distinctions were drawn between household credit for consumption and credit that facilitated business. Women's credit was for smaller sums and bound to commerce for consumption. Their credit networks were confined to their own parish both when acting as creditor and debtor and where evidence for established networks does exist, they indicate that credit was drawn through kinship networks. As sellers, they operated out of their home, workshops and shops where there was a fluidity between private domestic spaces and publicly regulated commerce. The biography of the durable homewares purchased by women shows an ongoing engagement with the secondhand market and pawning industry that demonstrated an entanglement of the domestic with the market as married women asserted their economic agency as asset managers within their household. When contracting credit, these married women were accessing 'support networks that enabled households to get by in the face of haphazard income streams and a limited cash flow'.[54] But as wives, they were entrusted with managing their household finances, handling larger sums of coin and demanding payments. Credit and its management was a significant part of a wife's duty in the household economy and the evidence here suggests that marital status was an important determinant in granting access to this nexus of household credit.

References

Primary Sources

Borthwick Institute of York, CP.H.1171, Edmondson v Bell, 1614.

Cheshire Record Office, EDC 5/1664/43, 1664; QJF/100/2/77, 1672; QJF/110/4/62, 1682.

Devon Record Office, Chanter 8299, 1688–92; Chanter 8299, Richards v Kerslake, 1691; Chanter 880, Bayly v Hele.

Devon Record Office, QS/4/Box 55, 1650; QS/4/Box24/Ep26–27, 1620; QS/4/Box32/B/30–28, 1630; QS/4/Box32/EP33, 1630.

Durham Diocesan Records, DDR/EJ/CCD/1/2, f.122v-123r, 1565–1573.

Hampshire Record Office, 21M65/C3/11, 1596; 21M65-C3-8, 1578–1582.

Lancashire Archive, QSB/1/1677.

[54] Shepard, 'Minding their own business', 55.

Lancashire Record Office, information of John Bruxton, QSB/1/1656.

Norfolk Record Office, DN/DEP/19/20/214–224, Collinson v Wright, 1581–1582.

Northamptonshire Archives, QSR/1/59/41, 1669.

Record Office, EDC 5/1664/43, 1664.

Somerset Record Office, D/D/Cd/55 1619–1621;

Suffolk Record Office, Q/SR/33/38, 1619

Wiltshire and Swindon History Centre, A1–110–1683H/127–8, 1638.

Printed Primary Material

'A goodfellowes complaint against strong beere, / OR / Take heed goodfellowes for heere you may see / How it is strong beere that hath vndone me', Printed for F. Groue, 1630, 1.439 Pepys Ballads, Magadlene College.

A very pleasant new Ditty', Printed at London for H. Gosson, 1625, Pepys Ballads 1.282–1.283.

Bell, Thomas, *The Speculation of Usurie* (London, 1596).

'JOAN's Ale is New; OR: / A new merry Medly, shewing the power, the strength, the operation, and the ver- / tue that remains in good Ale, which is accounted the Mother-drink of England, / All you that do this merry Ditty view, / Taste of Joan's Ale, for it is strong and new', printed for F. Coles, T. Vere, J. Wright / J. Clarke, W. Thackeray, & T. Passinger, 1678–1680, Crawford.EB.1130, National Library of Scotland.

'The Good Fellows Frolick', printed for I. Coniers in Duck-Lane, c.1682, Houghton library- Huth EBB65H

Secondary Material

Erickson, Amy. 2005. Coverture and Capitalism. *History Workshop Journal* 59: 1–16.

Fontaine, Laurence, and Jürgen. Schlumbohm. 2000. Household Strategies for Survival: An Introduction. *International Review of Social History* 45 (S8): 1–17.

Froide, Amy M. 2005. *Never Married: Singlewomen in Early Modern England*. Oxford: Oxford University Press.

Holderness, B. A. 1984. Widows in pre-industrial society: An essay upon their economic functions. In *Land, Kinship and Life-Cycle*, edited by Smith, Richard, 423–442. Cambridge: Cambridge University Press.

Lemire, Beverly. 2001. Introduction: Women, Credit and the Creation of Opportunity: A Historical Overview. In: *Women and Credit Researching the Past, Refiguring the Future*, edited by Beverly Lemire, Ruth Pearson and Gail Campbell, 3–14. Oxford: Berg Publishers.

Lemire, Beverly. 2005. *The Business of Everyday Life; Gender, Practice and Social Politics in England, c. 1600–1900*. London: Manchester University Press.

Lemire, Beverly. 1998. *Petty Pawns and Informal Lengind: Gender and the Transformation of Small-Scale Credit in England circa, 1600–1800, From Family Firms to Corporate Capitalism: Essays in Business and Industrial History in Honour of Peter Mathias*. Oxford: Oxford University press.

Ling, Sofia, Hassan Jansson, Karin, Lennersand, Marie, Pihl, Christopher, Ågren, Maria. 2016. Marriage and Work: Intertwined Sources of Agency and Authority. In: *Making a Living, Making a Difference: Gender and Work in Early Modern European Society*, edited by Maria Ågren, 80–102. Oxford: Oxford University Press.

McIntosh, Marjorie Keniston. 2005. Women, Credit and Family Relationships in England, 1300–1620. *Journal of Family History* 30 (2): 143–163.

McIntosh, Marjorie Keniston. 2005. *Working Women in English Society, 1300–1620*, 123–124. Cambridge: Cambridge University Press.

Muldrew, Craig. 2003. A Mutual Assent of Her Mind'? Women, Debt, Litigation and Contract in Early Modern England. *History Workshop Journal* 55: 47–71.

Muldrew, Craig. 1993. Credit and the Courts: Debt Litigation in a Seventeenth-Century Urban Community. *The Economic History Review* 46 (1): 23–38.

Muldrew, Craig. 2011. *Food, Energy and the Creation of Industriousness: Work and Material Culture in Agrarian England, 1550–1780*. Cambridge: Camrbidge University Press.

Muldrew, Craig. 1997. Rural Credit, Market Area and Legal Institutions in the Countryside in England, 1550–1700. In: *Commerce and Courts in Britain 1150–1900*, edited by Christopher Brooks and Michael Lobban, 155–178. London: Bloomsbury Publishing.

Postel-Vinay, Giles. 2021. Change and Transformation of Premodern Credit Markets. The Importance of Small-Scale Credits. In: *Change and Transformation of Premodern Credit Markets; The Importance of Small-Scale Credits*, edited by Stephan Nicolussi-Kohler. 23–38. Heidelberg: Heidelberg University Press.

Shepard, Alexandra. 2015. Crediting Women in the Early Modern English Economy. *History Workshop Journal* 79: 1–23.

Shepard, Alexandra. 2015. Minding their own Business: Married Women and Credit in Early Eighteenth-Century London. *Transactions of the Royal Historical Society* 25: 53–74.

Spence, Cathryn. 2016. *Women, Credit and Debt in Early Modern Scotland*. Manchester: Macnhester University Press.

Spicksley, Judith. 2018. Never-Married Women and Credit in Early Modern England. In *Women and Credit in Pre-Industrial Europe*, edited by Elise M. Dermineur, 227–251. Turnhout: Brepols.

Whittle, Jane and Elizabeth Griffiths. 2012. *Consumption and Gender in the Early Seventeenth-Century Household: The World of Alice Le Strange*. Oxford: Oxford University Press.

Whittle, Jane, and Mark Hailwood. 2020. The gender division of labour in early modern England. *The Economic History Review* 73 (1): 3–32.

CHAPTER 5

Credit and Social Networks in Late Fourteenth-Century Tyrol: The Village of Laas

Stephan Nicolussi-Köhler

1 Introduction[1]

This chapter aims to reconstruct the credit activities within the small village of Laas in Tyrol during the late fourteenth century .[2] A significant portion of Tyrol's credit market depended on notaries, who were

[1] The currency used in Tyrol were *Veronese denarii* (Berner): 1 *marca* (mr.) = 10 *librae* (lb.) = 120 *grossi* (gr.) = 200 *solidi* (sol.) = 2.400 *denarii* or *Berner* (d.). Helmut Rizzolli and Federico Pigozzo, *Der Veroneser Währungsraum: Verona und Tirol vom Beginn des 10. Jahrhunderts bis 1516* (= Runkelsteiner Schriften zur Kulturgeschichte 8) (Athesia, Bolzano, 2015), 23.

[2] The village of Laas is in modern day South-Tyrol. Stephan Nicolussi-Köhler, 'Between City and Countryside: Moneylending and Settling Debts in and around Meran (1388–1392)', in: Stephan Nicolussi-Köhler (ed.), *Change and Transformation of Pre-Modern Credit Markets: The Importance of Small-Scale Credits* (Heidelberg University Publishing, Heidelberg, 2021), 89–132.

S. Nicolussi-Köhler (✉)
University of Innsbruck, Innsbruck, Austria
e-mail: Stephan.Nicolussi-Koehler@uibk.ac.at

E. M. Dermineur and M. Pompermaier (eds.), *Credit Networks in The Preindustrial World*, Palgrave Studies in the History of Finance,
https://doi.org/10.1007/978-3-031-67117-3_5

responsible for issuing charters and recording transactions in their registers (so-called *imbreviaturae*).[3] As a result, many data on credit activities have survived. Using a complete register of the notary Jakob of Laas, which deals with business transactions for the year 1391 within the village of Laas, this study delves into the mechanisms of the credit market within a small-sized village in Tyrol.[4] The clientele of the notary consisted mostly of peasants, artisans, and parts of the sub-peasant strata (agricultural laborers) from Laas and its surroundings.[5] Only a small fringe belonged to the nobility or were burghers of the nearest bigger city of Meran. The relationships between the different actors were of diverse nature and consisted of marriages, leasehold contracts, granting of fiefs, legal disputes, and credit contracts. By analyzing the notary register and performing a network analysis, this chapter describes the participation of different social-economic groups to the credit market featuring the underlying social relations.[6]

[3] Richard Heuberger, 'Das deutschtiroler Notariat. Umrisse seiner mittelalterlichen Entwicklung', in: *Veröffentlichungen des Museum Ferdinandeum* 6 (1926), 27–122. For notarial credit see: François Menant and Odile Redon (eds.), *Notaires et crédit dans l'Occident méditerranéen médiéval* (École Française de Rome, Rome, 2004); Philipp T. Hoffman, Gilles Postel-Vinay, and Jean-Laurent Rosenthal, 'What do Notaries do? Overcoming Asymmetric Information in Financial Markets: The Case of Paris, 1751', in: *Journal of Institutional and Theoretical Economics* 154:3 (1998), 499–530.

[4] The register from the City Archive of Meran (StA) with the signature NI 22 has been edited by Raimund Senoner and published in a volume edited by Herbert Raffeiner in 2008. Herbert Raffeiner (ed.), *Noderbuch: Notariatsimbreviaturen des Jakob von Laas 1390–1392* (Provinz Verlag, Brixen, 2008). The edition has some significant shortcomings. See: Gustav Pfeifer, 'De arte edendi′, in: *Der Schlern* 82 (2009), 91–93; Volker Stamm, 'Kauf und Verkauf von Land und Grundrenten im hohen und späten Mittelalter: Eine Untersuchung zur historischen Wirtschaftsanthropologie', in: *Vierteljahrschrift für Sozial- und Wirtschaftsgeschichte* 96:1 (2009), 33–43, there 34. Therefore, the current research rests on the use of the original documents from the city archive. For the sake of simplicity, the numbering of the entries used in the edition of Raffeiner is used.

[5] Volker Stamm, 'Soziale Zwischengruppen in der mittelalterlichen Agrargesellschaft', in: *Historische Zeitschrift* 291:1 (2010), 1–22. Markus Cerman and Michael Mitterauer, 'The Sub-peasant Strata in the Late Medieval and Early Modern Eastern Alpine Region', in: Tore Iversen, John R. Myking, and Stefan Sonderegger (eds.), *Peasants, Lords, and State: Comparing Peasant Conditions in Scandinavia and the Eastern Alpine Region, 1000–1750* (=The Northern World 89) (Leiden, 2020), 269–291.

[6] Markus Gamper and Linda Reschke, 'Soziale Netzwerkanalyse: Eine interdisziplinäre Erfolgsgeschichte', in: Markus Gamper and Linda Reschke (eds.), *Knoten und Kanten: Soziale Netzwerkanalyse in Wirtschafts- und Migrationsforschung* (Bielefeld, 2010), 13–51; Eva Jullien, 'Netzwerkanalyse in der Mediävistik: Probleme und Perspektiven im Umgang

Credit relations were ubiquitous in medieval societies. But their overall importance is not reflected in the source material that survived. This is especially true for small-scale credits of local dimension. Unlike loans connected to long-distance trade, small-scale credits in the countryside were rarely formalized and were often poorly documented. Notarial acts and judicial sources are very often the only sources of these transactions. While the exact circumstances of credit transactions often elude us, we can gain better information about the individuals and social groups involved in the credit economy by applying social network analysis.[7] The network analysis captures actors (*nodes*) and their relationships (*edges*).[8] What is of interest about the actors or persons is not only their individual characteristics (absolute characteristics), but their connections to other actors (relational characteristics).[9] Pairs—so-called *dyads*—are generated through these connections, and the network is formed from the many pairs. The sum of all nodes and edges adds up to the so-called network-graph, which can be visualized and more importantly analyzed with statistical methods. This enables us to ask if different social groups resorted to different types of credit, how people were connected to each other within a village, or what persons were central in the network. The interpretation of the network, which consists in this case of all persons involved in a contract recorded by a single notary, broadens our understanding of patterns and connections. Here, the relationship network of a single person shows the opportunities of a specific person to raise or lend capital but at the same time also reveals financial burdens that can lead to dependence on other people (Fig. 1).

mit mittelalterlichen Quellen', in: *Vierteljahrschrift für Sozial- und Wirtschaftsgeschichte* 100:1 (2013), 135–153.

[7] Benjamin Hitz, *Ein Netz von Schulden: Schuldbeziehungen und Gerichtsnutzung im spätmittelalterlichen Basel* (=Vierteljahrschrift für Sozial- und Wirtschaftsgeschichte Beihefte 256) (Franz Steiner Verlag, Stuttgart, 2022), 11–22.

[8] A network consists of social structures that are characterized by a certain stability over time. Johannes Marx, 'Netzwerke als Quelle sozialen Kapitals: Zur kulturellen und strukturellen Einbettung vertrauensvoller Handlungen in Netzwerken', in: Markus Gamper and Linda Reschke (eds.), *Knoten und Kanten: Soziale Netzwerkanalyse in Wirtschafts- und Migrationsforschung* (Transcript Verlag, Bielefeld, 2010), 95–118, there 97.

[9] Robert Gramsch, *Das Reich als Netzwerk der Fürsten: Politische Strukturen unter dem Doppelkönigtum Friedrichs II. und Heinrichs (VII.) 1225–1235* (=Mittelalterforschungen 40) (Ostfildern, 2013), 21–34.

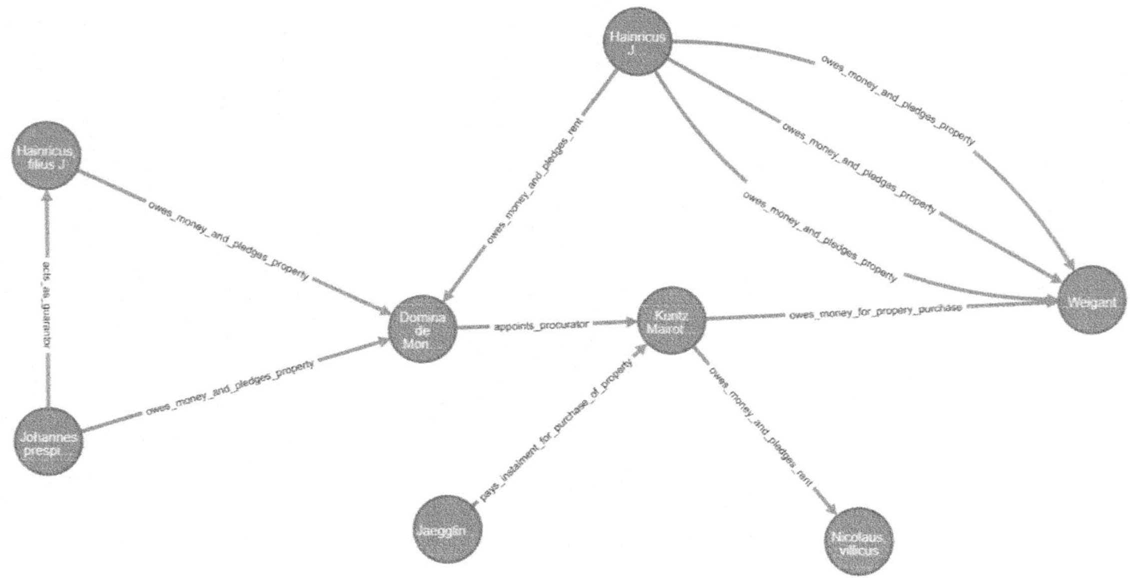

Fig. 1 Legal relations of Konrad (Kuntz) Mairott

The position of actors and their economic relations becomes immediately evident through the following example: Konrad Mairott was indebted to Jakob Weigand (alternatively spelled as Weigant), who appeared as one of the most important creditors in the community. Similarly, Konrad was also engaged in another credit transaction with Nicolaus and acted as procurator for a woman, Petrisie. As procurator, he acted as buyer in a purchase-contract of a rent for Petrisie from a certain Heinrich Mairjans. In this example, the network is of course very simple. In this concrete case, Konrad was connected directly to Jakob Weigand, the most important creditor in Laas, and indirectly to a member of the very influential Mairjans family, Heinrich. Konrad owed money to Nicolaus, who in turned also owed money to a married couple. Thus, within Laas, intricate chains of credit existed among various individuals, often not directly linked, underscoring the complexity of the network and the necessity of scrutinizing the broader context to unveil such connections.

Beyond the visual graph, social networks analysis enables us through statistical models to point at important actors (*nodes*) in the network. Here, Konrad, who owed several people money, had a central place in the (credit) network of the village of Laas as suggested by several statistical measures (e.g. betweenness centrality). Although he did not grant any credits at all, he was important to establish connections between different peers. Even if this example is very simple, social network analysis appears as a helpful methodological tool in addition to the qualitative analysis of credit contracts. The survey and presentation of networks is therefore not an objective in itself but a heuristic means to develop new questions. A discussion of network structures allows a better understanding of the functioning of credit markets.

The study proceeds in several steps. Initially, it examines the significance of pre-modern rural credit markets. Following this, it provides an economic overview of the late fourteenth-century village of Laas. Subsequently, the dataset and various types of credit transactions are outlined. The analysis then delves into a network analysis, offering insight into the credit activity within the village. Finally, the credit activities of this small community are reconstructed succinctly, facilitating a comprehensive understanding of the intertwined social and economic relationships at play.

2 Rural Credit Markets

It is well known that credit made up an important part of the medieval economy.[10] The rapidly growing economy from the tenth century onwards, with its shift from a manor economy to a market economy and increasing trade (both urban–rural and long-distance trade), is primarily responsible for the increased demand for money and the accompanying need for credit.[11] This credit was both urban and rural.[12] But for a long time, rural credit in medieval Europe has been either ignored—because of a lack of sources—or deemed not to be of importance.[13] This has partly been connected to the older assumption that an absence of banking institutions hampered the thriving of a vivid credit market and the lack of institutional credit in the countryside limited its extent. More recently, this view has been corrected by studies on the diversity of pre-modern

[10] Gabriela B. Clemens, 'Einleitung: Die Omnipräsenz von westeuropäischen Kreditbeziehungen', in: Gabriela B. Clemens (ed.), *Schuldenlast und Schuldenwert: Kreditnetzwerke in der europäische Geschichte 1300–1900* (Kliomedia, Trier, 2008), 9–20; Daniel L. Smail, 'The Materiality of Credit: Debt Collection as Pawnbroking in Late Medieval Mediterranean Europe', in: *Histoire urbaine* 51 (2018), 95–110; Bruno Kuske, 'Die Entstehung der Kreditwirtschaft und des Kapitalverkehrs', in: Bruno Kuske, *Köln, der Rhein und das Reich: Beiträge aus fünf Jahrhunderten wirtschaftsgeschichtlicher Forschung* (Böhlau, Cologne, 1956), 48–137; Julie Claustre, 'Vivre à crédit dans une ville sans banque (Paris XIVe–XVe siècle)', in: *Le Moyen Âge* 109 (2014), 567–596.

[11] Roberto S. López, *The Commercial Revolution of the Middle Ages 950–1350* (Cambridge University Press, Cambridge, 1971), 70–79; Shami Ghosh, 'Rural Commercialisation in Fourteenth-Century Southern Germany: The Evidence from Scheyern Abbey', in: *Vierteljahrsschrift für Sozial- und Wirtschaftsgeschichte* 104:1 (2017), 52–77; Thomas Ertl, 'Small Landlords: Land Transactions in and around Bozen (South Tirol) in the Mid-Thirteenth Century', in: *Vierteljahrschrift für Sozial- und Wirtschaftsgeschichte* 104:1 (2017), 7–28, there 8.

[12] Gilles Postel-Vinay, 'Change and Transformation of Pre-Modern Credit Markets: The Importance of Small-Scale Credits', in: Stephan Nicolussi-Köhler (ed.), *Change and Transformation of Pre-Modern Credit Markets: The Importance of Small-Scale Credits* (Heidelberg University Press, Heidelberg, 2021), 23–38.

[13] Jean-Laurent Rosenthal, 'Rural Credit Markets and Aggregate Shocks: The Experience of Nuits St. Georges, 1756–1776', in: *The Journal of Economic History* 54:2 (1994), 288–306, there 288; Chris Briggs, *Credit and Village Society in Fourteenth-Century England* (Oxford University Press, Oxford, 2009), 1–18.

credit institutions and actors.[14] It has been shown that outside the classical field of high finance, which consists of early banking institutions and their forerunners, informal credit markets mediated by informal agents prospered.[15] Capital markets already existed in the Middle Ages and had a great impact on the economic wellbeing of society.[16] Whereas access to credit could help people to bridge a shortage of cash or overcome harvest failures, a lack of access to credit or an imbalance in credit markets could lead to impoverishment or even expropriation.[17] Therefore, economists and historians alike are interested in pre-modern credit systems. Little is known about how these credit markets functioned. At least, two ways of obtaining credit from a would-be lender existed. Those who owned mobile goods or landed property could use it as collateral; those who possessed nothing of value could only pledge their reputation. In this case, much was at stake, including the future access to credit of the debtor. Usually, collateral was the easiest way to reduce the lender's anxiety to lend money.

[14] Philip T. Hoffman, Gilles Postel-Vinay, and Jean-Laurent Rosenthal, *Priceless Markets: The Political Economy of Credit in Paris, 1660–1870* (University of Chicago Press, Chicago and London, 2000); Philip T. Hoffman, Gilles Postel-Vinay, and Jean-Laurent Rosenthal, *Dark Matter Credit: The Development of Peer-to-Peer Lending and Banking in France* (Princeton University Press, Princeton, 2019); Laurence Fontaine, *Le marché: Histoire et usages d'une conquête sociale* (Gallimard, Paris, 2014); D'Maris Coffman, Cinzia Lorenzini, and Marcella Lorenzini, 'Introduction', in: D'Maris Coffman, Cinzia Lorenzini, Marcella Lorenzini (eds.), *Financing in Europe: Evolution, Coexistence and Complementarity of Lending Practices from the Middle Ages to Modern Times* (Palgrave Studies in the History of Finance) (Palgrave Macmillan, Cham, 2018), 1–18; Stephan Nicolussi-Köhler, 'Introduction', in: Stephan Nicolussi-Köhler (ed.), *Change and Transformation of Pre-Modern Credit Markets: The Importance of Small-Scale Credits* (Heidelberg University Publishing, Heidelberg, 2021), 1–21; Elise Dermineur, 'Trust, Norms of Cooperation, and the Rural Credit Market in Eighteenth-Century France', in: *The Journal of Interdisciplinary History* 45:4 (2015), 485–506.

[15] D'Maris Coffman, Cinzia Lorenzini, and Marcella Lorenzini, 'Introduction', 3–4. For other informal financial intermediaries see: Matteo Pompermaier, 'Credit and Poverty in Early Modern Venice', in: *Journal of Interdisciplinary History* 52:4 (2022), 513–536.

[16] Jaco Zuijderduijn, *Medieval Capital Markets: Markets for renten, State Formation and Private Investment in Holland (1300–1500)* (Brill, Leiden and Boston, 2009), 5–13.

[17] Philipp R. Schofield, 'Impediments to expropriation: Peasant property rights in medieval England and Marcher Wales', in: *Continuity and Change* 36 (2021), 211–232; Simon Teuscher, 'Schulden, Abhängigkeiten und politische Kultur: Das Beispiel der Kleinstadt Thun im Spätmittelalter', in: Gabriela Signori (ed.), *Prekäre Ökonomien: Schulden in Spätmittelalter und Früher Neuzeit* (=Spätmittelalterstudien 4) (UVK, Konstanz and Munich, 2014), 243–262, there 257.

Different sources are available: On the one hand, we have notary registers or municipal debt records, in which the granting of credit is controlled and recorded by the authorities, on the other hand, there are sources of the jurisdiction, in which the penalties for late payment or insolvency are documented.[18] Both sources cover only a very specific niche of the credit market. Besides these legal forms of credit existed a vast non-intermediated peer-to-peer capital market that involved individuals in dense networks. These networks made up an important part of the economic life and encompassed financial exchanges sustained through collaboration, fairness, solidarity, and trust.[19] Trust was mostly based on information about the debtor, his assets, his competences, his intentions, and his reputation. In a society with many shared social norms, such as a peasant society in a small village, the social and geographic proximity formed by family ties, a high rate of endogamy, and relative familiarity with each other created strong bonds.[20] These mechanisms helped to overcome information asymmetries within the community since lenders and debtors knew each other beforehand and uncertainty was mostly restricted to external and uncontrollable factors (bad harvests, death, catastrophic events, etc.). A peasant, who did not repay, would lose his reputation and would be unable to acquire further credit within the community. If the debtors and the creditors did not know each other, other forms of enforceability were needed, such as legal contracts with collateral or additional guarantees. Whereas the first type of (collateralized) credit can be reconstructed rather easily, reputational (or informal) credit is far more difficult to trace. The inhabitants were participating in different economic and social networks which included labor, rights to land, loans, and family bounds.[21] These networks are hard to reconstruct and can be easily overlooked. Analyzing these networks allows a better

[18] Gabriela Signori, 'Einleitung', in: Gabriela Signori (ed.), *Prekäre Ökonomien: Schulden in Spätmittelalter und Früher Neuzeit* (Konstanz and Munich, 2014), 11.

[19] Craig Muldrew, *The Economy of Obligation: The Culture of Credit and Social Relations in Early Modern England* (Palgrave Macmillan, New York, 1998), 2. This has been described as a 'moral economy'. Laurence Fontaine, *The Moral Economy: Poverty, Credit, and Trust in Early Modern Europe* (Cambridge University Press, Cambridge, 2014); Pompermaier, 'Credit and Poverty', 514.

[20] Dermineur, 'Trust', 487–489.

[21] Postel-Vinay, 'Change and Transformation', 33.

understanding of what role reputational and collateral credit played and how social and economic relationships were combined to acquire credit.

3 An Economic Summary of the Village of Laas

The village of Laas is located in the Vinschgau Valley, which extends along a heavily used trade route between the Reschenpass in the north and Meran in the south. The river Etsch flows through the city and divides the town in two parts.[22] The village was connected to the important regional Martini- (11 November) and Pentecost-Fairs of Meran and the Bartholomew-Fair (24 August) of Glurns, which both attracted merchants from southern Germany and northern Italy. These dates were of great importance for the local business activities, as is shown by several entries in the notary register. The notary Jakob of Laas himself was present at the Bartholomew-Fair of Glurns in 1391 and recorded business contracts there.[23] This shows the economic orientation of Laas toward the regional fairs and the city of Meran. Meran with approximately 2,000 inhabitants in the late fourteenth century was not only the central place of the court district (the so-called Landgericht Meran), but there was also the mint located and a pawnbroking bank (*casana*). Next to the city was the castle of Tyrol, where the counts and later some of the Habsburgian dukes had their residence.[24] Several times, the citizens of Meran appear as business partners, merchants, or creditors in Laas, granting credit or selling merchandise like drapery to dwellers from the countryside (Fig. 2).

The village of Laas was a rural community with a settlement nucleus around the main road and the bridge over the Etsch. In the late fourteenth century, around 80 people lived in the town.[25] Agriculture was

[22] Rainer Loose, 'Die Welt des Notars Jakob von Laas', in: Herbert Raffeiner (ed.), *Noderbuch: Notariatsimbreviaturen des Jakob von Laas 1390–1392* (Provinz Verlag, Brixen, 2008), 205–218, there 209; Nicolussi-Köhler, 'Between City and Countryside', 92–95.

[23] Raffeiner (ed.), *Noderbuch*, no. 69.

[24] Gertraud Zeindl, *Meran im Mittelalter: eine Tiroler Stadt im Spiegel ihrer Steuern* (=Tiroler Wirtschaftsstudien 57) (Universitätsverlag Wagner, Innsbruck, 2009), 39–42.

[25] A list of subjects (*Untertanenverzeichnis*) from the counts of Tirol from 1427 mentions 80 persons living in Laas. The overall population was probably a little bit higher since subjects of other feudal lords were not registered. The population probably did not change a lot within these three decades. Untertanenverzeichnis von Tirol, 1427: TLA IC 12, fol. 177r – 179v. Otto Stolz, 'Das Verzeichnis der Untertanen der Tiroler Landesfürsten im Inntal und Vintschgau vom Jahre 1427. Text bearbeitet von H. Bachmann, L.

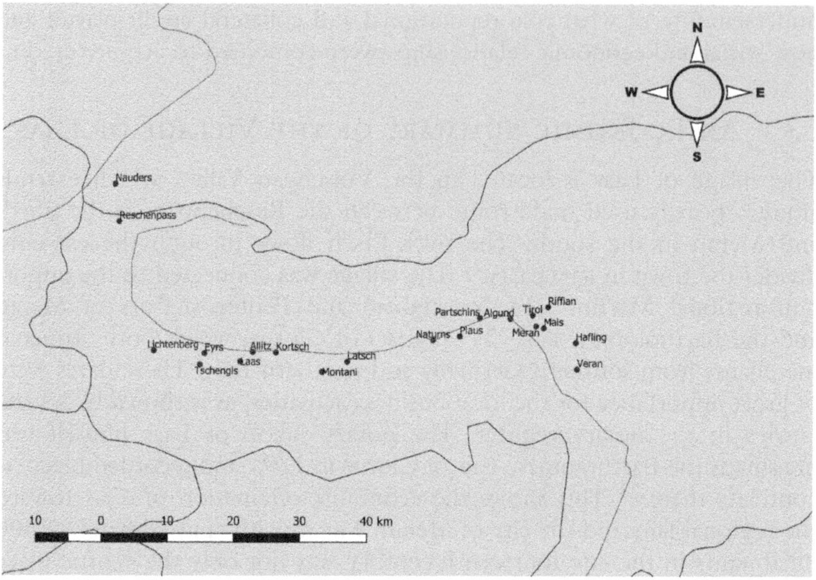

Fig. 2 The village of Laas in the Vinschgau

the dominant source of income for most people living in Laas.[26] The products mentioned in the sources were cereals (rye, barley, and some wheat) and dairy products (most notably cheese). Several times livestock are mentioned (cows, sheep, goats, horses, and pigs). Viniculture was only

von Berg, K. Dörrer, K. Finsterwalder, H. Kramer', in: *Quellen zur Steuer-, Bevölkerungs- und Sippengeschichte des Landes Tirol im 13., 14. und 15. Jahrhundert, bearb. v. mehreren Innsbrucker Historikern: Festschrift zu Oswald Redlichs achtzigstem Lebensjahr 1938/1939* (=Schlern-Schriften 44) (Universitätsverlag Wagner, Innsbruck, 1939), 159–200, there 188.

[26] Volker Stamm, 'Zur Bedeutung der Grundrente für die landesfürstlichen Einnahmen und bäuerlichen Abgaben in der Grafschaft Tirol (13./14. Jahrhundert)', in: *Vierteljahrschrift für Sozial- und Wirtschaftsgeschichte* 94:1 (2007), 47–56; Hannes Obermair and Volker Stamm, 'Alpine Ökonomie in Hoch- und Tieflagen: das Beispiel Tirol im Spätmittelalter und Früher Neuzeit', in: Yann Decorzant, Anne-Lise Head-König, and Luigi Lorenzetti (eds.), *Relire l'altitude: la terre et ses usages. Suisse et espaces avoisinants, XIIe-XXIe siècles* (Éditons Alphil-Presses universitaires suisses, Neuchâtel, 2019), 29–56.

of minor importance.[27] The size of the individual farms varied considerably, as both prices for property sales and the levies that had to be paid suggest. Most farmers held the land they cultivated as hereditary tenure, lease, or fiefdom, for which they owed rents and other duties.[28] A part of the land was owned by the peasants or the village elites themselves and the rest by the Count of Tyrol or clerical institutions. Most important is the fact that by the end of the fourteenth century, most peasants and leaseholders possessed the right to sell or pledge their property or the respective usage rights of their property.[29] Thus, in Tyrol existed a vivid market for land and rents.

Artisanal production was present to some extent in Laas, and the surnames of several people like *sartor*, *tornator*, or *calicator* could indicate that their number was not so small.[30] Many of these craftsmen also owned or leased land for agricultural production and did not rely solely on monetary wages for their living.[31] Besides, there existed the so-called sub-peasant strata, which included landless households, servants, or households with only small land ownership that relied on makeshift solutions to make a living. In a list of rents recorded by the notary, several inhabitants of the village are listed with the respective duties they owed. Here we get a very broad picture of the population that also included the lower social classes, like several servants (*kneht*) or a swineherd (*sweinhirt*).[32] Their low rent payments give us an indication of their modest economic situation.

However, most households in Laas had access to agricultural land to some extent, be it leased or owned. It can be assumed that approximately one-fourth of the overall population of roughly 80 people owned little or no real estate.[33] At the other end of the social stratum, we find

[27] Loose, 'Die Welt des Notars', 211.

[28] Nicolussi-Köhler, 'Between City and Countryside', 93; Volker Stamm, 'Lehnspraxis im spätmittelalterlichen Tirol', in: *Tiroler Heimat* NF 72 (2008), 63–72.

[29] Stamm, 'Kauf und Verkauf'.

[30] Loose, 'Die Welt des Notars', 212; Nicolussi-Köhler, 'Between City and Countryside', 100.

[31] Raffeiner, *Noderbuch*, nos. 63, 80, 87.

[32] Raffeiner (ed.), *Noderbuch*, no. 41; Loose, 'Die Welt des Notars', 214.

[33] A tax register from 1314 mentions 50 taxable persons in the village of Laas that paid between 10 and 240 sol. Eighteen persons paid 20 sol. or less. Since the ordinary tax was based on wealth respectively ownership of real estate, it can be assumed that

the village elite of Laas, which consisted of the parish priest and the members of important families.[34] They bore the ***dominus*** or (the middle-German) ***her*** title and held offices like that of a ***villicus*** or were appointed as sworn jurors to settle legal disputes.[35] In Laas, the most important family were the Mairjans, to which the notary Jakob belonged. His father, Johannes, was ***villicus*** of the town and owned a big manor (***Maierhof***) with vast possessions. The farm was directly in the center of the town.[36] He had four sons, Haupold, Heinrich, Jaenlin, and Jakob (the notary), and one daughter, Margaret. Johannes and his sons were involved in many legal and economic activities of the town, either as notaries, custom officers, creditors, debtors, or arbitrators.[37] Their wealth and social reputation allowed them to play a central role in the economy of the town. Other local rich families, like Jacob Weigand and his wife, were also of great importance as creditors in the village of Laas. Although external merchants from Meran, like Niklaus Spetziger, appear a few times doing business in Laas, they were by no means as important as local actors.

land ownership was unevenly distributed. Taken with the numbers from the population figures, it is reasonable to estimate that roughly one fourth belonged to the sub-peasant strata. Ferdinand Kogler, 'Das landesfürstliche Steuerwesen in Tirol bis zum Ausgang des Mittelalters', in: *Archiv für österreichische Geschichte* 90 (1901), 419–712, there 516–518 and 543–546; Stamm, 'Soziale Zwischengruppen'; Cerman and Mitterauer, 'The Sub-peasant Strata'.

[34] Kurt Andermann, 'Die Vornehmen der Gemeinde: Überlegungen zu dörflichen Oberschichten im deutschen Südwesten während des späten Mittelalters und der frühen Neuzeit', in: Gustav Pfeifer and Kurt Andermann (eds.), *Soziale Mobilität in der Vormoderne: Historische Perspektiven auf ein zeitloses Thema* (=Veröffentlichungen des Südtiroler Landesarchivs 48) (Universitätsverlag Wagner, Innsbruck, 2020), 129–144.

[35] Gustav Pfeifer, '"Nobis servire tenebitur in armis": Formen des Aufstiegs und Übergangs in den niederen Adel im Tirol des 14. Jahrhunderts', in: Kurt Andermann and Peter Johanek (eds.), *Zwischen Nicht-Adel und Adel* (=Vorträge und Forschungen 53) (Jan Thorbecke Verlag, Stuttgart, 2001), 49–103, there 54.

[36] The manor of the Mair Jans is already mentioned in a tax register from 1314, where it is assigned the highest tax sum of the entire village (12 lb.). BayHStA ASLT 25, fol. 14r; Loose, 'Die Welt des Notars', 208; Otto Stolz, 'Das Steuerbuch des Vintschgaus und Burggrafenamts von 1314. Text bearbeitet von K. Dörrer, H. Bachmann, H. Kramer und Otto Stolz', in: *Quellen zur Steuer-, Bevölkerungs- und Sippengeschichte des Landes Tirol im 13., 14. und 15. Jahrhundert, bearb. v. mehreren Innsbrucker Historikern: Festschrift zu Oswald Redlichs achtzigstem Lebensjahr 1938/1939* (Universitätsverlag Wagner, Innsbruck, 1939), 104–126, there 112.

[37] Loose, 'Die Welt des Notars', 208–209.

4 The Notary Register of 1391

The dataset consists of a notarial register from the city archive of Meran.[38] It is a paper codex, consisting of 45 folios, including altogether 95 entries. The register was written by the notary Jakob[39] and covers—with a few exceptions—the period from February 1391 to December 1391.[40] This source is remarkable, because unlike most of the other medieval *imbreviaturae* preserved in the city archive of Meran, it includes the business dealings of a small town.[41] Thus, the register is for two reasons of immense value: firstly, it covers the legal activities of the city of Laas over a whole year and allows us to reconstruct the seasonality of the local business activities. And secondly, in this single register, 143 individuals are mentioned in the 95 entries, encompassing a large part of the population of Laas and its surroundings in 1391. By analyzing this source in detail, a lot of information about credit networks can be gathered.

Jakob recorded overall 84 contracts (of which 45 were concerned with credits or debts) in his register over a period of roughly eleven months (not including the eleven fragments and other non-legal formulas).[42] He seems to be the only notary active in Laas, although some *notulae* in his register were written by a different notary.[43] People engaged the services of a notary in order to secure legal transactions and to facilitate any claims that they might have to make at a later point in court or somewhere else. If consulted for a legal transaction, the notary wrote

[38] (StA Meran NI 22)

[39] Seven cartularies from Jakob of Laas exist, covering the years 1390/1391, 1398, 1399, 1401, 1406, and 1407: StA Meran, NI 22–28 and MOE 22. His son Petrus also became a notary in Meran in the early fifteenth century. Three of his registers survived for the years 1412/13, 1414/15, and 1418: NI 33–35.

[40] A detailed description of the register is given by Raimund Senoner, 'Einleitung', in: Herbert Raffeiner (ed.), *Noderbuch: Notariatsimbreviaturen des Jakob von Laas 1390-1392* (rovinz Verlag, Brixen, 2008), 11–17, there 11–14; Nicolussi-Köhler, 'Between City and Countryside', 95–109.

[41] Out of the 40 oldest registers covering the period from 1328 to 1444, only this register includes the business activities of a small town. StA Meran, NI 1–NI 40. The only other exceptions are the registers of the Jacob of Zernez from 1400 to 1403, which deal with business activities from Glurns. StA Meran, MOE 21; 22; 23.1; 23.2; 23.3.

[42] Nicolussi-Köhler, 'Between City and Countryside', 98–99.

[43] The entries on fol. 40v and the following sheets were written in a different hand, probably by Heinrich Moser. Raffeiner (ed.), *Noderbuch*, no. 69.

a shortened text (*notula*) of the contract in his register (the so-called *imbreviatura*).[44] The entries in the register were already legally effective. If requested by the client, the notary would draw up a full notarial instrument based upon these entries and cancel the entry in the register by striking it out. However, only 20 to 25 percent of all entries have probably been reproduced as a full document.[45]

5 Sample Selection

Before going into detail, we have to tackle the question of sample selection. This register does naturally not include all business and legal activities that have taken place in Laas in 1391 but only those where both parties agreed to pay money and have the legal contract recorded by a notary. This mostly concerned two types of transactions: Firstly, if immovable property or rents were donated, sold, or pledged, a contract was usually drawn up to document the change of ownership.[46] Secondly, if the transaction was of big volume, people would more likely resort to a notary to safeguard their rights because of legal security. Legal transactions of a small volume were usually not recorded by a notary. This is confirmed by the fact that for small-scale loans and minor business transactions, people would hesitate to demand a notarial charter because of high transaction

[44] David Fliri, 'Das Meraner Notariat im Spätmittelalter', in: Gustav Pfeifer (ed.), *1317: Eine Stadt und ihr Recht: Meran im Mittelalter: Bausteine zur Stadtgeschichte. Akten der Internationalen Tagung, Meran, Kurhaus und Kurmittelhaus, 22. bis 25. Februar 2017 = 1317: una città e il suo diritto: Merano nel Medioevo: materiali di storia cittadina. Atti del convegno internazionale, Merano, Kurhaus e Vecchie Terme, 22–25 febbraio 2017* (=Veröffentlichungen des Südtiroler Landesarchivs 43) (Bozen, 2018), 213–228.

[45] Ertl, 'Small Landlords', 2017, 9; Kathrin Utz Tremp,*'Fiat littera ad dictamen sapientum': Notare, Lombarden und Juden in Freiburg im Üchtland (14. Jahrhundert)* (Dike, Zurich, 2012), 5.

[46] As can be seen, there was a tendency in Tyrol since the late Middle Ages to record land transactions in writing for better documentation and as a basis for taxation by the authorities. Hermann Wopfner, 'Zur Geschichte des tirolischen Verfachbuches', in: *Forschungen und Mitteilungen zur Geschichte Tirols und Vorarlbergs* (1904), 244–246; Kogler, 'Das landesfürstliche Steuerwesen', 568.

costs.[47] If the parties conducted their transactions on their own, registration was optional unless the contract later became part of a legal process. Thus, not all credit contracts appear in the register. Many of the small transactions, which were informally or orally conducted, elude us.[48] This is a serious problem. The co-existence of multiple and complementary credit markets that we observe with unequal accuracy makes it difficult to interpret the total volume of credit. However, the notary register probably covers a rather complete picture of the credit transactions linked to land.

6 The Clientele of Jakob of Laas

Nearly all social groups ranging from the nobility to peasants, artisans, and urban burghers (of Meran) appear in the register of the notary. The activities range from selling land, marriage contracts, wills, and pawning a cow, to swearing to give up the dice game. This means that almost all areas of life of different groups of people from all social classes are covered. However, there was a group of people who maintained close (personal, social, and economic) relations with the notary, which can be called the notary's *familia*.[49] The people actively participating in legal transactions belonged mostly to the local elite. The notary often dealt with persons from his own—the Mairjans—family and recorded 19 contracts that involved members of his family (cf. Fig. 3).[50] Another ten contracts were commissioned by Jakob Weigand (and his wife), who were also

[47] Nicolussi-Köhler, 'Between City and Countryside', 107. Next to the notarial fee, other costs such as the *arra*, a symbolic purchase price of a low amount, had to be paid. Unfortunately, no costs for the notarial services are mentioned in the register. In the register of the notary David of Meran from 1328, small amounts between 1 gr. and 3 lb. are mentioned in marginal notes in six cases. StA Meran NI 1, fol. 1r, 18r, 36v–37r, 60r, 70r, 97v–98r.

[48] Dermineur, 'Trust', 487–489; Ulrich Pfister, 'Le petit crédit rural en Suisse aux XVIe-XVIIIe siécles', in: *Annales. Histoire, Sciences Sociales* 49:6 (1994), 1339–1357.

[49] Jean L. Laffont, 'Introduction: Problèmes et enjeux de l'analyse de l'activité notariale', in: Jean L. Laffont (ed.), *Problèmes et méthodes d'analyse historique de l'activité notariale (XVe–XIXe siècle): Actes du colloque du Toulouse (15–16 septembre 1990), tenu dans le cadre de la Chambre départementale de Notaires de la Haute Garonne* (Presses Universitaires du Mirail, Toulouse-Le-Mirail, 1991), 22–26; Utz Tremp, *Fiat littera*, 3.

[50] Raffeiner (ed.), *Noderbuch*, nos. 10–11, 20, 22, 46, 47, 48, 50, 53, 55, 66, 73, 76, 79, 84, 86, 88.

members of the social and economic elite.[51] Besides, several other persons appear between one and several times in the cartulary. The monetary sums mentioned in diverse contracts range from 60 gr. to 4,440 gr. with 80 gr. being the wage of an unskilled worker per month (cf. Table 1).

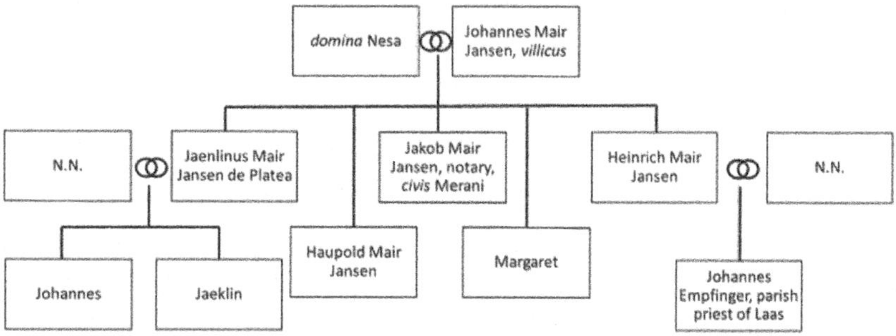

Fig. 3 Family Tree of the Mair Jansen Family

Table 1 Index of Prices and Wages. Source: StA Meran, NI 22, fol. 11v

Index of Prices and Wages (Laas, 1391)	
1 mark *(m.)* = *10* libra *(lb.)* = *120* grossi *(gr.)* = *200* solidi *(sol.)* = *2,400* denarii parvulorum *(den.)*	
	Prices and Wages
cow	84 gr
rye (pro ***modium*** *)	30 gr
barley (pro ***modium****)	24 gr
wine (pro ***carrata****)	180–250 gr
cheese (pro *schoett****)	6,8 gr
Wage of an unskilled worker (per day)	4 gr
Wage of a skilled craftsmen, i.e. mason or carpenter (per day)	8–10 gr
Average wage per month (approx. 20 days)	ca. 80–200 gr

* 1 modium = c. 171 l.; ** 1 carrata = c. 620 l.; *** 1 schoett = c. 5–8 kg
Cf. Lienhard Thaler, 'Wertewandel im spätmittelalterlichen Tirol: Wechselkurse, Münzgewicht, Maße und Preise zwischen 1290 und 1500', in: *Geschichte und Region* 29:2 (2020), 38–61

[51] Raffeiner (ed.), *Noderbuch*, nos. 8, 12, 50, 53, 58, 62, 72, 74, 81.

7 Types of Contracts and Credit Activity

The register includes diverse cases, ranging from the pledging of a cow to loans, debts for wine purchases, testaments, and the writing down of inventories. Transactions relating to credit and debt made up the biggest group of all entries. This category included loans, debt recognizances, purchases on credit, pawnbroking, and mortgage contracts. 45 out of 95 entries (roughly 47 percent) were related to credit. The second biggest group was acts relating primarily to transfers (buying and selling of property or goods) or to investments (roughly 26 percent). Here, land and property played an important role. Land for agriculture was the most common commodity, which is not surprising considering that land used for agriculture was an important source of income.[52] Finally, there are nine contracts relating to other rights and obligations, four court-related activities, and eleven miscellaneous contracts (including fragmentary entries). These last three categories accounted for 27 percent of all entries. Thus, we can observe a vivid land and capital market, in which a large part of the rural population participated. However, because no other register of a notary for Laas survived, it is hard to interpret these findings. People of different social backgrounds used the land market for investments or securing a credit. This seems to correspond with the findings of the land and capital market in Bozen.[53]

Before describing the dataset in detail, we must briefly discuss what kinds of credit contracts were registered by the notary. The majority of credit contracts were connected to collateral of some sort, e.g. income or property. This way, both parties could prove the change of ownership or the creditor could seize his debtors. Five types of credit transactions appear in the register: debt recognizances and loans; sales on credit; contracts of selling a rent or real estate with the right of repurchase; mortgage contracts; and pawnbroking. One finds both short-term credit instruments, like loans or sales on credit (with a runtime between a half and 18 months), and long-term contracts, like mortgage and sale-resale agreements (with a runtime from 14 to 72 months).

As Table 2 shows, roughly 70 percent of all credit transactions were carried out as loans collateralized with real estate or income stemming

[52] Ertl, 'Small Landlords', 9; Stamm, 'Kauf und Verkauf', 34.

[53] Roughly ten percent of the available assets in Bozen were invested annually into the local property market. Ertl, 'Small Landlords', 20.

from a property. Short-term credits were quite rare with only five loans, four sales on credit, and one pawnbroking contract, accounting only for ca. 26,5 percent of the total amount of credit. The median size of the credits taken out in Laas 1391 was 360 gr. or roughly two months wages of a skilled worker like a mason or carpenter. Mortgage contracts and sale-resale transactions were predominant, equating to 78 percent of all contracts and 73 percent of the total volume of loans taken out. Here, the seller or debtor received a certain sum and sold a property or rent to the buyer or creditor. Then, usually with another deed, the seller and his heirs received the right to buy their property back or rent it within a certain time (usually between six months and five years). The creditor or buyer would receive the revenues from the land in the meantime.[54] It is noteworthy that in some cases even the smallest plots of gardens or fields were pledged.[55] The predominance of credits secured with collateral forces us to confront the question of sample selection again. The problem is most obvious in the case of the notary register, where only contracts worth above a certain threshold were registered. The median sum of 360 gr. for all credit contracts recorded by the notary in Laas was much higher than the median sum (151 gr.) of unpaid debts and credits claimed in the court of Meran in the same period (1388–1391).[56] This might be because of two reasons: Firstly, that the number of landless persons was bigger in cities like Meran than in the countryside, and these persons would contract credits orally. And secondly, that the poorest parts of the rural population in Laas did not resort to notaries as credit intermediaries.

The overall value of credits, including both credits granted and liabilities claimed (but each case counted only once), recorded in the year 1391 in the village of Laas equated to 31,736 gr. To assess the scope of the credit market, some remarks about the overall wealth of the population in Laas are necessary. In the early fourteenth century (1314), the annual

[54] For a detailed analysis of the legal practices of mortgaging see: Markus J. Wenninger, *Zur Praxis des Geld- und Kreditgeschäftes im österreichischen Spätmittelalter* (diploma thesis, Institut für Österreichische Geschichtsforschung, University of Vienna, 1983), 15–41; Chris Briggs and Jaco Zuijderduijn, 'Introduction: Mortgages and Annuities in Historical Perspective', in: Chris Briggs and Jaco Zuijderduijn (eds.), *Land and Credit: Mortgages in the Medieval and Early Modern European Countryside* (ebook, Palgrave Macmillan, Cham, 2018), 1–17.

[55] Raffeiner (ed.), *Noderbuch*, no. 49; Nicolussi-Köhler, 'Between City and Countryside', 105.

[56] StA Meran, GP 1; Nicolussi-Köhler, 'Between City and Countryside', 111.

Table 2 Types of credit contracts mentioned in the register of Jakob of Laas

Type of Contract	*Numbers*		*Total Value of Credit*		*Value per Contract*	*Value per Contract*	*Duration (months)*	*Duration (months)*
	Numbers	*Percentage*	*Size (gr.)*	*Percentage*	*Mean (gr.)*	*Median (gr.)*	*Mean*	*Median*
loans, debt recognizances	5	11	4,032	18.5	806	720	8.3	5
mortgage contracts, sale-resale contracts of property or rents	35	78	15,856	73	466	360	41.5	36
sales on credit	4	9	1,728	8	432	456	5	6
pawnbroking contracts	1	2	120	0.5	120	120	3	3
total	45	100	21,736	100	/	/	/	/

Source: StA Meran, NI 22; Raffeiner (ed.), Noderbuch, nos. 1–5, 11–12, 16, 20, 31–33, 35, 37, 40, 43, 45–46, 48– 49, 51, 54–56, 58–63, 65–69, 72–74, 79–83, 86–87

and ordinary tax revenues from Laas equated to 16 mr. (or 1,920 gr.) paid by 50 households.[57] The direct tax had to be paid by all households that owned property or wealth and household assets were the basis for taxation. Since it is not known how exactly the tax in Laas was estimated, it is assumed that the tax rate was, like in Innsbruck or Bozen, presumably one percent.[58] In this case, the overall taxable wealth in fourteenth-century Laas would have been around 1,600 mr. (or 192,000 gr.), assuming the self-assessment of the taxpayers was true. Now the volume of the credit

[57] Laas was part of the larger *iudicium Laas* that was identical with the *Gericht Schlanders*. The tax revenues from the village of Laas were only a part of the overall revenues from the district. Tax register from 1314. BayHStA ASLT 25, fol. 14r–15r; Stolz, 'Das Steuerbuch', 104 and 112. Due to the lack of other sources, the figures from 1314 will be used here for an estimation of wealth.

[58] The tax in the office of Laas was set at 60 mr. from 1290 to 1304. Ertl, 'Small Landlords', 20; Kogler, 'Das landesfürstliche Steuerwesen', 456 and 492–495.

taken out in Laas in a single year (1391) was 21,736 gr. or approximately equal to 11.3 percent of the wealth of the population.[59]

The majority of the involved people is from Laas and its surroundings. Most creditors came from the Vinschgau or from small villages there, like Laas and its neighboring towns Eyrs, Tschengls, Tarnell, and Allitz. Local creditors lent 8,368 gr. (38.5 percent) out of the total value of credit contracts that were notarized before Jakob of Laas (cf. Fig. 4.). 20 different persons from Laas (8 creditors and 12 debtors) participated in the credit market, accounting for approximately 24 percent of the local population of 80 in the late fourteenth century. In Table 3, the social background of debtors and creditors as well as the volume of their loans are shown. Two groups dominated in providing credit: the village elite, consisting of *villici*, rich peasants, and most notably the members of the Mairjans family, and the merchants of Meran. Both groups together granted c. 38 percent of the overall credit in Laas. The credit granted by merchants from Meran was only used to buy drapery and wine and had to be repaid at Meran in a rather short term. And although it was a great volume, there were only two contracts granted by merchants. Besides that, the merchants of Meran did not engage in the land or capital market in Laas. The village elite on the other hand was heavily involved in lending and borrowing. Not only did they grant credits, pledge property, and sell rents, but they also played a vital role as credit intermediaries when they guaranteed for a loan or were appointed as arbiters to settle financial disputes.[60] This way, the village elite also provided information services to other people in the community. Since Jakob of Laas belonged to the family of the *villici* of Laas, it is hard to tell, to what extent the network of the notary and the network of the *villici* were separated. The scarce data collected from Laas points toward the direction that merchant moneylending and local lending did not compete with each other. Whereas merchant credit had a short duration and was usually granted when wares were sold on credit, local credit served different purposes. The annual rhythm of credit activity in Laas corresponeds to the usual agricultural rhythm, with a standstill during the harvest time in

[59] One must keep in mind that not all creditors and debtors lived directly in Laas, but the figures help to get an impression of the overall size of the capital market.

[60] Raffeiner (ed.), *Noderbuch*, nos. 23, 47, 53, 57. The importance of the local elites for the credit market has been pointed out by Simon Teuscher. Teuscher, 'Schulden', 257.

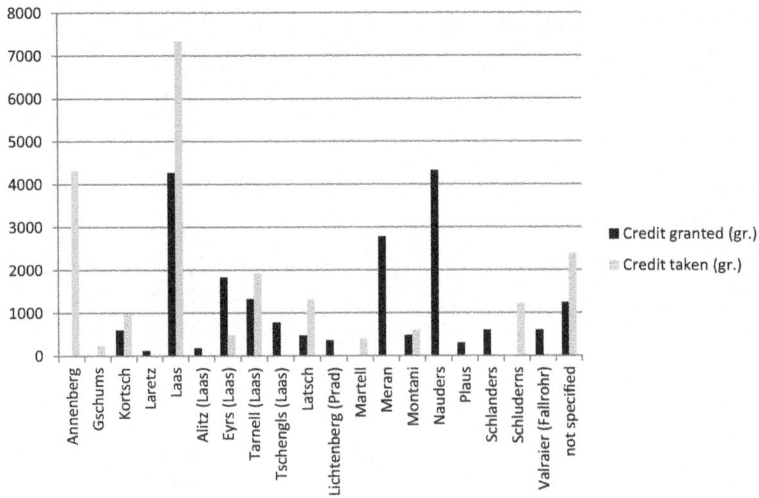

Fig. 4 Credit granted and taken by origin of the contracting parties. Source: StA Meran NI, 22

late summer and a very busy period after the harvest and winter time (cf. Fig. 5).

8 Credit Networks in Laas

At least twenty individuals from Laas participated in the local credit market. 22 persons came from villages within a radius of roughly five to ten kilometers (Alitz, Eyrs, Kortsch, Lichtenberg, Schluderns, Tarnell, Tschengels). Although lenders and borrowers were mostly local residents, it was not simply a bilateral credit system with peer-to-peer lending. Instead, lending was highly concentrated. As Table 4 shows, several people were engaged repeatedly in the credit market in 1391. Whereas 51 persons only once appear as borrowers or lenders, 13 persons appear several times. The most important lenders were Jakob Weigand and his wife, Katherina. They appear eight times as creditors and never as debtors and granted credits in one year worth 4,264 gr (equating to 21 month's wages of a skilled craftsman). The biggest actor in the section repeated activity as both lender and borrower was a member of the influential Mairjans family. Heinrich Mairjans participated in several contracts as a lender

Table 3 Creditors and Debtors by Social Group. (in total numbers and percentages), n = 45 (multiple entries per person counted)

	Numbers		*Value*	
Occupation Creditor	*total*	*in %*	*total (gr.)*	*in %*
Unknown	20	44	11,148	51
*Agriculture**	6	13	1,980	9
Artisans	2	4.5	420	2
Clergy	1	2	120	0.5
Merchants	2	4.5	2,064	9.5
Nobles	0	/	/	0
Village Elite	14	31	6,004	28
Occupation Debtor				
Unknown	11	24	4,884	22.5
*Agriculture**	13	29	4,624	21
Artisans	4	9	1,140	5
Clergy	1	2	360	1.5
Merchants	4	9	2,892	13
Nobles	1	2	4,320	20
Village Elite	11	24	3,516	16

* All persons living on or cultivating farmland were put in this group. Source: StA Meran, NI 22

and more importantly as a borrower. If we transfer the legal and social network mentioned in any of the contracts in a graph-database, we gain further insight into these relationships.

However, a joint participation in a legal transaction says nothing about motivation or interpersonal relations between several persons and in no way implies a greater willingness to borrow from these people. Rather, these relations can be seen as a potential channel for the exchange of information. It is safe to assume that persons, which participated in many legal transactions, were better informed and tended to have better access to information than those, which had only a few (legal) relations. People who appeared more frequently as creditors were often involved in debt chains. While people from all socio-economic categories are often found at the beginning of debt chains, a concentration of village elites can be seen at the end points of debt chains. These reveal a structure of dependency and hierarchy.

The visualization allows a first intuitive perception of the network of those individuals, which had a central social or economic position. As can be seen, the majority of actors (51) were only connected to each

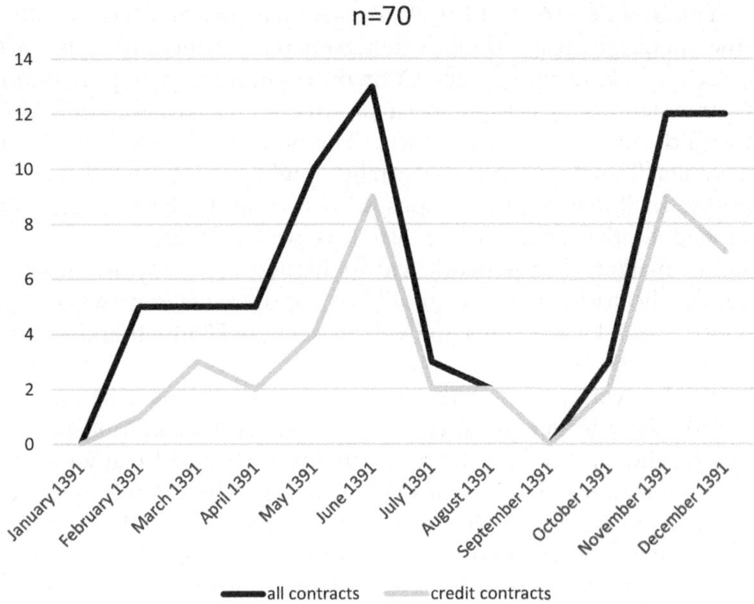

Fig. 5 Contracts recorded by Jakob of Laas. Copies of entries and fragments are not considered in this figure (n = 70). Source: StA Meran, NI 22

Table 4 Number of persons appearing in the notary registers one or more times as creditor, debtor or both. Source: StA Meran, NI 22

Credit Activity Indicators			
Single Activity on the Credit Market 1391	Only Borrows	Only Lends	Both Lends and Borrows
	24	27	6
Repeated Activity on the Credit Market 1391	Only Borrows	Only Lends	Both Lends and Borrows
	6	5	2

other, but there is a big central cluster around some actors like Jakob Weigand and his wife Katherina, Heinrich Mairjans, and Haupold Mairjans. The network has a high degree centrality clustered around Jakob Weigand (the difference between the mean centrality (1.1) and that of the most central node (16) is 14.9).[61] We see that specific offices or duties, like the appointment as arbiter, often go hand in hand with other activities, such as taking on guarantees or procurations or being involved in credit transactions. A certain social prestige seems to have been associated with the exercise of these offices. The office holders had the greatest social capital.[62] A high degree centrality might have mattered for credit networks. In Table 5, the persons with the most (legal) relationships mentioned in the cartulary are listed as well as their involvement in the credit market. The network had its highest centrality around Jakob Weigand (who had a degree centrality of 16, the average network degree centrality was 1.1) and other individuals such as Heinrich and Haupold Mairjans (Fig. 6).

As can be seen, some of the biggest actors in the credit market of Laas were also the persons involved in most legal arbitration processes (therefore, they had a high degree centrality). They had many incoming and outgoing relationships with other persons. Whereas the mean score for centrality of persons mentioned in the register was 1.1, the top ten connected persons had between 16 and 6 (see Table 5).[63] They owe their central position to their role as sworn jurors, arbiters, or other public offices they held. Jakob Weigand, Heinrich Mairjans, his brothers Haupold and Jaenlin Mairjans all were appointed two times as sworn jurors, together with several other people.[64] Additionally, the Mairjans were related to the notary and therefore maintained very close social and economic ties with him.

Their duty as sworn jurymen put them into direct contact with many people. But their central positions did not automatically turn them into big creditors. As Table 5 shows, the lending activity of these persons was not extraordinary (except for Jakob Weigand and his wife). Borrowing, on the other hand, seems to have been enforced by these relationships. Heinrich Mairjans pledged three properties to Jakob Weigand, and Jaenlin

[61] The degree centrality shows how many people a particular actor is directly connected to in the network. Jullien, 'Netzwerkanalye', 140.

[62] The importance of social capital for acquiring credit has been pointed out by: Dermineur, 'Trust'; Marx, 'Netzwerke', 98–99.

[63] On the mean degree see: Jullien, 'Netzwerkanalye', 147.

[64] Raffeiner 2008, nos. 47, 53, 57.

Table 5 The persons with the most relationships in the network (degree centrality, calculated with neo4j)

Name	*Relationships in Network*	*Credit Granted (gr.)*	*Credit Taken (gr.)*
Jakob Weigand	16	3,448*	0
Nikolaus, *gener* Chunradi Gresner	9	0	0
Heinrich Mairjans	9	420	2,124
Thomas, *filius q.* M. ex Martell	9	0	400
Jaenlin Mairjans	8	0	924
Katharina, *uxor* Weigandi	7	3,448*	0
Beta Muentzlin de Las	7	0	720
Haupold Mairjans	7	480**	0
Remigius, *filius q.* Jaklini de Auers	6	0	480
Konrad Pagnell de Las	6	276	0
minimum score (overall network)	0	/	/
mean score (overall network)	1.1041	/	/

* Credits granted together by Jakob and his wife. ** Includes the debts owed to him because of unpaid tolls

Mairjans pledged one.[65] The ties between Jakob Weigand and the Mairjans family were very close. Because of their social connections and their wealth, the Mairjans family had easy access to credit. Most of the loans they took out were secured by collateral. The repeated borrowing within a year did not seem to damage their reputation. Their position in the network helped others to assess their trustworthiness and reputation and was helpful in initiating credit transactions. Thus, the position in the network did matter a lot for obtaining credit.

Around the center are nodes with a high betweenness centrality (see Table 6). The betweenness centrality indicates the extent to which certain

[65] Raffeiner (ed.), *Noderbuch*, nos. 32, 48, 66 (Heinrich); no. 22 (Jaenlin).

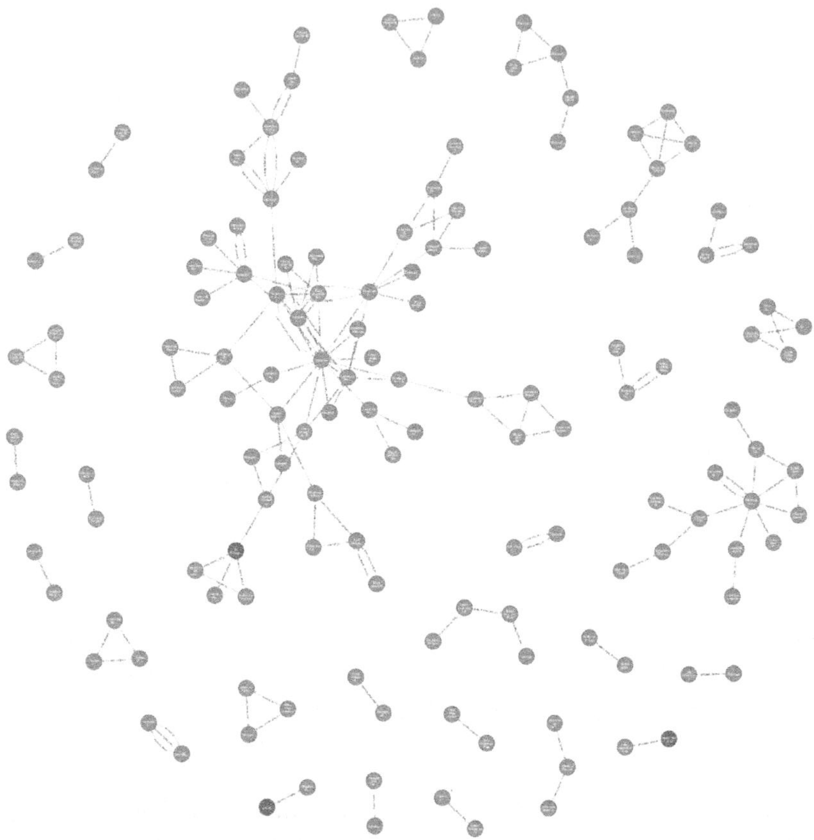

Fig. 6 Visual representation as one-mode network of all contracts recorded by Jakob of Laas in 1391(created with neo4j). The witnessing of a contract is not included in this figure. Node count: 144, relationship count: 159. Source: StA Meran, NI 22

nodes have strategically important positions in the network.[66] Persons with high betweenness centrality contributed to connecting different parts of the network. Next to the usual big lenders and creditors, there are several people, like Jagglein, or Nikolaus, who had a high betweenness

[66] Jullien, 'Netzwerkanalye', 141.

centrality and were not active in the credit market. However, removing individuals like them would create important structural damage to the network, damaging the interconnection of the system. They created chains of credit and connected the center with the periphery. Credit could flow throughout community (in both directions).

Besides, there were several dyads, a network where only two individuals are linked to each other, at the periphery. Outside the central cluster, there were many individuals at the periphery of this network. However, this does not mean they were necessarily poor or non-influential, they simply did not participate in the central cluster of the network. What can be seen here is that in many cases, the local community was the starting point to look for credit. People would take a credit from their neighbors, family, friends, or a leaseholder.[67] If land was pledged for a credit, often one of the neighbors or a relative appeared as the creditor. These relations indicate that social obligations (family, neighborhood) mattered for credit portfolios.[68] One could think about neighborly help in difficult times. Or maybe it was a good opportunity to expand one´s property on one's own doorstep. In at least four cases, the creditor is a direct neighbor of the

Table 6 Betweenness Centrality, top 10 results (calculated with Neo4j). Source: StA Meran, NI 22

Name	*Betweenness Centrality*
Jakob Weigand	54
Jagglein, Josten sun von Pagnell	38
Konrad (Kuntz) Mairotten	37
Petrisie, *domina* de Montani	28
Heinrich Mairjans	24
Remigius, *filius q.* Jaklini de Auers	18
Nicolaus, *villicus* de Weingarten	16
Jaenlin Mairjans	14
Konrad Pagnell de Las	14
Nikolaus, *gener* Chunrandi Gresner	12

67 Laurence Fontaine, 'Relations de crédit et surendettement en France: XVIIe–XVIIIe siècles', in: Laurence Fontaine, Gilles Postel-Vinay, Jean-Laurent Rosenthal, and Paul Servais (eds.), *Des persones aux institutions: Résaux et culture du crédit du XVIe aux XXe siècle en Europe* (Bruylant-Academia, Louvain-la-Neuve, 1997), 212–217.

68 Teuscher, 'Schulden', 250.

debtor (or owns a property next to the debtor).[69] Once again, it can be assumed that the neighborhood would have been rather good informed about each other, which would have reduced the problem of trust and asymmetric information.

9 Economic Strategies and Need for Credit

It has been shown that credit was mostly local, e.g. creditor and debtor were neighbors or lived in adjacent villages (that is within a one-day's journey of 20km or less, cf. Figure 3). Since credit was local, information asymmetries were small. Nevertheless, the parties regularly resorted to the (expensive) services of a notary. There were two main reasons: Firstly, the notary produced written evidence that was necessary to secure the possession of the land pledged or rents sold. Even if the sums involved were small, the parties did not refrain from putting the legal transaction in writing. Secondly, the notary could have acted as a broker. As he knew the economic situation of his clientele well, he may have been involved in the mediation of lenders and borrowers, especially if both parties came from different places. No fewer than 26 transactions were contracted in the house or shop of the notary, which can be considered a public place.[70] The notary may have been the first port of call when someone wanted to buy or sell a property or needed a loan. His close relationships with the village elites, but also with the town of Meran, where he was later documented as a notary, certainly contributed to his position as intermediary.

The liquidation of capital was uncomplicated. Because property rights were well protected through notarial records, people could use their assets very easily as collateral to obtain credit.[71] This economic strategy can be witnessed several times in Laas. Mark Mesner pledged a meadow for a

[69] It is not always possible to reconstruct the ownership around a piece of land. Raffeiner (ed.), *Noderbuch*, nos. 51, 56, 66, 74.

[70] Steven A. Epstein, 'Secrecy and Genoese commercial practices', in: *Journal of Medieval History* 20 (1994), 313–325, there 319.

[71] For a discussion of the importance of property rights and transactions costs, see Jan L. van Zanden, Jaco Zuijderduijn, and Tine De Moor, 'Small Is Beautiful: The Efficiency of Credit Markets in the Late Medieval Holland', in: *European Review of Economic History* 16 (2012), 3–22, there 3–6.

credit of 15 lb. to Gall von Allitz. If he would not redeem his property within the agreed period, he promised to hand over the ownership of the property and to provide a notarial charter. Besides, it was stated that if the good was not redeemed, the debtor should also receive the value of his pledged property above the debt amount of 15 lb.[72] This way, several problems were circumvented: the costs of a notarial instrument were saved, and the property did not have to be assessed at market value in advance, making the pledging of property not too costly. As a result, households were engaged heavily in the land market to obtain credit and pledged even the smallest plots of land. Financial assets (such as property) were used to increase liquidity and bridge cash shortages. This also allowed the households to carry out more complex credit transactions, such as debt restructuring. Although land was very often pledged, studies suggest that expropriation rarely happened.[73] Besides, peasants could create new rents, sell them to obtain cash, and restructure their debts, or make investments with the money.[74] Landlords and feudal lords were just as involved in this long-term credit network as peasants.[75]

Next to these mortgage contracts, there were several short-term loans with a runtime between two weeks and six months registered by the notary. These transactions were of a different nature, foremost sales on credit.[76] In Laas, in three cases, the seller agreed to receive the payments in kind instead of cash.[77] This might point to a shortage of cash in the countryside.[78] This short-term credit is clearly distinguishable from the

[72] Raffeiner (ed.), *Noderbuch*, no. 2.

[73] Jaco Zuijderduijn, 'The Other Fundamental Problem of Exchange: Mortgages, Defaults and Debtor Protection in Sixteenth-Century Holland', in: Chris Briggs and Jaco Zuijderduijn (eds.), *Land and Credit. Mortgages in the Medieval and Early Modern European Countryside* (ebook, Palgrave Macmillan, Cham, 2018), 281–308, there 284–288 and 300–301; Schofield, 'Impediments to expropriation'; Hans-Jörg Gilomen, 'L'endettement paysan et la question du crédit dans les pays d'Empire au Moyen Âge', in: Maurice Berthe (ed.), *Endettement paysan et credit rural dans L'Europe medievale et moderne* (Presses universitaires du Midi, Toulouse, 1998), 99–137.

[74] Nicolussi-Köhler, 'Between City and Countryside', 101; Stamm, 'Kauf und Verkauf', 39.

[75] Nicolussi-Köhler, 'Between City and Countryside', 103, table 2. See the similar findings of Thomas Ertl for the land and capital market in Bozen. Ertl, 'Small Landlords'.

[76] Teuscher, 'Schulden', 249.

[77] Raffeiner (ed.), *Noderbuch*, nos. 11, 12, 65, 69.

[78] Loose, 'Die Welt des Notars', 213.

local land and capital market. Payments were due after a short period of time and the means of payment played a role. All the mentioned products—wine, iron, horses, or cereals—could be easily marketed and sold. These short-term credits were provided by (wine) merchants, like Peter de Angaro, Niklaus Spetziger, but also by Jakob Weigand.

10 Conclusion

Credit relations were diverse. A large part of the liquid assets that circulated was based on mutual relations within the village community. How well the network could be used to obtain credit depended not least on individual conditions: trust and wealth. The network analysis of legal and credit relations in Laas in 1391 suggests an interdependency between network position and social reputation. A central position in the network did indeed matter for credit. The most active lenders and borrowers had a high degree centrality in the network, meaning that people engaged in legal transactions were significantly more active in the capital market. The results obtained here must be interpreted with caution. However, some general patterns can be identified.

(1) Social relations can be seen as a potential channel for the exchange of information. This especially mattered for persons who were engaged several times in credit activities, like Jakob Weigand or the Mairjans family.
(2) When credit was secured with (immobile) collateral, credit activity remained mostly local. In several cases, the neighbors acted as creditors. This might relate to the low information asymmetry within a community and helped to avoid the problem of asymmetric information (for example, to assess the value of the collateral) and monitoring costs. Debts incurred within the family were also fixed in writing with a high degree of commitment and publicity.[79]
(3) The confidence put into the reputation was a major part of the local credit market. The network had its highest density around the legal dealings of the social elite of the *villici*. The trust created through these legal relations migrated to economic activities.

[79] Teuscher, 'Schulden', 253.

(4) Thanks to his position and his professional network, the notary was the first port of call for real estate loans. Jakob was apparently the center of the real estate secured loan market in the village, he was part of several social networks, member of the Mairjans family and intermediated business contracts.

The network analytical tools improve our understanding of (social and economic) structures and help to visualize relationships. This way, new questions can be addressed which would not have popped up otherwise. The limited scope of interregional capital markets forced individuals to borrow within the local community. A network analysis shows that what mattered for this local credit was reputation that was established through stable relationships.

References

Primary Sources

BayHStA = Bayerisches Hauptstaatsarchiv
TLA = Tiroler Landesarchiv, Innsbruck
StA Meran = Stadtarchiv Meran

Secondary Material

Andermann, Kurt. 2020. Die Vornehmen der Gemeinde: Überlegungen zu dörflichen Oberschichten im deutschen Südwesten während des späten Mittelalters und der frühen Neuzeit. In: *Soziale Mobilität in der Vormoderne: Historische Perspektiven auf ein zeitloses Thema* (=Veröffentlichungen des Südtiroler Landesarchivs 48), edited by Gustav Pfeifer and Kurt Andermann, 129–144. Universitätsverlag Wagner, Innsbruck.

Beimrohr, Wilfried. 1994. *Mit Brief und Siegel: Die Gerichte Tirols und ihr ältestes Schriftgut im Tiroler Landesarchiv* (=Tiroler Geschichtsquellen 43). Tiroler Landesarchiv, Innsbruck.

Briggs, Chris. 2009. *Credit and Village Society in Fourteenth-Century England.* Oxford University Press, Oxford.

Briggs, Chris and Jaco Zuijderduijn. 2018. Introduction: Mortgages and Annuities in Historical Perspective. In: *Land and Credit: Mortgages in the Medieval and Early Modern European Countryside*, edited by Chris Briggs and Jaco Zuijderduijn, 1–17. Palgrave Macmillan, Cham.

Cerman, Markus and Michael Mitterauer. 2020. The Sub-peasant Strata in the Late Medieval and Early Modern Eastern Alpine Region. In: *Peasants, Lords, and State: Comparing Peasant Conditions in Scandinavia and the Eastern Alpine Region, 1000–1750* (=The Northern World 89), edited by Tore Iversen, John R. Myking, and Stefan Sonderegger, 269–291. Brill, Leiden and Boston.

Claustre, Julie. 2014. Vivre à crédit dans une ville sans banque (Paris XIVe–XVe siècle). *Le Moyen Âge* 109: 567–596.

Clemens, Gabriela B. 2008. Einleitung: Die Omnipräsenz von westeuropäischen Kreditbeziehungen. In: *Schuldenlast und Schuldenwert: Kreditnetzwerke in der europäischen Geschichte 1300–1900*, edited by Gabriela B. Clemens, 9–20. Kliomedia, Trier.

Coffman, D'Maris, and Cinzia Lorenzini, Marcella Lorenzini. 2018. Introduction. In: *Financing in Europe: Evolution, Coexistence and Complementarity of Lending Practices from the Middle Ages to Modern Times*, edited by D'Maris Coffman, Cinzia Lorenzini, Marcella Lorenzini, 1–18. Palgrave Macmillan, Cham.

Dermineur, Elise. 2015. Trust, Norms of Cooperation, and the Rural Credit Market in Eighteenth-Century France. *The Journal of Interdisciplinary History* 45 (4): 485–506.

Epstein, Steven A. 1994. Secrecy and Genoese commercial practices. *Journal of Medieval History* 20: 313–325.

Ertl, Thomas. 2017. Small Landlords: Land Transactions in and around Bozen (South Tirol) in the Mid-Thirteenth Century. *Vierteljahrschrift für Sozial- und Wirtschaftsgeschichte* 104 (1): 7–28.

Fliri, David. 2018. Das Meraner Notariat im Spätmittelalter. In: *1317: Eine Stadt und ihr Recht: Meran im Mittelalter: Bausteine zur Stadtgeschichte*, edited by Gustav Pfeifer, 213–228. Akten der Internationalen Tagung, Meran, Kurhaus und Kurmittelhaus, 22. bis 25. Februar 2017 = 1317: una città e il suo diritto: Merano nel Medioevo: materiali di storia cittadina. Atti del convegno internazionale, Merano, Kurhaus e Vecchie Terme, 22–25 febbraio 2017 (=Veröffentlichungen des Südtiroler Landesarchivs 43). Athesia, Bolzano.

Fontaine, Laurence. 1997. Relations de credit et surendettement en France: XVIIe–XVIIIe siècles. In: *Des personnes aux institutions: Réseaux et culture du crédit du XVIe aux XXe siècle en Europe*, edited by Laurence Fontaine, Gilles Postel-Vinay, Jean-Laurent Rosenthal, and Paul Servais, 212–217. Bruylant-Academia, Louvain-la-Neuve.

Fontaine, Laurence. 2014a. *Le marché. Histoire et usages d'une conquête sociale*. Gallimard, Paris.

Fontaine, Laurence. 2014b. *The Moral Economy: Poverty, Credit, and Trust in Early Modern Europe*. Cambridge University Press, Cambridge.

Gilomen, Hans-Jörg. 1998. L'endettement paysan et la question du crédit dans les pays d'Empire au Moyen Âge. In: *Endettement paysan et credit rural dans L'Europe medievale et moderne*, edited by Maurice Berthe, 99–137. Presses universitaires du Midi, Toulouse.

Gosh, Shami. 2017. Rural Commercialisation in Fourteenth-Century Southern Germany: The Evidence from Scheyern Abbey. *Vierteljahrsschrift für Sozial- und Wirtschaftsgeschichte* 104 (1): 52–77.

Gramsch, Robert. 2013. *Das Reich als Netzwerk der Fürsten: Politische Strukturen unter dem Doppelkönigtum Friedrichs II.* und Heinrichs (VII.) 1225–1235 (=Mittelalterforschungen 40). Jan Thorbecke Verlag, Ostfildern.

Heuberger, Richard. 1926. Das deutschtiroler Notariat: Umrisse seiner mittelalterlichen Entwicklung. *Veröffentlichungen des Museum Ferdinandeum* 6: 27–122.

Hitz, Benjamin. 2022. *Ein Netz von Schulden: Schuldbeziehungen und Gerichtsnutzung im spätmittelalterlichen Basel* (=Vierteljahrschrift für Sozial- und Wirtschaftsgeschichte Beihefte 256). Franz Steiner Verlag, Stuttgart.

Hoffman, Philipp T., Gilles Postel-Vinay, and Jean-Laurent. Rosenthal. 1998. What do Notaries do? Overcoming Asymmetric Information in Financial Markets: The Case of Paris, 1751. *Journal of Institutional and Theoretical Economics* 154 (3): 499–530.

Hoffman, Philipp T., Gilles Postel-Vinay, and Jean-Laurent Rosenthal. 2000. *Priceless Markets: The Political Economy of Credit in Paris, 1660–1870*. University of Chicago Press, Chicago and London.

Hoffman, Philipp T., Gilles Postel-Vinay, and Jean-Laurent Rosenthal. 2019. *Dark Matter Credit: The Development of Peer-to-Peer Lending and Banking in France*. Princeton University Press, Princeton.

Jullien, Eva. 2013. Netzwerkanalyse in der Mediävistik. Probleme und Perspektiven im Umgang mit mittelalterlichen Quellen. *Vierteljahrschrift für Sozial- und Wirtschaftsgeschichte* 100 (1): 135–153.

Kogler, Ferdinand. 1901. Das landesfürstliche Steuerwesen in Tirol bis zum Ausgang des Mittelalters. *Archiv für österreichische Geschichte* 90: 419–712.

Kuske, Bruno. 1956. Die Entstehung der Kreditwirtschaft und des Kapitalverkehrs. In: *Köln, der Rhein und das Reich: Beiträge aus fünf Jahrhunderten wirtschaftsgeschichtlicher Forschung*, edited by Bruno Kuske, 48–137. Böhlau, Cologne.

Laffont, Jean L. 1991. Introduction: Problèmes et enjeux de l'analyse de l'activité notariale. In: *Problèmes et méthodes d'analyse historique de l'activité notariale (XVe–XIXe siècle): Actes du colloque du Toulouse (15–16 septembre 1990), tenu dans le cadre de la Chambre départementale de Notaires de la Haute Garonne*, edited by Jean L. Laffont, 19–28. Presses Universitaires du Mirail, Toulouse-Le-Mirail.

Loose, Rainer. 2008. Die Welt des Notars Jakob von Laas. In: *Noderbuch: Notariatsimbreviaturen des Jakob von Laas 1390–1392*, edited by Herbert Raffeiner, 204–218. Provinz Verlag, Brixen.

López, Roberto S. 1971. *The Commercial Revolution of the Middle Ages 950–1350*. Cambridge University Press, Cambridge.

Marx, Johannes. 2010. Netzwerke als Quelle sozialen Kapitals: Zur kulturellen und strukturellen Einbettung vertrauensvoller Handlungen in Netzwerken. In: *Knoten und Kanten: Soziale Netzwerkanalyse in Wirtschafts- und Migrationsforschung*, edited by Markus Gamper and Linda Reschke, 95–116. Transcript Verlag, Bielefeld.

Menant, François and Odile Redon (eds.). 2004. *Notaires et crédit dans l'Occident méditerranéen médiéval* (=Publications de l'École française de Rome 343). École Française de Rome, Rome.

Muldrew, Craig. 1998. *The Economy of Obligation: The Culture of Credit and Social Relations in Early Modern England*. Palgrave Macmillan, New York.

Nicolussi-Köhler, Stephan. 2021a. Between City and Countryside: Moneylending and Settling Debts in and around Meran (1388–1392). In: *Change and Transformation of Pre-Modern Credit Markets: The Importance of Small-Scale Credits*, edited by Stephan Nicolussi-Köhler, 89–132. Heidelberg University Publishing, Heidelberg.

Nicolussi-Köhler, Stephan. 2021b. Introduction. In: *Change and Transformation of Pre-Modern Credit Markets: The Importance of Small-Scale Credits*, edited by Stephan Nicolussi-Köhler, 1–21. Heidelberg University Publishing, Heidelberg.

Obermair, Hannes and Volker Stamm. 2019. Alpine Ökonomie in Hoch- und Tieflagen: das Beispiel Tirol im Spätmittelalter und Früher Neuzeit. In: *Relire l'altitude: la terre et ses usages. Suisse et espaces avoisinants, XIIe-XXIe siècles*, edited by Yann Decorzant, Anne-Lise Head-König, and Luigi Lorenzetti, 29–56. Éditons Alphil-Presses universitaires suisses, Neuchâtel.

Pfeifer Gustav. 2001. "Nobis servire tenebitur in armis": Formen des Aufstiegs und Übergangs in den niederen Adel im Tirol des 14. Jahrhunderts. In: *Zwischen Nicht-Adel und Adel* (=Vorträge und Forschungen 53), edited by Kurt Andermann and Peter Johanek, 49–103. Jan Thorbecke Verlag, Stuttgart.

Pfeifer, Gustav. 2009. De arte edendi. *Der Schlern* 82: 91–93.

Pfister, Ulrich. 1994. Le petit crédit rural en Suisse aux XVIe-XVIIIe siècles. *Annales. Histoire, Sciences Sociales* 49 (6): 1339–1357.

Pompermaier, Matteo. 2022. Credit and Poverty in Early Modern Venice. *Journal of Interdisciplinary History* 52 (4): 513–536.

Postel-Vinay, Gilles. 2021. Change and Transformation of Pre-Modern Credit Markets: The Importance of Small-Scale Credits. In: *Change and Transformation of Pre-Modern Credit Markets: The Importance of Small-Scale Credits*, edited by Stephan Nicolussi-Köhler, 23–38. Heidelberg University Press, Heidelberg.

Raffeiner, Herbert (Ed.). 2008. *Noderbuch: Notariatsimbreviaturen des Jakob von Laas 1390–1392*. Provinz Verlag, Brixen.

Rizzolli, Helmut and Federico Pigozzo. 2015. *Der Veroneser Währungsraum: Verona und Tirol vom Beginn des 10. Jahrhunderts bis 1516* (=Runkelsteiner Schriften zur Kulturgeschichte 8). Athesia, Bolzano.

Rosenthal, Jean-Laurent. 1994. Rural Credit Markets and Aggregate Shocks: The Experience of Nuits St. Georges, 1756–1776. *The Journal of Economic History* 54 (2): 288–306.

Schofield, Philipp R. 2021. Impediments to expropriation: Peasant property rights in medieval England and Marcher Wales. *Continuity and Change* 36: 211–232.

Senoner, Raimund. 2008. Einleitung. In: *Noderbuch: Notariatsimbreviaturen des Jakob von Laas 1390–1392*, edited by Herbert Raffeiner, 11–14. Provinz Verlag, Brixen.

Signori, Gabriela. 2014. Einleitung. In: *Prekäre Ökonomien: Schulden in Spätmittelalter und Früher Neuzeit* (=Spätmittelalterstudien 4), edited by Gabriela Signori, 6–14. UVK, Konstanz and Munich.

Smail, Daniel L. 2018. The Materiality of Credit: Debt Collection as Pawnbroking in Late Medieval Mediterranean Europe. *Histoire urbaine* 51: 95–110.

Stamm, Volker. 2007. Zur Bedeutung der Grundrente für die landesfürstlichen Einnahmen und bäuerlichen Abgaben in der Grafschaft Tirol (13./14. Jahrhundert). *Vierteljahrschrift für Sozial- und Wirtschaftsgeschichte* 94 (1): 47–56.

Stamm, Volker. 2008. Lehnspraxis im spätmittelalterlichen Tirol. *Tiroler Heimat NF* 72: 63–72.

Stamm, Volker. 2009. Kauf und Verkauf von Land und Grundrenten im hohen und späten Mittelalter: Eine Untersuchung zur historischen Wirtschaftsanthropologie. *Vierteljahrschrift für Sozial- und Wirtschaftsgeschichte* 96 (1): 33–43.

Stamm, Volker. 2010. Soziale Zwischengruppen in der mittelalterlichen Agrargesellschaft. *Historische Zeitschrift* 291 (1): 1–22.

Stolz, Otto. 1939a. Das Verzeichnis der Untertanen der Tiroler Landesfürsten im Inntal und Vintschgau vom Jahre 1427. Text bearbeitet von H. Bachmann, L. von Berg, K. Dörrer, K. Finsterwalder, H. Kramer. In: *Quellen zur Steuer-, Bevölkerungs- und Sippengeschichte des Landes Tirol im 13., 14. und 15. Jahrhundert, bearb. v. mehreren Innsbrucker Historikern: Festschrift zu Oswald Redlichs achtzigstem Lebensjahr 1938/1939* (=Schlern-Schriften 44), 159–200. Universitätsverlag Wagner, Innsbruck.

Stolz, Otto. 1939b. Das Steuerbuch des Vintschgaus und Burggrafenamts von 1314. Text bearbeitet von K. Dörrer, H. Bachmann, H. Kramer und Otto Stolz0. In: *Quellen zur Steuer-, Bevölkerungs- und Sippengeschichte des Landes Tirol im 13., 14. und 15. Jahrhundert, bearb. v. mehreren Innsbrucker Historikern: Festschrift zu Oswald Redlichs achtzigstem Lebensjahr 1938/1939* (=Schlern-Schriften 44), 104–126. Universitätsverlag Wagner, Innsbruck.

Teuscher, Simon. 2014. Schulden, Abhängigkeitrn und politische Kultur. In: *Prekäre Ökonomien. Schulden in Spätmittelalter und Früher Neuzeit* (=Spätmittelalterstudien 4), edited by Gabriela Signori, 243–262. UVK, Konstanz and Munich.

Thaler, Lienhard. 2020. Wertewandel im spätmittelalterlichen Tirol: Wechselkurse, Münzgewicht, Maße und Preise zwischen 1290 und 1500. *Geschichte und Region* 29 (2): 38–61.

Utz Tremp, Kathirn. 2012. *"Fiat littera ad dictamen sapientum": Notare, Lombarden und Juden in Freiburg im Üchtland (14. Jahrhundert)* (=Europäische Rechts- und Regionalgeschichte 17). Dike, Zurich.

van Zanden, Jan L., Jaco Zuijderduijn, and Tine De Moor. 2012. Small Is Beautiful: The Efficiency of Credit Markets in the Late Medieval Holland. *European Review of Economic History* 16: 3–22.

Wenninger, Markus J. 1983. *Zur Praxis des Geld- und Kreditgeschäftes im österreichischen Spätmittelalter.* Diploma thesis, Institut für Österreichische Geschichtsforschung, University of Vienna.

Wopfner, Hermann. 1904. Zur Geschichte des tirolischen Verfachbuches. *Forschungen und Mitteilungen zur Geschichte Tirols und Vorarlbergs*, 241–263.

Zeindl, Gertraud. 2009. *Meran im Mittelalter: eine Tiroler Stadt im Spiegel ihrer Steuern* (=Tiroler Wirtschaftsstudien 57). Universitätsverlag Wagner, Innsbruck.

Zuijderduijn, Jaco. 2009. *Medieval Capital Markets: Markets for renten, State Formation and Private Investment in Holland (1300–1500).* Brill, Leiden and Boston.

Zuijderduijn, Jaco. 2018. The Other Fundamental Problem of Exchange: Mortgages, Defaults and Debtor Protection in Sixteenth-Century Holland. In: *Land and Credit. Mortgages in the Medieval and Early Modern European Countryside*, edited by Chris Briggs and Jaco Zuijderduijn, 281–307. Palgrave Macmillan, Cham.

CHAPTER 6

More than Merchant Bankers: Second-Class Financial Intermediation in Eighteenth-Century Amsterdam

Alberto Feenstra

1 Introduction

This chapter examines the case of the Dutch province of Friesland to study how relatively small and non-domestic public debtors behaved on the Amsterdam capital market in the eighteenth century. So far, the literature has focused on the emergence of Amsterdam as an international capital

A. Feenstra (✉)
Leiden University, Leiden, The Netherlands
e-mail: alberto_feenstra@yahoo.co.uk

E. M. Dermineur and M. Pompermaier (eds.), *Credit Networks in The Preindustrial World*, Palgrave Studies in the History of Finance,
https://doi.org/10.1007/978-3-031-67117-3_6

market for European major powers in the eighteenth century.[1] Smaller borrowers did not have the same financial options as major powers, yet they were also more plentiful than the handful of large ones. On the other hand, information about small borrowers' creditworthiness was even more difficult to obtain than about the great powers. Intermediaries may have played a role in reducing this information asymmetry.[2] Studying smaller public debtors, like Friesland, offers insight into how information was transmitted, who was involved, and what financial mechanisms applied to foster sovereign lending.

Why external sovereign lending exists at all is puzzling. External creditors lack the political or juridical means to ensure payments that domestic creditors have, for instance through parliaments or courts.[3] In the absence of third-party contract enforcement, the question is why a sovereign lender would honor the agreement after creditors provided a loan.[4] In the literature, two explanations stand out as to why cross-border borrowing

[1] James C. Riley, *International Government Finance and the Amsterdam Capital Market, 1740–1815* (Cambridge, 1980); Larry Neal, *The Rise of Financial Capitalism: International Capital Markets in the Age of Reason*, Studies in Monetary and Financial History (Cambridge, 1990); Ann M. Carlos and Larry Neal, 'Amsterdam and London as Financial Centers in the Eighteenth Century', in: *Financial History Review* 18:1 (2011), 21–46; Joost Jonker, 'Klem tussen de lokale en mondiale markt. De Amsterdamse Haute Banque vanaf het midden van de zestiende tot het begin van de twintigste eeuw (deel 1, 1550–1763)', in: *Amstelodamum* 106:1 (2019), 25–45; Joost Jonker, 'Klem tussen de lokale en mondiale markt. De Amsterdamse haute banque vanaf het midden van de zeventiende tot het begin van de twintigste eeuw (deel 2, 1763–1914)', in: *Amstelodamum* 106:2 (2019), 63–87.

[2] Riley, *International Government Finance*; Marc Flandreau and Juan H. Flores, 'Bonds and Brands', in: *The Journal of Economic History* 69:3 (2009), 646–684; Alejandra Irigoin and Regina Grafe, 'Bounded Leviathan: Fiscal Constraints and Financial Development in the Early Modern Hispanic World', in: D'Maris Coffman, Adrian Leonard, and Larry Neal, *Questioning Credible Commitment: Perspectives on the Rise of Financial Capitalism* (Cambridge, 2013), 199–227.

[3] Douglas C. North and Barry R. Weingast, 'Constitutions and Commitment: The Evolution of Institutions Governing Public Choice in Seventeenth-Century England', in: *The Journal of Economic History* 49:4 (1989), 803–832; David Stasavage, *States of Credit: Size, Power, and the Development of European Polities* (Princeton, 2011); Kim Oosterlinck, Loredana Ureche-Rangau, and Jacques-Marie Vaslin, 'Aristocratic Privilege. Exploiting "Good" Institutions', in: *CEPR Discussion Paper Series*, DP 140,771 (v.2) (2019); Anne L. Murphy, 'Demanding "Credible Commitment": Public Reactions to the Failures of the Early Financial Revolution' in: *The Economic History Review* 66:1 (2013), 178–197.

[4] Michael Tomz, *Reputation and International Cooperation: Sovereign Debt across Three Centuries* (Princeton, 2007); Mauricio Drelichman and Hans-Joachim Voth, 'Serial

exists. On the one hand, various sanctions may be imposed, including trade sanctions, of which 'gunboat diplomacy', speaks most to the imagination.[5] On the other hand, reputation and the loss thereof when not honoring financial obligations would discipline debtor states. Creditors could, eventually, adopt a credit rationing strategy that prevented the defaulting state from issuing new loans.[6] Nevertheless, inadequate or incomplete information caused losses for lenders and creditors in eighteenth-century Amsterdam.[7]

Not just the reputation of the borrower mattered. The reputation of the intermediary was also relevant to assess the defaulting risk. In London's early nineteenth-century capital market, the reputation of the underwriters solved part of the information asymmetry for investors. In this emerging capital market, default risk was lower for sovereign loans marketed by leading banking houses than those serviced by second-rate banking houses.[8] Riley, Flandreau, and Flores suspect that the reputation of the banker was equally important in eighteenth-century Amsterdam, as London's predecessor.[9] Starting with Deutz in 1695, merchant banking houses, such as Pels & Sons, Hope & Co., and Clifford & Sons, matched international borrowers to private wealth owners in the Dutch

Defaults, Serial Profits: Returns to Sovereign Lending in Habsburg Spain, 1566–1600', in: *Explorations in Economic History* 48:1 (2011).

[5] Tomz, *Reputation and International Cooperation*; Kris James Mitchener and Marc D. Weidenmier, 'Supersanctions and Sovereign Debt Repayment', in: *Journal of International Money and Finance* 29:1 (2010), 19–36; Drelichman and Voth, 'Serial Defaults, Serial Profits', there 1–2.

[6] Peter Temin and Hans-Joachim Voth, 'Credit Rationing and Crowding out during the Industrial Revolution: Evidence from Hoare's Bank, 1702–1862', in: *Explorations in Economic History* 42:3 (2005), 325–348; Tomz, *Reputation and International Cooperation*, there 6, 10, 53–54.

[7] Riley, *International Government Finance*, there 41.

[8] Flandreau and Flores, 'Bonds and Brands'.

[9] Flandreau and Flores, 'Bonds and Brands', there 656; Riley, *International Government Finance*; Tomz, *Reputation and International Cooperation*; Neal, *The Rise of Financial Capitalism*, there 223; Carlos and Neal, 'Amsterdam and London'.

Republic.[10] Next to the bankers, Riley also identified brokers, and the commission agents as key players.[11]

Although we do have information on the leading bankers, we hardly know anything about the lower-ranking merchant bankers or intermediaries. Gelderblom, Hup, and Jonker showed that notaries in the Dutch Republic did not acquire the commanding intermediary position they gained in France.[12] Petram found that officially sworn brokers became important intermediaries for the Amsterdam stock market only in the last quarter of the seventeenth century. These official brokers were members of the brokers' guild and had taken an oath. Interlopers also performed brokerage services, but transactions brokered by them were legally void.[13] The brokers' guild jealously guarded its position. Due to its lobby, innkeepers were forbidden to act as brokers or intermediaries—services they had performed for travelers until the sixteenth century, as a natural extension of their business, as did innkeepers elsewhere.[14] So,

[10] Jonker, 'Klem 1'; Jonker, 'Klem 2'; Joost Jonker and Keetie E Sluyterman, *Thuis op de wereldmarkt: Nederlandse handelshuizen door de eeuwen heen* (Den Haag, 2000); Riley, *International Government Finance*, there 42; Alice Clare Carter, *Getting, Spending and Investing in Early Modern Times: Essays on Dutch, English and Huguenot Economic History* (Assen, 1975); Carlos and Neal, 'Amsterdam and London', there 31; Peter George Muir Dickson, *Finance and Government under Maria Theresia 1740–1780* (Oxford, 1987), there 42; Tomz, *Reputation and International Cooperation.*

[11] Riley, *International Government Finance*, there 41.

[12] Oscar Gelderblom, Mark Hup, and Joost Jonker, 'Public Functions, Private Markets: Credit Registration by Aldermen and Notaries in the Low Countries, 1500–1800', in: Marcella Lorenzini, Cinzia Lorandini, and D'Maris Coffman (eds.), *Financing in Europe: Evolution, Coexistence and Complementarity of Lending Practices from the Middle Ages to Modern Times*, (Cham, 2018), 163–194; Philip T. Hoffman, Gilles Postel-Vinay, and Jean-Laurent Rosenthal, *Priceless Markets: The Political Economy of Credit in Paris, 1660–1870* (Chicago, 2000); Philip T. Hoffman, Gilles Postel-Vinay, and Jean-Laurent Rosenthal, *Dark Matter Credit: The Development of Peer-to-Peer Lending and Banking in France* (Princeton, 2019).

[13] Lodewijk Petram, *The World's First Stock Exchange: How the Amsterdam Market for Dutch East India Company Shares Became a Modern Securities Market, 1602–1700*, Unpublished PhD-thesis Universiteit van Amsterdam (Amsterdam, 2011), there 36–37, 41, 44–45; Joost Jonker, *Merchants, Bankers, Middlemen: The Amsterdam Money Market during the First Half of the 19th Century* (Amsterdam, 1996), 145–147.

[14] Maarten Hell, *De Amsterdamse herberg 1450–1800: geestrijk centrum van het openbare leven* (Nijmegen, 2017), there 51–55, 139–141; Anke Greve, 'Brügger Hosteliers und hansische Kaufleute: ein Netzwerk vorteilhafter Handelsbeziehungen oder programmierte Interessenkonflikte?', in: Werner Paravicini, Horst Wernicke, and Nils Jörn, Kieler Werkstücke (eds), *Hansekaufleute in Brügge. Tl. 4: Beiträge der internationalen Tagung*

the sub-question is whether Dutch provinces relied on brokers or other intermediaries and if so, how they should be understood or characterized. Understanding the position and reputation of the intermediary is crucial in addressing the debt market's information asymmetry, which further adds to the subject's relevance.

The case of eighteenth-century Friesland is particularly relevant because a dramatic increase in the provincial debt during the War of the Spanish Succession was followed by a default in 1711.[15] How the province first gained access to the market and then maintained its relation is based on a database of 347 newspaper advertisements. In the case of Friesland, disadvantaged creditors do not appear to have taken action in public media. This contrasts with Britain around the same time, where newspapers were used to voice public discontent about inadequate payments.[16] The phenomenon was not unknown in the Dutch Republic, however. After a default in payment by the Dutch province of Groningen, the Amsterdam merchant Roeters called on other Holland and Zeeland creditors in advertisements to come forward to unite in collective sanctions.[17,18] In the case of Friesland, newspaper advertisements only show communication on the part of the Frisian government.

in Brügge April 1996 (Frankfurt am Main, 2000), 151–161; Anke Greve, 'Hoteliers en Hanzekooplieden in Brugge in de 14de en 15de eeuw', in: A. Vandewalle, *Hanzekooplui en Medicibankiers: Brugge, wisselmarkt van Europese culturen*, (Oostkamp 2002), 99–104; Matteo Pompermaier, 'Credit and Poverty in Early Modern Venice', in: *The Journal of Interdisciplinary History* 52:4 (2022), 513–536.

[15] Alberto Feenstra, 'De Lange Schaduw van de Spaanse Successieoorlog (1701–1713) in Friesland', in: Victor Enthoven, *Nederland in Last. Vijfhonderd Jaar Overheidsfinanciën in de Lage Landen, 1500–2000* (Leiden, 2021), 89–109.

[16] Murphy, 'Demanding'.

[17] Alberto Feenstra, 'Hiding in a Twilight Zone: Credible Commitment in the Dutch Republic and Groningen's 1680s Default', in: *Histoire & Mesure* 30:2 (2015), 79–116; Alberto Feenstra and Sabine Muller, 'Wie wil wachten op het zoet? De laatste adem van Amsterdamse kopers van Groningse lijfrenten, 1660–1760', in: *Historisch Jaarboek Groningen*, (2016), 46–65, there 56.

[18] Advertentie. "Leydse courant". Te Leyden, 08-12-1755, p. 2. Geraadpleegd op Delpher op 05-12-2023, https://resolver.kb.nl/resolve?urn=ddd:010910185:mpeg21:p002; Advertentie. "Leydse courant". Te Leyden, 08-12-1755, p. 2. Geraadpleegd op Delpher op 05-12-2023, https://resolver.kb.nl/resolve?urn=ddd:010910185:mpeg21:p002; Advertentie. "Amsterdamse courant". Amsterdam, 02-10-1760, p. 2. Geraadpleegd op Delpher op 05-12-2023, https://resolver.kb.nl/resolve?urn=ddd:010708213:mpeg21:p002.

Friesland's payment policy and interaction with the market offer insight into the position of lower-ranking public debtors and intermediation in eighteenth-century Amsterdam. This study thus contributes to the literature on non-bank credit markets and specifically on the role of intermediation for public debt.

The chapter proceeds as follows. Section 1 explains the fiscal structure of the Dutch Republic and positions the province of Friesland within that framework. Section 2 analyzes Friesland's payment behavior in Amsterdam, in general terms. Section 3 then focuses on the position of intermediaries for the execution of the actual payments. Section 4 singles out the most important intermediary for Friesland since the 1760s, Johannes Menkema, and scrutinizes his business. Section 5 concludes.

2 Friesland's Public Finance within the Dutch Republic

The Dutch fiscal system was layered. The shared expenses, mostly those for warfare, were almost exclusively financed from provincial contributions. Central taxes hardly existed. Each of the Seven Provinces that constituted the Dutch Republic was fiscally autonomous. Of the shared expenses, Friesland paid the second largest contribution of 11.5% of the total; Holland was the largest contributor, paying 58% according to the fixed distribution key. Each province was completely free to choose the means to pay its contribution.[19] Borrowing was frequent, especially during wartime when tax incomes fell short of expenditure.[20] Each

[19] Hans. L. Zwitzer, 'Het quotenstelsel onder de Republiek der Verenigde Nederlanden alsmede enkele beschouwingen over de generale petitie, de staat van oorlog en de repartitie', in: *Mededelingen van de Sectie Militaire Geschiedenis, Landmachtstaf* 5 (1982), 5–57, there 17; Feenstra, 'Lange Schaduw', there 90: Friesland paid around one-fifth of Holland's, while its population was merely one-sixth.

[20] Wantje Fritschy, *Public Finance of the Dutch Republic in Comparative Perspective: The Viability of an Early Modern Federal State (1570s-1795)* (Leiden, 2017); Marjolein C. 't Hart, *The Making of a Bourgeois State: War, Politics and Finance during the Dutch Revolt* (Manchester, 1993); Marjolein C. 't Hart, *The Dutch Wars of Independence: Warfare and Commerce in the Netherlands 1570–1680* (London, 2014); Oscar Gelderblom and Joost Jonker, 'Public Finance and Economic Growth', *The Journal of Economic History* 71:1 (2011), 1–40; E. H. M. Dormans, *Het tekort: staatsschuld in de tijd der Republiek*, (Amsterdam, 1991); R. Liesker, 'Tot zinkens toe bezwaard. De schuldenlast van het Zuiderkwartier van Holland 1672–1794', in: Jan Juliaan Woltjer, Simon Groenveld, and Marianne Elisabeth Henriette Nicolette Mout (eds.) *Bestuurders en geleerden: opstellen*

province was responsible for several regiments, which they paid directly.[21] To smooth and ensure prompt payments to the troops in the field, intermediaries, known as 'military solicitors', advanced short-term credit to regiment captains. Eventually, the tax receiver of the responsible province had to repay these advances.[22]

In Holland, the wealthiest and most studied province, eighteen district tax receivers issued loans locally and serviced the debt from taxes, also collected locally.[23] Their private credit provided additional surety to investors within their network, as a form of fiscal intermediation.[24] This allowed the States of Holland to benefit widely from the wealth that accumulated since the sixteenth century.[25] A drawback of the system was that

over onderwerpen uit de Nederlandse geschiedenis van de zestiende, zeventiende en achttiende eeuw, aangeboden aan Prof. Dr. J.J. Woltjer bij zijn afscheid als hoogleraar van de Rijksuniversiteit te Leiden (Amsterdam, 1985), 151–160.

[21] 't Hart, *The Making of a Bourgeois State*, there 192–193; 't Hart, *The Dutch Wars of Independence*, there 154–155.

[22] Pepijn Brandon, *War, Capital, and the Dutch State (1588–1795)*, (Leiden, 2015); Pepijn Brandon, '"The Whole Art of War Is Reduced to Money": Remittances, Short-Term Credit and Financial Intermediation in Anglo-Dutch Military Finance, 1688–1713', in: *Financial History Review* 25:1 (2018), 19–41, there 33.

[23] Fritschy, *Public Finance*, there 60–62; R. Liesker and W. Fritschy, *Gewestelijke financiën ten tijde van de Republiek der Verenigde Nederlanden. Deel IV. Holland (1572–1795)*, (Den Haag, 2004), there 33–34; Gelderblom and Jonker, 'Public Finance', there 6.

[24] Wantje Fritschy, 'A "financial Revolution" Reconsidered: Public Finance in Holland during the Dutch Revolt, 1568–1648', in: *The Economic History Review* 56:1 (2003): 57–89, there 76, 78–79; Marjolein C. 't Hart, 'Staatsfinanciën als familiezaak tijdens de Republiek: de ontvangers-generaal Doubleth', in: J. Th de Smidt (ed.), *Fiscaliteit in Nederland. 50 jaar Belastingmuseum 'Prof. Dr. Van der Poel'*, (Zutphen/Deventer, 1987), 56–65; Marjolein 't Hart, 'Mutual Advantages: State Bankers as Brokers between the City of Amsterdam and the Dutch Republic', in: Oscar Gelderblom (ed.) *The Political Economy of the Dutch Republic* (Farnham, 2009), 115–142; 't Hart, *The Making of a Bourgeois State*, 174; On the medieval roots of fiscal intermediation in Holland: Jaco Zuijderduijn and Dries Raeymaekers, (eds.), *Publieke financiën in de Lage Landen (1300–1800)*, (Maastricht, 2015); Jaco Zuijderduijn, 'De laatmiddeleeuwse crisis van de overheidsfinanciën en de financiële revolutie in Holland', in: *Bijdragen en mededelingen betreffende de geschiedenis der Nederlanden* 125:4 (2010), 3–24; Jaco Zuijderduijn, 'The Emergence of Provincial Debt in the County of Holland (Thirteenth–Sixteenth Centuries)', in: *European Review of Economic History* 14:3 (2010), 335–359.

[25] Jan De Vries and Ad Van der Woude, *The First Modern Economy: Success, Failure, and Perseverance of the Dutch Economy, 1500–1815* (Cambridge, 1997), there 124–125; Jan De Vries and Ad Van der Woude, *Nederland 1500–1815: de eerste ronde van*

the other provinces could not use this system for issuing and servicing debt. They had to find alternatives to tap into Holland's capital surplus.

Friesland's first short-lived experiment with borrowing in Holland ended during a simultaneous and fierce conflict with the States-General in the 1630s. From the onset, Friesland objected to its allotted share and continued to dispute this during the seventeenth and eighteenth centuries. The results were regularly belated or incomplete payments. Amid the conflict with the States-General, in the 1630s, Friesland defaulted on its external debt in Holland. The States-General enforced a fiscal reform and redemption of the external debt in the 1640s.[26] As a consequence of the superimposed fiscal reform, Friesland could manage its public finances largely without borrowing, until the end of the seventeenth century.[27]

In the 1660s, Friesland returned to the Amsterdam capital market. The conditions and process remained opaque, until the 1690s, when the first interest payments were announced.[28] By then the debt had risen substantially and comprised both redeemable and life annuities. Both credit instruments were issued in parallel by two different Frisian tax receivers,

moderne economische groei (Amsterdam, 1995), there 157–158; Wantje Fritschy, *De patriotten en de financiën van de Bataafse Republiek: Hollands krediet en de smalle marges voor een nieuw beleid (1795–1801)* ('s-Gravenhage, 1988), there 42, 72; Gelderblom and Jonker, 'Public Finance', there 13–14, 26–27; Kees Zandvliet, *De 250 rijksten van de Gouden Eeuw: kapitaal, macht, familie en levensstijl*, (Amsterdam, 2006); Christiaan van Bochove, Christopher L. Colvin, and Oscar Gelderblom, 'Detecting the Function of Finance through History: An Essay in Celebration of the Work of Joost Jonker', in: *TSEG - The Low Countries Journal of Social and Economic History* 18:3 (2021), 125–166, there 141.

[26] Hotso Spanninga, *Gulden vrijheid?: politieke cultuur en staatsvorming in Friesland, 1600–1640* (Hilversum, 2012), there 180, 212–63, 312–320, 355–368; Alberto Feenstra, *Between Shared and Conflicting Interests. The Political Economy of the Markets for Public Debt in the Dutch Republic, 1600–1795*, Unpublished Ph.D. thesis Universiteit van Amsterdam, (Amsterdam, 2018), there 163–66, 199–200; A. Th. Van Deursen, 'De plaats van het gewest Friesland in de Republiek', in: Jouke Arend Frieswijk et al. (eds), *Fryslân, staat en macht 1450–1650: bijdragen aan het historisch congres te Leeuwarden van 3 tot 5 juni 1998*, (Hilversum, 1999), 218–231; 't Hart, *The Making of a Bourgeois State*, there 37.

[27] Feenstra, 'Between Shared', there 189–91.

[28] Cor Trompetter, *Gewestelijke financiën ten tijde van de Republiek der Verenigde Nederlanden. Deel VI. Friesland (1587–1795)*, 221 (Den Haag: Instituut voor Nederlandse Geschiedenis, 2007), there 39–40, 184–91; Feenstra, 'Between Shared', there 200–201.

the receiver of the redeemable annuities and the receiver of the life annuities. In Friesland, four separate offices executed specific fiscal tasks, each headed by a tax receiver-general.[29] Each acted relatively independently of the others. Their relative autonomy may explain why in the 1660s, only redeemable annuities had been issued in Amsterdam. This amounted to less than a million guilders.[30] The real increases in the debt only began with the Nine Years' War (1688–1697) for both life and redeemable annuities.

Before the war, Friesland's provincial public debt had been relatively modest; amounting to less than 5 million guilders against 2 million in tax revenues. The war more than doubled the debt to 11 million. The War of the Spanish Succession dealt the real blow to the provincial public finances, even though the Dutch Republic's territories remained untouched. By 1710, hence even before peace was made, the debt had risen to a staggering 28 million guilders and continued to increase to 37 million in 1720—to add some perspective: an unskilled wage worker in Holland earned a guilder per day, in Friesland, some 30% less.[31]

The amounts the States of Friesland required exceeded the capacity of its receivers and their domestic networks and of that of the entire province. Therefore, the States turned to the Amsterdam capital market. By 1715, half of the debt was issued in Holland. The accompanying debt service had equally increased from around half a million guilders per year in 1688 to over 2 million in 1710.[32] The fiscal income had not increased accordingly, even though the 25% increase to 2.5 guilders was a remarkable achievement.[33] It was clear that this was no sustainable situation for Friesland when more than 80% of the income was spent on debt service.

As a result, Friesland again selectively defaulted on its external debt in 1711. This was a substantial relief of fiscal pressure since half of the debt

[29] Trompetter, *Gewestelijke financiën: vol 6. Friesland*, there 24–40, 60–62.

[30] Tresoar, Staten van Friesland, inv.nr. 1788, f. 45.

[31] De Vries and Van der Woude, *The First Modern Economy*, there 610–611; Harm Tjeerd Nijboer, *De fatsoenering van het bestaan: consumptie in Leeuwarden tijdens de Gouden Eeuw* (Leeuwarden, 2007), there 129, 131–32.

[32] Feenstra, 'Lange Schaduw', there 91–92. 94; Trompetter, *Gewestelijke financiën: vol 6. Friesland*, there 223–27, 258–60; Feenstra, 'Between Shared', there 191.

[33] Trompetter, *Gewestelijke financiën: vol 6. Friesland*, there 83–86; Feenstra, 'Between Shared', there 172.

was issued in Holland. The default was followed by protests from creditors in Holland. Without overarching legal or political institutions that had a say in Friesland's fiscal affairs, there was little else they could do. On their behalf, the States of Holland requested their Frisian counterparts to resume payments, who in turn claimed impoverishment. In 1716, 1717, and 1718 the States of Friesland promised to resume interest payments in Holland, as soon as it saw the opportunity. Meanwhile, the States of Friesland first reduced the official coupon for all bonds to 4%. Then it introduced a withholding tax over the bonds, which reduced the effective coupon from 4 to 2% and reduced the payment of life annuities by 20%.[34] The main consequence was that Friesland suffered from credit rationing, as the receiver Knock experienced when his attempt failed to issue a new loan in Amsterdam in 1725 and 1726. The province now felt forced to issue an expensive life annuity within Friesland.[35] Credit rationing appeared the only effective sanction that the external creditors had to discipline a defaulter. The absence of public announcements in newspapers to subscribe to the loans suggests that the tax receivers attempted to issue loans through personal networks or that of the brokers in Amsterdam.

The effectiveness of the sanction of credit rationing was limited, however. Some thirty years before Friesland, the province of Groningen had defaulted on debt issued in Holland. Confronted with credit rationing, it found a backdoor to the Holland capital market: the States-General's receiver issued and guaranteed loans for Groningen since 1688.[36] However, during the War of the Austrian Succession (1740–1748) credit rationing was also applied to Friesland loans guaranteed by the Generality. Desperate for funds, it asked the States of Holland to secretly issue a loan for Friesland, on Holland's account, in 1746. Once word got out, this displeased the creditors, who assumed to have invested in safe Holland debt. A year after Holland's 3% loan, the States-General granted another loan to Friesland, although this was not a smooth process either.[37] The credit rationing was not watertight as individuals could still lend money to a defaulting province. At some point during the War of

[34] Nationaal Archief, Den Haag (NL-HaNA), Provinciale resoluties, inv.nr. 484, p. 11.

[35] Feenstra, 'Lange Schaduw', there 97–99.

[36] Feenstra, 'Hiding'.

[37] Feenstra, 'Lange Schaduw', there 102–3.

the Austrian Succession, the banking houses of Pels and Clifford had advanced money to Friesland. Although the details remain obscure, Friesland owed them money they had advanced for troop payments. Similarly, the banker Boas from The Hague held a claim on Friesland, in 1747.[38] These must have been short-term military loans requiring replacement by long-term debt. Like in 1725–1726, public announcements of loan subscriptions were absent around the end of the War of the Austrian Succession.

Friesland thus still suffered from the effects of the default, which prevented the issuing of loans in Amsterdam until the 1770s. The province either borrowed expensively within Friesland or with the intermediation of the States of Holland or the States-General. Between 1767 and 1770, it issued multiple 3% loans to redeem the States of Holland debt, domestically, within Friesland. It was not until the 1770s that it could float a loan on its own account in Holland.[39] Unlike the 1740s, the loan issue was not born out of a financial need for war costs but was intended to redeem the older loans. The Republic had remained neutral in the Seven Years' War (1756–1763), the crisis of 1763 its aftermath was over and there was money in abundance.[40] Although these were favorable conditions, it does not entirely explain Friesland's return to the Amsterdam capital market, without the aid of public intermediaries such as the States of Holland or the States-General.

3 Friesland Debt Service in Amsterdam

Having outlined Friesland's main fiscal developments, this section analyzes the practice of debt issuance and interest payments before and after the default of 1711 to see how and what changed. Figure 1 shows the time between the due date of the interest installment and the actual interest payment. These data are derived from newspaper advertisements. The figure shows that from the earliest advertisements in 1696 until 1711, the interest was paid on time. Thereafter, the default resulted in

[38] Feenstra, 'Lange Schaduw', there 104.

[39] Feenstra, 'Lange Schaduw', there 107.

[40] Elisabeth Emmy De Jong-Keesing, *De Economische Crisis van 1763 Te Amsterdam* (Amsterdam: Intern. Uitgevers en Handelsmaatschappij (Systemen Keesing), 1939); Riley, *International Government Finance*, there 15–16, 84.

a temporary halt of payments that were only resumed in 1719, with one exceptional payment in 1714 over the life annuities in between (Fig. 2).

Two results stand out. First, once the interest payments resumed, there was a delay that persisted until the end of the eighteenth century. Second, the overdue time for life annuities and redeemable annuities differed. The

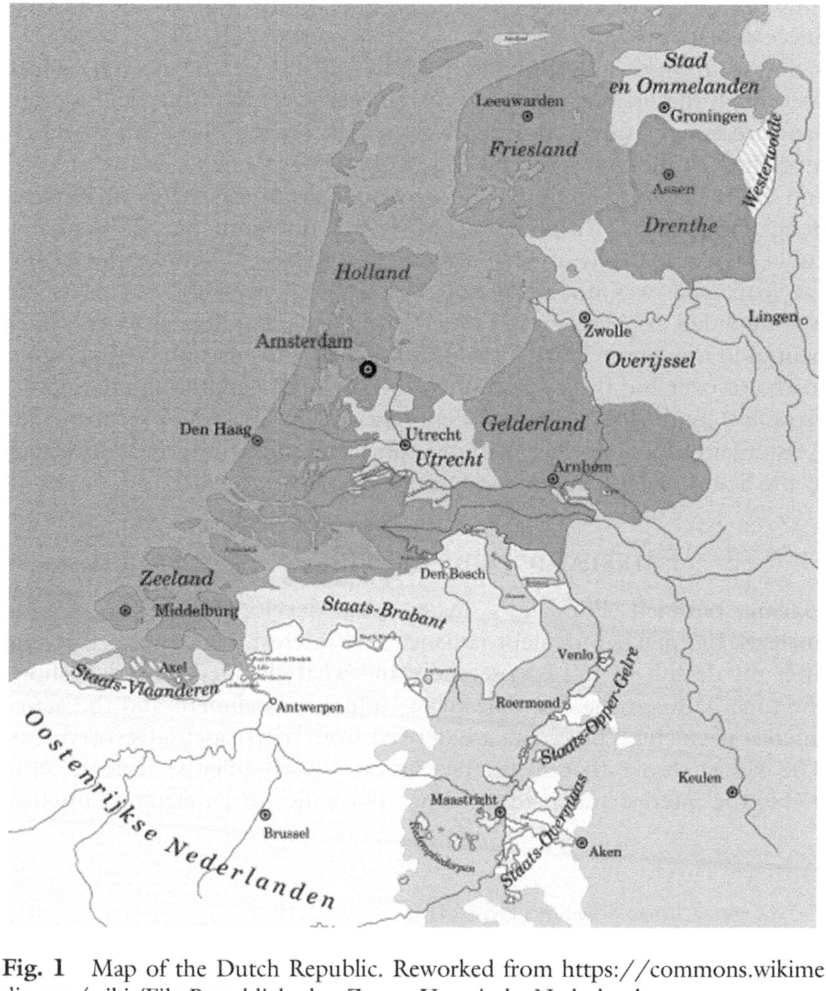

Fig. 1 Map of the Dutch Republic. Reworked from https://commons.wikimedia.org/wiki/File:Republiek_der_Zeven_Verenigde_Nederlanden.svg

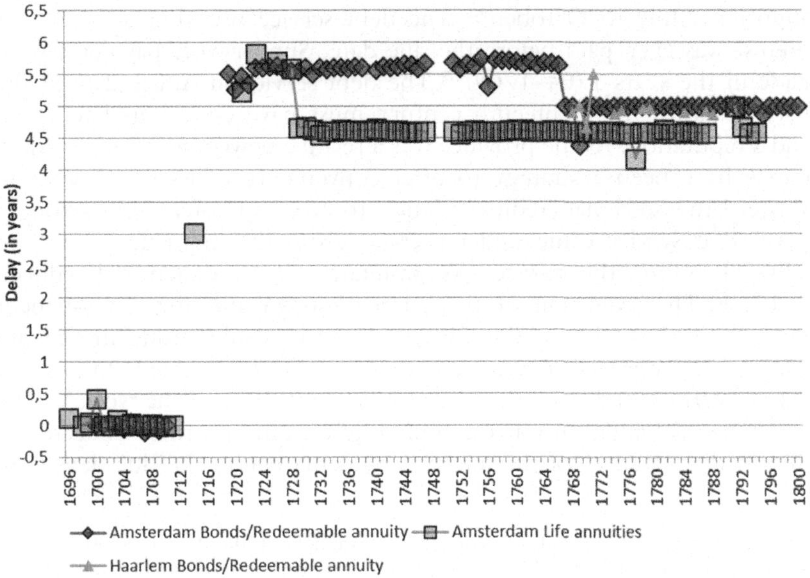

Fig. 2 Timing Friesland's Debt Service in Holland (Source Database, Friesland newspaper 347 advertisements, based on Delpher.nl)

former was paid with an overdue time of four and a half years. The latter was first paid with an overdue time of five and a half years, which dropped to five years after 1767. From around that period, interest payments in the town of Haarlem—some 20 kilometers west of Amsterdam—began to appear. The striking persistence of constant belated payments must have offered a curious form of reliability: every year a full year's installment was paid, even though it concerned an overdue term.

So, until 1711 all interest was paid neatly, for bonds and life annuities. Rather, the receivers of both types of annuities paid multiple times per year and partly in advance.[41] For instance, Receiver Johan Knock paid the interest concerning March to June in March and April and again in

[41] Advertentie. "Amsterdamse courant". Amsterdam, 29-08-1705, p. 2. Geraadpleegd op Delpher op 20-06-2022, https://resolver.kb.nl/resolve?urn=MMSAA06:166474104:mpeg21:p00002.

August for July to October.[42] The debt service was thus so neat that interest was even paid before the due date. Similar early payments were made in the years 1704–1709.[43] The debt service in Amsterdam in the first decade of the eighteenth century must have contributed to Friesland's reputation. As the province was a relative newcomer to the market, it may have been a strategy to offer convenience of local payments in Amsterdam and signal creditworthiness to new and potential investors.[44]

Yet that service came under pressure from the dramatic increase in debt. Therefore, the service was simultaneously extended and reduced in 1710. The extension of the service was by offering a permanent presence in Amsterdam; the Receiver's clerk would reside in the inn named *Het Wapen van Groningen and Ommelanden*, located in the street *Warmoesstraat*, and pay interest every first four days of the week.[45] The simultaneous limitation was that only interest due was to be collected.[46] Hence, the advances of the interest payments before the due date were

[42] "Advertentie". "Amsterdamse courant". Amsterdam, 1705/03/24 00:00:00, p. 2. Geraadpleegd op Delpher op 03-12-2019, http://resolver.kb.nl/resolve?urn=ddd:010708040:mpeg21:p002;

[43] Advertentie. "Amsterdamse courant". Amsterdam, 25-11-1704, p. 2. Geraadpleegd op Delpher op 20-06-2022, https://resolver.kb.nl/resolve?urn=MMSAA06:166473142:mpeg21:p00002; Advertentie. "Amsterdamse courant". Amsterdam, 06-08-1705, p. 2. Geraadpleegd op Delpher op 20-06-2022, https://resolver.kb.nl/resolve?urn=MMSAA06:166474094:mpeg21:p00002; Advertentie. "Amsterdamse courant". Amsterdam, 21-01-1706, p. 2. Geraadpleegd op Delpher op 20-06-2022, https://resolver.kb.nl/resolve?urn=MMSAA06:165530009:mpeg21:p00002; Advertentie. "Amsterdamse courant". Amsterdam, 23-07-1707, p. 2. Geraadpleegd op Delpher op 20-06-2022, https://resolver.kb.nl/resolve?urn=MMSAA06:166465088:mpeg21:p00002; Advertentie. "Amsterdamse courant". Amsterdam, 28-03-1709, p. 2. Geraadpleegd op Delpher op 20-06-2022, https://resolver.kb.nl/resolve?urn=MMSAA06:165531038:mpeg21:p00002.

[44] Compare Tomz for his ideas about building reputations, esp. Ch. 2 and 3: Tomz, *Reputation and International Cooperation*; Compare Van Bochove for the phenomenon that public securities were retraded to the places of origin in the Dutch Republic. Christiaan van Bochove, 'Configuring Financial Markets in Preindustrial Europe', in: *The Journal of Economic History* 73: 1 (2013), 247–78.

[45] Translates as: "The Groningen and Ommelanden Arms", often shortened to "*Groningen en Omlanden*" or "*Groningen en Ommelanden*", and in the period up to 1711 also as "*Karels Kroon in Sweden, of gekroond Groningen en Omlanden*". *Warmoesstraat* runs from the port to Dam Square, where the City Hall, with the Amsterdam Exchange Bank and Amsterdam Exchange (Beurs), was located.

[46] Advertentie. "Amsterdamse courant". Amsterdam, 18-03-1710, p. 2. Geraadpleegd op Delpher op 20-06-2022, https://resolver.kb.nl/resolve?urn=MMSAA06:166470033:mpeg21:p00002.

suspended. The reduction of the service became a foreshadowing of what was to come the next year.

The suspension of payments was not announced in the newspapers, there is simply a lack of announcements of the interest payments. Yet the absence of interest payments did not mean absolute silence in these sources. For other matters, the States of Friesland advertised in the period until 1719. For instance, the loss of bonds and withdrawal of bad alloy coins. For these purposes, interested parties in Amsterdam could turn to either a messenger (*Boode*), in alley *Zoutsteeg* (running between *Nieuwendijk* and *Damrak*), or the broker Jonas de Voogt, living in *Nes* (an extension of *Warmoestraat*).[47] The selective default on the Holland-issued debt resulted in a selective absence of newspaper advertisements that announced interest payments.

From 1719, the consistency of the installments was only interrupted during the period 1748–1750 when no advertisements were found for either bonds or life annuities. This presumably had to do with the fiscal pressure from the War of the Austrian Succession, discussed above. This time, however, the absence of advertisements does not reflect another formal and deliberate default on Friesland's external debt; the total amount of interest paid dropped only slightly.[48] Alternatively, changes in the proprietorship of the inns and functions of the messengers in Amsterdam distorted the ordinary organization of interest payments, as will be detailed below. Finally, the interest payments over the bonds continued five years after the dissolution of the 'old' Dutch Republic in 1795, whereas the payments over the life annuities halted as soon as 1795, underlining the fiscal fragmentation within Friesland.

[47] Advertentie. "Amsterdamse courant". Amsterdam, 07-12-1713, p. 2. Geraadpleegd op Delpher op 19-10-2022, https://resolver.kb.nl/resolve?urn=MMSAA06:166463146:mpeg21:p00002; Advertentie. "Amsterdamse courant". Amsterdam, 09-12-1713, p. 2. Geraadpleegd op Delpher op 19-10-2022, https://resolver.kb.nl/resolve?urn=MMSAA06:166463147:mpeg21:p00002; Advertentie. "Amsterdamse courant". Amsterdam, 11-12-1714, p. 2. Geraadpleegd op Delpher op 29-09-2022, https://resolver.kb.nl/resolve?urn=MMSAA06:166476146:mpeg21:p00002; Advertentie. "Amsterdamse courant". Amsterdam, 26-01-1715, p. 2. Geraadpleegd op Delpher op 29-09-2022, https://resolver.kb.nl/resolve?urn=MMSAA06:166477012:mpeg21:p00002; Advertentie. "Amsterdamse courant". Amsterdam, 23-03-1715, p. 2. Geraadpleegd op Delpher op 29-09-2022, https://resolver.kb.nl/resolve?urn=MMSAA06:166477036:mpeg21:p00002.

[48] Trompetter, *Gewestelijke financiën: vol 6. Friesland*, there 223–24, 258–60; Feenstra, 'Lange Schaduw', there 91.

4 Interest Payers and Their Venues

With the pattern of the interest payments laid out, this section focuses on intermediaries and their activities. More specifically, it addresses the question of who issued the debt, who executed the payments, where, and how. The loans issued since the 1660s are surrounded by uncertainty. It is known that the Friesland Receivers turned to brokers in Amsterdam in 1672, for which they offered a brokerage fee of 0.25%. It remains unclear how much debt they issued, and when, and where they did so.[49] Again there is a difference between the redeemable annuities and the life annuities. Payments concerning the life annuities began during the 1690s. Those over the redeemable annuities started in 1700, simultaneous with the appointment of Johan Knock as Receiver. His predecessor as Receiver of the redeemable annuities, Gerhardus Beilanus, paid interest in Leeuwarden. He only advertised that lost bonds could be returned to either his office or to the widow of Aart Dirksz. Oossaen, in Amsterdam.[50] She ran a bookstore cum post office on Dam Square, on the corner of *Beursstraat* (Amsterdam Exchange).[51] Except for this correspondence address, the Receiver of the redeemable annuities appears not to have had any presence in Amsterdam, until Johan Knock's appointment in 1700.

The broker Jonas de Voogt played a part in handling that part of Friesland's debt in Amsterdam. He first appears in 1695 at the occasion of the issuance of a lottery for the orphanage in Leeuwarden, the capital of Friesland.[52] Soon after, in 1701, creditors could collect the interest

[49] Trompetter, *Gewestelijke financiën: vol 6. Friesland*, there 186.

[50] Advertentie. "Oprechte Haerlemsche courant". Haerlem, 03-11-1693, p. 2. Geraadpleegd op Delpher op 09-12-2023, https://resolver.kb.nl/resolve?urn=ddd:011227005:mpeg21:p002; Advertentie. "Amsterdamse courant". Amsterdam, 15-07-1694, p. 2. Geraadpleegd op Delpher op 19-10-2022, https://resolver.kb.nl/resolve?urn=MMSAA06:165525083:mpeg21:p00002.

[51] Advertentie. "Amsterdamse courant". Amsterdam, 29-04-1688, p. 2. Geraadpleegd op Delpher op 09-12-2023, https://resolver.kb.nl/resolve?urn=ddd:010759044:mpeg21:p002; Advertentie. "Amsterdamse courant". Amsterdam, 19-05-1689, p. 2. Geraadpleegd op Delpher op 09-12-2023, https://resolver.kb.nl/resolve?urn=MMSAA06:165521215:mpeg21:p00002; Amfterdam den 25 Iuly Brieven van den 19 defer. "Amsterdamse courant". Amsterdam, 26-07-1689, p. 2. Geraadpleegd op Delpher op 09-12-2023, https://resolver.kb.nl/resolve?urn=MMSAA06:165521245:mpeg21:p00002.

[52] Advertentie. Oprechte Haerlemsche courant. Haerlem, 29-12-1695, p. 2. Geraadpleegd op Delpher op 29-09-2022, https://resolver.kb.nl/resolve?urn=MMNHA02:164948156:mpeg21:p00002; Advertentie. "Amsterdamse courant". Amsterdam, 20-12-1695,

payments over the Friesland redeemable annuities at his house.[53] This suggests that his reputation as a financial intermediary in Amsterdam had spread through Leeuwarden's administrative networks.

The broker Voogt appeared as soon as a more specialist service was demanded. For instance, in 1708, redeemable annuities or bonds were called that had a 6% coupon; Voogt would pay the interest due and reimburse the creditors.[54] Two years later, in 1710, he informed the States of Friesland about the market prices for Friesland bonds on the Amsterdam Exchange. He thus had access to information that the Friesland Receivers lacked. The 5% bonds sold just under par, which signaled the precariousness of Friesland's credit on the secondary market. This declaration substantiated the Receiver Knock's claim that he was unable to attract money at 5% in Amsterdam. In signing the note, Voogt mentioned his capacity as a sworn broker.[55] This then illustrates the authority and position of Voogt as an official broker, offering a more specialist service in issuing and reimbursing debt.

p. 2. Geraadpleegd op Delpher op 19-10-2022, https://resolver.kb.nl/resolve?urn=MMSAA06:166468152:mpeg21:p00002; Advertentie. "Amsterdamse courant". Amsterdam, 27-12-1695, p. 2. Geraadpleegd op Delpher op 19-10-2022, https://resolver.kb.nl/resolve?urn=MMSAA06:166468155:mpeg21:p00002.

[53] Advertentie. "Amsterdamse courant". Amsterdam, 10-09-1701, p. 2. Geraadpleegd op Delpher op 29-09-2022, https://resolver.kb.nl/resolve?urn=MMSAA06:165528265:mpeg21:p00002; Advertentie. "Amsterdamse courant". Amsterdam, 13-09-1701, p. 2. Geraadpleegd op Delpher op 29-09-2022, https://resolver.kb.nl/resolve?urn=MMSAA06:165528266:mpeg21:p00002.

[54] Advertentie. "Amsterdamse courant". Amsterdam, 11-02-1708, p. 2. Geraadpleegd op Delpher op 29-09-2022, https://resolver.kb.nl/resolve?urn=MMSAA06:166466018:mpeg21:p00002.

[55] Tresoar, Archive 5, Gewestelijke bestuursinstellingen van Friesland 1580–1795, inv.nr. 453, 4 February 1710: "Verklaere ick ondergeschreve, Beedigden makelaar, binen de stadt Amsterdam, waer en warachtigh te weese, dat d'obligaties a vijff per cento losrente, lopen tot laste van de provintie van Vrieslant, alhier ter bursse dagelijckz worden gelaaten en verhandelt, tot 97: 97 1/2 en uijterlijck 98 per cento, tot welke verklaringhe van den heer ontfanger generaal der losrent, Johan Knock, versoecht sijnde hebben gepasseert, om te strecken na behooren, in Amsterdam, den 21 Januarij 1710, J.S. Voogt 1710 Makelaare"Translation: "I, the undersigned sworn broker in the city of Amsterdam, declare, to be true and faithful, that the bonds issued as five per cent annuities, debited for the province of Friesland, here at the Exchange are sold and traded daily at 97, 97 ½ and 98 per cent at most, being requested to declare likewise by the Receiver of the annuities, Johan Knock, did so to provide [this information] properly, in Amsterdam, 21 January 1710, J.S. Voogt, 1710 Broker.".

For most of the eighteenth century, the Friesland tax receivers paid the interest in Amsterdam, in person. To that end, they would normally reside in an inn, for a week during the summer. Only in a few cases until the 1760s, someone else paid, like the broker Voogt, who paid once. In the earliest period, the receivers' clerks incidentally arranged the payments. Their permanent availability to the creditors, as announced in 1710, was of course canceled with the entire suspension of the debt service in 1711. After 1711, only in four more years, the clerks paid, and none after 1729.[56] The Friesland tax receivers did not rely on a system of brokers or agents that would have required the use of bills of exchange.

How the Friesland Receivers obtained the money to pay the interest remains uncertain. On the one hand, using bills of exchange was an option to transfer money from Friesland to Amsterdam.[57] On the other hand, in 1689, a Friesland official traveled with physical cash from Friesland to Holland, for troop payments in Brussels.[58] Also in the eighteenth century, Friesland's neighboring province of Groningen physically shipped money to Holland, even though they had previously relied on bills of exchange too.[59] Whatever the precise form, the Friesland tax receivers traveled to Amsterdam to personally pay the interest, throughout the eighteenth century.

That the tax receivers came to make the payment in person suggests that personal presence had added value compared to the alternative of agents or brokers. They could not rely on a personal network in Amsterdam to issue the debt, as the Holland Receivers in their respective districts. The newspaper advertisements form an expression of the scale of the loans and the impersonal character of the exchange.

Nevertheless, the Friesland tax receivers built long-term relationships with their hosts in Amsterdam. This was made easier by relatively few changes on the part of the tax receivers, who were also partly family. Two families and two receivers stand out. Father and son Everhardus

[56] 1709, 1710, 1714, 1721, 1726, 1729.

[57] Advertentie. "Amsterdamse courant". Amsterdam, 27-02-1744, p. 1. Geraadpleegd op Delpher op 02-04-2023, https://resolver.kb.nl/resolve?urn=ddd:010712619:mpeg21:p001.

[58] NL-HaNA, Staten van Holland, inv.nr. 5121, pp. 412–413, 428–430, pp. 607–608.

[59] Feenstra, 'Hiding', there 109; Regionaal Historisch Centrum, Groninger Archief (RHC-GrA), archieven der Staten van Stad en Lande (SvSL), inv.nr. 96, p. 56, 3 March 1699.

and Epeus Wieinga served as receivers of the life annuities, from 1702 to 1785. The family Knock served as counterparts for the redeemable annuities, from 1700 to 1766. Within each family and function, Epeus Wielinga (in office: 1728–July 1785) and Gulbartus Knock (in office: 1718-Febr. 1762) served seventy-five and forty-four years, respectively. The stability on the part of the Friesland Receivers may have contributed to stable long-term relationships with the inns and innkeepers.

4.1 Venues

To have an impression of the social context of debt-related payments, we focus on the locations and changes therein. The venues, in which the payments were made, can be categorized into three types. The first and most common is the inn or lodge house, as indicated in Table 2. The second type is the post office or messengers' office. The third is the office of Johannes Menkema. The first two types are naturally related to long-distance relations. Inns offered travelers a place to stay. The offices of the messenger, which were later described as post offices, served to send letters and also take packages to more distant places. These two types of venues show most prominently in the period up to the 1760s. From then on Johannes Menkema began hosting from his office, starting with the redeemable annuities, which will be discussed in detail in the next section. The question discussed here is why the tax receivers changed payment locations and how the relationship between messengers and innkeepers developed.

First, we examine the position of the innkeepers, then the messengers, and finally their relationship. Even though they could no longer act as brokers, the innkeepers facilitated travelers with financial services. For instance, innkeepers and shopkeepers in Amsterdam also offered sailors the possibility to pledge future incomes to pay for boarding,

Table 1 Tax annuities and redeemable tax annuities, detail

Life annuities, tax receivers			*Redeemable annuities, tax receivers*		
Name	*Period*	*Remark*	*Name*	*Period*	*Remark*
Sjuk van Burmania	1685–1699		Gerhardus Beilanus	1679–1700	
Hendrik Recalff	1699–1702				
Everhardus Wielinga	1702–1728		Johan Knock	1700–1718	
Epeus Wielinga	1728–1785	Son of his predecessor	Gulbartus Knock	1718–1762	Son-in-law of his predecessor
Hans Willem Baron van Plettenberg	1785–1791		Bernhardus Hermanus Knock	1762–1766	Son of his predecessor
Michiel de With	1791–1797		Jacob Boreel van Haersma	1766–1800	

(Source Tresoar, Archive 5, Gewestelijke bestuursinstellingen van Friesland 1580–1795, inv.nrs. 787391, 787392, 787393, 787394, 787395, 787403, 787404, 787405, 787406, 787,407, 787,408.)

lodging, and necessities purchased before boarding a ship.[60] They sometimes promoted their services in newspaper advertisements.[61] Offering and promoting additional services to facilitate travelers would normally help to attract customers and generate more business.

Analyzing the changes in payment locations reveals something about the innkeepers, and whether their terms and conditions were attractive enough to maintain their relations with tax receivers. Most payments were made from four locations: the Inns *Oudezijds Heerenlogement*, *Het Wapen van Groningen en Ommelanden*, *Het Wapen van Friesland*, and the office of Johannes Menkema. The inns and messenger or post offices were located a short distance from each other. They were mainly found in

[60] Christiaan van Bochove and Ton van Velzen, 'Loans to Salaried Employees: The Case of the Dutch East India Company, 1602–1794', in: *European Review of Economic History* 18 (2014), 19–38; Daan Verwaaij and Christiaan van Bochove, 'Credit without Banks: The Amsterdam Water Bailiff's Ledger of 1856', in: *Financial History Review* 26:2 (August 2019), 171–195; Christiaan van Bochove, 'Seafarers and Shopkeepers: Credit in Eighteenth-Century Amsterdam', in: *Eighteenth-Century Studies* 48:1 (2014), 67–88.

[61] Hell, *De Amsterdamse herberg 1450–1800*, there 360.

Table 2 Venues and people

<table>
<tr><th colspan="2">Life annuities</th><th colspan="2">Redeemable annuities</th><th>Life annuities</th><th>Redeemable annuities</th></tr>
<tr><th>Host</th><th>Name venue</th><th>Host</th><th>Name location</th><th>Name</th><th>Name</th></tr>
<tr><td>Anthony Swaenenburg (1696-1697)</td><td>Oudezijds Heerenlogement</td><td colspan="2" rowspan="2">[none]</td><td rowspan="2">Sjuk van Burmania (1685-1699)</td><td rowspan="2">Gerhardus Beilanus (1679-1700)</td></tr>
<tr><td>Evert Haverkamp (1699-1698)</td><td>House next to Old Church</td></tr>
<tr><td rowspan="4">Gerard de Ruyter (1700-1711)</td><td rowspan="4">Het Wapen van Groningen en Ommelanden</td><td>Evert Haverkamp (1700)</td><td>House next to Old Church</td><td rowspan="2">Hendrick Recalff (1699-1702)</td><td rowspan="8">Johan Knock (1700-1718)</td></tr>
<tr><td rowspan="2">Gerard de Ruyter (1701-1710)</td><td rowspan="2">Het Wapen van Groningen en Ommelanden</td></tr>
<tr><td rowspan="13">Everhard Wielinga (1702-1728)</td></tr>
<tr><td colspan="2" rowspan="6">[none]</td></tr>
<tr><td colspan="2">[none]</td></tr>
<tr><td>Willem Onk (messenger) (1714)</td><td>House</td></tr>
<tr><td>Widow of Gerard de Ruyter (1714)</td><td>Groningen en Ommelanden</td></tr>
<tr><td colspan="2" rowspan="3">[none]</td></tr>
<tr><td rowspan="8">Gulbartus Knock (1718-1762)</td></tr>
<tr><td rowspan="3">Jan Christoffel Schrader (1719-1724)</td><td rowspan="3">Groningen en Ommelanden</td></tr>
<tr><td>Jan Christoffel Schrader (1721-1723)</td><td>Groningen en Ommelanden</td></tr>
<tr><td colspan="2" rowspan="2">[none] (1724-175)</td></tr>
<tr><td rowspan="2">Jan Christoffel Schrader (1725-1726)</td><td rowspan="2">Het Hof van Holland</td></tr>
<tr><td>Jan Christoffel Schrader (1726)</td><td>Het Hof van Holland</td></tr>
<tr><td colspan="2">[none] (1727)</td><td rowspan="2">Jan Spyker (1727-1733)</td><td rowspan="2">Groningen & Omlanden</td></tr>
<tr><td>Jan Spyker (1728-1736)</td><td>Groningen en Ommelanden</td><td>Epeus Wielinga (1728-1785)</td></tr>
</table>

(continued)

Table 2 (continued)

		Nicolaus Menkema (1734-1738)	Wepen van Friesland, office of Jan van Schayk, 'Bode' of Friesland		
Huybert de Wit (1737-1742)	Oudezijds Heerenlogement	*[none] 1739*			
		Nicolaus Jans Campstrup (1740-1747)	Groningen & Omlanden		
Johannes Hageman (1743)	Kloveniersdoelen				
Huybert de Wit (1744-1747)	Oudezijds Heerenlogement				
[none] (1748-1750)					
Huybert de Wit (1751-1759)	Oudezijds Heerenlogement (1751-1785)	Nicolaes Menkema	House of Nicolaas Menkema		
[none] (1760-1785)		Pieter Bernard Texier	Frisian Post Office		Bernhardus Hermanus Knock (1762-1766)
		Johannes Menkema and Sons (1767-1800)	Office		Jacob Boreel van Haersma (1766-1800)

(continued)

Table 2 (continued)

Johannes Menkema and Sons (1785-1787)	Office			Hans Willem Baron Van Plettenberg (1785-1791)	
[none]					
Johannes Menkema and Sons (1791-1795)	Office			Michiel de With (1791-1797)	
[none]				*[none]*	
					E. Roorda

the streets of *Warmoesstraat* and *Nieuwendijk*, their side streets or extensions: *Nes* and *Kalverstraat*. These two ran on either side of the water connection between the port and Dam Square, the Damrak. *Nieuwendijk*, *Warmoesstraat*, and *Kalverstraat* were important shopping streets, with medium–high rents.[62] The *Burgwallen* ran parallel, on the east, the Old Side, and on the west the New Side, named after the Old and New Churches (Fig. 3).

The limited number of places suggests a certain predictability and stability, which is in line with Friesland's payment policy since 1719. Most changes occurred in the period up to 1750. Further, the payment locations differed for either life or redeemable annuities between 1734 and 1781. Between 1700 and 1734, both life and redeemable annuities were paid from the inn, *Het Wapen van Groningen and Ommelanden*.

[62] Clé Lesger, Marco H. D. van Leeuwen, and Bart Vissers, 'Residentiële Segregatie in Vroegmoderne Steden. Amsterdam in de Eerste Helft van de Negentiende Eeuw', in: *TSEG - The Low Countries Journal of Social and Economic History* 10:2 (2013), 126–127.

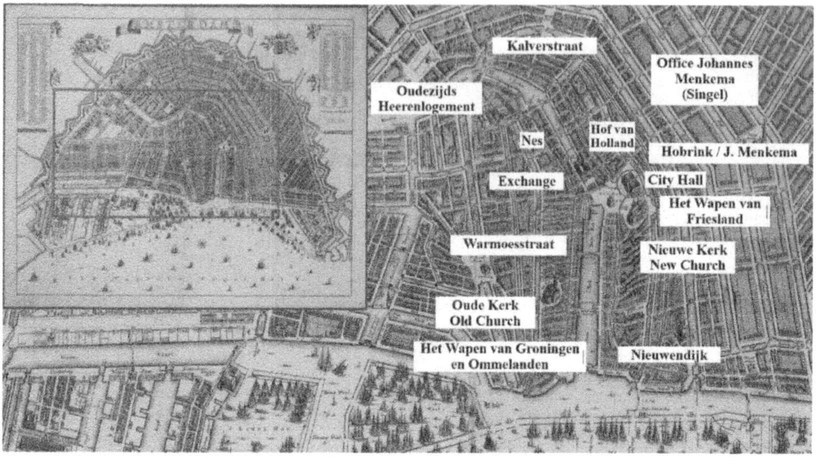

Fig. 3 City plan Amsterdam (Source reworked from Gerrit de Broen jr., 1728–1737, Collectie Atlas Splitgerber, Stads Archief Amsterdam, beeldbank nr. 010,001,001,033)

From 1785, both were paid from the office of Johanes Menkema. In the meantime, the various tax receivers preferred different venues.

Personal relations and preferences of the tax receivers probably explain part of the changes in venues. This was related to changes on the part of either the innkeeper or the tax collector, for example, due to death, or changes in proprietorship or appointment. For instance, Hendrick Recalff relocated interest payments over the life annuities to *Het Wapen van Groningen en Ommelanden*, after his predecessor Van Burmania died in 1699. Van Burmania appears to have explored options. He first stayed in the famous inn, the *Oudezijds Heerenlogement*, at Grimburgwal and then at the house of Evert Haverkamp, the bell ringer of the Old Church. Johan Knock also opted for the latter's house, when he started paying interest over the redeemable annuities in 1700.

Further, Epeus Wielinga left *Het Wapen van Groningen en Ommelanden*, when the innkeeper Jan Spyker died, in late 1736 or early 1737, even though his widow, Jacoba Vermeulen, continued the business.[63] Conversely, the succession of Gulbartus Knock by Bernard Knock in 1763 coincided with the relocation from the house of Nicolaas Menkema to the Frisian post office of Pieter Berhard Texier. Likewise, Jacob Boreel van Haersma's appointment was followed by the relocation to Johannes Menkema, in 1767. Finally, when Van Plettenberg succeeded Epeus Wielinga, in 1785, he also relocated to the office of Johannes Menkema.

Sometimes the payment location remained unchanged, and sometimes the payment location changed but not the people. The inn *Het Wapen van Groningen and Ommelanden* became the prominent payment location until 1748, despite varying people. For, in 1701, Johan Knock followed Recalff to this, which was not far from the Old Church, where he had paid the previous year.[64] There, innkeeper Gerard de Ruyter facilitated the tax receivers until he died in 1712. Neither his death nor that of Hendrick Recalff and Johan Knock breached the bond between the inn

[63] Advertentie. "Amsterdamse courant". Amsterdam, 05-02-1737, p. 2. Geraadpleegd op Delpher op 10-12-2023, https://resolver.kb.nl/resolve?urn=ddd:010710795:mpeg21:p002; Advertentie. "Amsterdamse courant". Amsterdam, 12-02-1737, p. 2. Geraadpleegd op Delpher op 10-12-2023, https://resolver.kb.nl/resolve?urn=ddd:010710798:mpeg21:p002; Advertentie. "Amsterdamse courant". Amsterdam, 19-02-1737, p. 2. Geraadpleegd op Delpher op 10-12-2023, https://resolver.kb.nl/resolve?urn=ddd:010710801:mpeg21:p002; Advertentie. "Amsterdamse courant". Amsterdam, 21-02-1737, p. 2. Geraadpleegd op Delpher op 10-12-2023, https://resolver.kb.nl/resolve?urn=ddd:010710802:mpeg21:p002; Advertentie. "Amsterdamse courant". Amsterdam, 21-02-1737, p. 2. Geraadpleegd op Delpher op 10-12-2023, https://resolver.kb.nl/resolve?urn=ddd:010710802:mpeg21:p002; Advertentie. "'s Gravenhaegse courant". 's-Gravenhage, 11-03-1737, p. 2. Geraadpleegd op Delpher op 10-12-2023, https://resolver.kb.nl/resolve?urn=ddd:010724076:mpeg21:p002.

[64] When the inn was sold, in 1737, it was described as being located between *Oudebrugsteeg* and *Nieuwebrugsteeg*. Later, in 1738, Jacoba Vermeulen (Widow of Jan Spyker) moved the inn ten houses toward the Oudebrug, so that it was located diagonally opposite *Niezel* another alley. Advertentie. "Amsterdamse courant". Amsterdam, 21-02-1737, p. 2. Geraadpleegd op Delpher op 10-12-2023, https://resolver.kb.nl/resolve?urn=ddd:010710802:mpeg21:p002; Advertentie. "'s Gravenhaegse courant". 's-Gravenhage, 11-03-1737, p. 2. Geraadpleegd op Delpher op 10-12-2023, https://resolver.kb.nl/resolve?urn=ddd:010724076:mpeg21:p002; Advertentie. "Leydse courant". Te Leyden, 30-06-1738, p. 2. Geraadpleegd op Delpher op 28-11-2023, https://resolver.kb.nl/resolve?urn=ddd:010907372:mpeg21:p002; "Advertentie". "Amsterdamse courant". Amsterdam, 1738/07/01 00:00:00, p. 2. Geraadpleegd op Delpher op 09-03-2020, http://resolver.kb.nl/resolve?urn=ddd:010712364:mpeg21:p002; "Advertentie". "Amsterdamse courant". Amsterdam, 1738/07/01 00:00:00, p. 2. Geraadpleegd op Delpher op 13-02-2020, http://resolver.kb.nl/resolve?urn=ddd:010712364:mpeg21:p002.

and the Friesland's tax receivers. Rather, De Ruyter's widow continued the business until she died in late 1718. Meanwhile, she facilitated the single payment of 1714, during Friesland's default. Jan Christoffel Schrader succeeded her as proprietor.[65] When both tax receivers resumed interest payments, they did so from *Het Wapen van Groningen and Ommelanden*, as their predecessors had done before the 1711 default, even though the proprietorship had changed even as the Friesland public officials.

In 1725 and 1726, the reason for relocation was that Jan Christoffel Schrader moved to *Het Hof van Holland*, in *Kalverstraat*, near Dam Square.[66] The receivers of both the redeemable and life annuities followed the innkeeper, albeit temporarily. Remarkably both receivers returned to *Het Wapen van Groningen en Ommelanden* in 1727. Why they stopped paying from Schrader's new inn remains unclear. Perhaps it was too upmarket and more expensive than the receivers deemed fitting for their creditors. At least the *Hof van Holland* was considered an inn of a certain standing, among the higher end of the hierarchy of the Amsterdam inns (Fig. 4).[67]

[65] "Advertentie". "Oprechte Haerlemsche courant". Haerlem, 1712/03/03 00:00:00, p. 2. Geraadpleegd op Delpher op 24-12-2019, http://resolver.kb.nl/resolve?urn=ddd:011222386:mpeg21:p002; "Advertentie". "'s Gravenhaegse courant". 's-Gravenhage, 1712/03/07 00:00:00, p. 2. Geraadpleegd op Delpher op 27-11-2019, http://resolver.kb.nl/resolve?urn=ddd:010725161:mpeg21:p002; Advertentie. "Amsterdamse courant". Amsterdam, 12-03-1712, p. 2. Geraadpleegd op Delpher op 28-11-2023, https://resolver.kb.nl/resolve?urn=MMSAA06:165533031:mpeg21:p00002; Advertentie. Oprechte Haerlemsche courant. Haerlem, 25-08-1714. Geraadpleegd op Delpher op 23-01-2017, http://resolver.kb.nl/resolve?urn=ddd:011220671:mpeg21:a0005; "Advertentie". "Oprechte Haerlemsche courant". Haerlem, 1712/03/15 00:00:00, p. 2. Geraadpleegd op Delpher op 27-11-2019, http://resolver.kb.nl/resolve?urn=ddd:011222391:mpeg21:p002; Advertentie. "Amsterdamse courant". Amsterdam, 15-12-1718, p. 2. Geraadpleegd op Delpher op 16-10-2022, https://resolver.kb.nl/resolve?urn=MMSAA06:165537150:mpeg21:p00002; Advertentie. "Amsterdamse courant". Amsterdam, 09-02-1719, p. 2. Geraadpleegd op Delpher op 16-10-2022, https://resolver.kb.nl/resolve?urn=MMSAA06:166461017:mpeg21:p00002.

[66] "Advertentie". "Amsterdamse courant". Amsterdam, 1724/11/16 00:00:00, p. 2. Geraadpleegd op Delpher op 24-12-2019, http://resolver.kb.nl/resolve?urn=ddd:010708606:mpeg21:p002; Advertentie. "Amsterdamse courant". Amsterdam, 1724/12/05 00:00:00, p. 2. Geraadpleegd op Delpher op 07-10-2019, http://resolver.kb.nl/resolve?urn=ddd:010708614:mpeg21:p002.

[67] Hell, *De Amsterdamse herberg 1450–1800*, there 85–86, 252, 254, 319.

Fig. 4 Newspaper advertisement for the payment of Life and Reedemable annuities (Source 1734-07-29 Amsterdamse Courant (Delpher))

When Schrader moved out, Jan Spyker moved in from the *Wapen van Deventer* (the Arms of Deventer), an inn only four doors away in *Warmoesstraat*.[68] He hosted the interest payments by both receivers until Knock relocated the payment of the redeemable annuities to *Het Wapen van Friesland*, in 1734. Knock's reason for relocating to this inn, run by Nicolaas Menkema, probably had to do with the role of the messengers, detailed below. As mentioned, the presence of Epeus Wielinga ended, when Jan Spyker died, in late 1736 or early 1737.

Wielinga permanently moved the interest payment over the life annuities to the *Oudezijds Heerenlogement*, except for 1743. That year Wielinga paid from the nearby *Kloveniersdoelen*, run by Johannes Hageman.[69] The proprietors of both establishments belonged to the more well-to-do bourgeoisie and were among the highest-earning tavern- and innkeepers.[70] The position of these two inns and their owners was not representative of the majority of inns, who belonged to the lower strata of society.[71] Perhaps the *Oudezijds Heerenlogement* was not available that year and he therefore had to move to another location on a one-off basis. For the rest, Wielinga continued to make all payments from that location until he died in 1784.

[68] "Advertentie". "Amsterdamse courant". Amsterdam, 1724/11/16 00:00:00, p. 2. Geraadpleegd op Delpher op 24-12-2019, http://resolver.kb.nl/resolve?urn=ddd:010708606:mpeg21:p002; Advertentie. "Amsterdamse courant". Amsterdam, 1724/12/21 00:00:00, p. 2. Geraadpleegd op Delpher op 07-10-2019, http://resolver.kb.nl/resolve?urn=ddd:010708621:mpeg21:p002.

[69] Advertentie. Amsterdamse courant. Amsterdam, 01-08-1743. Geraadpleegd op Delpher op 30-04-2016, http://resolver.kb.nl/resolve?urn=ddd:010712533:mpeg21:a0008; Advertentie. Amsterdamse courant. Amsterdam, 03-08-1743. Geraadpleegd op Delpher op 30-04-2016, http://resolver.kb.nl/resolve?urn=ddd:010712534:mpeg21:a0010.

[70] Hell, *De Amsterdamse herberg 1450–1800*, there 294–95.

[71] Hell, *De Amsterdamse herberg 1450–1800*, there 377–78.

Whereas Wielinga had permanently relocated, Knock returned to *Het Wapen van Groningen en Ommelanden*, in 1740. Jacoba Vermeulen, Jan Spyker's widow was remarried to Nicolaas Jans. Campstrup, who now ran the place. Knock paid until the temporary halt of payments in 1748–1750. Meanwhile, Camstrup and Vermeulen moved to The Hague in 1749.[72] *Het Wapen van Groningen en Ommelanden* was offered for rent.[73] A certain Dirk Smit relocated from the inn '*Mey Boom*' in the nearby street *Lange Niezel*.[74] Upon resumption of the personal interest payments, in 1751, the Friesland Receivers preferred other locations. Wielenga continued to pay from the *Oudezijds Heerenlogement*, Knock returned to Nicolaas Menkema.[75] Hence, the relocation of Jacoba

[72] "Advertentie". "Amsterdamse courant". Amsterdam, 1749/03/13 00:00:00, p. 2. Geraadpleegd op Delpher op 13-02-2020, http://resolver.kb.nl/resolve?urn=ddd:010714938:mpeg21:p002; Advertentie. "Opregte Groninger courant". Groningen, 1749/04/15 00:00:00, p. 2. Geraadpleegd op Delpher op 23-10-2019, http://resolver.kb.nl/resolve?urn=ddd:010410416:mpeg21:p002; "Advertentie". "Opregte Groninger courant". Groningen, 1749/04/29 00:00:00, p. 2. Geraadpleegd op Delpher op 13-02-2020, http://resolver.kb.nl/resolve?urn=ddd:010410420:mpeg21:p002; "Advertentie". "Amsterdamse courant". Amsterdam, 1749/05/03 00:00:00, p. 2. Geraadpleegd op Delpher op 13-02-2020, http://resolver.kb.nl/resolve?urn=ddd:010714960:mpeg21:p002; "Advertentie". "Opregte Groninger courant". Groningen, 1749/05/06 00:00:00, p. 2. Geraadpleegd op Delpher op 13-02-2020, http://resolver.kb.nl/resolve?urn=ddd:010410422:mpeg21:p002; "Advertentie". "Amsterdamse courant". Amsterdam, 1749/05/08 00:00:00, p. 2. Geraadpleegd op Delpher op 13-02-2020, http://resolver.kb.nl/resolve?urn=ddd:010714962:mpeg21:p002; "Advertentie". "'s Gravenhaegse courant". 's-Gravenhage, 1749/05/09 00:00:00, p. 2. Geraadpleegd op Delpher op 13-02-2020, http://resolver.kb.nl/resolve?urn=ddd:010725057:mpeg21:p002; Advertentie. "Oprechte Haerlemsche courant". Haerlem, 10-05-1749, p. 2. Geraadpleegd op Delpher op 03-12-2023, https://resolver.kb.nl/resolve?urn=ddd:010811460:mpeg21:p002; Advertentie. "'s Gravenhaegse courant". 's-Gravenhage, 16-05-1749, p. 2. Geraadpleegd op Delpher op 03-12-2023, https://resolver.kb.nl/resolve?urn=ddd:010725060:mpeg21:p002; "Advertentie". "'s Gravenhaegse courant". 's-Gravenhage, 1749/08/01 00:00:00, p. 2. Geraadpleegd op Delpher op 13-02-2020, http://resolver.kb.nl/resolve?urn=ddd:010725091:mpeg21:p002.

[73] Advertentie. "Amsterdamse courant". Amsterdam, 13-02-1749, p. 2. Geraadpleegd op Delpher op 03-12-2023, https://resolver.kb.nl/resolve?urn=ddd:010714926:mpeg21:p002.

[74] Advertentie. "Amsterdamse courant". Amsterdam, 15-05-1749, p. 2. Geraadpleegd op Delpher op 16-10-2022, https://resolver.kb.nl/resolve?urn=ddd:010714965:mpeg21:p002.

[75] Advertentie. "Amsterdamse courant". Amsterdam, 05-08-1751, p. 2. Geraadpleegd op Delpher op 19-06-2022, https://resolver.kb.nl/resolve?urn=MMSAA06:165538093:mpeg21:p00002; Advertentie. "Amsterdamse courant". Amsterdam, 04-09-1751, p. 2.

Vermeulen and Nicolaas Jans. Campstrup ended the position of *Het Wapen van Groningen en Ommelanden* as the preferred payment location for Friesland's debt.

The second type is the post office or messengers' office. The city messengers were appointed by the city council. As a daily service, they offered primarily to accept letters and packages that people could send to Friesland. In addition, these messengers traveled a few times per month to Leeuwarden. For such trips, they accepted bonds and money throughout the year.[76] The messengers to Friesland were not unique in offering financial services besides sending packages and letters, judging similar advertisements of Dirk ten Brink, messenger of the town of Nijmegen to Amsterdam. When in Amsterdam, he stayed in a place where a sign hung from the building that read that money, packages, and bonds could be sent and delivered.[77] Hence, the messengers offered a parallel service that was more flexible and constantly available than the interest payments that the Friesland tax receivers made once a year.

The relationship between messengers and innkeepers could be either competitive or cooperative. So far, four messengers are known from the sources. The first is Willem Onk. Living in the alley *Zoutsteeg*, he was probably the messenger, mentioned in the advertisement in 1713. In 1714, life annuity holders could turn to his office for payment in

Geraadpleegd op Delpher op 15-06-2022, https://resolver.kb.nl/resolve?urn=MMSAA06:165538106:mpeg21:p00002.

[76] Advertentie. Amsterdamse courant. Amsterdam, 03-12-1733. Accessed at Delpher 29-04-2016, http://resolver.kb.nl/resolve?urn=ddd:010710300:mpeg21:a0007; "Advertentie". "Amsterdamse courant". Amsterdam, 1748/01/02 00:00:00, p. 2. Geraadpleegd op Delpher op 09-03-2020, http://resolver.kb.nl/resolve?urn=ddd:010797660:mpeg21:p002; Advertentie. Amsterdamse courant. Amsterdam, 20-01-1748. Accessed at Delpher 29-04-2016, http://resolver.kb.nl/resolve?urn=ddd:010797668:mpeg21:a0009; Advertentie. "Amsterdamse courant". Amsterdam, 07-05-1750, p. 2. Geraadpleegd op Delpher op 01-04-2023, https://resolver.kb.nl/resolve?urn=MMSAA06:165536368:mpeg21:p00002.

[77] Advertentie. "Amsterdamse courant". Amsterdam, 10-08-1734, p. 2. Geraadpleegd op Delpher op 17-04-2023, https://resolver.kb.nl/resolve?urn=ddd:010710406:mpeg21:p002; Advertentie. "Amsterdamse courant". Amsterdam, 14-08-1734, p. 2. Geraadpleegd op Delpher op 18-04-2023, https://resolver.kb.nl/resolve?urn=ddd:010710408:mpeg21:p002.

May, before the payments were made by the Receiver Wielinga.[78] A few months later, Wielinga announced his coming to Amsterdam. He did not reside at the house of the messenger, however. Instead, he stayed and paid from the inn *Het Wapen van Groningen en Ommelanden.*[79] Here the messenger and the inn offered complementary and parallel services to the creditors and the tax receiver.

The second messenger is Jan van Schayk. He succeeded the deceased Willem Onk in late 1733.[80] Upon his appointment, he advertised that he was to deliver packages and collect bonds and money destined for Friesland. He held his office at the *Vergulde Zaal* (Golden Saloon) in the house of Mr. Munnikhof, in the *Oudezijds Armsteeg*, an alley off *Warmoesstraat*.[81] Again his service was parallel to the interest payments in the inns by the Friesland tax receivers.

This changed within a year. Both the messenger's office and the tax receiver of the redeemable annuities relocated to the inn, *Het Wapen van Friesland*, ran by master carpenter Nicolaas Menkema. This inn was located at *Nieuwzijds Voorburgwal*, opposite the New Church, on the west side of Dam Square. Upon moving the office, Van Schayk advertised that he also placed a letterbox, next to the entrance of the Amsterdam

[78] Advertentie. Oprechte Haerlemsche courant. Haerlem, 01-05-1714. Geraadpleegd op Delpher op 14-01-2017, http://resolver.kb.nl/resolve?urn=ddd:011220621:mpeg21:a0005; Advertentie. "Amsterdamse courant". Amsterdam, 01-05-1714, p. 2. Geraadpleegd op Delpher op 20-06-2022, https://resolver.kb.nl/resolve?urn=MMSAA06:166464052:mpeg21:p00002; Advertentie. "Amsterdamse courant". Amsterdam, 03-05-1714, p. 2. Geraadpleegd op Delpher op 20-06-2022, https://resolver.kb.nl/resolve?urn=MMSAA06:166464053:mpeg21:p00002.

[79] Advertentie. Oprechte Haerlemsche courant. Haerlem, 25-08-1714. Geraadpleegd op Delpher op 23-01-2017, http://resolver.kb.nl/resolve?urn=ddd:011220671:mpeg21:a0005. Although the source describes this venue as 'house', the rest suggests it was a public house or an inn.

[80] Advertentie. *Amsterdamse courant*. Amsterdam, 21–11-1733. Accessed at Delpher 29-04-2016, http://resolver.kb.nl/resolve?urn=ddd:010710295:mpeg21:a0005; Advertentie. "Amsterdamse courant". Amsterdam, 28-11-1733, p. 2. Geraadpleegd op Delpher op 17-11-2022, https://resolver.kb.nl/resolve?urn=ddd:010710298:mpeg21:p002; Advertentie. *Amsterdamse courant*. Amsterdam, 03-12-1733. Accessed at Delpher 29-04-2016, http://resolver.kb.nl/resolve?urn=ddd:010710300:mpeg21:a0007.

[81] Advertentie. *Amsterdamse courant*. Amsterdam, 05-12-1733. Accessed at Delpher 29-04-2016, http://resolver.kb.nl/resolve?urn=ddd:010710301:mpeg21:a0005.

Exchange, to the convenience of the merchants.[82] This implied an improvement of the existing service by Jan van Schayk. In a similar vein, the movement of the messengers' office suggests that attracting such offices in an inn may have been lucrative and hence subject to competition among innkeepers.

The other way around, the loss of certain functions may have caused Knock to return to *Het Wapen van Groningen and Ommelanden* in 1740, for arranging interest payments.[83] In 1739, no interest payments were advertised over the redeemable annuities.[84] By 1748, Nicolaas Menkema had left *Het Wapen van Friesland* behind and had begun to live as a butter merchant on *Nieuwedijk*.[85] When he took up his new occupation remains opaque. Yet considering that changes in staffing caused relocations in other cases, this may well explain why Knock returned to *Het Wapen van Groningen en Ommelanden*.

[82] Advertentie. "Amsterdamse courant". Amsterdam, 09-02-1734, p. 2. Geraadpleegd op Delpher op 17-04-2023, https://resolver.kb.nl/resolve?urn=ddd:010710328:mpeg21:p002; Advertentie. "Amsterdamse courant". Amsterdam, 11-02-1734, p. 2. Geraadpleegd op Delpher op 17-04-2023, https://resolver.kb.nl/resolve?urn=ddd:010710329:mpeg21:p002; Advertentie. Amsterdamse courant. Amsterdam, 27-07-1734. Geraadpleegd op Delpher op 30-04-2016, http://resolver.kb.nl/resolve?urn=ddd:010710400:mpeg21:a0005; "Familiebericht." "Amsterdamse courant". Amsterdam, 1738/08/05 00:00:00, p. 2. Geraadpleegd op Delpher op 23-10-2019, http://resolver.kb.nl/resolve?urn=ddd:010712379:mpeg21:p002.

[83] Advertentie. "Amsterdamse courant". Amsterdam, 1740/07/23 00:00:00, p. 2. Geraadpleegd op Delpher op 23-10-2019, http://resolver.kb.nl/resolve?urn=ddd:010713292:mpeg21:p002.

[84] I checked all the *Amsterdamse Couranten*, by hand from 15 June 1739 to 12 September 1739. In total 34 newspapers: 16-06-1739, 18-06-1739, 20-06-1739, 23-06-1739, 25-06-1739, 30-06-1739, 02-07-1739, 04-07-1739, 07-07-1739, 09-07-1739, 11-07-1739, 16-07-1739, 18-07-1739, 21-07-1739, 23-07-1739, 25-07-1739, 30-07-1739, 01-08-1739, 04-08-1739, 08-08-1739, 11-08-1739, 13-08-1739, 15-08-1739, 18-08-1739, 20-08-1739, 22-08-1739, 25-08-1739, 27-08-1739, 29-08-1739, 01-09-1739, 03-09-1739, 05-09-1739, 08-09-1739, 10-09-1739.

[85] In 1748, Nicolaas Menkema was now described as a 'butter merchant', no longer a Master Carpenter. Advertentie. Amsterdamse courant. Amsterdam, 20-01-1748. Accessed at Delpher 29-04-2016, http://resolver.kb.nl/resolve?urn=ddd:010797668:mpeg21:a0009; "Advertentie". "Amsterdamse courant". Amsterdam, 1748/01/23 00:00:00, p. 2. Geraadpleegd op Delpher op 21-10-2019, http://resolver.kb.nl/resolve?urn=ddd:010797669:mpeg21:p002; "Advertentie". "Amsterdamse courant". Amsterdam, 1748/01/25 00:00:00, p. 2. Geraadpleegd op Delpher op 21-10-2019, http://resolver.kb.nl/resolve?urn=ddd:010797670:mpeg21:p002.

This brings the third and fourth messengers to the story. In late 1747, Jan van Schayk died and was succeeded in the office by Pieter Bernard Texier. When advertising his appointment, he emphasized the collection of interest and only secondarily the sending and receiving of documents. He finally informed the general public that he relocated his office from 'behind the New Church' to *St. Luciensteeg*, an alley of *Kalverstraat*.[86] Simultaneously, a certain D. Tebbitman identified himself as Leeuwarden's city messenger to Amsterdam and advertised the continuation of paying and receiving interest payments in the house of Nicolaas Menkema, at *Nieuwendijk*.[87] Tebbitman had thus acted as Jan van Schayk's Frisian counterpart and hoped to take over this part of his business, following the latter's death.[88] This also implies that Nicolaas Menkema had retained some of the financial services in the network between Amsterdam and Friesland. In 1750, Texier relocated his post office again, to nearby the canal *Nieuwezijds Achterburgwal*.[89] This situation of two competing messengers and venues coincided with the paucity of advertisements by the Friesland tax receivers. Perhaps their parallel services provided just enough collection options to the creditors, while the Frisian tax receivers were desperately looking for new loans.

[86] The St. Luciensteeg runs between the *Kalverstraat* and the *Nieuwezijds Voorburgwal*, the office was the fourth house from the City Orphanage. "Advertentie". "Amsterdamse courant". Amsterdam, 1747/12/26 00:00:00, p. 2. Geraadpleegd op Delpher op 09-03-2020, http://resolver.kb.nl/resolve?urn=ddd:010797657:mpeg21:p002; Advertentie. "'s Gravenhaegse courant". 's-Gravenhage, 29-12-1747, p. 1. Geraadpleegd op Delpher op 13-04-2023, https://resolver.kb.nl/resolve?urn=ddd:010723213:mpeg21:p001; "Advertentie". "Amsterdamse courant". Amsterdam, 1748/01/02 00:00:00, p. 2. Geraadpleegd op Delpher op 09-03-2020, http://resolver.kb.nl/resolve?urn=ddd:010797660:mpeg21:p002.

[87] Advertentie. Amsterdamse courant. Amsterdam, 20-01-1748. Accessed at Delpher 29-04-2016, http://resolver.kb.nl/resolve?urn=ddd:010797668:mpeg21:a0009; "Advertentie". "Amsterdamse courant". Amsterdam, 1748/01/23 00:00:00, p. 2. Geraadpleegd op Delpher op 21-10-2019, http://resolver.kb.nl/resolve?urn=ddd:010797669:mpeg21:p002; "Advertentie". "Amsterdamse courant". Amsterdam, 1748/01/25 00:00:00, p. 2. Geraadpleegd op Delpher op 21-10-2019, http://resolver.kb.nl/resolve?urn=ddd:010797670:mpeg21:p002.

[88] Advertentie. "Amsterdamse courant". Amsterdam, 27-02-1744, p. 1. Geraadpleegd op Delpher op 02-04-2023, https://resolver.kb.nl/resolve?urn=ddd:010712619:mpeg21:p001.

[89] Advertentie. "Amsterdamse courant". Amsterdam, 07-05-1750, p. 2. Geraadpleegd op Delpher op 01-04-2023, https://resolver.kb.nl/resolve?urn=MMSAA06:165536368:mpeg21:p00002.

Neither receiver opted for a messenger or a post office when interest payments resumed. Wielinga resumed payments from the *Oudezijds Heerenlogement*. Knock returned to the hospitality of Nicolaas Menkema, this time in 'house at the front of *Nieuwendijk*'.[90] Nicolaas Menkema hosted the interest payments until he died in 1762 (Fig. 5).[91]

Fig. 5 Het Oude Zijds Herenlogement te Amsterdam, by G Berck Heyde, ca. 1660–1680 (Source RijksMuseum Amsterdam: SK-A-681 (Public domain))

[90] Advertentie. "Amsterdamse courant". Amsterdam, 04-09-1751, p. 2. Geraadpleegd op Delpher op 15-06-2022, https://resolver.kb.nl/resolve?urn=MMSAA06:165538106:mpeg21:p00002.

[91] The absence of the description may indicate that Nicolaas Menkema was primarily active as a butter merchant. "Advertentie". "Amsterdamse courant". Amsterdam, 1761/08/27 00:00:00, p. 2. Geraadpleegd op Delpher op 28-11-2019, http://resolver.kb.nl/resolve?urn=ddd:010708344:mpeg21:p002; Stads Archief Amsterdam (SAA, Amsterdam City Archive), Archief van de Burgerlijke Stand: doop-, trouw- en begraafboeken van Amsterdam (retroacta van de Burgerlijke Stand) (DTB, Toegang 5001), inv.nr. 1072 (Nicolaas Menkema is buried on 26 January 1762).

Texier reappeared in 1762 as the host for the interest payments over the redeemable annuities, until 1766.[92] The return of Texier facilitating the interest payments raises questions of why Johannes Menkema did not succeed his father Nicolaas and why he did in 1766. In other cases, an innkeeper's relatives advertised the continuation of the business, for example by the widow.[93] Perhaps Texier's promotion of his business drew the attention of the newly appointed Tax receiver, Bernhardus Hermanus Knock. At least, Texier advertised his service to pay interest on Friesland bonds, between the death of Nicolaas Menkema and the payment of the annual installment by the Tax receiver. To this end, bondholders and life annuity holders could turn daily to what he now described as the 'Frisian post office', instead of the messenger's office.[94] The relocation from 1766 cannot be attributed to changes on the part of Texier; he exploited the Frisian post office in Amsterdam until he died in 1789.[95] Rather, this must be attributed to changes on the part of the Friesland tax receivers, where Boreel van Haersma replaced B.H. Knock.

Moreover, Texier began an advertising campaign to promote his services in 1767, when Receiver Knock moved his business to the office of Johannes Menkema. It is not hard to imagine that this implied a loss for Texier. He put at least eight advertisements in three different newspapers. In these ads, he assured the bondholders an immediate service and emphasized that his post office was open five days a week, in the morning. He accepted a range of financial instruments, from bills of exchange to

[92] "Advertentie". "Amsterdamse courant". Amsterdam, 09-09-1762. Geraadpleegd op Delpher op 26-01-2017, http://resolver.kb.nl/resolve?urn=ddd:010709970:mpeg21:a0006.

[93] Advertentie. "Amsterdamse courant". Amsterdam, 15-12-1718, p. 2. Geraadpleegd op Delpher op 16-10-2022, https://resolver.kb.nl/resolve?urn=MMSAA06:165537150:mpeg21:p00002; Advertentie. "Amsterdamse courant". Amsterdam, 09-02-1719, p. 2. Geraadpleegd op Delpher op 16-10-2022, https://resolver.kb.nl/resolve?urn=MMSAA06:166461017:mpeg21:p00002; Advertentie. "Opregte Groninger courant". Groningen, 1749/04/15 00:00:00, p. 2. Geraadpleegd op Delpher op 23-10-2019, http://resolver.kb.nl/resolve?urn=ddd:010410416:mpeg21:p002.

[94] Advertentie. "Amsterdamse courant". Amsterdam, 23-03-1762, p. 2. Geraadpleegd op Delpher op 06-04-2023, https://resolver.kb.nl/resolve?urn=ddd:010709904:mpeg21:p002; Advertentie. "Amsterdamse courant". Amsterdam, 25-03-1762, p. 2. Geraadpleegd op Delpher op 06-04-2023, https://resolver.kb.nl/resolve?urn=ddd:010709905:mpeg21:p002.

[95] SAA, DTB, Inv.nr. 1072, f180r, (Pieter Bernard Texier 15 January 1789).

interest payments and *assignaties* ('paper money').[96] When he acquired the same function for the province of Groningen, in 1770, he issued similar promotion advertisements.[97] He nevertheless irreversibly lost his position to Johannes Menkema.

All this indicates competition among innkeepers and messengers to facilitate the payments of interest on the Friesland debt. The interest payments were made by the Friesland tax receivers themselves. For the issuance and reimbursement of the debt, they turned to official brokers as intermediaries. The inns and post offices functioned as natural nodes or hubs for travelers and correspondence in long-distance networks. Hence, the innkeepers facilitated a different service, mostly a place to stay and pay. Relocations often coincided with changes in staffing of either the inns or the public offices of the tax receivers. This suggests that such events opened negotiations about the terms and conditions of the hosting facilities and compensation, which was otherwise customarily continued. However, brokers, innkeepers, and messengers ultimately lost out to the office of Johannes Menkema, who offered the Friesland tax receivers a more specialist financial service.

[96] Advertentie. "Haerlemse courante". Haerlem, 07-07-1767, p. 2. Geraadpleegd op Delpher op 01-04-2023, https://resolver.kb.nl/resolve?urn=ddd:010799424:mpeg21:p002; Advertentie. "Oprechte Haerlemsche courant". Haerlem, 07-07-1767, p. 2. Geraadpleegd op Delpher op 06-04-2023, https://resolver.kb.nl/resolve?urn=ddd:011230968:mpeg21:p002; Advertentie. "Haerlemse courante". Haerlem, 11-07-1767, p. 2. Geraadpleegd op Delpher op 06-04-2023, https://resolver.kb.nl/resolve?urn=ddd:010799426:mpeg21:p002; Advertentie. "Leydse courant". Te Leyden, 15-07-1767, p. 2. Geraadpleegd op Delpher op 06-04-2023, https://resolver.kb.nl/resolve?urn=ddd:010911543:mpeg21:p002; Advertentie. "Haerlemse courante". Haerlem, 16-07-1767, p. 2. Geraadpleegd op Delpher op 06-04-2023, https://resolver.kb.nl/resolve?urn=ddd:010799428:mpeg21:p002; Advertentie. "Oprechte Haerlemsche courant". Haerlem, 16-07-1767, p. 2. Geraadpleegd op Delpher op 06-04-2023, https://resolver.kb.nl/resolve?urn=ddd:011230973:mpeg21:p002; Advertentie. "Leydse courant". Te Leyden, 17-07-1767, p. 2. Geraadpleegd op Delpher op 06-04-2023, https://resolver.kb.nl/resolve?urn=ddd:010911544:mpeg21:p002; Advertentie. "Oprechte Haerlemsche courant". Haerlem, 18-07-1767, p. 2. Geraadpleegd op Delpher op 06-04-2023, https://resolver.kb.nl/resolve?urn=ddd:011231132:mpeg21:p002.

[97] Advertentie. "Amsterdamse courant". Amsterdam, 15-03-1770, p. 2. Geraadpleegd op Delpher op 01-04-2023, https://resolver.kb.nl/resolve?urn=ddd:010713386:mpeg21:p002; Advertentie. "Leydse courant". Te Leyden, 16-03-1770, p. 2. Geraadpleegd op Delpher op 11-04-2023, https://resolver.kb.nl/resolve?urn=ddd:010911960:mpeg21:p002; Advertentie. "Amsterdamse courant". Amsterdam, 20-03-1770, p. 2. Geraadpleegd op Delpher op 11-04-2023, https://resolver.kb.nl/resolve?urn=ddd:010713388:mpeg21:p002.

5 Johannes Menkema

The question is why the Friesland Receivers shifted their payments from the inns and post offices to Menkema's office. As the son of Nicolaas Menkema, Johannes must have been familiar with the Friesland tax receivers' practices.[98] Yet he did not succeed in his father's business but started a business of his own in the early 1750s. He continued in this business until he died in 1797.[99] From the late 1770s, the firm is mostly referred to as Johannes Menkema and Son.[100] This section scrutinizes his business to understand why he eventually became Friesland's central intermediary.

Menkema's business consisted of at least four types of activities. The first is facilitating debt-related transactions for smaller public borrowers, such as interest payments. The second is trading securities for others.[101] The third is trading in securities for his own account. And finally, he also invested directly in projects. In the absence of a family archive, a patchwork of alternative sources offers insight into the development of his business.

Public debt was the first type of activity for Johannes Menkema when he started his business in late 1751 or early 1752. In July 1751, he purchased a house from the Widow L. Hobrink, at *Nieuwezijds Agterburgwal* between the alley *Stilsteeg* and *Huiszittensteeg*—this was opposite the New Church, almost neighboring Texier's post office and *Het Wapen van Friesland*.[102] He also took over at least three parts of their business. First, in January 1752, Menkema advertised that he was the successor in

[98] SAA, DTB, inv. nr. 592, p.125: Johannes Menkema married Anna Haring, soon after 31 January 1748, his father Nicolas acted as a witness. He married at the age of 21 since he was born on 17 January 1727: SSA, DTB Dopen, Inv. nr. 69, p. 373, folio195, nr. 5.

[99] The advertisement was made by the Widow Anna Munnikhuyzen, which implies that Johannes Menkema remarried. "Familiebericht". "Amsterdamse courant". Amsterdam, 30-05-1797, p. 4. Geraadpleegd op Delpher op 17-11-2022, https://resolver.kb.nl/resolve?urn=ddd:010716221:mpeg21:p004; "Familiebericht". "Rotterdamse courant". Rotterdam, 1797/06/03 00:00:00, p. 3. Geraadpleegd op Delpher op 03-12-2019, http://resolver.kb.nl/resolve?urn=ddd:010731718:mpeg21:p003.

[100] "Advertentie". "Haerlemse courante". Haerlem, 1779/12/14 00:00:00, p. 2. Geraadpleegd op Delpher op 01-12-2020, http://resolver.kb.nl/resolve?urn=ddd:010800586:mpeg21:p002.

[101] Riley, *International Government Finance*, there 44: Riley names Johannes Menkema as a trade relation of Hope & Co.

[102] SAA, 5062 Archief Schepenen: kwijtscheldingen, Inv.nr. 125, f. 208r.

the business of the Widow L. Hobrink and Sons, in arranging the interest payments from the lottery loan by the Dutch province of Zeeland.[103] He was not alone in this kind of offer, as in the same newspaper the brothers Jan and Dirk Wattens advertised a similar service, also in Amsterdam.[104] Secondly, he had taken over the debt service for the Saxon bonds from the office of Widow L. Hobrink.[105] Thirdly, the firm of Widow L. Hobrink and Sons had established a financial derivate, called *contract van overleving* (a private tontine loan: a mutual fund based on life annuities). Public bodies often relied on official brokers for issuing tontine loans, the *contracten van overleving* often involved alternative intermediaries.[106] This *contract* was established in 1750 and was based on a Saxony loan.[107] For some years, the firm of Hobrink continued to pay interest over the *contract van overleving*.[108] At least from 1764, Menkema had also taken over this financial instrument.[109] The business probably thrived, since in 1768 he announced that he would continue his 'office for the receipt

[103] The firm of the Widow L. Hobrink and Sons, yet offered some service to public bodies directly. At least, in 1748, the Quarter of Veluwe—part of the province of Gelderland—hired the form to issue a loan in Holland. Gelders Archief (GldA), 2000 Oud Archief Arnhem (OAA)' (n.d.) inv. nr. 5420.

[104] Advertentie. "Amsterdamse courant". Amsterdam, 01-01-1752, p. 2. Geraadpleegd op Delpher op 18-06-2022, https://resolver.kb.nl/resolve?urn=MMSAA06:165538157:mpeg21:p00002.

[105] Advertentie. "Amsterdamse courant". Amsterdam, 10-02-1752, p. 2. Geraadpleegd op Delpher op 07-11-2022, https://resolver.kb.nl/resolve?urn=MMSAA06:165538174:mpeg21:p00002.

[106] Herman Wagenvoort, *Tontines: een onderzoek naar de geschiedenis van de lijfrenten bij wijze van tontine en de contracten van overleving in de Republiek der Verenigde Nederlanden*, (Utrecht, 1961), there 21; Jonker, 'Klem 1', there 40.

[107] Advertentie. "Amsterdamse courant". Amsterdam, 30-07-1750, p. 2. Geraadpleegd op Delpher op 07-11-2022, https://resolver.kb.nl/resolve?urn=MMSAA06:165536404:mpeg21:p00002; Advertentie. "Amsterdamse courant". Amsterdam, 01-08-1750, p. 2. Geraadpleegd op Delpher op 08-11-2022, https://resolver.kb.nl/resolve?urn=MMSAA06:165536405:mpeg21:p00002.

[108] Advertentie. "Amsterdamse courant". Amsterdam, 22-01-1754, p. 2. Geraadpleegd op Delpher op 08-11-2022, https://resolver.kb.nl/resolve?urn=MMSAA06:165539010:mpeg21:p00002.

[109] Advertentie. "Amsterdamse courant". Amsterdam, 18-10-1764, p. 2. Geraadpleegd op Delpher op 08-11-2022, https://resolver.kb.nl/resolve?urn=ddd:010711044:mpeg21:p002.

of interests, etc.,' on the canal *Singel*.[110] Hence, Menkema began by acquiring activities from another firm, focused on privately collecting interest payments from debtors outside of Amsterdam.

His activities for the interest of Saxon *Steuer* deserve more detailed scrutiny. In February 1752, Menkema first called investors to bring their bonds to his office. Since the bonds had to be presented in Leipzig, he offered to travel there. A few months later, he called the investors again. This time he offered the payment of the 5% coupon. Meanwhile, he had traveled back and forth to Leipzig, to collect the interest personally for the Amsterdam investors.[111] A few years later, he called the investors to submit their bonds, so that he could send them to Leipzig, by mail.[112] Hence, his personal traveling was replaced by mail.

Later in the eighteenth century, he expanded his activities from the Electorate of Saxony to the city of Leipzig itself. In 1764, he acted as the underwriter of a loan for Leipzig issued in Amsterdam.[113] In 1780, Menkema and Son paid the interest and redemption for the bonds that had been drawn. The drawing of lots was done by a notary.[114] This shows a division of labor between an underwriter and a notary, thus fulfilling different functions. Later reimbursements did not involve a notary and

110 " "Advertentie". "Leydse courant". Te Leyden, 1768/01/18 00:00:00, p. 2. Geraadpleegd op Delpher op 17-06-2020, http://resolver.kb.nl/resolve?urn=ddd:010911622:mpeg21:p002.

111 Advertentie. "Amsterdamse courant". Amsterdam, 02-09-1752, p. 2. Geraadpleegd op Delpher op 18-04-2023, https://resolver.kb.nl/resolve?urn=MMSAA06:165538262:mpeg21:p00002.

112 Advertentie. "Oprechte Haerlemsche courant". Haerlem, 14-02-1764, p. 2. Geraadpleegd op Delpher op 20-04-2023, https://resolver.kb.nl/resolve?urn=ddd:011230731:mpeg21:p002.

113 Familiebericht. "Oprechte Haerlemsche courant". Haerlem, 26-01-1769, p. 2. Geraadpleegd op Delpher op 20-04-2023, https://resolver.kb.nl/resolve?urn=MMNHA02:164950011:mpeg21:p00002.

114 Advertentie. "Oprechte Haerlemsche courant". Haerlem, 10-10-1780, p. 2. Geraadpleegd op Delpher op 18-04-2023, https://resolver.kb.nl/resolve?urn=ddd:010800715:mpeg21:p002.

were wholly arranged by Menkema and Son.[115] The lasting relationship with Leipzig, even continued after Johannes senior died in 1797.[116]

Menkema's involvement with German polities exceeded than the strong connection with the Electorate of Saxony and its capital city of Leipzig. At least two other German polities relied on his services. The first was the German town of Embden, in East Frisia, and the second was the principality Anhalt-Cöthen. For Embden, he acted as a correspondent for investors in Amsterdam. He collected the bonds, sent them to Embden, and paid interest when he received them back.[117] This did not always go well. In 1756, Menkema called investors to convene at the inn *Het Hof van Holland*, in *Kalverstraat*, to discuss the matter. Investors who wished to participate first had to obtain a ticket from his office in the morning.[118] He presumably planned to coordinate the action of a lenders' coalition in response to a default.[119]

For the German Prince of Anhalt-Cöthen, he facilitated the issue of a loan, in 1769, whereto the investors could collect the scrips in anticipation of the official bonds.[120] The loan ran at least until 1791 when

[115] Advertentie. "Amsterdamse courant". Amsterdam, 30-05-1786, p. 2. Geraadpleegd op Delpher op 14-11-2022, https://resolver.kb.nl/resolve?urn=ddd:010718401:mpeg21:p002.

[116] Advertentie. "Oprechte Haarlemse courant". Haarlem, 31-10-1799, p. 3. Geraadpleegd op Delpher op 21-04-2023, https://resolver.kb.nl/resolve?urn=ddd:010729468:mpeg21:p003.

[117] Advertentie. "Leydse courant". Te Leyden, 27-09-1754, p. 2. Geraadpleegd op Delpher op 14-11-2022, https://resolver.kb.nl/resolve?urn=ddd:010909914:mpeg21:p002; Advertentie. "Amsterdamse courant". Amsterdam, 01-01-1756, p. 2. Geraadpleegd op Delpher op 14-11-2022, https://resolver.kb.nl/resolve?urn=ddd:010715064:mpeg21:p002.

[118] Advertentie. "Oprechte Haerlemsche courant". Haerlem, 01-04-1756, p. 2. Geraadpleegd op Delpher op 18-04-2023, https://resolver.kb.nl/resolve?urn=ddd:011224408:mpeg21:p002.

[119] Rui Esteves, 'Quis Custodiet Quem? Sovereign Debt and Bondholders' Protection Before 1914', in: *SSRN Electronic Journal*, (2007); Flandreau and Flores, 'Bonds and Brands', there 649; Jonker, *Merchants, Bankers, Middlemen*, there 157.

[120] Advertentie. "Amsterdamse courant". Amsterdam, 08-06-1769, p. 2. Geraadpleegd op Delpher op 18-04-2023, https://resolver.kb.nl/resolve?urn=ddd:010712976:mpeg21:p002; Advertentie. "Oprechte Haerlemsche courant". Haerlem, 17-06-1769, p. 2. Geraadpleegd op Delpher op 14-11-2022, https://resolver.kb.nl/resolve?urn=MMNHA02:164950072:mpeg21:p00002.

Menkema and Son partially repaid it.[121] In 1770, Menkema grouped the announcement of interest payments for various debtors: Friesland, Anhalt-Cöthen, and Leipzig. Each could turn to his office to receive the installment on the respective maturity dates: a whole year for Friesland and Leipzig, half a year from the Prince of Anhalt-Cöthen.[122] By 1770, he thus cared for loans of smaller public borrowers within the German Empire and the Dutch province of Friesland.

Within the Dutch Republic, he also continued to extend his business. Around 1780, he appeared as an intermediary for the Holland town of Medemblik, concerning a loan issue.[123] More importantly, in 1774 Menkema was appointed *'agendaris'* (agent) of the province of Zeeland.[124] Whereas in 1752 he had still privately arranged the interest payment, he now held an official position. The bankers Abraham and Simeon Boas fulfilled a similar position in The Hague.[125] In this capacity, Menkema paid the interest on Zeeland bonds in Amsterdam. Moreover, potential investors could consult the conditions over Zeeland's proposed loan issue for new 2.5%-bonds in 1775.[126] Menkema and Sons continued to service Zeeland's debt in Amsterdam at least until 1797 with their

[121] Advertentie. "Oprechte Haerlemsche courant". Haerlem, 28-04-1791, p. 3. Geraadpleegd op Delpher op 17-11-2022, https://resolver.kb.nl/resolve?urn=ddd:010801162:mpeg21:p003.

[122] Advertentie. "Leydse courant". Te Leyden, 23-04-1770, p. 2. Geraadpleegd op Delpher op 14-11-2022, https://resolver.kb.nl/resolve?urn=ddd:010911977:mpeg21:p002.

[123] Advertentie. "Amsterdamse courant". Amsterdam, 02-10-1781, p. 2. Geraadpleegd op Delpher op 25-09-2022, https://resolver.kb.nl/resolve?urn=ddd:010813223:mpeg21:p002.

[124] Advertentie. "Oprechte Haerlemsche courant". Haerlem, 02-08-1774, p. 2. Geraadpleegd op Delpher op 21-04-2023, https://resolver.kb.nl/resolve?urn=ddd:010800371:mpeg21:p002.

[125] Advertentie. "Amsterdamse courant". Amsterdam, 25-06-1789, p. 2. Geraadpleegd op Delpher op 17-10-2022, https://resolver.kb.nl/resolve?urn=ddd:010716071:mpeg21:p002.

[126] Advertentie. "Haarlemse Courant". Haarlem, 11-07-1775, p. 2. Geraadpleegd op Delpher op 16-11-2021, https://resolver.kb.nl/resolve?urn=ddd:010799113:mpeg21:p002; Advertentie. "Oprechte Haerlemsche courant". Haerlem, 27-02-1776, p. 2. Geraadpleegd op Delpher op 14-11-2022, https://resolver.kb.nl/resolve?urn=MMNHA02:164953196:mpeg21:p00002.

official status as *agendarissen*.[127] Each of the agencies Menkema entered into resulted in long-term and stable relationships, implying that he was a reliable partner who offered what these public debtors were looking for.

Menkema was not unique. Two consecutive advertisements in the *Amsterdamse Courant* of 18 October 1764 offer another glimpse into the practices of debt service in Amsterdam. First, the broker Jan Wattens announced the payment of the coupons over the Saxon *Steuer*. Then, Menkema announced the same, yet added the payment of other loans too. The first is the payment of interest over bills of exchange issued by the heads of merchants in Leipzig. Then, he called entitled parties to collect their interest, concerning a *contract van overleving* founded by the firm of Widow L. Hobrink and Sons.[128]

Also, the more famous merchant banking houses announced similar interest payments in newspapers. For instance, in 1765 Clifford and Sons advertised the interest payments on Austrian redeemable annuities and life annuities, issued by the same firm and the merchant bank house of Deutz.[129] In 1774, the firm of Andries Pels & Sons advertised the interest payments concerning the city of Hamburg, in Germany. In this case, the cashier Johannes van der Hooght made the actual interest payment.[130] Here, we see a division of labor between a payment window and the underwriting banker. Despite the difference in hierarchy in the Amsterdam capital market, the method to inform creditors was similar to that of Friesland as a smaller public debtor.

Competition in servicing the interest over the Saxon *Steuer* loans meanwhile remained and was even more intensive than in 1764. On 19 August 1776, no less than six intermediaries advertised the payment of interest on this loan: Jan Wattens, Abraham van Ketwich, Brunel and

[127] Advertentie. "Haagsche courant". 's Gravenhage, 22-03-1797, p. 2. Geraadpleegd op Delpher op 18-04-2023, https://resolver.kb.nl/resolve?urn=ddd:010808177:mpeg21:p002.

[128] Advertentie. "Amsterdamse courant". Amsterdam, 18-10-1764, p. 2. Geraadpleegd op Delpher op 08-11-2022, https://resolver.kb.nl/resolve?urn=ddd:010711044:mpeg21:p002.

[129] NEDERLANDEN.. "Oprechte Haerlemsche courant". Haerlem, 18-06-1765, p. 1. Geraadpleegd op Delpher op 13-05-2022, https://resolver.kb.nl/resolve?urn=ddd:011231280:mpeg21:p001.

[130] Advertentie. "Oprechte Haerlemsche courant". Haerlem, 28-07-1774, p. 2. Geraadpleegd op Delpher op 10-04-2023, https://resolver.kb.nl/resolve?urn=MMNHA02:164952259:mpeg21:p00002.

Brothers, Wouter Zeelt, Johannes Menkema, and Eberlein and Joukes. Each announced that creditors could obtain interest payments in their respective offices. Except for Menkema, each of them identified themselves as 'brokers'.[131] Offering an identical financial service suggests that even though Menkema was not a broker, he was no stranger in the social circles of Amsterdam's financial sector.

During the 1770s and 1780s, the firm of Menkema and Son acted as commission agents for Amsterdam's most prominent banking house Hope & Co. The latter relied on some fifty intermediaries to market larger loans issued for Sweden, Poland, Russia, and Spain. Menkema and Son subscribed for almost 2 million guilders, which made it one of the more active and important commission agents.[132] This implies on one hand that he possessed a personal network that was large enough to absorb such large amounts of public debt. On the other hand, this made him valuable for Amsterdam's most prominent banker, which implied a good reputation.

Menkema's second type of business was catering investments of private persons, outside of Amsterdam. He, for instance, handled the securities for the Widow, Jacoba Catharina van Schoonhoven, from Rotterdam. She possessed Friesland bonds and 2% Dutch East India Company (VOC) bonds from the chambers in Amsterdam and Enkhuizen. The payment of 2% interest over the Friesland bonds, concerned 1764 and was paid in 1769, which confirms the standard delay. Menkema reserved a small fee for himself for handling it. For the purchase of Austrian bonds, in 1766, Menkema paid a fee to a broker.[133] Hence, there was a division of labor between him and the broker and Menkema's function may best described as a correspondent.

Similarly, the firm of Menkema and Son arranged several transactions for the nobleman, Baron Dedem in the town of Zwolle in the province of Overijssel. Most transactions concern the collection of interest over various loans. This included French and Russian life annuities, interest

[131] Advertentie. "Leydse courant". Te Leyden, 19-08-1776, p. 2. Geraadpleegd op Delpher op 11-04-2023, https://resolver.kb.nl/resolve?urn=ddd:010912962:mpeg21:p002.

[132] Riley, *International Government Finance*, there 44–45; Marten Gerbertus Buist, *At Spes Non Fracta: Hope and Co. 1770–1815, Merchant Bankers and Diplomats at Work* (Den Haag, 1974), there 498–501.

[133] NL-HaNA, Van der Staal van Piershil, 1636–1904, inv.nr. 364.

over loans by Zeeland, Anhalt-Cöthen, and Mecklenburg in Germany, and even French-Canadian loans. Menkema recorded all transactions for the Baron in a current account. This record shows on the one hand the purchases and expenses Menkema made and on the other hand the income from the investments. The expenses included a fee or commission for Menkema, as a reward for his services. These transactions not only concerned securities; the firm also purchased wine for the Baron. Surpluses on the current account were transferred by bills of exchange.[134] The combination of trade in both commodities and securities suggests that he fits in a larger group of merchants that did so in exchange for a fee or commission from his clients.[135] The banking activities of the major bankers generally emerged from trading activities and were hence not created as deposit-taking institutions.[136]

Thirdly, Menkema's trade in securities was not limited to trading for others. He appears to have been an active trader for himself. For instance, in March 1763, he sold two Austrian bonds he purchased a week before. Menkema is referred to as 'merchant' in the notarial deed.[137] Also in 1766, he sold bonds and identified himself as a merchant. This time it concerned Union bonds issued by the States-General's Receiver.[138] Between 1749 and 1797, his name showed up at least 530 times in the notarial archives in Amsterdam; in 1766 alone he appeared 39 times.[139]

[134] Collectie Overijssel, Toegang 1447.1 Dedem, familie Van, Huis den Berg te Dalfsen, Inv.nr.287.

[135] Jonker, *Merchants, Bankers, Middlemen*, 146; Riley, *International Government Finance*, there 44.

[136] Jonker and Sluyterman, *Thuis op de wereldmarkt*; Jonker, 'Klem 1'; Jonker, 'Klem 2'; Dickson, *Finance and Government under Maria Theresia 1740–1780*, there 42; Tomz, *Reputation and International Cooperation.*

[137] SAA, 5075 Notarieel Archief, Inv.nr. 14,079, aktenummer 250,903, 25 March 1763.

[138] SAA, Notariële archieven 5075, inventarisnummer 14,090, aktenummer 283,743, 3juni 1766 "Koopman in deze stede".

[139] SAA, https://archief.amsterdam/indexen/persons?f=%7B%22search_i_datum%22:%7B%22v%22:%5B%2217270000%22,%2217979999%22%5D,%22d%22:%221727%20-%201797%22%7D%7D&ss=%7B%22q%22:%22johannes%20menkema%22%7D&sa=%7B%22person_1%22:%7B%22search_t_geslachtsnaam%22:%22Menkema%22,%22search_t_voornaam%22:%22Johannes%22%7D,%22search_s_register_type_title%22:%5B%22Boedelpapieren%22,%22Notari%C3%ABle%20archieven%22%5D%7D&sort=%7B%22order_i_datum%22:%22asc%22%7D&rows=250.

Since only a fraction of the securities trade was recorded with the notaries, his business must have been substantial.[140] A more detailed study would be worthwhile exploring in future research to reveal how much he traded as a commission agent and how much for his own account.

Finally, Menkema also was involved in direct investment, in this case with partners. In 1780, Menkema established a new society with Abraham van Ketwich, to finance a land reclamation project in the Austrian Low Countries. The project consisted of an investment of 250,000 guilders, divided over 1800 shares. The planning had been on the way for some time, as the first concepts dated back to 1771.[141] Already in 1779, Baron van Dedem, mentioned above, made a 1,000 guilders investment in *Moerland*.[142] Menkema's partner Van Ketwich was a well-known broker and merchant, who had established the first mutual fund in 1774.[143] This confirms that Menkema commanded a good network and was considered a serious partner within Amsterdam's financial circles (Fig. 6).

5.1 Friesland Debt Handling

When Menkema became the correspondent for Friesland in 1767, he introduced improvements to creditors, probably building on previous experiences for German debtors. Firstly, he expanded the interest payments to Haarlem, which were paid from the house of a broker that was part of his network.[144] Secondly, the overdue term was reduced

[140] Gelderblom, Hup, and Jonker, 'Public Functions, Private Markets'.

[141] SAA, Toegang 600, Archief van de Firma Ketwich & Voomberg en Wed. W. Borski, Inv.nr. 771, 791,

[142] Collectie Overijssel, Toegang 1447.1 Dedem, familie Van, Huis den Berg te Dalfsen, Inv.nr.287.

[143] K. Geert Rouwenhorst, 'The Origins of Mutual Funds', in: William N. Goetzmann and K. Geert Rouwenhorst, *The Origins of Value: The Financial Innovations That Created Modern Capital Markets*, (Oxford, 2005), there 249–269; Jonker, 'Klem 2', there 65; Jonker, *Merchants, Bankers, Middlemen*, there 146.

[144] Advertentie. "Leydse courant". Te Leyden, 21-10-1768, p. 2. Geraadpleegd op Delpher op 26-10-2022, https://resolver.kb.nl/resolve?urn=ddd:010911741:mpeg21:p002; Advertentie. Oprechte Haerlemsche courant. Haerlem, 23-11-1784. Geraadpleegd op Delpher op 15-09-2016, http://resolver.kb.nl/resolve?urn=ddd:010802288:mpeg21:a0008; "Advertentie". "Oprechte Haerlemsche courant". Haerlem, 1788/11/11 00:00:00, p. 2. Geraadpleegd op Delpher op 03-12-2019, http://resolver.kb.nl/resolve?urn=ddd:010801715:mpeg21:p002.

Fig. 6 Johannes Menkema (1727–1797) (Source https://www.geneanet.org/media/public/johannesmenkema-6917846)

by six months. Thirdly, Menkema sometimes paid the interest himself, for instance in November 1767 when he first assumed his position for Friesland.[145] Fourthly, he offered additional services besides the interest payments. For instance, those liable for the Death Taxes (*Collaterale Successie*) over Frisian bonds could make the payment at his office.[146] For this matter, he was the central address, although people could also turn to alternative addresses in towns outside of Amsterdam.[147] Menkema

145 Advertentie. *Amsterdamse courant*. Amsterdam, 17-11-1767. Geraadpleegd op Delpher op 29-04-2016, http://resolver.kb.nl/resolve?urn=ddd:010711639:mpeg21:a0009.

146 Advertentie. *Haerlemse courante*. Haerlem, 03-12-1767. Accessed at Delpher 15-09-2016, http://resolver.kb.nl/resolve?urn=ddd:010799488:mpeg21:a0008.

147 "Advertentie". "Haerlemse courante". Haerlem, 1768/09/27 00:00:00, p. 2. Geraadpleegd op Delpher op 01-12-2020, http://resolver.kb.nl/resolve?urn=ddd:010799771:mpeg21:p002.

offered Friesland tax receivers more comprehensive financial services than innkeepers and post office holders, was more accommodating toward creditors, and had good connections within Amsterdam's financial circles.

This cannot be separated from Friesland's re-entry to the Amsterdam capital market. Although Friesland's consistency in its belated payments offered the creditors some surety, Menkema's involvement might have been precisely the necessary part that allowed for a return on the Amsterdam capital market. In 1770, Friesland issued a 3% loan from the office of Menkema.[148] Contrary to the pre-1711 debt, these new loans were tax-exempt and promptly paid. From then on, Menkema's office facilitated the payment of the coupons of this new loan next to the old pre-1711 debt.[149]

Menkema's services concerning life annuities were only called in from 1785 onwards. Epeus Wielinga continued to pay the annuities from *Oudezijds Heerenlogement* until his death. A few years prior he issued new annuities, in Friesland, with subscriptions only open in in Leeuwarden.[150] Also under his successor as Receiver of the life annuities, Baron Van Plettenberg, Friesland did not return to Amsterdam for the issuance of life annuities. Van Plettenberg, did, however, relocate the interest payments to Johannes Menkema, in 1785.[151]

[148] Advertentie". "*Oprechte Haerlemsche courant*". Haerlem, 18-07-1771. Accessed at Delpher 30-01-2017, http://resolver.kb.nl/resolve?urn=ddd:010799898:mpeg21:a0007.

[149] Advertentie. Amsterdamse courant. Amsterdam, 26-07-1774. Accessed at Delpher 30-04-2016, http://resolver.kb.nl/resolve?urn=ddd:010714372:mpeg21:a0014; "Advertentie". "Amsterdamse courant". Amsterdam, 29-07-1777. Geraadpleegd op Delpher op 31-01-2017, http://resolver.kb.nl/resolve?urn=ddd:010712219:mpeg21:a0007; "Advertentie". "Oprechte Haarlemsche courant". Haarlem, 02-08-1777. Geraadpleegd op Delpher op 31-01-2017, http://resolver.kb.nl/resolve?urn=ddd:010798810:mpeg21:a0003; "Advertentie". "Oprechte Haarlemsche courant". Haarlem, 28-07-1778. Geraadpleegd op Delpher op 31-01-2017, http://resolver.kb.nl/resolve?urn=ddd:010798651:mpeg21:a0006; "Advertentie". "Amsterdamse courant". Amsterdam, 31-07-1779. Geraadpleegd op Delpher op 31-01-2017, http://resolver.kb.nl/resolve?urn=ddd:010712843:mpeg21:a0009.

[150] Advertentie. Leeuwarder courant. Leeuwarden, 02-08-1783. Geraadpleegd op Delpher op 30-04-2016, http://resolver.kb.nl/resolve?urn=ddd:010576349:mpeg21:a0004; Advertentie. Leeuwarder courant. Leeuwarden, 09-08-1783. Geraadpleegd op Delpher op 30-04-2016, http://resolver.kb.nl/resolve?urn=ddd:010576351:mpeg21:a0004.

[151] Advertentie. Amsterdamse courant. Amsterdam, 23-07-1785. Geraadpleegd op Delpher op 15-09-2016, http://resolver.kb.nl/resolve?urn=ddd:010715927:mpeg21:a0009; Advertentie. Amsterdamse courant. Amsterdam, 26-07-1785. Geraadpleegd

Arguably the best illustration of Johannes Menkema's commanding position for Friesland is the issuance of another 3% loan, in 1782. The province announced that it would float a one-million-guilder loan, in Amsterdam from the office of Menkema and Son.[152] What is most striking is the absence of the option to subscribe to the loan, within Friesland. An advertisement in Friesland's capital Leeuwarden that year underlines this. A certain R. Storm, a 'bonds merchant', in Leeuwarden offered the sale of 3% Friesland bonds that were issued by the office of Johannes Menkema and Son in Amsterdam. Investors could purchase these bonds for 99.75% of the face value.[153] The advertisement by stock jobber Storm suggests that these bonds must have been in demand in Leeuwarden too. Furthermore, Storm must have been able to purchase the bonds at a price below 99.75% of the face value, assuming that he was a professional profit-seeking businessman. And, if so, Menkema would have sold the bonds below the nominal value and hence created a certain run-up profit for professional investors, which is much similar to the technique used in London, some forty years later.[154] In 1795, the year of the 'old' Dutch Republic's dissolution, creditors could turn to his office for the rollover of the 1782 loan against 3.5%.[155] Menkema was thus not merely a payment window, but a professional financial who offered a specialized service that incited Friesland to issue debt entirely outside their jurisdiction, in Amsterdam. From this central point, he sold and distributed this in his network.

Menkema's office had become indispensable for Friesland's relation to the Amsterdam capital market in the latter part of the eighteenth century. It facilitated Friesland's return to the Amsterdam capital market,

op Delpher op 25-01-2017, http://resolver.kb.nl/resolve?urn=ddd:010715928:mpeg21:a0006.

152 NEDERLANDEN.. "Amsterdamse courant". Amsterdam, 13-04-1782, p. 1. Geraadpleegd op Delpher op 13-04-2023, https://resolver.kb.nl/resolve?urn=ddd:010714484:mpeg21:p001.

153 "Advertentie". "Leeuwarder courant". Leeuwarden, 1782/05/18 00:00:00, p. 5. Geraadpleegd op Delpher op 13-02-2020, http://resolver.kb.nl/resolve?urn=ddd:010576224:mpeg21:p005.

154 Flandreau and Flores, 'Bonds and Brands'.

155 Advertentie. *Amsterdamse courant*. Amsterdam, 16-04-1795. Geraadpleegd op Delpher op 15-09-2016, http://resolver.kb.nl/resolve?urn=ddd:010716520:mpeg21:a0008

by issuing new loans, debt service, prolongations, and above all understanding financial techniques. In this way, his office offered more and different to the Frisian tax collectors than the post office keepers and innkeepers had done. Perhaps he also offered a place to sleep, but that was not the reason to use his office. Instead, he was part of the Amsterdam financial circles, yet he was not part of this first-ranking group.

6 Conclusion

This chapter examined the question of how smaller non-domestic public debtors operated on the Amsterdam capital market in the eighteenth century. The case of the Dutch province of Friesland shows that even in this large and impersonal market, people and their mutual relations continued to matter, even though the scale of the loans forbade them from knowing all of the creditors. The focus on the venues and their proprietors demonstrates an evolution in payment methods in the eighteenth century. This changed from the dependency on brokers and innkeepers to the office of Johannes Menkema, which functioned as a one-stop shop.

Around 1700, brokers were the main intermediaries for loan issues. Friesland's default reduced their importance because creditors would no longer lend the province any money. They must have had a role in failed loan issues of 1725–1726 and around 1750. Yet the outcome was that the market, and hence their networks, did not absorb the proposed loans. Temporarily, Friesland relied on fiscal intermediation of Holland and the States-General to obtain loans despite the credit rationing it encountered. The reputation of Friesland prevented other forms of borrowing and even negatively affected Holland's reputation.

The consistency of the annual interest payments must have improved Friesland's reputation in the Amsterdam capital market. The tax receivers paid the interest on the provincial debt in person in Amsterdam, mostly by members of two families. They did so from various inns, which sometimes also hosted messengers or post offices. Both functioned as physical nodes or hubs in long-distance networks. Relocations were primarily related to changes in the staffing of either innkeepers or tax receivers. The advantage of messengers was that their presence was more continuous than the annual payments by the Friesland tax receivers. Either way, the service of both inns and post offices was largely practically facilitating and not so much financial. This was in part because Friesland did little else than make interest payments. Innkeepers and messengers eventually had to concede their position as hosts and facilitators to the specialist service of financial agent Johannes Menkema.

He started his business in 1751 as a facilitator of interest payments of various smaller public debtors. He did not succeed his father Nicolaas Menkema who had facilitated Friesland's interest payments until 1762. Meanwhile, Johannes Menkema gradually expanded his business and became well-known within Amsterdam's financial circles. His position was of second rank. There was a clear hierarchy in the Amsterdam capital market in the second half of the eighteenth century. On top were the major merchant bankers, followed by brokers and commission agents, including Johannes Menkema. As a commission agent for Hope & Co., he marketed the loan issues, since he possessed a network that could absorb and distribute the large amounts involved in that trade. Hence, when Menkema took over the interest payments for Friesland in 1767, he had something to offer.

The firm of Johannes Menkema & Son formed the necessary link between the world of High Finance and smaller non-domestic debtors. Major merchant banking houses, like Clifford & Sons and Pels, provided short-term credit to Friesland for troop payments, they did not underwrite provincial loans, as they did for major European powers. This suggests specialization, and segmentation of the market for sovereign debt, where the large banking houses served the major powers and second-rank financial intermediaries second-rank sovereign debtors. Next to that, there was also a division of labor. Notaries primarily registered public and private financial transactions, brokers matched buyers and sellers on the Amsterdam Exchange and possessed valuable information about market developments. The firm of Johannes Menkema & Son worked with all of these other intermediaries, based on their respective specialisms to service its public and private clients. Menkema & Son not only had a good reputation, but it also commanded a network that was able to absorb serious amounts of debt, which made it invaluable for Friesland as a smaller debtor state.

References

Primary Sources

List of newspaper in the database:

Amsterdamse courant: 1688-4-29, 1689-5-19, 1689-7-26, 1694-7-15, 1695-12-20, 1695-12-27, 1701-9-10, 1701-9-13, 1704-11-25, 1705-3-24, 1705-8-6, 1705-8-29, 1706-1-21, 1707-7-23, 1708-2-11, 1709-3-28, 1710-3-18, 1712-3-12, 1713-12-7, 1713-12-9, 1714-5-1, 1714-5-3, 1714-12-11, 1715-1-26, 1715-3-23, 1718-12-15, 1719-2-9, 1724-1-16, 1724-2-5, 1724-2-21, 1733-11-21, 1733-11-28, 1733-12-3, 1733-12-5, 1734-2-9, 1734-2-11, 1734-7-27, 1734-8-10, 1734-8-14, 1737-2-5, 1737-2-12, 1737-2-19, 1737-2-21, 1738-7-1, 1738-8-5, 1740-7-23, 1743-8-1, 1743-8-3, 1744-2-27, 1747-2-26, 1748-1-2, 1748-1-20, 1748-1-23, 1748-1-25, 1749-2-13, 1749-3-13, 1749-5-3, 1749-5-8, 1749-5-15, 1750-5-7, 1750-7-30, 1750-8-1, 1751-8-5, 1751-9-4, 1752-1-1, 1752-2-10, 1752-9-2, 1754-1-22, 1756-1-1, 1761-8-27, 1762-3-23, 1762-3-25, 1762-9-9, 1764-10-18, 1767-11-17, 1769-6-8, 1770-3-15, 1770-3-20, 1774-7-26, 1777-7-29, 1779-7-31, 1781-10-2, 1782-4-13, 1785-7-23, 1785-7-26, 1786-5-30, 1789-6-25, 1795-4-16, 1797-5-30

Haagsche courant: 1797-3-22

Haerlemse courante: 1767-7-7, 1767-7-11, 1767-12-3, 1768-9-27, 1775-7-11, 1779-2-14.

Leeuwarder courant: 1782-5-18, 1783-8-2, 1783-8-9

Leydse courant: 1738-6-30, 1754-9-27, 1767-7-15, 1768-10-21, 1768-1-18, 1770-3-16, 1770-4-23, 1776-8-19.

Oprechte Haerlemsche courant: 1780-10-10, 1784-11-23, 1788-1-11, 1791-4-28, 1799-10-31, 1693-11-3, 1695-12-29, 1712-3-3, 1712-3-15, 1714-8-25, 1749-5-10, 1756-4-1, 1764-2-14, 1765-6-18, 1769-1-26, 1769-6-17, 1771-7-18, 1774-7-28, 1774-8-2, 1776-2-27, 1777-8-2, 1778-7-28.

Opregte Groninger courant: 1749-4-15, 1749-4-29, 1749-5-6.

Rotterdamse courant: 1797-6-3

's Gravenhaegse courant: 1712-3-7, 1737-3-11, 1747-12-29, 1749-5-16, 1749-5-9, 1749-8-1.

Archival Collections

Collectie Overijssel, Toegang 1447.1 Dedem, familie Van, Huis den Berg te Dalfsen, Inv.nr.287.

Gelders Archief (GldA), 2000 Oud Archief Arnhem (OAA), inv. nr. 5420.

Nationaal Archief, Den Haag (NL-HaNA), Provinciale resoluties, inv.nr. 484

NL-HaNA, Van der Staal van Piershil, 1636–1904, inv.nr. 364.

NL-HaNA, Staten van Holland, inv.nr. 5121
Regionaal Historisch Centrum, Groninger Archief (RHC-GrA), Archieven der Staten van Stad en Lande (SvSL), inv.nr. 96
Stads Archief Amsterdam (SAA, Amsterdam City Archive), Archief van de Burgerlijke Stand: doop-,
trouw- en begraafboeken van Amsterdam (retroacta van de Burgerlijke Stand) (Toegang 5001), inv.nr. 1072.
SAA, Notariële archieven 5075, Inv.nr. 14079, aktenummer 250903, 25 March 1763.
SAA, Notariële archieven 5075, inventarisnummer 14090, aktenummer 283743
SAA, 5062 Archief Schepenen: kwijtscheldingen, Inv.nr. 125
SAA, 600 Archief van de Firma Ketwich & Voomberg en Wed. W. Borski, Inv.nr. 771, 791,
https://archief.amsterdam/beeldbank/detail/d657c12a-e445-55cd-8a6c-1c6893d789df
Tresoar, 5 Gewestelijke bestuursinstellingen van Friesland 1580–1795, inv.nrs. 453, 787391, 787392, 787393, 787394, 787395, 787403, 787404, 787405, 787406, 787407, 787408

Secondary sources

Bochove, Christiaan van. 2014. Seafarers and Shopkeepers: Credit in Eighteenth-Century Amsterdam. *Eighteenth-Century Studies* 48 (1): 67–88.
Bochove, Christiaan van, Christopher L. Colvin, and Oscar Gelderblom. 2021. Detecting the Function of Finance through History: An Essay in Celebration of the Work of Joost Jonker. *TSEG - The Low Countries Journal of Social and Economic History* 18 (3): 125–166. https://doi.org/10.52024/tseg.11076
Brandon, Pepijn. 2018. “The Whole Art of War Is Reduced to Money”: Remittances, Short-Term Credit and Financial Intermediation in Anglo-Dutch Military Finance, 1688–1713. *Financial History Review* 25 (1): 19–41. https://doi.org/10.1017/S0968565017000282
———. 2015. *War, Capital, and the Dutch State (1588–1795).* Historical Materialism Book Series, ISSN 1570-1522 101. Leiden: Brill.
Buist, Marten Gerbertus. 1974. *At Spes Non Fracta : Hope and Co. 1770–1815, Merchant Bankers and Diplomats at Work.* Den Haag: Nijhoff.
Carlos, Ann M., and Larry Neal. 2011. Amsterdam and London as Financial Centers in the Eighteenth Century. *Financial History Review* 18 (1): 21–46. https://doi.org/10.1017/S0968565010000338
Carter, Alice Clare. 1975. *Getting, Spending and Investing in Early Modern Times: Essays on Dutch, English and Huguenot Economic History.* Aspects of Economic History: The Low Countries 1. Assen: Van Gorcum.

De Jong-Keesing, Elisabeth Emmy. 1939. *De Economische Crisis van 1763 Te Amsterdam*. Amsterdam: Intern. Uitgevers en Handelsmaatschappij (Systemen Keesing).

De Vries, Jan and Ad Van der Woude. 1995. *Nederland 1500–1815: de eerste ronde van moderne economische groei*. Amsterdam: Balans.

———. 1997. *The First Modern Economy: Success, Failure, and Perseverance of the Dutch Economy, 1500–1815*. Cambridge etc.: Cambridge University Press.

Dickson, Peter George Muir. 1987. *Finance and Government under Maria Theresia 1740–1780*. Oxford: Clarendon Press.

Dormans, E. H. M. 1991. *Het tekort: staatsschuld in de tijd der Republiek*. NEHA-series III 14. Amsterdam: NEHA.

Drelichman, Mauricio, and Hans-Joachim. Voth. 2011. Serial Defaults, Serial Profits: Returns to Sovereign Lending in Habsburg Spain, 1566–1600. *Explorations in Economic History* 48 (1): 1–19. https://doi.org/10.1016/j.eeh.2010.08.002

Esteves, Rui. 2007. Quis Custodiet Quem? Sovereign Debt and Bondholders. Protection Before 1914. *SSRN Electronic Journal*. https://doi.org/10.2139/ssrn.2025023

Feenstra, Alberto. 2015. Hiding in a Twilight Zone: Credible Commitment in the Dutch Republic and Groningen's 1680s Default. *Histoire & Mesure* 30 (2): 79–116.

———. 2018. *Between Shared and Conflicting Interests. The Political Economy of the Markets for Public Debt in the Dutch Republic, 1600–1795*, (Unpublished Ph.D. thesis Universiteit van Amsterdam). Amsterdam.

Feenstra, Alberto and Sabine Muller. 2016. Wie wil wachten op het zoet? De laatste adem van Amsterdamse kopers van Groningse lijfrenten, 1660–1760. *Historisch Jaarboek Groningen*, 46–65.

Feenstra, Alberto. 2021. De Lange Schaduw van de Spaanse Successieoorlog (1701–1713) in Friesland. In: *Nederland in Last. Vijfhonderd Jaar Overheidsfinanciën in de Lage Landen, 1500–2000*, edited by Victor Enthoven 89–109. Leiden: Primavera Pers.

Flandreau, Marc, and Juan H. Flores. 2009. Bonds and Brands. *The Journal of Economic History* (3): 646–684.

Fritschy, Wantje. 1988. *De patriotten en de financiën van de Bataafse Republiek: Hollands krediet en de smalle marges voor een nieuw beleid (1795–1801)*. 's-Gravenhage: Stichting Hollandse Historische Reeks.

———. 2003. A "financial Revolution" Reconsidered: Public Finance in Holland during the Dutch Revolt, 1568–1648. *The Economic History Review* 56 (1): 57–89.

———. 2017. *Public Finance of the Dutch Republic in Comparative Perspective: The Viability of an Early Modern Federal State (1570s-1795)*. Leiden: Brill.

Gelderblom, Oscar, and Joost Jonker. 2011. Public Finance and Economic Growth. *The Journal of Economic History* 71 (1): 1–40.

Gelderblom, Oscar, Mark Hup and Joost Jonker. 2018. Public Functions, Private Markets: Credit Registration by Aldermen and Notaries in the Low Countries, 1500–1800. In: *Financing in Europe: Evolution, Coexistence and Complementarity of Lending Practices from the Middle Ages to Modern Times*, edited by Marcella Lorenzini, Cinzia Lorandini, and D'Maris Coffman, 163–194. Cham: Springer International Publishing. https://doi.org/10.1007/978-3-319-58493-5_7

Greve, Anke. 2000. Brügger Hosteliers und hansische Kaufleute: ein Netzwerk vorteilhafter Handelsbeziehungen oder programmierte Interessenkonflikte? In: *Hansekaufleute in Brügge. Tl. 4: Beiträge der internationalen Tagung in Brügge April 1996*, edited by Werner Paravicini, Horst Wernicke, and Nils Jörn, 151–161. Frankfurt am Main [etc.]: Lang.

———. 2002. Hoteliers en Hanzekooplieden in Brugge in de 14de en 15de eeuw. In: *Hanzekooplui en Medicibankiers: Brugge, wisselmarkt van Europese culturen*, edited by A. Vandewalle, 99–104. Oostkamp: Stichtung Kunstboek.

Hart Marjolein, C. 1987. t, 'Staatsfinanciën als familiezaak tijdens de Republiek: de ontvangers-generaal Doubleth. In: *Fiscaliteit in Nederland. 50 jaar Belastingmuseum 'Prof. Dr. Van der Poel'*, edited by J. Th de Smidt, 56–65. Zutphen/Deventer.

———. 1993. *The Making of a Bourgeois State: War, Politics and Finance during the Dutch Revolt*. Manchester etc.: Manchester University Press.

———. 2014. *The Dutch Wars of Independence: Warfare and Commerce in the Netherlands 1570–1680*. London: Routledge.

Hart, Marjolein 't. 2009. Mutual Advantages: State Bankers as Brokers between the City of Amsterdam and the Dutch Republic. In: *The Political Economy of the Dutch Republic*, edited by Oscar Gelderblom, 115–142. Farnham etc.: Ashgate.

Hell, Maarten. 2017. *De Amsterdamse herberg 1450–1800: geestrijk centrum van het openbare leven*. Nijmegen: Uitgeverij Vantilt.

Hoffman, Philip T., Gilles Postel-Vinay, and Jean-Laurent Rosenthal. 2000. *Priceless Markets: The Political Economy of Credit in Paris, 1660–1870*. Chicago etc.: The University of Chicago Press.

Hoffman, Philip T., Gilles Postel-Vinay, and Jean-Laurent Rosenthal. 2019. *Dark Matter Credit: The Development of Peer-to-Peer Lending and Banking in France*. Princeton, NJ: Princeton University Press.

Irigoin, Alejandra, and Regina Grafe. 2013. Bounded Leviathan: Fiscal Constraints and Financial Development in the Early Modern Hispanic World. In: *Questioning Credible Commitment: Perspectives on the Rise of Financial Capitalism*, edited by D'Maris Coffman, Adrian Leonard, and Larry Neal, 199–227. Cambridge: Cambridge University Press.

Jonker, Joost. 1996. *Merchants, Bankers, Middlemen: The Amsterdam Money Market during the First Half of the 19th Century. NEHA-Series III 24*. Amsterdam: NEHA.

Jonker, Joost. 2019a. Klem tussen de lokale en mondiale markt. De Amsterdamse Haute Banque vanaf het midden van de zestiende tot het begin van de twintigste eeuw (deel 1, 1550–1763). *Amstelodamum* 106 (1): 25–45.

———. 2019b. Klem tussen de lokale en mondiale markt. De Amsterdamse haute banque vanaf het midden van de zeventiende tot het begin van de twintigste eeuw (deel 2, 1763–1914). *Amstelodamum* 106 (2): 63–87.

Jonker, Joost and Keetie E Sluyterman. 2000. *Thuis op de wereldmarkt: Nederlandse handelshuizen door de eeuwen heen*. Den Haag: Sdu Uitgevers.

Lesger, Clé., Marco H. D. van Leeuwen, and Bart Vissers. 2013. Residentiële Segregatie in Vroegmoderne Steden. Amsterdam in de Eerste Helft van de Negentiende Eeuw. *TSEG - The Low Countries Journal of Social and Economic History* 10 (2): 102–132. https://doi.org/10.18352/tseg.201

Liesker, R. 1985. Tot zinkens toe bezwaard. De schuldenlast van het Zuiderkwartier van Holland 1672–1794. In: *Bestuurders en geleerden: opstellen over onderwerpen uit de Nederlandse geschiedenis van de zestiende, zeventiende en achttiende eeuw, aangeboden aan Prof. Dr. J.J. Woltjer bij zijn afscheid als hoogleraar van de Rijksuniversiteit te Leiden*, edited by Jan Juliaan Woltjer, Simon Groenveld, and Marianne Elisabeth Henriette Nicolette Mout, 151–160. Amsterdam etc.: De Bataafsche Leeuw.

Liesker, R., and Wantje Fritschy. 2004. *Gewestelijke financiën ten tijde van de Republiek der Verenigde Nederlanden. Deel IV. Holland (1572–1795)*. Den Haag: Instituut voor Nederlandse Geschiedenis.

Mitchener, Kris James, and Marc D. Weidenmier. 2010. Supersanctions and Sovereign Debt Repayment. *Journal of International Money and Finance* 29 (1): 19–36. https://doi.org/10.1016/j.jimonfin.2008.12.011

Murphy, Anne L. 2013. Demanding "Credible Commitment": Public Reactions to the Failures of the Early Financial Revolution. *The Economic History Review* 66 (1): 178–197.

Neal, Larry. 1990. *The Rise of Financial Capitalism: International Capital Markets in the Age of Reason*. Cambridge etc.: Cambridge University Press.

Nijboer, Harm Tjeerd. 2007. *De fatsoenering van het bestaan: consumptie in Leeuwarden tijdens de Gouden Eeuw*.

North, Douglas C., and Barry R. Weingast. 1989. Constitutions and Commitment: The Evolution of Institutions Governing Public Choice in Seventeenth-Century England. *The Journal of Economic History* 49 (4): 803–832.

Oosterlinck, Kim, Loredana Ureche-Rangau, and Jacques-Marie Vaslin. 2019. Aristocratic Privilege. Exploiting "Good" Institutions. *CEPR Discussion Paper Series* DP 140771 (v.2). https://cepr.org/active/publications/discussion_papers/dp.php?dpno=14071

Petram, Lodewijk. 2011. *The World's First Stock Exchange: How the Amsterdam Market for Dutch East India Company Shares Became a Modern Securities Market, 1602–1700*. Unpublished Ph.D. thesis Universiteit van Amsterdam. Amsterdam.

Pompermaier, Matteo. 2022. Credit and Poverty in Early Modern Venice. *The Journal of Interdisciplinary History* 52 (4): 513–536. https://doi.org/10.1162/jinh_a_01765

Riley, James C. 1980. *International Government Finance and the Amsterdam Capital Market, 1740–1815*. Cambridge etc.: Cambridge University Press.

Rouwenhorst, K. Geert. 2005. The Origins of Mutual Funds. In: *The Origins of Value: The Financial Innovations That Created Modern Capital Markets*, edited by William N. Goetzmann and K. Geert Rouwenhorst, 249–269. Oxford etc.: Oxford University Press.

Spanninga, Hotso. 2012. *Gulden vrijheid? Politieke cultuur en staatsvorming in Friesland, 1600–1640*. Hilversum: Verloren.

Stasavage, David. 2011. *States of Credit: Size, Power, and the Development of European Polities*. Princeton, NJ etc.: Princeton University Press.

Temin, Peter, and Hans-Joachim. Voth. 2005. Credit Rationing and Crowding out during the Industrial Revolution: Evidence from Hoare's Bank, 1702–1862. *Explorations in Economic History* 42 (3): 325–348.

Tomz, Michael. 2007. *Reputation and International Cooperation: Sovereign Debt across Three Centuries*. Princeton, NJ etc.: Princeton University Press.

Trompetter, Cor. 2007. *Gewestelijke financiën ten tijde van de Republiek der Verenigde Nederlanden. Deel VI. Friesland (1587–1795)*. Den Haag: Instituut voor Nederlandse Geschiedenis.

Van Bochove, Christiaan. 2013. Configuring Financial Markets in Preindustrial Europe. *The Journal of Economic History* 73 (1): 247–278.

Van Bochove, Christiaan, and Ton Van Velzen. 2014. Loans to Salaried Employees: The Case of the Dutch East India Company, 1602–1794. *European Review of Economic History* 18: 19–38.

Van Deursen, A. Th. 1999. De plaats van het gewest Friesland in de Republiek. In: *Fryslân, staat en macht 1450–1650: bijdragen aan het historisch congres te Leeuwarden van 3 tot 5 juni 1998*, edited by Jouke Arend Frieswijk, A.H. Huussen jr. Y.B. Kuiper and J.A. Mol, 218–231. Hilversum: VerlorenLeeuwarden : Frys Akademy.

Verwaaij, Daan, and Christiaan van Bochove. 2019. Credit without Banks: The Amsterdam Water Bailiff's Ledger of 1856. *Financial History Review* 26 (2): 171–195. https://doi.org/10.1017/S0968565019000076

Wagenvoort, Herman. 1961. *Tontines: een onderzoek naar de geschiedenis van de lijfrenten bij wijze van tontine en de contracten van overleving in de Republiek der Verenigde Nederlanden*. Utrecht.

Zandvliet, Kees. 2006. *De 250 rijksten van de Gouden Eeuw: kapitaal, macht, familie en levensstijl*. Edited by Paulien Retèl. Amsterdam: RijksmuseumAmsterdam : Nieuw Amsterdam.

Zuijderduijn, C. Jaco. 2010. De laatmiddeleeuwse crisis van de overheidsfinanciën en de financiële revolutie in Holland. *Bijdragen en mededelingen betreffende de geschiedenis der Nederlanden* 125 (4): 3–24.

Zuijderduijn, Jaco. 2010. The Emergence of Provincial Debt in the County of Holland (Thirteenth–Sixteenth Centuries). *European Review of Economic History* 14 (3): 335–359. https://doi.org/10.1017/S1361491610000055

Zuijderduijn, C. Jaco and Dries Raeymaekers (eds.). 2015. *Publieke financiën in de Lage Landen (1300–1800)*. Maastricht: Shaker Publishing.

Zwitzer, Hans L. 1982. Het quotenstelsel onder de Republiek der Verenigde Nederlanden alsmede enkele beschouwingen over de generale petitie, de staat van oorlog en de repartitie. *Mededelingen van de Sectie Militaire Geschiedenis, Landmachtstaf* 5: 5–57.

CHAPTER 7

A Differentiated Access to Credit in a Merchant Network in the 1780s (Philadelphia and Its Region)

Louis Bissières

1 Introduction

Social network analysis (SNA) offers a powerful set of tools to grasp the systems of credit in which actors were involved in the early modern period.[1] It can be applied to transactions recorded in account books, actors owning individual accounts then constituting the nodes of the

[1] Pierre Gervais, 'Crédit et filières marchandes au XVIIIe siècle', in: *Annales. Histoire, Sciences Sociales*, 67:4 (2012), 1011–48; Elise M. Dermineur, 'Peer-to-peer lending in pre-industrial France', in: *Financial History Review*, 26:3 (2019), 359–88; Louis Bissieres, 'Les ressources économiques du réseau au défi de la mesure: les commerces de Levi

L. Bissières (✉)
Université Paris 1-Panthéon Sorbonne, IDHES, Paris, France
e-mail: Louis.Bissieres@univ-paris1.fr

E. M. Dermineur and M. Pompermaier (eds.), *Credit Networks in The Preindustrial World*, Palgrave Studies in the History of Finance,
https://doi.org/10.1007/978-3-031-67117-3_7

network and transactions the edges.[3] SNA is used to characterize the structure of a merchant network and to distinguish between different kinds of actors within it. Exploring this structure, I use other quantitative methods (mainly simple graphs and linear or bimodal regressions) that help characterize a differentiated access to credit. The goal is to tackle quantitatively an issue that has already been studied by scholars: there would be a close relation between credit and trust.[4] In other words, the fear of a partner's default strongly influenced credit practices.[5] My systematic analysis of a trade network both confirms and expands this idea. Trade and trust are linked but their articulation needs to be thought within a complex structure and not as something that is bilateral between a lender and a borrower.

Several works in economic history have stressed the extent to which access to credit was affected by a whole range of determinants, particularly social ones. The study of Florentine credit, for example, has shown how credit practices were correlated with non-economic factors, such as

Hollingsworth (Philadelphie, fin XVIIIe siècle)' (PhD dissertation, Université Paris 1 Panthéon-Sorbonne, 2022). On a more general approach of SNA in history, see Markus Gamper, 'The history of 'relational science' and social network analysis', in Andreas Gestrich and Martin Stark (eds.), *Debtors, Creditors, and Their Networks: Social Dimensions of Monetary Dependence from the Seventeenth to the Twentieth Century*, (London, 2015), 11–42; Claire Lemercier, 'Formal network methods in history: why and how?', in Georg Fertig (ed.), *Social networks, political institutions, and rural societies*, (Turnhout, 2015), 281–310; Kate Davison, 'Early Modern Social Networks: Antecedents, Opportunities, and Challenges', in: *The American Historical Review*, 124:2 (2019), 456–82.

[3] Cheryl S. McWatters and Yannick Lemarchand, 'Accounting as story telling: Merchant activities and commercial relations in eighteenth century France', in: *Accounting, Auditing & Accountability Journal*, 23:1 (2010), 14–54; Cheryl S. McWatters and Yannick Lemarchand, 'Merchant networks and accounting discourse: the role of accounting transactions in network relations', in: *Accounting History Review*, 23:1 (2013), 49–83.

[4] Craig Muldrew, *The economy of obligation: the culture of credit and social relations in early modern England*, (Houndmills, 1998); Ellen Hartigan-O'Connor, *Ties That Buy: Women and Commerce in Revolutionary America*, (Philadelphia, PA, 2009); M. Capelo, P. Araújo, and C. Álvarez-Dardet, 'Management control systems, trust and risk in inter-organisational relationships: The case of Francisco González de la Sierra and its partner Rivas y Cantallops (1847–1864)', in: *Business History*, 57:4 (2015), 528–63.

[5] Bruce H. Mann, *Republic of debtors: bankruptcy in the age of American independence* (Cambridge, MA, 2002); Pierre Gervais, 'A Game of Claims and Expectations: Credit, failure, and personal relationships across the Atlantic', in: *Commonplace*, 10:3 (2010).

religious affiliation or matrimonial strategies.[6] In this paper, I show empirically that positioning within a relational structure affects access to credit. Thus, I establish how merchant networks were paramount structures of finance in the end of the eighteenth century.[7] Their importance was twofold: credit flows were massive in networks, and they were differentiated according to the position actors held in them. The use of credit to support day-to-day transactions or large-scale trade was frequent in 1780s United States since the country faced shortages of metallic currency and that it counted only one bank (the Bank of North America).[8] William T. Baxter refers to this process as a form of time-extended barter, through credit.[9]

Merchant records offer a particularly rich access to these credit practices. To do so, I study transactions recorded in Levi Hollingsworth's journal from the year 1786.[10] As it was common in early modern business, Hollingsworth's books did not only record transactions between him and other traders (760 actors involved in 5548 transactions in 1786),

[6] John F. Padgett and Paul D. McLean, 'Economic Credit in Renaissance Florence', in: *The Journal of Modern History*, 83:1 (2011), 1–47; Paul D. McLean and Neha Gondal, 'The Circulation of Interpersonal Credit in Renaissance Florence', in: *European Journal of Sociology / Archives Européennes de Sociologie / Europäisches Archiv für Soziologie*, 55:2 (2014), 135–76.

[7] The role of merchant network is already stressed in multiple works. Among them, see David J. Hancock, *Citizens of the world: London merchants and the integration of the British Atlantic community, 1735 - 1785* (Cambridge, 1995); Francesca Trivellato, *The familiarity of strangers: the Sephardic diaspora, Livorno, and cross-cultural trade in the early modern period*, (New Haven, CT, 2009); Andrea Caracausi and Christof Jeggle (eds.), *Commercial networks and European cities, 1400–1800* (London, 2014).

[8] John J. McCusker and Russell R. Menard (eds.), *The economy of British America, 1607–1789*, (Chapel Hill, NC, 1985); Stanley L. Engerman and Robert E. Gallman (eds.), *The Cambridge economic history of the United States: the Colonial Era*, (Cambridge, 1996); Andrew D. Edwards, 'Money and the American Revolution: Changing Concepts of Money and Wealth, 1765–1786', PhD dissertation, Princeton University 2018; Howard Bodenhorn, *State banking in early America: a new economic history*, (New York, NY, 2003); Joshua R. Greenberg, *Bank Notes and Shinplasters: the Rage for Paper Money in the Early Republic*, (Philadelphia, PA, 2020).

[9] William T. Baxter, 'Observations on Money, Barter and Bookkeeping', in: *The Accounting Historians Journal*, 31:1 (2004), 129–39.

[10] Historical Society of Pennsylvania (HSP), Hollingsworth family papers, collection 289 (HFP), 2.c. Daybooks and Journals: Journal L (1786–1788, vol. 86). Hollingsworth's Ledger was also used to add some information about accounts. HSP, HFP, 2.a. Ledgers: Ledger L (1786–1788, vol. 21).

but they also recorded transfers of credit between those traders.[11] For instance, a miller from Delaware could buy supplies from a Baltimore merchant, settling the purchase using credit given by Levi Hollingsworth who would record the transaction. Thus, a single account book allows for the observation of a whole network of credit. This way of reconstructing a business network has its limitations since some transactions that happened between the members of the network cannot be observed (those that were recorded outside the books of Hollingsworth). Still it allows an in-depth exploration of the credit flows involving a major American businessman of the eighteenth century.

Born in 1739, Levi Hollingsworth was a large flour dealer in Philadelphia where he moved in the 1760s from Maryland. Philadelphia was the largest city in the United States in the aftermath of the American Independence and it was a vibrant place for commerce. There, Hollingsworth was one of the most important merchants in the 1780s and 1790s, his business quickly developing.[12] His trade network combined partners living in the region's urban centers like New York, Baltimore, or Richmond. Since the Philadelphian specialized in flour, his network also counted numerous backcountry millers and farmers.[13] It then helped connecting rural consumers to the Atlantic world of goods, through a massive circulation of credit.[14] There was a wide variety of actors involved in this network that allows for the exploration of a differentiated access to credit.

Complementing SNA with other methods allows to discuss how social networks could affect economic behavior by the end of the early modern period. In the following section, I establish that credit flows were organized around specific actors within a merchant network that was both segmented and hierarchical. This is a primary step that allows for a comparison of the access to credit for actors situated in different parts of the network. In the subsequent section, I demonstrate that the actors that were the most invested in the network obtained a better (more frequent

[11] Robert Bloom and John Solotko, 'Barter accounting in the US during the late eighteenth and early nineteenth centuries', in: *Accounting History*, 9:1 (2004), 91–108.

[12] Thomas M. Doerflinger, *A vigorous spirit of enterprise: merchants and economic development in revolutionary Philadelphia*, (Chapel Hill, NC, 1986).

[13] Brooke Hunter, 'Rage for Grain: Flour Milling in the Mid-Atlantic', PhD dissertation, University of Delaware 2001.

[14] Ann Smart Martin, *Buying into the world of goods: early consumers in backcountry Virginia* (Baltimore, MD, 2010).

and more intense) access to credit. In the fourth part, I discuss the differentiated use of means of payment to back credit flows. I conclude that the involvement in a complex commercial structure was a resource in the early modern period since it improved access to credit.

2 A Hierarchical and Segmented Merchant Network

Reconstructed from account books, a merchant network is a structure of trade in which goods, services, means of payment like cash, paper instruments, and credit are circulated. The 1786 Hollingsworth network is composed of 761 nodes (a node is an individual or a firm so it can be a collection of several account) and 1492 edges (a relation between two nodes that can be weighted according to the number or value of transactions).[15] Since the network under study is drawn from one of Levi Hollingsworth's account book, the merchant of Philadelphia holds an extremely strong position of centrality in it. Indeed, his books do not give access to every transaction that happened between the other members of his network and that contributes to the overestimation of his centrality. Still, Levi Hollingsworth is absent in about 25% of the transactions recorded in his own books. In these cases, it is not one of his accounts that was debited or credited but two of his partners'. What his partners then did was trading the credit they accumulated with the Philadelphian in order, for instance, to buy and sell goods.

Among many options offered by SNA, it is possible to define a hierarchy of actors in the merchant network from the number of relations they had with others (this is the notion of degree centrality).[16] If Hollingsworth traded with almost everyone else, the rest of the actors in the network had a wide range of partners. As shown in Fig. 1, the degree distribution (the number of accounts reaching a certain score of

[15] The network density is 0.0052, its diameter 7, and the average path length 2.23. In this chapter, network metrics are obtained using the igraph package in R. On network metrics, see David Easley and Jon Kleinberg, *Networks, crowds, and markets: reasoning about a highly connected world*, (Cambridge, 2010); Eric D. Kolaczyk and Gábor Csárdi, *Statistical analysis of network data with R*, (Cham, 2020).

[16] For a conceptual approach of centrality, see Sébastien De Valeriola, 'Can historians trust centrality? Historical network analysis and centrality metrics robustness', in: *Journal of Historical Network Research*, 6:1 (2021), 85–125.

degree centrality) is strongly decreasing for centralities between 1 and 10 and then only reaching small numbers (one to three) for some values above. This distribution suggests that merchant networks were highly hierarchical. Indeed, there is Levi Hollingsworth at one end of the scope (whose centrality was massive but not as much as the network reconstructed from his own records tends to suggest) and 367 actors at the other end that reached a centrality of 1 and thus only used the Philadelphian's account books to trade with him. In between, there were 383 actors who used the merchant's books to (also) trade with each other (centralities of 2–62). They were using credit granted by the Philadelphian to organize their trade and make some transactions that were recorded in his account books.

Among the 383 actors who traded with each other, it can be interesting to make a distinction between those who held an important role

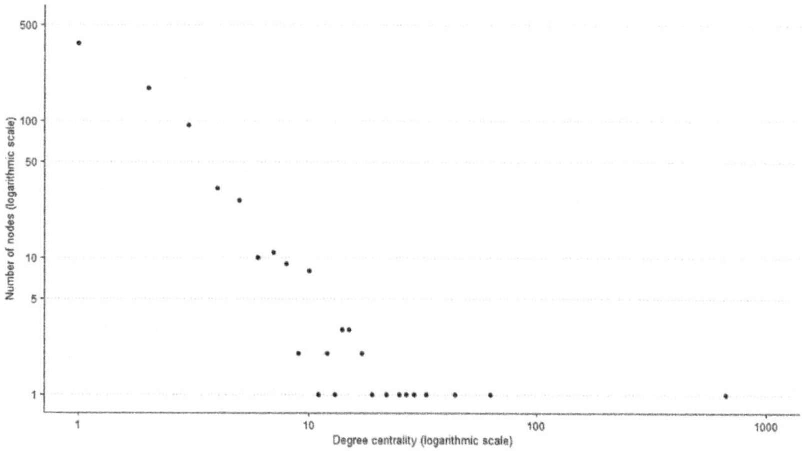

Fig. 1 The degree distribution in Hollingsworth's merchant network in 1786 (Source HSP, HFP, 2.c. Daybooks and Journals: Journal L (1786–1788, vol. 86), 2.a. Ledgers: Ledger L (1786–1788, vol. 21). The scales are logarithmic. For instance, one node obtained a degree centrality of 11, meaning that only one actor had 11 partners in the Hollingsworth network in 1786. Note: Levi Hollingsworth's presence strongly affects the scale of the graph. Still, removing him from the network would lead to the disappearance of the 367 actors who only traded with him (those with a degree centrality of 1). Indeed, removing Hollingsworth means each node loses 1 unit of centrality)

in the overall structure and the others. To do so, a threshold is set at 3% to distinguish between the most central nodes and the others (the 3% of the nodes reaching the higher degrees of centrality are defined as central).[17] According to the overall number of nodes, we get 23 central actors in 1786. These central actors maintained close relations with each other since they collectively organized the commercial network. In the network visualization (Fig. 2), it appears that the central actors belonged to a single connected component. This means that no central actor was isolated from the rest of the group, enhancing this idea of collaboration.

Then, I define a clientele as the set of non-central nodes attached to a central node. This happened when a non-central actor traded with a central one, or traded with one of his clients, while not directly trading with any central actor. What is remarkable is that these clienteles were highly segmented, meaning that central actors did not share many clients and that members of a same clientele traded with each other rather than with members of other clienteles, over and over.[18] There was also a strong spatial component in the clienteles: a central actor and his clients had a strong tendency to live close to each other (a client from Maryland had a highly higher chance to be attached to a central actor living in Baltimore rather than New York).[19] Solely reconstructed through the transactions recorded in Levi Hollingsworth's account books, the shape of the clienteles could be altered by the observation of the full set of transactions between the totality of the nodes in the network. Still, the spatial component of the clienteles and their stability through time tend to suggest that

[17] After a series of comparisons (with 1, 2, 4, 5, and 10%) it appears the 3% threshold is the one that best captures the distinction between central and not central nodes in Hollingsworth's network. Beyond 4%, the population of central actors would be too large and lose its internal coherence. On the other hand, some actors who appear to play an important role in the commercial structure (as observed, especially, through Hollingsworth's correspondence) would not make the cut with the 1% and 2% thresholds. The weight of nodes is included in this process. On this issue, see Tore Opsahl, Filip Agneessens, and John Skvoretz, 'Node centrality in weighted networks: Generalizing degree and shortest paths', in: *Social Networks*, 32:3 (2010), 245–51; Tore Opsahl, 'tnet, analyse of Weighted, Two-mode and Longitudinal Networks', (2011).

[18] Louis Bissières, "Taking time seriously': an empirical approach to an American merchant network at the end of the eighteenth century', in: *Journal of Historical Network Research*, 8 (2023), 58–92.

[19] Bissières, 'Les ressources économiques du réseau'.

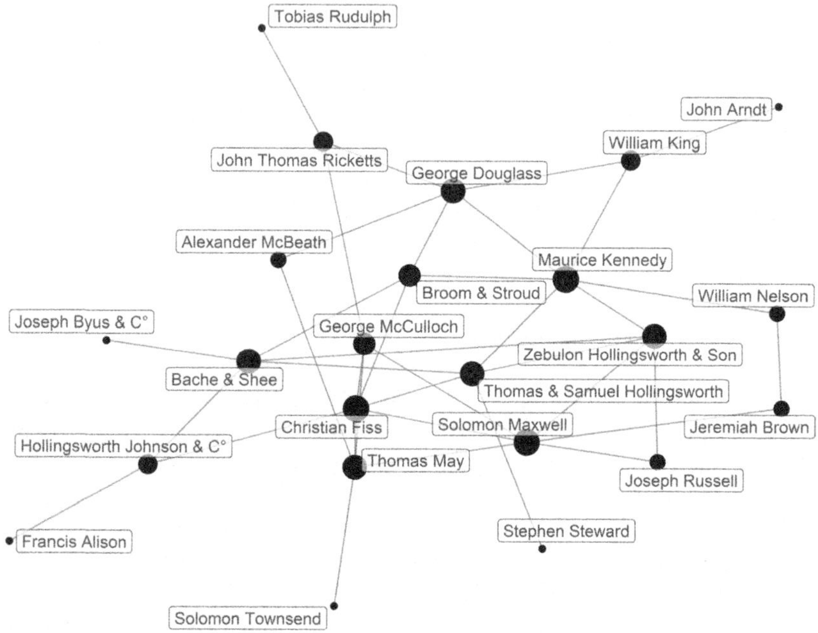

Fig. 2 The central actors' network in 1786 (Source *ibid*. Network analysis is done with R's package igraph. The package ggraph is used for the visualization (On ggraph see Thomas Lin Pedersen, 'Data Imaginist' (https://www.data-imaginist.com.0//, accessed on June 19th 2023)). The size of the nodes is proportional to their degree centrality)

the credit flows observed in these Hollingsworth-based clienteles would be very similar to the actual clienteles'.

Then, it appears that an eighteenth-century merchant network can be divided into several types of members. Figure 3 consists in a visualization representing these populations in Levi Hollingsworth's network. In this very case, Hollingsworth is the most central actor around which the other revolve (square-shaped node). Very different populations can then be identified: his exclusive clients on the right-hand side (cross-shaped nodes) being those who did not use his books to trade with anyone else than the Philadelphian, and those who did and are on the left-hand side. Among them, I make a distinction between the central actors (circle-shaped nodes) and their clients (triangle-shaped nodes).[20] The two next sections consist in an exploration of the differences between the three types of partners regarding their access to credit with Levi Hollingsworth. I put an emphasis on the two types of clients (whether they were Hollingsworth's or central actors' i.e., cross-shaped and triangle-shaped nodes) for comparability purposes. From now on, I refer to Hollingsworth's exclusive clients as outsiders and the central actors' clients as insiders. The outsiders were not taking advantage of Hollingsworth's credit to trade with anyone else in his books, while the insiders did. Besides this major difference, all of them were peripheral in the overall structure. For instance, major and minor partners of Hollingsworth; millers, artisans, and retailers; urban and rural people can be found both among the insiders and the outsiders.[21]

3 A Differentiated Access to Credit

The aim of this section is to demonstrate that it is possible to observe that the insiders (the actors that were more involved in the trade structure, i.e., those who did not only transact with Hollingsworth) had a better access to credit than the outsiders. This is critical since credit was the main way to gain access to commodities and services in the end of the eighteenth century.[22] This difference between insiders and outsiders can be established through the study of the intensity of their trade in the overall network and with Levi Hollingsworth (3.1), the amount of credit they could get (3.2), their use of credit in purchasing merchandise (3.3), and their chances of obtaining a credit on common operations (3.4).

3.1 The Intensity of Trade

First, Table 1 shows that the central actors' clients transacted for larger amounts than Hollingsworth's exclusive clients (this total amount of

[20] The idea underlying this visualization is to properly differentiate the four populations. This is why the central actors' clienteles seem so entangled.

[21] Bissières, 'Les ressources économiques du réseau'.

[22] Muldrew, *The economy of obligation*; Elise M. Dermineur (ed.), *Women and credit in pre-industrial Europe* (Turnhout, 2018); Philip T. Hoffman, Gilles Postel-Vinay, and Jean-Laurent Rosenthal, *Dark matter credit: the development of peer-to-peer lending and banking in France* (Princeton, NJ, 2019); Sara T. Damiano, *To her credit: women, finance, and the law in eighteenth-century New England cities* (Baltimore, MD, 2021).

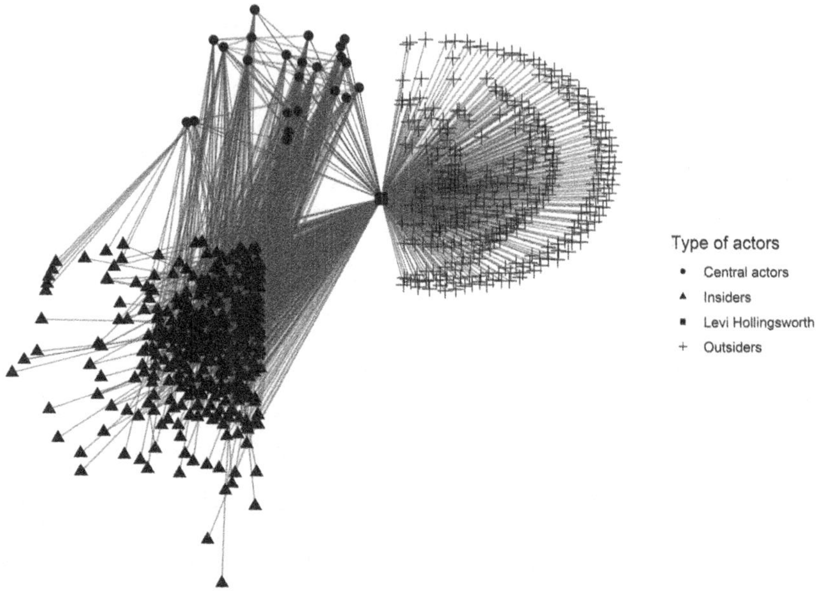

Fig. 3 The different populations in Hollingsworth's merchant network in 1786 (Source *ibid*. Network analysis is done with R's package igraph. The package ggraph is used for the visualization)

trade is the sum of every debit and credit from the account(s) an actor owned in Hollingsworth's books). Indeed, the outsiders' business in Hollingsworth's books amounted to less than 100£ on average while the insiders' reached 339£. Studying the median is even more illuminating since half of the outsiders traded for less than 21£ which is very small in comparison with the 122£ of the insiders. There was a lot more outsiders than insiders that did very little business. If we focus on the very big traders that transacted for more than 1,000£, only four out of thirty-four were outsiders.

Still, there is a limitation in focusing on the total amount of trade to discriminate the insiders and the outsiders. While the firsts could have had several partners, the seconds only traded with Hollingsworth. This limited their trade opportunities within the Philadelphian's books. A solution to this problem can be to focus the study on their transactions with Levi Hollingsworth. This way, the potential difference in terms of amount

Table 1 A differentiated amount of trade

Characteristic	*Type of actor*		
	Outsiders, N = 377[1]	*Insiders, N = 360*[1]	*Total, N = 737*[1]
Total amount of trade	92 (21)	339 (122)	212 (55)

[1] Mean (Median) in Pennsylvania £[a]

(Source *ibid*)

[a] A Pennsylvania Pound was worth 0,56 £ sterling in 1786. See John J. McCusker, 'Colonial statistics', in Susan B. Carter (ed.), *Historical statistics of the United States: earliest times to the present* (New York, NY, 2006), 1155–1200

Table 2 A differentiated amount of trade with Levi Hollingsworth

Characteristic	*Type of actor*		
	Outsiders, N = 377[1]	*Insiders, N = 360*[1]	*Total, N = 737*[1]
Total amount of trade	92	246	167

[1] Mean in Pennsylvania £

(Source *ibid*)

of trade cannot be explained by the number of partners. Table 2 shows that the difference of business with Hollingsworth is still major between insiders and outsiders. Indeed, while the Philadelphian traded for 92£ in average with an insider in 1786, he traded for 246£ with an outsider. Being a part of the core of the merchant network (i.e., having integrated the clientele of a central actor) seems to have granted a better access to Levi Hollingsworth (and his business).

3.2 *Larger Amounts of Credit for the Insiders*

Since a huge part of transactions was conducted on credit, this difference in activity could suggest that a merchant like Levi Hollingsworth granted larger credits to the insiders in his network. To confirm this hypothesis, it is necessary to assess which transactions were associated with a credit and which ones were not. To do so, I use a typology of transactions that

I have, in collaboration with Pierre Gervais, explored elsewhere.[23] The main principle consists in defining a transaction as the transfer of forms of value (or their conversion) between two accounts.[24] For instance, when Solomon Maxwell (a merchant from Delaware) buys a box of lemons from Levi Hollingsworth on credit on the 18th of March in 1786, the transaction is categorized as "Book credit for merchandise" (alphabetically).[25] If Maxwell had reimbursed this amount in cash a few weeks later, it would have been categorized as "Book credit for cash" since cash was converted into book credit. The subtlety of this typology is that—when trading together—two personal accounts can only transfer book credit. Indeed, in the account book, one will simply credit the other. I can then integrate a motive in some cases to characterize why the transfer of book credit occurred. A purchase of shoes by Levi Adams (another Delaware merchant) to Samuel Richards on the 20th of March will then appear as "Book credit for book credit for merchandise."[26] Indeed, Adams' transfers some of his book credit (whether it was previously accumulated with Hollingsworth or obtained at that moment) to Richards.

Using this typology enables the study of credit practices in the end of the eighteenth century. Especially, it allows to distinguish between their conversions of Book Credit into means of payment and the conversion of Book Credit into other forms of assets. In the first case, the use of a means of payment meant that a transaction was immediately settled (for instance, an actor gave cash to pay for a barrel of sugar) or that a previous credit was reimbursed. In the second case, it meant that a transaction was made on credit (for instance, an actor bought the same barrel of sugar on a credit, whether to Hollingsworth or to one of his partners). Table 3 shows a decomposition of the business of Hollingsworth's partners. It appears he granted larger amounts of credit to the insiders (104£ on average) than to outsiders (35£).

[23] Louis Bissières and Pierre Gervais, 'Means of payment in Early Modern double-entry merchant accounting: an exploration using multilayer network analysis', Accounting History Review Conference, 2021.

[24] I define eight types of value that can be found in Hollingsworth's books capital, merchandize, services, lands, cash, bank credit, (financial) paper instruments, and book credit.

[25] HSP, HFP, 2.c. Daybooks and Journals: Journal L (1786–1788, vol. 86), p. 18.

[26] HSP, HFP, 2.c. Daybooks and Journals: Journal L (1786–1788, vol. 86), p. 18.

Table 3 A differentiated use of credit

Characteristic	*Type of actor*		
	Outsider, N = 377[1]	*Insider, N = 360*[1]	*Overall, N = 737*[1]
Total business (all partners)	92	339	212
Total payments	57	142	98
Book Credit for Cash	30	49	39
Bank Credit for Book Credit	22	73	47
Book Credit for Paper Instruments	5	20	12
Total business on credit (all partners)	35	197	114
Total credit with Levi Hollingsworth	35	104	69
Total credit with other partners	0	93	45

[1] Mean

(Source *ibid)*
All transactions involving insiders and outsiders in 1786 are taken into consideration in this chart. "Total business (all partners) [the total amount of transactions for an individual or firm expressed in £]" is the sum of "Total payments" and "Total business on credit (all partners)". "Total business on credit (all partners)" is the sum of "Total credit with Levi Hollingsworth" and "Total credit with other partners." By definition, the outsiders have a total credit with other partners of 0 since they only trade with Hollingsworth

This is a decisive result to understand how business and consumption were financed in the end of the early modern period. The involvement in trade structures (networks) was rewarded with larger amounts of credit. For a merchant like Hollingsworth, it was safer to lend credit to a partner that was deeply involved in the network since he could assume that this partner had incentives to reimburse his credit to keep his position in the structure and that the central actor he was associated with could guarantee his probity. Another argument consists in the fact that Hollingsworth knew that when he lent credit to an insider, this insider could be supported by others within the network. The risk associated with the credit was then spread inside a clientele and not solely put on an individual as was the case with outsiders.

It is possible to run a regression model in order to assess the importance of belonging to a specific part of a merchant network in the access to credit.[27] The linear model below (Table 4) estimates the relationship between the amount of credit granted by Hollingsworth (the value of commercial transactions categorized as "Total Credit with Levi Hollingsworth" in Table 3) to an actor and several explanatory variables regarding this actor (his position in the network, his presence in Hollingsworth account books before and/or after 1786, the fact that he was involved in Hollingsworth's major trade—flour—his specialization, his location, and his preferred means of payment).[28] In this model, we find that the position held in the network is significantly correlated with the amount of credit that Hollingsworth could lend. Indeed, all other things being equal, an insider would obtain 57£ more than an outsider, and a central actor would obtain almost 800£ more.

[27] On the use of regression models in history, see Charles H. Feinstein and Mark Thomas, *Making history count: a primer in quantitative methods for historians* (Cambridge, 2002); Keith McNulty, 'Handbook of Regression Modeling in People Analytics: With Examples in R and Python', (https://peopleanalytics-regression-book.org/gitbook/, 2021, accessed June 19, 2023). For an example of the use of regression models in Early modern economic history, see Julien Villain, *Le commode et l'accessoire: le commerce des biens de consommation au XVIIIe siècle Lorraine, v. 1690-v. 1790*, (Rennes, 2021).

[28] In this case, there are three possible positions in the network: outsider, insider, or central (central actors are integrated in this model). The specialization variable is drawn from the observation of the trade of actors in Hollingsworth's book. An actor is considered as a specialist if the trade of his major merchandize is twice as important as the rest of his trade in merchandize, otherwise he is a generalist. If he never trades for goods, the specialization is "none." It is possible to locate more than half of Hollingsworth's partners thanks to his correspondence, some other books, and complementary sources (especially directories). I make a distinction between foreign (mostly from the Caribbean, Ireland, or England), urban (from Philadelphia, New York, Baltimore, Richmond), and rural actors (the rest that can be located). The preferred means of payment refers to the means of payment that is most used by an actor in terms of value (not in terms of number of transactions). For the location of actors, see HSP, HFP, 1.a. Correspondence, Incoming, boxes 22–57; HSP, HFP, 2.b. Correspondence, Outgoing, Letterbooks, vol. 2–3; 2.a., Financial, Ledgers: Settlement of Ledger M, vol. 62; 2.e., Orders, box 174; 2.g., Invoices; box 185; 2.h., Shipping: Freight Journal K, vol. 205; 2.o., Bills and Receipts, box 259–260. HSP, Miscellaneous Professional and Personal Business Papers, 1732–1945 (collection 2001), Thomas, Samuel and Miers Fisher Journals (1784–1788 and 1792–1796); Delaware Historical Society, Hollingsworth Maxwell & Adams company ledger, 1787–1798, vol. 1; Francis White, *Philadelphia Directory* (Philadelphia, PA, 1785); Clement Biddle, *The Philadelphia Directory* (Philadelphia, PA, 1791); Edmund Hogan, *The prospect of Philadelphia and check on the next Directory* (Philadelphia, PA, 1795); T. W. Jones et S. S. Moore, *The Traveller's Directory* (Philadelphia, PA, 1804).

Table 4 The determinants of the quantity of credit lent by Levi Hollingsworth (linear regression model)

Characteristic	*n()*	*freq*	*Beta*	*95% CI*[1]	*p value*
Position in the network	760				
Outsider client	377	49.6	–	–	
Insider client	360	47.4	**57**	18, 96	0.004
Central actor	23	3.0	**789**	677, 901	<0.001
Appearance around 1786	760				
None	214	28.2	–	–	
1785	151	19.8	-7.3	-60, 46	0.8
1785 & 1787	257	33.8	**52**	1.0, 103	0.046
1787	138	18.2	-2.2	-57, 53	>0.9
Major trade: flour	760				
No	530	69.7	–	–	
Yes	230	30.3	**122**	75, 168	<0.001
Specialization	760				
Generalist	90	11.8	–	–	
Specialist	403	53.0	-29	-88, 31	0.3
None	267	35.2	-38	-106, 29	0.3
Location	760				
Rural	185	24.3	–	–	
Foreign	14	1.8	102	-36, 240	0.15
Urban	264	35.3	-45	-92, 1.7	0.059
Unknown	293	38.6	-47	-95, -0.05	0.050
Preferred means of payment	760				
Cash	376	49.5	–	–	
Bank Credit	133	17.5	31	-19, 82	0.2
Paper Instruments	251	33.0	**55**	15, 96	0.008

[1] CI = Confidence Interval

(Source *ibid*)
In bold are the value of the factors that are significant at the 0.95 threshold

Among the other factors, only few are significant: those involved in the flour trade (230 actors, 108 being insiders) were favored over those who were not (530 actors, 252 being insiders), as was the case of those who dealt with paper instruments rather than cash and those who were involved with Hollingsworth in the long run. On the other hand, the kind of specialization and, more surprisingly, the location, did not seem to make any difference in the access to credit. In other words, an urban merchant like Hollingsworth did not favor other urban actors over rural ones.[29] What was critical was not the actual location, but the position held within an economic configuration called a merchant network.

3.3 Credit for Consumption: Financing the Purchase of Merchandise

This first set of results shows that the involvement in a merchant network had some effect on the overall access to credit. Indeed, a rural producer or an urban consumer had better chances to obtain a credit with Levi Hollingsworth if she also used her account in Hollingsworth's books to deal with other of his partners. It is possible to study if, on two almost identical occasions, a credit was as easily obtained for an insider as an outsider. To do so, I develop a case study on the trade of goods. I do not distinct between sales and purchases but between the ways a good could be traded through Hollingsworth's books. Thanks to the typology of transactions, I can make a distinction between immediate payments of goods, on the one hand, and sales on credit, on the other. Indeed, while some actors bought (or sold) merchandise by giving (or receiving) cash, bank credit, or papers instruments, others got their merchandise on credit given by Hollingsworth whether because they got their goods from him or one of his partners.

Studying the arbitrations between granting credit and asking for an immediate payment (usually in cash), historians of the early modern economy have highlighted the existence of differentiated pricing practices. Thus, for a given commodity, the price would be lower if the transaction was settled immediately (in cash) than if it was carried out on credit.[30] This reflects the fact that credit was not free, insofar as those who used cash would obtain some form of discount.[31] This phenomenon can be observed in Levi Hollingsworth's correspondence. For instance, Herman

[29] On the question of the specificities of urban trade in Early modern America, see Emma Hart and Cathy Matson, 'Situating Merchants in Late Eighteenth-Century British Atlantic Port Cities', in: *Early American Studies: An Interdisciplinary Journal*, 15:4 (2017), 660–82; Emma Hart, *Trading spaces: the colonial marketplace and the foundations of American capitalism*, (Chicago, IL, 2019).

[30] Basil S. Yamey, 'The 'particular gain or loss upon each article we deal in': an aspect of mercantile accounting, 1300–1800', in: *Accounting, Business & Financial History*, 10:1 (2000), 1–12; Clare Haru Crowston, *Credit, fashion, sex: economies of regard in Old Regime France*, (Durham, NC, 2013).

[31] Yannick Lemarchand, Cheryl S. McWatters, and Laure Pineau-Defois, 'The current account as cognitive artefact: stories and accounts of La Maison Chaurand', in Pierre

Stump tells him in 1795: "I sold 300 [Barrels] of Superfine Flour in [Baltimore] at 12,5 Dollars payable in 5 Months & 700 [Barrels] at 12,75 Dollars payable in 6 Months to Men I suppose safe & punctual 11,5 Dollars is the price at 60 days & 4£ [i.e., 10,67$] the Cash Price."[32] In this letter, the link between price and payment term is explicit. The longer the delay, the higher the price needed for the seller to agree to the transaction. Cash transactions were then characterized by lower prices, insofar as they allowed immediate settlement and sellers could re-use the cash immediately. Still, these arbitrations were not always possible in an economy characterized by the scarcity of cash. This next section shows there was a preference for credit within the network. Insiders were willing to structure their trade around credit, meaning that they paid a price to integrate a clientele giving them access to regular buyers and suppliers, as well as support and information.[33]

In Table 5, I study the 332 insiders and outsiders involved in the purchases of merchandise that can be observed in Levi Hollingsworth's Journal in 1786. The outsiders could only trade with Hollingsworth but that was not the case for the insiders (who could trade with each other or with central actors). The difference in access to credit between insiders and outsiders is massive. Indeed, insiders beneficiated from almost 84% of the amount of credit in the purchase of merchandise while they were only involved in 41% of the immediate payments. Furthermore, for each insider making an immediate payment for his merchandise, more than 15 got a credit, while the number goes down to 4 for the outsiders. Overall, for each pound an insider had to pay immediately he got 4.1 £ on credit on average while an outsider only got 2.1 £. This leads to the conclusion that it was much easier to finance the purchases of goods on credit in the end of the eighteenth century for an insider than an outsider. Indeed, outsiders had to immediately pay their transactions much more often than insiders who were rewarded for their participation in the network with easily obtainable credit.

Gervais, Yannick Lemarchand, and Dominique Margairaz (eds.), *Merchants and profit in the age of commerce, 1680–1830*, (London, 2014), 13–32.

[32] HSP, HFP, 1.a. Incoming Letters, Box 56 fol. 6: Letter from Herman Stump to Levi Hollingsworth from the 30th of November 1795.

[33] Bissières, 'Les ressources économiques du réseau'.

Table 5 The trade of merchandise and the access to credit

Characteristic	*Type of actor*		
	Outsider, N = 80	*Insider, N = 252*	*Overall, N = 332*
Transaction on credit			
Total amount [£ Pa] (part)	3,576.93 (16.1%)	18,583.15 (83.9%)	22,160.08 (100%)
Number of actors (part)	66 (21.0%)	249 (79.0%)	315 (100%)
Mean credit per actor [£ Pa]	54.2	74.6	70.3
Immediate payment			
Total amount [£ Pa] (part)	407.21 (58.6%)	287.34 (41.4%)	694.55 (100%)
Number of actors (part)	16 (50.0%)	16 (50.0%)	32 (100%)
Mean immediate payment per actor [£ Pa]	25.5	18.0	21.7
Rates of usage of credit compared to immediate payment			
Total amount	8.8	64.7	31.9
Number of actors	4.1	15.6	9.8
Mean amount	2.1	4.1	3.2

(Source *ibid*)
The sum of the number of actors buying on credit and giving an immediate payment is superior to the total of actors since some of them were involved in both ways of getting goods. The rates of usage are to be read the following way: outsiders received 8.8 times more credit than the amount they had to immediately pay (rate of usage: total amount); for each insider making an immediate payment for his merchandise, 15.6 (249/16) got a credit (rate of usage-number of actors); for each pound spent on an immediate payment for merchandise by an insider, 4.1 £ were granted on credit (rate of usage: mean amount)

3.4 *Obtaining a Credit*

It is possible to shift the focus from actors to transactions. Rather than studying the average credit an actor got, I determine what was the behavior of Levi Hollingsworth when he dealt with insiders and outsiders when it came to credit lending. To do so, I only focus on transactions the Philadelphian was involved in (in this case, purchases of goods and services). In 1786, insiders were involved in 1,202 exchanges with Hollingsworth concerning goods or services, compared to 460 for outsiders (Table 6). Purchases were financed on a credit in 88% of cases for insiders, compared to 78% for outsiders. In other words, an insider obtained a credit 7 times more often than he paid immediately, compared to 3.5 times for an outsider.

A regression model allows to establish that the position held in the network was, indeed, significantly correlated with obtaining a credit (Table 7). Unlike the previous model, the assessment of the access to credit is based on a binomial regression. In a binomial regression, the aim is not to assess the contribution of a variable to a numerical value (e.g., how many more transactions a generalist makes than a specialist) but to compare two possible outcomes (in this case: obtaining a credit rather than settling the transaction immediately). Each of the coefficients proposed in such an analysis (taking the form of odds ratios, "OR" in the table) allows to evaluate the chances of obtaining (or granting) a credit rather than not obtaining one (and therefore of settling immediately). Thus, all other things being equal, an insider was 2.33 times more likely to obtain a credit than an outsider, rather than having to make an immediate payment. This score is significant and indicates that network membership and easy access to credit were correlated.

Two additional explanatory variables are added to the model. First, the motive of the transaction controls whether it was a purchase of goods or services.[34] Its coefficient can be interpreted as follows: a transaction

Table 6 The type of transaction in the sales and purchases of goods and services with Levi Hollingsworth according to the position in the network

Characteristic	*Type of actor*	
	Outsider, N = 460[1]	*Insider, N = 1202*[1]
Type of transaction		
Crédit	358 (78%)	1,054 (88%)
Immediate payment	102 (22%)	148 (12%)
1 n (%)		

(Source *ibid*)

[34] Levi Hollingsworth offered many services to his partners. The main one was his service of transportation since he carried goods between the countryside and Philadelphia on his shallops. He also offered other services like gauging and weighing. See, Louis Bissières, 'Une route à travers champs: la mise en relation de l'Amérique rurale (Maryland, Delaware, Pennsylvanie) au commerce atlantique à la fin du XVIIIe siècle', in: *Bulletin de l'AHMUF*, 44 (2024).

Table 7 The determinants of the chances of obtaining a credit with Levi Hollingsworth (binomial regression model)

Variable	*n()*	*freq*	*OR*	*95% CI*	*p value*
Position in the network	1,662				
Outsider client	460	27.7	–	–	
Insider client	1,202	72.3	**2.33**	1.60, 3.40	<0.001
Appearance around 1786	1,662				
None	290	17.5	–	–	
1785	246	14.8	1.12	0.64, 1.98	0.7
1785 & 1787	810	48.7	0.73	0.46, 1.15	0.2
1787	316	19.0	**0.56**	0.35, 0.91	0.020
Major trade: flour	1,662				
No	1,210	72.8	–	–	
Yes	452	27.2	0.70	0.48, 1.00	0.051
Motive of transaction	1,662				
Merchandise	734	44.2	–	–	
Service	928	55.8	**0.48**	0.32, 0.73	<0.001
Specialization	1,662				
Generalist	630	37.9	–	–	
Specialist	812	48.9	1.01	0.70, 1.46	>0.9
None	220	13.2	**0.49**	0.29, 0.84	0.009
Location	1,662				
Rural	450	27.1	–	–	
Foreign	72	4.3	0.85	0.41, 1.88	0.7
Urban	632	38.0	**1.52**	1.06, 2.17	0.022
Unknown	508	30.6	**1.99**	1.34, 2.97	<0.001
Value of transaction (£ Pa)	1,662				
(0, 1]	534	32.1	–	–	
(1, 5]	354	21.3	0.93	0.65, 1.33	0.7
(5, 10]	244	14.7	1.63	1.00, 2.72	0.057
(10, 20]	210	12.6	**2.82**	1.52, 5.57	0.002
(20, 50]	184	11.1	**4.87**	2.35, 11.5	<0.001
(50, 100]	66	4.0	**7.75**	2.25, 48.9	0.006
(100, 1000]	70	4.2	**7.74**	2.23, 49.0	0.006

(Source *ibid*)
In bold are the value of the factors that are significant at the 0.95 threshold

involving services was 2.1 times less likely (which amounts to 0.48 times more likely) to be paid on credit rather than immediately. In other words, sales of goods lead to much more credit than sales of services. Second, the amount of the transaction is included in the model to ensure that there was a network effect independent of it (this is the case since the p-value associated with the network position is far under 0.05). The amount of transactions had an effect for transactions above 10 £ and it very strongly increased the probability of using credit.

This regression allows to establish that Levi Hollingsworth granted credit much more easily to members of the central actors' clienteles (insiders) than to his exclusive clients (outsiders). Reciprocally, it was easier for Levi Hollingsworth to obtain credit from the former than from the latter. This work confirms the idea that the granting of credit in the early modern period was based on the position occupied in a merchant network. The historiography of the merchant world has long emphasized that credit stems from network position, but this was either an axiomatic assertion or a conclusion based on discrete observations.[35] Here this work provides both empirical evidence of the existence of this effect, and a quantitative order of magnitude. This can be interpreted as follows: the embedding of commercial relations in a merchant network allowed for a reduction of transaction costs that made the relative interest in turning to immediate settlements negligible, due to the trust placed in the members of the network.[36] Since the credit provider did not have to worry about short-term repayment (since the beneficiary was an insider who could get the support of his partners already embedded in the network), the premium for immediate settlement disappeared (unless the lender had an immediate need for cash).

[35] Pierre Gervais, 'De la discontinuité historique: économie, politique et temporalités, XVIIIe-XIXe siècles', HDR dissertation, Université Paris 1 Panthéon-Sorbonne 2012.

[36] On the articulation of networks and transaction costs, see Oliver E. Williamson, *Markets and hierarchies, analysis and antitrust implications: a study in the economics of internal organization* (New York, NY, 1975); Laurel Smith-Doerr and Walter W. Powell, 'Networks and Economic Life', in Neil J. Smelser and Richard Swedberg (eds.), *The handbook of economic sociology* (Princeton, NJ, 2005), 379–402; Forbes Munro and Tony Slaven, 'Networks and Markets in Clyde Shipping: The Donaldsons and the Hogarths, 1870–1939', in: *Business History*, 43:2 (2001), 19–50.

4 Credit and the Use of Means of Payment

Financing trade through credit was very common in the American economy in the end of the eighteenth century.[37] One important feature for the system of credit not to collapse lay in the ability of actors to punctually reimburse a part or the totality of their credit. Indeed, since most of early modern merchant credit did not mention any duration, credits could go on for years, but the lack of reimbursement could increase the risk of default of several members of the network.[38] Hollingsworth's partners could rely on cash, bank credit (that was very restricted since there was only one bank in the United States in 1786—the Bank of North America) and paper instruments (like promissory notes or bills of exchange) in order to compensate their credits (in getting their debtor or creditor account closer to zero).[39] This section establishes that, if their position in the network affected the amount of credit they got, it also influenced their tendencies to use one means of payment over the other.[40] Especially, insiders and central actors did not solely depend on cash. In other

[37] Jacob M. Price, 'What Did Merchants Do? Reflections on British Overseas Trade, 1660–1790', in: *The Journal of Economic History*, 49:2 (1989), 267–84; Cathy D. Matson, 'The revolution, the constitution, and the new nation', in Stanley L. Engerman and Robert E. Gallman (eds.), *The Cambridge economic history of the United States: the Colonial Era*, (Cambridge, 1996), 363–401; Robert S. DuPlessis, 'Conclusion: Reorienting early modern economic history: Merchant economy, merchant capitalism and the age of commerce', in: Pierre Gervais, Yannick Lemarchand, and Dominique Margairaz (eds.), *Merchants and profit in the age of commerce, 1680–1830* (London, 2014), 171–80; Damiano, *To her credit*.

[38] Tom Cutterham, "'A Very Promising Appearance': Credit, Honor, and Deception in the Emerging Market for American Debt, 1784–92', in: *The William and Mary Quarterly*, 75:4 (2018), 623–50; Julian Hoppit, *Risk and failure in English business 1700–1800* (Cambridge, 1987).

[39] On the Bank of North America see, Lawrence Lewis, *A History of the Bank of North America, The First Bank Chartered in the United States* (Philadelphia, PA, 1882); Robert E. Wright, *Origins of commercial banking in America, 1750–1800* (Lanham, MD, 2001).

[40] It is not obvious from the correspondence that insiders were aware of their privileged position, even if their business practices were different from those of the outsiders. Still, if the position held in a trade structure was not discussed, many insiders thanked Levi Hollingsworth for the opportunities he gave them access to. See, for instance, HSP, HFP, 1.a. Incoming Letters, Box 28 fol° 11: Letter from Charles Ghequiere to Levi Hollingsworth from the 8th of November 1785; Box 44 fol° 6: Letter from Herman Stump to Levi Hollingsworth from the 20th of July 1791; Box 45 fol° 8: Letter from Joseph England to Levi Hollingsworth from the 2th of January 1792.

words, centrality in the network allowed for the diversification of the use of means of payment, easing the compensation of credit.

Table 8 first shows general differences in the use of the three means of payment according to the position held within a merchant network. Overall, Hollingsworth's partners used cash 74% of the time, compared to 20% for bank credit and only 6% for commercial paper. This is a reminder of the massive use of cash in the American economy. This table confirms cash was the principal means of payment backing the credit system.[41] However, a comparison of the three types of partners allows to refine this observation. The imbalance in favor of cash is much more visible among the outsiders than among the insiders or the central actors. Indeed, an outsider used cash 86% of the time when it was less than 70% for the others. The difference between central actors and their clients (the insiders) lies in the fact that the former used a lot more paper instruments (especially drafts and promissory notes) in proportion. This is consistent with the fact that central actors were major players at a regional scale, giving them access to more sophisticated means of payment. In an economy in which metallic currency was scarce, they were willing to lose the premium associated with payments in cash (sometimes at a lesser cost), to get involved in large-scale transactions using bank credit, promissory notes, or bills of exchange in order to take advantage of controlling large clienteles. What transpires from this table is that the more central an actor was in the network, the greater the variety of means of payment he used would be. The systems of finance through credit were then backed by very differentiated circuits of payment.

These three binomial regression models allow to account for the correlation of the choice of one of the means of payment (over the other two) with the position held in a merchant network (Table 9). This position is a significant factor in the choice of any of the three means of payment available to actors participating in exchanges with Hollingsworth (except for the use of bank credit for which there was no significant difference between outsiders and central actors). The choice of cash was negatively correlated with the presence in the heart of the network (insiders and central actors) while the choice of bills of exchange or bank credit was positively correlated with it, all other things being equal (especially the amount of the transaction which means a large transaction would likely

[41] For an in-depth analysis, see Bissières, 'Les ressources économiques du réseau'.

Table 8 The use of means of payment according to the position held within Hollingsworth's network in 1786

Characteristic	*Type of actor*			
	Outsider, N = 1400[1]	*Insider, N = 1948*[1]	*Central actor, N = 884*[1]	*Total, N = 4232*[1]
Type of payment				
Bank Credit	162 (12%)	502 (26%)	164 (18%)	828 (20%)
Paper Instruments	28 (2%)	108 (5%)	122 (14%)	258 (6%)
Cash	1,210 (86%)	1,338 (69%)	598 (68%)	3,146 (74%)
[1] n (%)				

(Source *ibid*)
This table shows the number of occurrences of a type of actor mobilizing a type of transaction. This means that transactions between insiders and or central actors are counted twice, once for the debtor and once for the creditor

be compensated with cash for an outsider and with another means of payment for an insider).

Compared to the other two, cash is the means of payment that has the most intrinsic value since trust in cash was based on the monetary instrument itself, not the person holding it. It was mostly chosen by outsiders and Hollingsworth when they traded together. Conversely, paper instruments (for which the value depended on who wrote or held them) were more likely to be used by insiders and central actors. This confirms that the mutual trust between Hollingsworth and an insider (whether he was central or not) was stronger than that between Hollingsworth and one of his exclusive clients. For insiders compared to outsiders, bank credit was more similar to paper instruments in this situation, in that Hollingsworth must have had trusted that his partner would be able to fund his account at the Bank of North America.

This data shows that, through their position, the insiders and central actors gained the confidence of a merchant like Hollingsworth to handle more sophisticated means of payment than cash. This allowed them to have a greater issuing power to reimburse their credits. In doing so, they emancipated themselves from the constraints of the lack of cash in post-revolutionary America and could more easily finance their trade than outsiders (since it eased their access to credit). A letter written a few years later by two of Levi's brothers, Thomas and Samuel, who were also merchants in Baltimore, illustrates the way trust, credit, and means

Table 9 The determinants of the chances of using a specific means of payment (three binomial regression models)

Variable	*Cash*		*Bank Credit*		*Paper Instruments*	
	OR[1]	*p value*	*OR*[1]	*p value*	*OR*[1]	*p value*
Position in the network						
Outsider client	–		–		–	
Insider client	**0.45**	<0.001	**1.88**	<0.001	**2.02**	0.004
Central actor	**0.46**	<0.001	1.00	>0.9	**5.95**	<0.001
Appearance around 1786						
None	–		–		–	
1785	**2.51**	<0.001	**0.33**	<0.001	1.40	0.4
1785 & 1787	1.33	0.11	0.80	0.2	0.85	0.7
1787	0.95	0.8	1.08	0.7	0.95	0.9
Major trade: flour						
No	–		–		–	
Yes	**0.78**	0.031	**1.28**	0.030	0.98	>0.9
Specialization						
Generalist	–		–		–	
Specialist	1.04	0.7	0.84	0.13	1.30	0.2
None	0.87	0.5	1.03	0.9	1.19	0.6
Location						
Rural	–		–		–	
Foreign	**0.34**	0.018	2.45	0.051	1.94	0.4
Urban	1.06	0.6	0.98	0.9	0.98	>0.9
Unknown	**1.61**	<0.001	0.86	0.3	**0.31**	<0.001
Value of the transaction (£ Pa)						
(0,20]	–		–		–	
(20,50]	**0.11**	<0.001	**6.39**	<0.001	**28.0**	<0.001
(50,100]	**0.04**	<0.001	**12.8**	<0.001	**57.2**	<0.001
(100,1000]	**0.02**	<0.001	**22.5**	<0.001	**63.0**	<0.001
[1] OR = Odds Ratio, CI = Confidence Interval						

(Source *ibid*)
In bold are the value of the factors that are significant at the 0.95 threshold

of payment were articulated in the minds of traders from the end of the eighteenth century:

> Cash very scarce, indeed there is [next] to none here, it is all gone to the Country for Produce and our Merchants have been buying up Flour from the Millers on Credit many of which are now due & they're without Cash to support their Contracts. The excessive high prices of Produce together with the low rate of Exchange renders our Town very distressed. Our T[homas] H[ollingsworth] wrote you on the 23rd [of February] respecting the particular situation of our affairs. It is extremely painful to us that you should experience the present embarrassments and the more so as it happens at an unlucky period from the very extensive & wild circulation of our [property] and to undertake at this time to give you the support required, would deprive us of almost all the Property we now can Command in Trade. We have just been obliged to pay a Considerable Sum of Money for A Vessel [bought] last Fall and Our Notes will be due in Two Months for the [Amount] of a Snow we purchased last Summer [...] nothing would give us greater pain than that the Credit of any of our Family should suffer or their reputation in any manner be impeached, Particularly yours.[42]

In this letter, Levi's brothers explained why they could not help him with cash in a time of need. This explanation is twofold. First, they did not have access to cash, as it was being used by Baltimore merchants to reimburse purchases of flour bought on credit in the countryside. Facing a situation where cash was scarce, and since prices were high, trade came to a standstill in Baltimore. Mentioning the fact that the Baltimore merchants' credits were running out was also a way of justifying the fact that Thomas and Samuel could not collect the debts that some other partners owed them in order to help Levi. Second, they were also unable to finance their brother with paper instruments. This is what they suggested when they mentioned the past and forthcoming repayment of several promissory notes. Facing these obligations, they could not take on new loans without risking their own default. This clearly shows that arbitrations between different means of payment were sometimes difficult for merchants. Even if the position held in a network were a strong factor,

[42] HSP, HFP, 1.a. Incoming Letters, Box 40 fol° 10: Letter from Thomas & Samuel Hollingsworth to Levi Hollingsworth from the 2nd of March 1790.

these arbitrations were (at least partly) constrained by the general context or the state of traders' business.[43]

However, the threat was clear for Thomas and Samuel's brother in Philadelphia: his credit could be damaged if he found himself unable to repay his debts due to a lack of liquidity. This notion of reputation is essential and is mentioned directly in the words of Thomas and Samuel Hollingsworth. The question remains: To whom would Hollingsworth's reputation be impaired? I make the assumption that it would be much more impaired with his exclusive clients (outsiders) than with the other members of his network (insiders and central actors). Indeed, the granting of credit was easier with the latter and the longer duration of the relationship suggests that arrangements regarding means of payment could be made. While network membership played a very important role in the repayment of loans, it did not prevent all forms of repayment difficulties, as this letter shows. Still, if network membership did not remove all the risks inherent in credit practices, it did make it much easier to grant and repay credit.

5 Conclusion: The Involvement in a Network as a Resource

This paper consisted in an in-depth analysis of merchant credit practices. It showed that early modern finance (that, for many actors, only came from merchant credit) was deeply embedded in economic structures of trade, namely merchant networks. Indeed, the amount of credit a producer or a consumer could be granted depended on a series of relations he maintained, not only with the lender, but also with several partners of the lender. In the case of Levi Hollingsworth's merchant network, an actor would get more credit if he was in relation with others (central actors and their clients). Conversely, it means that an important merchant like Hollingsworth would discriminate between his partners when it came to credit. His behavior and his strategies were influenced by the position they held in the network.

Furthermore, credit systems were backed by a specific use of means of payment. Indeed, actors holding different positions in the network would use different means of payment to settle their debts. As it was

[43] Crowston, *Credit, fashion, sex.*

showed, cash was the main tool for outsiders while insiders would use bank credit or paper instruments more. This is coherent with the fact that Levi Hollingsworth put more trust in the latter than the former. In the end, when it came to finance, the activity of an individual and his history (his "track record" in contemporary terms) were not the only elements that mattered. The way he was connected to others was (maybe even more) decisive. Indeed, before they could massively turn to banks, American had to rely on impersonal relations to get credit. And these relations were not as much thought as bilateral than as a part of a larger system. A merchant network consisted in a system of control that overshadowed the simple notion of trust between two partners.

References

Primary sources

Historical Society of Pennsylvania (HSP), Hollingsworth family papers, collection 289 (HFP), 1.a. Letters, boxes 22–57.
HSP, HFP, 2.a. Ledgers: Ledger L, vol 21, and M, vol. 62.
HSP, HFP, 2.b. Correspondence, Outgoing, Letter books, vol. 2–3.
HSP, HFP, 2.c. Daybooks and Journals: Journal L, vol. 86.
HSP, HFP, 2.e., Orders, box 174.
HSP, HFP, 2.g., Invoices; box 185.
HSP, HFP, 2.h., Shipping: Freight Journal K, vol. 205.
HSP, HFP, 2.o., Bills and Receipts, boxes 259–260.
HSP, Miscellaneous Professional and Personal Business Papers, 1732–1945 (collection 2001), Thomas, Samuel and Miers Fisher Journals (1784–1788 and 1792–1796).
Delaware Historical Society, Hollingsworth Maxwell & Adams company ledger, 1787–1798, vol. 1.

Printed primary material

Francis White, *Philadelphia Directory* (Philadelphia, PA, 1785).
Clement Biddle, *The Philadelphia Directory* (Philadelphia, PA, 1791).
Edmund Hogan, *The prospect of Philadelphia and check on the next Directory* (Philadelphia, PA, 1795).
T. W. Jones et S. S. Moore, *The Traveller's Directory* (Philadelphia, PA, 1804).

Secondary material

Baxter, William T. 2004. Observations on Money, Barter and Bookkeeping. *The Accounting Historians Journal* 31 (1): 129–139.

Bissières, Louis. 2022. Les ressources économiques du réseau au défi de la mesure : les commerces de Levi Hollingsworth (Philadelphie, fin XVIIIe siècle). PhD dissertation, Université Paris 1 Panthéon-Sorbonne.

Bissières, Louis. 2023. 'Taking time seriously': An empirical approach to an American merchant network at the end of the 18th century. *Journal of Historical Network Research* 8: 58–92.

Bissières, Louis. 2024. Une route à travers champs: la mise en relation de l'Amérique rurale (Maryland, Delaware, Pennsylvanie) au commerce atlantique à la fin du XVIIIe siècle. *Bulletin de l'AHMUF* 44.

Bloom, Robert, and John Solotko. 2004. Barter accounting in the US during the late eighteenth and early nineteenth centuries. *Accounting History* 9 (1): 91–108.

Bodenhorn, Howard. 2003. *State Banking in Early America: A New Economic History*. New York, NY, Oxford University Press.

Capelo, M., P. Araújo, and C. Álvarez-Dardet. 2015. Management control systems, trust and risk in inter-organisational relationships: The case of Francisco González de la Sierra and its partner Rivas y Cantallops (1847–1864). *Business History* 57 (4): 528–563.

Caracausi, Andrea, and Christof Jeggle (eds.). 2014. *Commercial Networks and European Cities, 1400–1800*. London, Pickering & Chatto.

Crowston, Clare Haru. 2013. *Credit, Fashion, Sex: Economies of Regard in Old Regime France*. Durham, NC, Duke University Press.

Cutterham, Tom. 2018. 'A Very Promising Appearance': Credit, Honor, and Deception in the Emerging Market for American Debt, 1784–92. *The William and Mary Quarterly* 75 (4): 623–650.

Damiano, Sara T. 2021. *To Her Credit: Women, Finance, and the Law in Eighteenth-Century New England Cities*. Baltimore, MD, Johns Hopkins University Press.

Davison, Kate. 2019. Early modern social networks: Antecedents, opportunities, and challenges. *The American Historical Review* 124 (2): 456–482.

de Valeriola, Sébastien. 2021. Can historians trust centrality? Historical network analysis and centrality metrics robustness. *Journal of Historical Network Research* 6 (1): 85–125.

Dermineur, Elise M. (ed.). 2018. *Women and Credit in Pre-industrial Europe*. Turnhout, Brepols.

Dermineur, Elise M. 2019. Peer-to-peer lending in pre-industrial France. *Financial History Review* 26 (3): 359–388.

Doerflinger, Thomas M. 1986. *A Vigorous Spirit of Enterprise: Merchants and Economic Development in Revolutionary Philadelphia*. Chapel Hill, NC, University of North Carolina Press.

DuPlessis, Robert S. 2014. Conclusion: Reorienting early modern economic history: Merchant economy, merchant capitalism and the age of commerce. In *Merchants and Profit in the Age of Commerce, 1680–1830*, edited by Pierre Gervais, Yannick Lemarchand, and Dominique Margairaz, 171–80. London, Pickering & Chatto.

Easley, David, and Jon Kleinberg. 2010. *Networks, Crowds, and Markets: Reasoning About a Highly Connected World*. Cambridge, Cambridge University Press.

Edwards, Andrew D. 2018. Money and the American Revolution: Changing Concepts of Money and Wealth, 1765–1786. PhD dissertation, Princeton University.

Engerman, Stanley L., and Robert E. Gallman (eds.). 1996. *The Cambridge Economic History of the United States: The Colonial Era*. Cambridge, Cambridge University Press.

Feinstein, Charles H., and Mark Thomas. 2002. *Making History Count: A Primer in Quantitative Methods for Historians*. Cambridge, Cambridge University Press.

Gamper, Markus. 2015. The history of 'relational science' and social network analysis. In *Debtors, Creditors, and Their Networks: Social Dimensions of Monetary Dependence from the Seventeenth to the Twentieth Century*, edited by Andreas Gestrich and Martin Stark, 11–42. London, German Historical Institute London Bulletin.

Gervais, Pierre. 2010. A game of claims and expectations: Credit, failure, and personal relationships across the Atlantic. *Commonplace* 10: 3.

Gervais, Pierre. 2012a. Crédit et filières marchandes au XVIIIe siècle. *Annales. Histoire, Sciences Sociales* 67 (4): 1011–1048.

Gervais, Pierre. 2012b. De la discontinuité historique : économie, politique et temporalités, XVIIIe-XIXe siècles, HDR dissertation, Université Paris 1 Panthéon-Sorbonne.

Greenberg, Joshua R. 2020. *Bank Notes and Shinplasters: The Rage for Paper Money in the Early Republic*. Philadelphia, PA, University of Pennsylvania Press.

Hancock, David J. 1995. *Citizens of the World: London Merchants and the Integration of the British Atlantic Community, 1735–1785*. Cambridge, Cambridge University Press.

Hart, Emma. 2019. *Trading Spaces: The Colonial Marketplace and the Foundations of American Capitalism*. Chicago, IL, University of Chicago Press.

Hart, Emma, and Cathy Matson. 2017. Situating Merchants in Late Eighteenth-Century British Atlantic Port Cities. *Early American Studies: An Interdisciplinary Journal* 15 (4): 660–682.

Hartigan-O'Connor, Ellen. 2009. *Ties That Buy: Women and Commerce in Revolutionary America*. Philadelphia, PA, University of Pennsylvania Press.

Hoffman, Philip T., Gilles Postel-Vinay, and Jean-Laurent Rosenthal. 2019. *Dark Matter Credit: The Development of Peer-to-Peer Lending and Banking in France*. Princeton, NJ, Princeton University Press.

Hoppit, Julian. 1987. *Risk and Failure in English Business 1700–1800*. Cambridge, Cambridge University Press.

Hunter, Brooke. 2001. Rage for Grain: Flour Milling in the Mid-Atlantic. PhD dissertation, University of Delaware.

Kolaczyk, Eric D., and Gábor Csárdi. 2020. *Statistical Analysis of Network Data with R*. Cham, Springer.

Lemarchand, Yannick, Cheryl S. McWatters, and Laure Pineau-Defois. 2014. The current account as cognitive artefact: Stories and accounts of La Maison Chaurand. In *Merchants and profit in the age of commerce, 1680–1830*, edited by Pierre Gervais, Yannick Lemarchand, and Dominique Margairaz, 13–32. London, Pickering & Chatto.

Lemercier, Claire. 2015. Formal network methods in history: why and how? In *Social Networks, Political Institutions, and Rural Societies*, edited by Georg Fertig, 281–310. Turnhout, Brepols.

Lewis, Lawrence. 1882. *A History of the Bank of North America, The First Bank Chartered in the United States*. Philadelphia, PA, J. B. Lippincott & Company.

Mann, Bruce H. 2002. *Republic of Debtors: Bankruptcy in the Age of American Independence*. Cambridge, MA, Harvard University Press.

Martin, Ann Smart. 2010. *Buying into the World of Goods: Early Consumers in Backcountry Virginia*. Baltimore, MD, Johns Hopkins University Press.

Matson, Cathy D. 1996. The revolution, the constitution, and the new nation. In *The Cambridge Economic History of the United States: The Colonial Era*, edited by Stanley L. Engerman and Robert E. Gallman, 363–401. Cambridge, Cambridge University Press.

McCusker, John J. 2006. Colonial statistics. In: *Historical Statistics of the United States: Earliest Times to the Present*, edited by Susan B. Carter, 1155–1200. New York, NY, Cambridge University Press.

McCusker, John J., and Russell R. Menard (eds.). 1985. *The Economy of British America, 1607-1789*. Chapel Hill, NC, Omohundro Institute of Early American History and Culture.

McLean, Paul D., and Neha Gondal. 2014. The Circulation of Interpersonal Credit in Renaissance Florence. *European Journal of Sociology/Archives Européennes de Sociologie / Europäisches Archiv für Soziologie* 55 (2): 135–176.

McNulty, Keith. 2021. Handbook of Regression Modeling in People Analytics: With Examples in R and Python. https://peopleanalytics-regression-book.org/gitbook/

McWatters, Cheryl S., and Yannick Lemarchand. 2010. Accounting as story telling: Merchant activities and commercial relations in eighteenth century France. *Accounting, Auditing & Accountability Journal* 23 (1): 14–54.

McWatters, Cheryl S., and Yannick Lemarchand. 2013. Merchant networks and accounting discourse: The role of accounting transactions in network relations. *Accounting History Review* 23 (1): 49–83.

Muldrew, Craig. 1998. *The Economy of Obligation: The Culture of Credit and Social Relations in Early Modern England*. Houndmills, Palgrave.

Munro, Forbes, and Tony Slaven. 2001. Networks and Markets in Clyde Shipping: The Donaldsons and the Hogarths, 1870–1939. *Business History* 43 (2): 19–50.

Opsahl, Tore. 2011. tnet, analyse of Weighted, Two-mode and Longitudinal Networks. https://toreopsahl.com/tnet/

Opsahl, Tore, Filip Agneessens, and John Skvoretz. 2010. Node centrality in weighted networks: Generalizing degree and shortest paths. *Social Networks* 32 (3): 245–251.

Padgett, John F., and Paul D. McLean. 2011. Economic Credit in Renaissance Florence. *The Journal of Modern History* 83 (1): 1–47.

Pedersen, Thomas Lin. Data Imaginist. https://www.data-imaginist.com//

Price, Jacob M. 1989. What Did Merchants Do? Reflections on British Overseas Trade, 1660–1790. *The Journal of Economic History* 49 (2): 267–284.

Smith-Doerr, Laurel, and Walter W. Powell. 2005. Networks and Economic Life. In *The Handbook of Economic Sociology*, edited by Neil J. Smelser and Richard Swedberg, 379–402. Princeton, NJ, Princeton University Press.

Trivellato, Francesca. 2009. *The Familiarity of Strangers: The Sephardic Diaspora, Livorno, and Cross-Cultural Trade in the Early Modern Period*. New Haven, CT, Yale University Press.

Villain, Julien. 2021. *Le commode et l'accessoire: le commerce des biens de consommation au XVIIIe siècle Lorraine, v. 1690-v. 1790*. Rennes, Presses Universitaires de Rennes.

Williamson, Oliver E. 1975. *Markets and Hierarchies, Analysis and Antitrust Implications: A Study in the Economics of Internal Organization*. New York, Free Press.

Wright, Robert E. 2001. *Origins of Commercial Banking in America, 1750–1800*. Lanham, MD, Rowman & Littlefield.

Yamey, Basil S. 2000. The 'particular gain or loss upon each article we deal in': An aspect of mercantile accounting, 1300–1800. *Accounting, Business & Financial History* 10 (1): 1–12.

CHAPTER 8

Financial Intermediation and Networks in Early Modern Castile Fairs

David Carvajal

1 Introduction

The Nobel Prize in Economic Sciences 2022 was awarded to economists Ben S. Bernanke, Douglas W. Diamond, and Philip H. Dybvig, in recognition of their research on financial intermediation and banking. The prize honored a series of contributions that focused on the study of banking activity in times of economic crisis, particularly during the Great Depression. Among the reflections of the laureates, one of the most valued by the Committee refers to the importance that all the three have attributed to banking as a vital institution in financial intermediation and its key role in the real economy, favoring the contact between supply and demand of capital. Few people are aware that the absence or destruction of financial intermediation tends to have important consequences in the short and long term.[1] Just as the generation of financial networks has a positive

[1] Ben S. Bernanke, 'Nonmonetary effects of the financial crisis in the propagation of the Great Depression', in: *American Economic Review* 73 (1983), 257–276.

D. Carvajal (✉)
University of Valladolid, Valladolid, Spain
e-mail: david.carvajal@uva.es

E. M. Dermineur and M. Pompermaier (eds.), *Credit Networks in The Preindustrial World*, Palgrave Studies in the History of Finance,
https://doi.org/10.1007/978-3-031-67117-3_8

effect, a breakdown in intermediation means a breakdown in the relational structure that supports the circulation of money. Trust disappears and it takes a long time to rebuild these ties, return to normality, and allow money to flow again.[2] Although some of the award-winning studies are based on the analysis of American banking during the 1930s, a large part of the reflections on the importance of intermediation and the capacity to mobilize money from savings and deposits to those economic activities that demand it can be extrapolated, with nuances, to past times.

This chapter aims to investigate the role of bankers (moneychangers in Castile) in a period, the beginning of the sixteenth century, which historiography has marked the division between two ages, but which really represents a transition between two connected worlds. Identifying the origins of European banking is a complex issue, but it requires us to go back to medieval times. Although the roots are diffuse and the definition of the European banker and his activity was slow and gradual, it is inevitable to mention the importance of the Italian world. In its cities we find references to the first medieval merchant-bankers, pioneers in their activity[3] who demonstrated the importance of having capital providers or intermediaries able to promote the rise of a complex financial system and to generate and maintain banking networks throughout Europe.[4] The presence of bankers became more common from the fourteenth century onward in various European territories and kingdoms, from Flanders to Barcelona, Paris, and so on. In Castile, however, the emergence of banking as an economic activity seems to have taken place later. From the fifteenth century onward, there are references about the presence of moneychangers in cities such as Seville and Burgos who, beyond mercantile business, carried out activities proper to bankers and settled in the main streets and squares. In other words, the term moneychanger was similar to the concept of medieval and early modern bankers, as its main activities consisted in lending, currency exchange, and financial intermediation. The activity of moneychangers as intermediaries was consolidated

[2] Scientific Background on the Sveriges Riksbank Prize in Economic Sciences in Memory of Alfred Nobel 2022, 'Financial Intermediation and the Economy' (2022), 5–6.

[3] Raymond de Roover, *Money, Banking and Credit in Medieval Bruges* (Cambridge [Ma], 1948).

[4] John F. Padgett and Christopher. K. Ansell, 'Robust Action and the Rise of the Medici, 1400–1434', in: *American Journal of Sociology* 98:6 (1993) 1259–1319.

as they became present in the main European and Castilian markets and fairs. Thanks to their ability to attract deposits, they became a key part of the financial system, granting credit and facilitating economic activities such as consumption and investment. As in the case of the merchants, moneychangers and bankers soon realized the need to generate local, regional, and European networks adapted to their business and their role as financial intermediaries.[5]

The second objective of this chapter is to study this capacity of moneychangers to generate networks and to intermediate, trying to understand the typologies of the networks according to their configuration, to study their objectives and other aspects that we consider key to determine to what extent their role as financial intermediaries was effective. The interest of studying the formation of commercial and financial networks in Castile is not new, as shown by the studies of H. Casado on the Castilian commercial network in Europe in the fifteenth-sixteenth centuries, or the information networks analyzed from the dispatch of mercantile correspondence and the letters of exchange in the company of the merchant-banker Simón Ruiz in the second half of the sixteenth century.[6] The existence of networks based on the creation of companies and the alliances between merchant families through marriage were fundamental to ensure the cohesion and success of mercantile communities in local but also in foreign markets. The creation of information networks was also crucial to ensure the correct development of business between distant markets, avoiding asymmetric information.

Related to the increasing interest in the study of networks in late medieval and modern age, a decade ago Social Network Analysis (SNA) became a common methodology in many studies on the economic and

[5] David Carvajal, 'The "économie sans travail" in early modern Castile Credit and moneychangers', in: Luisa Brunori et al. (eds.) Le Droit face à l'économie sans travail, Tome II, 'L'approche internationale' (Paris, 2020), 47–68.

[6] Hilario Casado, *El triunfo de Mercurio. La presencia Castellana en Europa (Siglos XV y XVI)* (Burgos, 2003); Hilario, Casado, 'Los flujos de información en las redes comerciales castellanas de los siglos XV y XVI', in: *Investigaciones de Historia Económica* 10 (2008), 35–68; Hilario Casado, 'Crecimiento económico, redes de comercio y fiscalidad en Castilla a fines de la Edad Media', in: Juan A. Bonachía and David Carvajal (eds.), Los negocios del hombre. Comercio y rentas en Castilla. Siglos XV y XVI (Valladolid, 2012), 17–36; Ana Sofia Ribeiro, *Early Modern Trading Networks in Europe. Cooperation and the case of Simon Ruiz* (New York, 2016).

social history of the Crown of Castile.[7] Among the new contributions to the study of trade and finance in Castile, some works provided new approaches that have led researchers to better understand some of the realities already described in traditional analyses, as the case of the communities of financers who managed the royal taxation.[8] SNA approach has also allowed the study of the relationships between Castilian merchant families, or the evolution of urban oligarchies based on the links created between them to ensure their social and political escalation.[9] After these first experiences, SNA has been relegated to a secondary level in the study of the economic relations of this period, but it continues to be an important tool in other fields of contemporary economic history[10] and in the social and political history of Spain in the eighteenth century.[11]

The choice of SNA as a method is based on three key reasons. First, SNA allows for a systematic mapping of the relationships between actors, considering different structural variables such as financial relationships (lending, intermediation, etc.) in a single analysis. Second, the SNA allows to recognize to what extent actors' attributes were key in generating or enhancing relationships. Finally, the use of SNA opens an opportunity for future studies that delve deeper into the relationships between known individuals, incorporating new relationships and attributes; or new studies that extend the time frame presented in this chapter. Understanding the generation of networks in annual or biannual meetings, such

[7] Sanjay Subrahmanyam, *Merchant Networks in the Early Modern World* (London and New York, 2016).

[8] Pablo Ortego, ' Financieros y redes financieras en tiempos de Juan II: posibilidades de estudio del libro de "recepta" de 1440', in: David Carvajal et al. (eds.), Redes sociales y económicas en el mundo bajomedieval (Valladolid, 2011), 105–129.

[9] María A. Martín Romera, 'Nuevas perspectivas para el estudio de las sociedades medievales: el análisis de redes sociales', in: *Studia Histórica. Historia Medieval* 28 (2010), 217–239; David Carvajal, 'Redes socioeconómicas y mercaderes castellanos a fines de la Edad Media e inicios de la Moderna', in: David Carvajal et al. (eds.), Redes sociales y económicas en el mundo bajomedieval (Valladolid, 2011), 79–102; David Carvajal, 'Merchant Networks in the Cities of the Crown of Castile', in: Andrea Caracausi and Christoff Jeggle (eds.), Commercial Networks and European Cities, 1400–1800 (London, 2014), 137–152.

[10] Juan Antonio Rubio, *Andalucía durante la segunda revolución tecnológica: ciclos de inversión, sociedades mercantiles y grupos empresariales* (Granada, 2014).

[11] José M. Imízcoz and Antoni Artola, 'Redes sociales, procesos de cambio cultural y conflicto en las provincias vascas y navarra (1700–1839)', in: *Historia Social* 89 (2017), 73–77.

as the Medina del Campo fairs, and their maintenance will allow us to recognize important channels of economic cooperation or transmission of information that go beyond the temporal and geographical limits of these markets.

This chapter aims to take up the principles of SNA to understand some of the characteristics of financial relations and intermediation through the study of financial networks, understanding the development of relationships between agents—moneychangers and merchants—based on the available sources of documentation. This last question is fundamental since the sources available for the study of financial relations in the Crown of Castile at the beginning of the sixteenth century are scarce. Spanish archives offer the researcher public documentation from government and judicial archives, as well as notarial archives, but there is also private documentation, such as some private accounting books, etc., which can help us to reconstruct the financial intermediation networks. Of all the available sources, we know from previous studies that notarial sources have great potential since notaries carried out key intermediation work in their offices as network-makers.[12] Therefore, in this work we have chosen notarial records to analyze in a serialized way the relationships established by the Castilian moneychangers in the main fairs of the north of the Crown. This analysis is based on the study of 7,180 notarial contracts signed in Castilian fair centers dated between 1509 and 1520—obtained after the analysis of more than 17,000 notarial records from the *Archivo Provincial de Valladolid* and published in 2014—and from which a considerable number of financial relationships have been extracted.[13]

The chapter is organized into three sections. The first section explains the reasons for the economic and financial rise in Castile at the beginning of the sixteenth century and then discusses the importance of the fairs as financial markets. The second section explains the importance of the financial intermediation developed by the moneychangers in the fairs, focusing on the financial instruments they used and the type of relationships they created with others. Finally, the third and most important part of the paper analyses the networks generated by the moneychangers in the

[12] Philip. T. Hoffman, Giles Postel-Vinay and Jean-Laurent Rosenthal, *Priceless Markets. The Political Economy of Credit in Paris. 1660–1870* (Chicago, 2000).

[13] David Carvajal, Mauricio Herrero, Francisco Javier Molina and Irene Ruiz, *Mercaderes y cambiadores en los protocolos notariales de la provincia de Valladolid (1486–1520)* (Valladolid, 2015).

Castilian fairs from three perspectives. The first focuses on analyzing how the moneychangers acted as a channel for credit between Castilian and foreign merchants; the second is oriented toward the study of communities based on the geographical origin and other SNA tools. The third perspective is devoted to the study of the networks of the three main actors of the network detected in the analysis.

2 The Rise of Castile: Economy, Markets, and Fairs

During the fifteenth century and, above all, at the beginning of the sixteenth century, mercantile and financial activities grew intensely. The territorial expansion of Castile and endogenous development, based on the growth of factors such as population and agricultural and craft production, explain the high rates of urbanization achieved in the Crown and the flourishing of important local, regional, peninsular, and international markets and fairs.[14] All of this led to an important increase in mercantile traffic, both domestic and international.[15] In this context, the Castilian financial system underwent significant development. From an institutional point of view, the advances in the codification of Castilian legislation, the regulation of markets, the consolidation of certain financial instruments, and the notary's office provided security to the economic actors and drove the expansion of financial activities and credit throughout Castilian territory.[16] Beyond the strictly institutional framework, it is worth highlighting the emergence of important groups of merchants and financiers who, at the local, regional, and peninsular level, showed a growing capacity to generate companies and extensive mercantile networks, as well as advanced technical and practical knowledge when negotiating.

As we have noted above, one of the most significant changes at the mercantile and financial level was the creation and consolidation of

[14] Bartolomé Yun, *Marte contra Minerva. El precio del Imperio Español, ca. 1450–1600* (Barcelona, 2004).

[15] Casado, *El Triunfo*.

[16] David Carvajal, 'Ley, justicia y cambio económico en Castilla a fines de la Edad Media e inicios de la Edad Moderna', in: *Ricerche di Storia Economica e Sociale* 2 (2018), 35–60.

numerous markets and fairs in Medieval Europe, the appropriate environment for the development of networks. In Castile we find parallel influences in the two phenomena cited by S. R. Epstein when analyzing the rise of the European fairs: demographic-economic growth and institutional changes.[17] Economic growth and the search for opportunities on the part of lords and cities were behind the rise of numerous fairs and markets in the Crown of Castile. Castilian kings, important noblemen, and some city councils promoted the holding of fairs and markets granting privileges, first as a complement to daily commercial activities and, later, as a source of income thanks to the taxes imposed on mercantile activities and other revenues. Thus, in the mid-fifteenth century, Castile had important manorial fairs such as that of Villalón, under the control of the Count of Benavente; those of Medina de Rioseco, promoted by the Admiral of Castile, or those of Valladolid and Medina del Campo, closely linked to royal power. The proliferation of the fairs was accompanied by the granting of privileges and the issuing of new ordinances that affected the timing of the fairs, the organization of spaces, the regulation of taxation, the role of justice, etc., consolidating commercial activity and the development of capital markets.[18]

The integration of the fairs increased after Isabella I granted the Medina del Campo fairs the status of general fairs and payment fairs of Castile in 1491, making them the core of the commercial and financial system of the northern region of Castile. At these fairs, for example, the leasing of royal taxes was negotiated, the Crown made some of its main payments and large-scale buying and selling operations were carried out between Castilian and foreign merchants and businessmen.[19] The notaries of Medina acted as guarantors of thousands of contracts in their offices, guaranteeing the correct functioning of the market and enhancing trust among the participants. The seasonality in the celebration of the main Castilian fairs generated, not without significant conflicts, a calendar defined as the Castilian fair cycle, dominated by the most important markets the fairs of Medina del Campo, and the secondary ones,

[17] Stephan R. Epstein, 'Fairs, Institutional Innovation, and Economic Growth in Late Medieval Europe', in: *The Economic History Review* 47–3 (1994), 459–482.

[18] Miguel Á. Ladero Quesada, *Las ferias en Castilla. Siglos XII-XV* (Madrid, 1994).

[19] Falah Hassan Abed H. A. Al-Hussein, 'Las ferias de Medina y el comercio de la lana: 1514–1573', in: Eufemio Lorenzo (ed.), Historia de Medina del Campo y su Tierra (Valladolid, 1986), vol. II, 15–30.

Villalón at Easter and Medina de Rioseco in August. The cycle extended throughout the year, except for the winter months when traveling was a complex due to the difficulties caused by the weather and the conditions of the routes of transport that structured a large territory. The fair cycle not only included the three major fairs, but also other smaller fairs, such as those of Béjar, held between 1st and 15th August, those of Zafra and Plasencia, held in May. The aim of scheduling the fairs in successive months was to facilitate negotiation between merchants and the payment among moneychangers, who acted as intermediaries and bankers. The fairs allowed to make the capital flows more regular and secure, and the financial markets took the fair cycle as a time point for making payments and paying off debts, for which the closing periods of the fairs were reserved.[20] For example, the Medina del Campo fairs reserved their last weeks and the days after the fair for merchants and moneychangers to settle operations through their accounting books, compensating or transferring capital.

It is possible that the institutional balance achieved between the monarchy and the lords—a key aspect for Epstein—when it came to maintaining fair privileges and control over certain economic activities allowed the survival of this system throughout the sixteenth century and established the fairs of northern Castile as an organized market where stable commercial and financial networks could be cultivated.[21] The Castilian markets, and especially the fairs such as that of Medina del Campo, were ideal contexts for the generation of important mercantile networks at different levels.

We know the importance of local networks in fostering the growth of retail trade. These networks became channels for the distribution of products from the fairs to the surrounding villages, promoting the growth of consumption.[22] On a second level, there were wider geographical networks—regional and peninsular—such as those that connected the

[20] Ramón Carande, *Carlos V y sus banqueros. La vida económica en Castilla (1516–1556)* (Madrid, 1965); Yun, Bartolomé, *Sobre la transición al Capitalismo en Castilla: economía y sociedad en Tierra de Campos (15,001–1830)* (Valladolid, 1987).

[21] Epstein, 'Fairs', 473.

[22] Hilario Casado, 'Crédito y comercio en las ferias de Medina del Campo en la primera mitad del siglo XVI', in: Elena María García and Giuseppe de Luca (eds.), Il mercato del crédito in Età Moderna. Reti e operatori finanziari dello spazio europeo (Milano, 2009), 21–48.

north of the Crown of Castile—Medina del Campo, Valladolid, Burgos, or Segovia—with the main cities and ports of the south—Sevilla, Jerez de la Frontera, Cádiz.[23] Finally, the fairs were also the epicenter of important international commercial and financial networks, leading one of the great changes observed in many European markets: the transition from being local markets to international markets,[24] which brought merchants from all over Europe—Genoa, Florence, Milan, France, England, or Flanders—into contact with Castilians, especially those from Burgos, specialized in the export of wool and other products.[25]

The economic expansion of trade and financial activity led Castilian fairs to turn into important international markets during the sixteenth century. Markets where large amounts of money were demanded, where financial intermediation was fundamental, and where it was necessary to have a solid and trustworthy business network. In this context, moneychangers played a key role, given that their role as simple changers had mutated into one of financial intermediaries, into small and medium-sized bankers who facilitated credit operations, granted loans, or ensured the payment and drawing of bills of exchange to markets such as Bruges, Antwerp, Florence, Genoa, or La Rochelle.

3 Financial Intermediation: Actors, Instruments, and Relationships

The main objective of this chapter is to explore the generation of financial networks based on the activity of the moneychangers (or bankers) operating in the fairs of Medina del Campo and Medina de Rioseco at the beginning of the sixteenth century. Therefore, it is essential to define the main actors of the network, as well as the relationships generated through the signature of different financial instruments and contracts.

The origins of banking activity in Castile date back to the Middle Ages and are related to the figure of the moneychanger, whose activity was increasingly mentioned in the sources. Originally, they were agents

[23] Hilario Casado', Comercio, crédito y finanzas públicas en Castilla en la época de los Reyes Católicos', in: Antonio Miguel Bernal (ed.), Dinero, moneda y crédito en la monarquía hispánica (Madrid, 2000), 135–156.

[24] Laurence Fontaine, *Le marché. Histoire et usages d'une conquête sociale* (Paris, 2014), there 102.

[25] Casado, *El Triunfo.*

specializing in currency exchange, established in trade centers and on routes such as the Camino de Santiago—an important pilgrimage and trade route that connected French territory with the north of the Iberian Peninsula. During the 15th the number of moneychangers, as well as the size and variety of their activities, grew exponentially.This was a significant sign of the development of financial and banking activities in the towns, markets and fairs of Castile.[26]

Although the moneychangers gradually consolidated their role as specialists in intermediation, it should be noted that many of them also worked not only as bankers, but also as merchants, buying and selling all kinds of products, or as small financiers who, at different levels, rented and managed local or royal taxes. In this chapter, due to the diffuse nature of their economic interests, we have considered the relationship established between moneychangers and the relationships between moneychangers and merchants at the fairs, whom they represented in numerous businesses. It is logical to suppose that a moneychanger from Valladolid would represent and intermediate for merchants from his own city. The Medina del Campo fairs, held in the months of May–June and October–November, were a meeting place for moneychangers from the economic centers in the surrounding area, especially Burgos, Valladolid, and Segovia.[27] In these markets there were operators named as "*cambiadores de feria*", financiers with an institutional status, known by the great majority of the merchants and actors who traded there. These were professionals of good reputation and with proven financial solvency. Moreover, these moneychangers acted as guarantors for each other so that much of their capital and the capital circulating at the fair was insured through a system of community liability. This aspect became fundamental as the fairs grew and, as an institution, they could not afford the failure of this cog in the wheel.[28]

[26] Felipe Ruiz, 'La Banca en España hasta 1782', in: *El Banco de España: Una historia Económica* (Madrid, 1970), 1–196; David Carvajal, 'En los precedentes de la banca castellana moderna: cambiadores al norte del Tajo a inicios del siglo XVI', in: Ernesto García and Juan A. Bonachía (eds.), *Hacienda, Mercado y Poder al norte de la Corona de Castilla en el tránsito del medievo a la modernidad* (Valladolid, 2015), 17–38.

[27] Carvajal, 'En los precedentes', there 20–21.

[28] An example of the system of mutual bonds between exchangers at the fairs in Medina del Campo in David Carvajal, 'La banca privada castellana y el fin de una generación: diversificación, crisis de liquidez y quiebra en el cambio de Gaspar Enríquez (1531- ca.

Moneychangers attended the fairs regularly. There they kept their account books where recorded their daily contacts and business. In fact, many moneychangers kept a daily book and a ledger called "fair books" exclusively for this time, distinguishing them from the other books and registers. Their daily book and ledgers recorded the accounts of their depositors and hundreds of transactions with their customers using the "double entry". In besides spending a good part of their fair days absorbed in their mercantile documentation, it was relatively common to find many moneychangers in the offices of the notaries at the fairs of Medina del Campo or Medina de Rioseco—we have not preserved notarial testimonies for the fairs of Villalón in this period—signing contracts with their customers, with creditors and, above all, with debtors to whom they had lent capital.

At the end of the fifteenth century, the activity of notaries in Castile seemed to be inadequate and had significant limitations. The absence of notaries in their offices, the irregularity of their activity, the overpricing of their services, and the inadequate management of the registry of notarial protocols were some of the problems. For this reason, since the reform in 1503, Castilian notaries were legally obliged to preserve all their registers, as well as improving other organizational aspects. This change has allowed us to consult notarial sources from this period, although the documents preserved during the first decades of the sixteenth century in the north of Castile are quite scarce. Among the diversity of mercantile contracts and businesses signed in the presence of notaries, two contracts or financial instruments stand out and allow us to investigate the financial intermediation capacity of the moneychangers: the obligation (*obligación*) and the power or letter of attorney (*carta de poder*).[29] From these instruments, located among the 7,180 documents analyzed, and the recorded relationships—a total of 444—we have reconstructed the structure of a network on which the moneychangers carried out a significant part of their financial intermediation work, and which allows us to address some of the

1562)', in: Ramón Lanza (ed.), Finanzas y crisis financieras en la Monarquía Hispánica, siglos XVI-XVII (Madrid, 2023), there 100–101.

[29] The letter of exchange is another fundamental contract regarding intermediation. However, as it was a private contract, there are few references to this document in notarial records. There are "protests" at the notary's office for non-payment of letters of exchange, which became more common as the sixteenth century progressed.

proposed objectives regarding the type of network, the characteristics of the dominant groups, and the role of certain moneychangers as nodes.

The obligation was the most common financial and credit instrument in Castile from the sixteenth to the beginning of the nineteenth century. The contract at the financial level was based on the commitment acquired by the debtor with the creditor to whom he had to pay back an amount within the established terms. This public instrument was the most frequently used in credit purchase and sale operations or in loans. Its study at the Medina del Campo fairs allows us, among other things, to reconstruct the rates at which debts were signed and paid. Obligations also provide us the opportunity to analyze financial relationships between agents, either as creditors or as debtors. From the point of view of SNA, each obligation represents a directed relationship, a financial flow involving the transfer of capital or a credit sale to the debtor. Credit relationships are particularly significant for the study of intermediation as they start from an economic agreement that reveals other links such as mutual trust or the recognition of reputation and honor between the two parties, etc. In any case, these relationships are based on a public contract, which makes all the relationships recorded here homogeneous from a legal and economic point of view.

The second instrument used in this work is the power or letter of attorney. This instrument was used by creditors to transfer economic rights against their debtors to a third-party participant. The reasons for these transfers were diverse: to secure the recovery of rights in other geographical locations or at future times, to sell the rights to obtain capital, and so on. The delivery of this instrument was very common in Castilian fairs and allows us to reconstruct three financial flows: the original relationship between creditor and debtor, the delivery of the right, and the new financial relationship between the transferee—new creditor—and the debtor. This instrument is also interesting for the study of intermediation based on the transferees that, in many cases, were moneychangers able to claim debts where others could not. Again, we are dealing with a notarial contract that shows relationships under the same conditions of homogeneity.

Notarial sources allow us to identify and study more relationships through other types of financial instruments such as bills of exchange (which appear in the notarial sources via protests), letters of payment, or notarial testimonies on operations carried out by moneychangers. However, thanks to the two contracts mentioned, we have been able to reconstruct direct relations, which are embodied in a public contract, i.e., we have been able to reconstruct the creation of "strong ties" established, at a financial level, between moneychangers, merchants, etc. However, equally interesting are other types of relationships or the generation of "weak ties" based on these same documents and others that allow us to reconstruct, indirectly, economic, professional, and unneighborly relationships established at the Castilian fairs.[30] For example, the witnesses who attend the signing of the contracts included in this work could be considered a weak tie for the moneychangers. The witnesses were usually merchants or local agents who came to the notary's office to certify the agreements. In this way, exchangers and witnesses met on an occasional business deal, which favored mutual acquaintance but without a financial exchange as a basis. But this issue will be the subject for future studies.

4 Financial Intermediation: Networks

Financial intermediation is based on the ability to connect agents with different financial needs (lenders, borrowers, sellers, buyers, etc.). Castilian moneychangers played a fundamental role in terms of intermediation as they connected those who demanded capital with those who deposited it in banks, as well as providing liquidity to consumers and merchants in their commercial dealings. In addition, the moneychangers became representatives of many Castilians who relied on them to manage their businesses or to collect unpaid debts on time. The role of financial intermediation began to be fundamental in the Castilian fairs and markets because it also had a positive effect on improving the speed of money circulation, as well as boosting economic activity and generating ideal conditions of trust for exchanges.

Moneychangers tended to work alone or in small companies but, given the characteristics of their businesses, they tended to maintain constant relationships with other agents and moneychangers. They show a constant dialogue between individual and community.[31] Daily contacts between them built up a relatively well-connected and cohesive group, although

[30] Mark S. Granovetter, 'The Strength of Weak Ties', in: *American Journal of Sociology* 78:6 (1973), 1360–1380.

[31] Charles H. Parker, 'Introduction. Individual and Community in the Early Modern World', in: Charles H. Parker and Jerry H. Bentley (eds.), Between the Middle Ages and Modernity. Individual and Community in the Early Modern World (Lanham, 2007), 1–9.

each moneychanger represented his own interests at the fairs and developed different networking strategies. The network of moneychangers operating at the Castilian fairs, generated from two relationships (creditor-debtor from obligations, and transfer of payment rights from powers of attorney), shows us the generation of different types and the orientation of the relationships of each moneychanger and each community.

In this first approach the size of the nodes corresponds to their total degree and the size of the labels is linked to their intermediation index (betweenness). We consider betweenness a useful indicator for intermediation. In addition to being a standard indicator, we consider it to be appropriate in this context given that in a financial market such as the Castilian one, and in the fairs in particular, the strength of individual intermediation was key. The network of moneychangers allows us to observe two different interaction spheres as we can see in Fig. 1: on the one hand, the relationships established between them and, on the other hand, the relationships established with other businessmen, generating wider and better interrelated networks. According to the extent of the relationships, measured as the number of interactions, we can distinguish different groups of moneychangers: those such as Antonio de Paredes, Diego Díaz, or Sebastián Romero, who maintained numerous links between them with very close businesses and networks, as we will see more in detail below, and others such as Bernardino de Santa María, whose relationships with other moneychangers were minimal, perhaps he did not need it. The moneychanger privileged his relations with merchants. These transactions for sizeable sums of money were related to international trade, which shows that his interests, as we shall see, were not focused on local and regional traders and their circuits. In general, the network demonstrates the prevalence of relations between moneychangers as opposed to relations with merchants, and the existence of communities of moneychangers according to their place of origin and the importance of certain actors within the network thanks to their intermediary capacity. These relations made possible that moneychangers could settle operations among themselves or the operations of their respective clients through the clearing or payment of debts at the end of the fair or in their respective villages if they were neighbors.

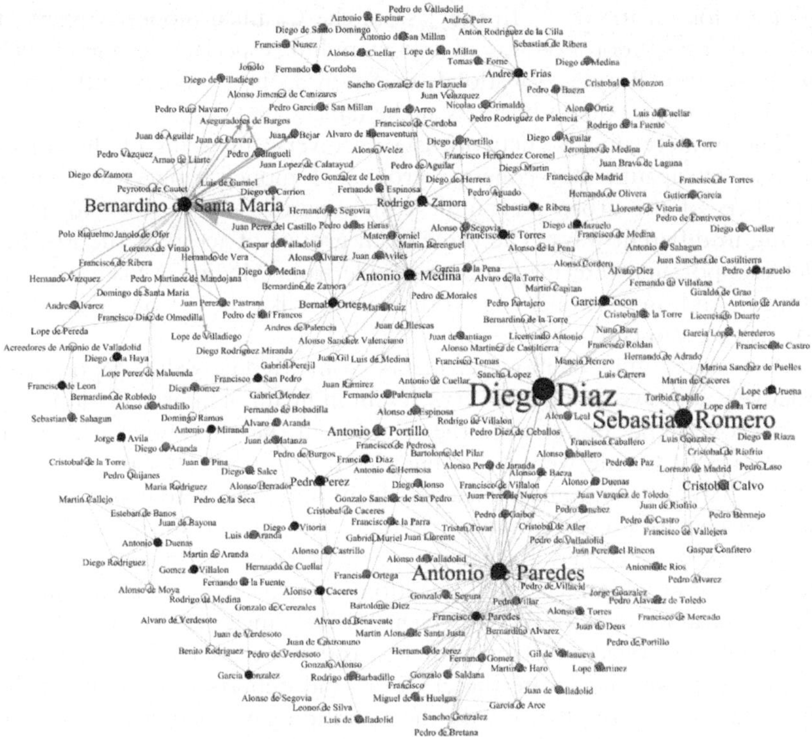

Fig. 1 Moneychangers and Merchants in Medina del Campo (1509–1520). Source: Notarial records from the Archivo Histórico Provincial de Valladolid (AHPV), section *Protocolos Notariales*, numbers 1, 2, 29, 30, 32, 253, 1380/2, 4351, 4394, 6095, 6318, 7330, 7838–7840, 8433–8441, 8448, 14,065, 20,152–20,154, 20,205, collected in Carvajal et al., *Mercaderes y cambiadores*. Nodes: Moneychangers (Black), Merchants (Grey)

4.1 Communities

It is well known that merchants and financiers tended to foster social and economic relations with those who shared the same geographical origin. This phenomenon is behind the emergence of important mercantile communities outside their place of origin, communities which, with a greater or lesser degree of institutional organization, were an important support for expatriates.[32] In the case of the Castilian moneychangers, it seems that neighborhood was an important link, especially for agents such as those from Burgos, Valladolid, or Segovia, who spent months away from their homes doing business at the fairs.

The moneychangers' network is very diverse in terms of the origin of its participants. But cohesive groups of moneychangers as well as members of the urban mercantile communities can be observed interacting in different ways. The three main groups of actors at the Medina del Campo fairs were made up of people from Medina, Valladolid, and Burgos, and, in a second stage, other groups like those from Segovia or Medina de Rioseco.

The community of moneychangers from Medina del Campo was a relatively cohesive group and very present in financial intermediation relations, something logical since they resided in the same town where the main fairs of Castile were held (Fig. 2). It was relatively easy for many of the merchants and moneychangers from other places to come to them as intermediaries, especially because they were sure to meet them again in the town every fair. Exchangers such as Diego Díaz and Sebastián Romero show a high level of integration and capacity for relationships in the financial network of the fair. Their business included receiving letters of attorney to collect outstanding debts, as they were the agents best positioned to know and locate the creditors and debtors who attended the fairs year by year. In other words, their position gave them great ability to find out about the presence of many merchants or the economic situation of trading companies (Fig. 2).

The second community with an important presence at the fairs were moneychangers from the neighboring village of Valladolid. The town had been the political and institutional epicenter of Castile since the time of the Catholic Kings. Despite having lost its struggle to host the main fair of Castile against Medina del Campo, it maintained an important mercantile activity and the presence of its businessmen in the surrounding fairs was continuous. At the end of the fifteenth century, the high number of public moneychangers in Valladolid was a clear symptom of the financial orientation of the town, a strategy that resulted in the formation of important banking companies among families of moneychangers such as

[32] Jacques Bottin and Donatella Calabi (eds.), *Les étrangers dans la ville. Minorités et espace urbain du bas Moyen Âge à l'époque moderne* (Paris, 1999); Sheilagh Ogilvie, Institutions and European Trade. Merchant Guilds, 1000–1800 (Cambridge, 2011).

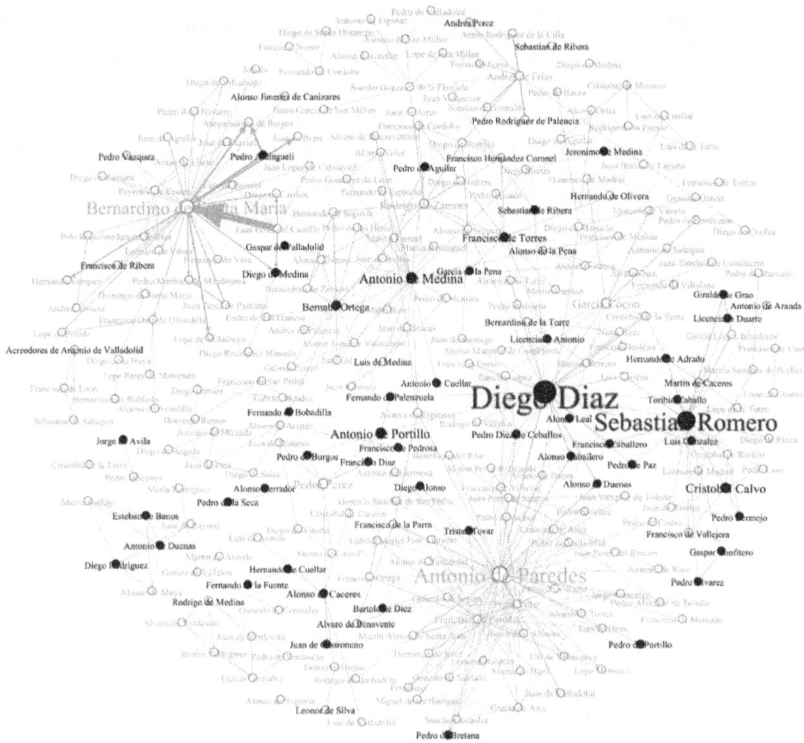

Fig. 2 Medina del Campo neighbors, black nodes (1509–1520). Source: Notarial records from the Archivo Histórico Provincial de Valladolid, section *Protocolos Notariales*, numbers 1, 2, 29, 30, 32, 253, 1380/2, 4351, 4394, 6095, 6318, 7330, 7838–7840, 8433–8441, 8448, 14,065, 20,152–20,154, 20,205, collected in Carvajal et al., *Mercaderes y cambiadores*

the Verdesoto, the Cocón, the León, and the Paredes. The members of these families formed a particularly well-knit community as they shared, among other things, common political objectives. Important members of these families belonged to the Valladolid oligarchy and held positions in the city council, controlling rents, and other businesses in the town.[33] This interest in the local economy and politics did not affect the increasing presence of Valladolid citizens at the neighboring fairs. The network shows the weight of the presence of Valladolid through the two instruments studied (Fig. 3), but we know that the moneychangers also carried out important financial intermediation tasks with Italian merchants who moved between the fairs and the Court, which frequently resided in Valladolid. For example, moneychangers, such as Francisco de San Pedro, appear as an important intermediary transferring high amounts, 578.700 mrs (1,543.2 ducats), between two Italians, Galvan Buoniseni to Pantaleon Vieri, for the liquidation of a company,[34] or transferring the repayment of a loan of 975,000 mrs. (2,600 ducats) between the Florentine Pedro Belache to his creditor, the Valladolid-born Diego Ruiz.[35]

Both communities of moneychangers, the one in Medina del Campo and the one from Valladolid, stood out for being well-knit communities and especially integrated with each other and with merchants from other nearby cities and towns. For example, relations with moneychangers and merchants from the neighboring city of Segovia, an important textile-producing center at the beginning of the sixteenth century, stand out. The Segovian merchants were regulars at the fairs where they sold raw materials of great interest for export, such as wool, or cloth produced in the city for the domestic market, but they also had their own group of moneychangers headed by men such as Andrés de Frías, Rodrigo de Zamora, or Pedro Pérez who, in turn, were mainly connected with the financiers of Medina del Campo and Valladolid, as shown in Fig. 1.[36]

In difference to what has been observed so far, the third community of moneychangers that was prominent in the Castilian fairs was the Burgos community. Burgos businessmen were a very important community in Medina del Campo. Their support was fundamental in the struggle

[33] Víctor Arenzana, *Los libros de actas del concejo de Valladolid (1497–1520). Estudio y descripción* (Valladolid, 2019).

[34] Archivo Histórico Provincial de Valladolid (AHPV), Section *Protocolos Notariales*, num. 7839, 474–475 (1515).

[35] AHPV, Section *Protocolos Notariales*, num. 7840, 263–264 (1519).

[36] María Asenjo, 'Participación de las mujeres en las compañías comerciales castellanas a fines de la Edad Media. Los mercaderes segovianos', in: Ángela Muñoz and Cristina Segura (eds.), El trabajo de las mujeres (Madrid, 1988), there 223–234.

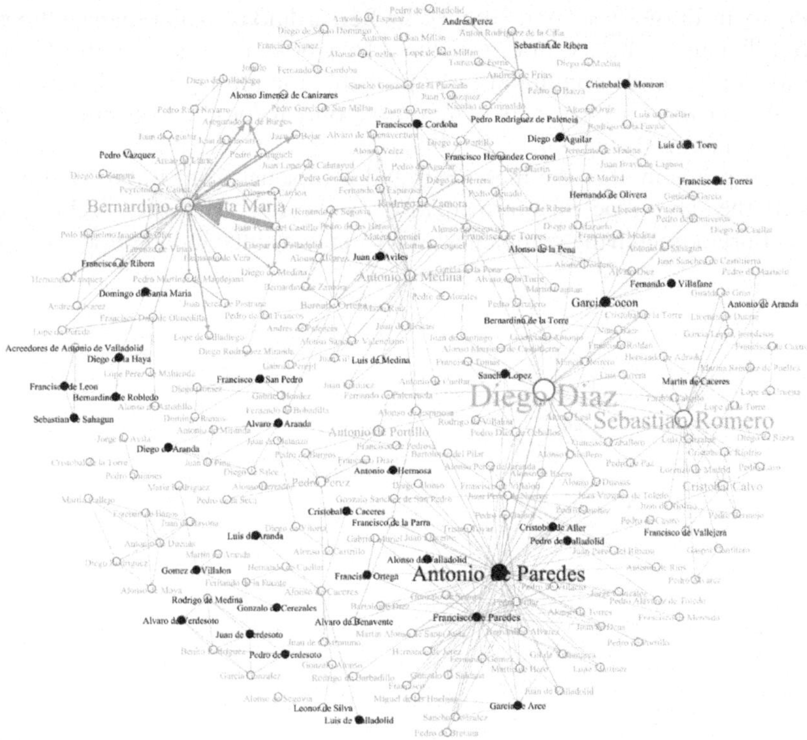

Fig. 3 Valladolid neighbors, black nodes (1509–1520). Source: Notarial records from the Archivo Histórico Provincial de Valladolid, section *Protocolos Notariales*, numbers 1, 2, 29, 30, 32, 253, 1380/2, 4351, 4394, 6095, 6318, 7330, 7838–7840, 8433–8441, 8448, 14,065, 20,152–20,154, 20,205, collected in Carvajal et al., *Mercaderes y cambiadores*

against Valladolid to host the main fairs of the Crown.[37] Furthermore, this group was a very well-integrated community, both at an institutional level, given that many of its merchants were members of the Consulate of Burgos, and at a mercantile and social level through the founding of companies, marriage alliances, etc.[38] In Medina del Campo, the banking

[37] Adeline Rucquoi, *Valladolid en la Edad Media* (Valladolid, 1997).

[38] Carvajal, 'Merchant Networks'.

activity in Burgos was monopolized by Bernardino de Santa María, whom we will mention below. But the data we have obtained raise a doubt. If the Burgos mercantile community was probably the most powerful of those present at the Castilian fairs, why do we only record a small number of moneychangers? (Fig. 4).

It is probably that the merchants and companies from Burgos did not need the same type of intermediation as the rest. The size reached by the Burgos merchant companies, with many agents and representatives

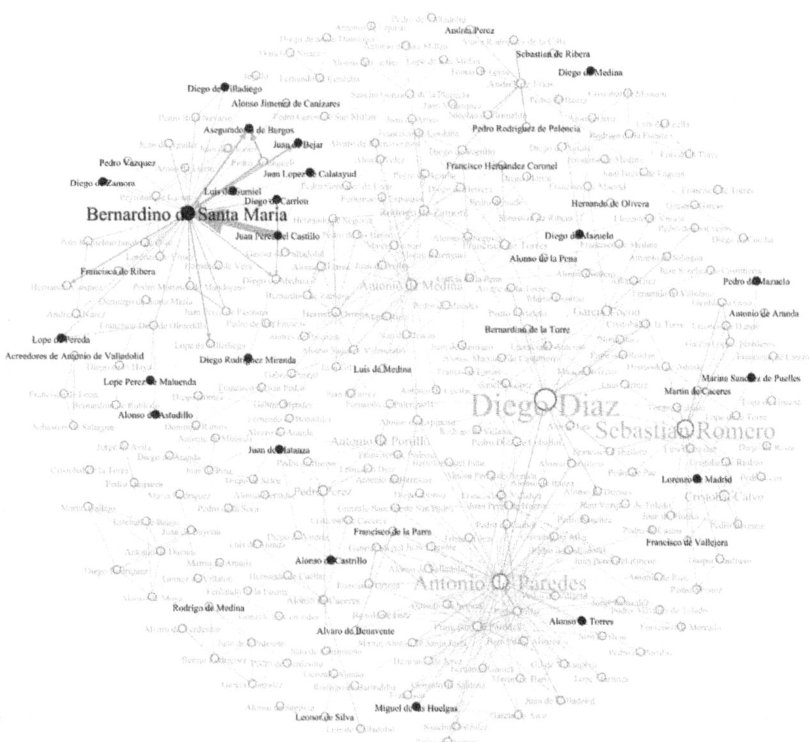

Fig. 4 Burgos neighbors, black nodes (1509–1520). Source: Notarial records from the Archivo Histórico Provincial de Valladolid, section *Protocolos Notariales*, numbers 1, 2, 29, 30, 32, 253, 1380/2, 4351, 4394, 6095, 6318, 7330, 7838–7840, 8433–8441, 8448, 14,065, 20,152–20,154, 20,205, collected in Carvajal et al., *Mercaderes y cambiadores*

dispersed throughout Castile and Europe, would make intermediation less necessary. Moreover, their negotiation skills and knowledge probably made it less necessary to have a wide number of moneychangers, so that their contact with bankers seems to be limited at the fairs beyond the Santa María or Mazuelo banks, which appear to be scarcely integrated with the rest of the moneychangers and merchants. To this we must add another reality: although the companies demanded significant amounts of capital, it seems that they were able to obtain important sums from the collaboration between families and from their business in other markets such as the Italian or Flemish cities.[39]

In opposition to the network formed by the Burgos, the financial networks of Medina and Valladolid show a greater connection between merchants and moneychangers from these centers and others such as Segovia, Toledo, Villalón, or Medina de Rioseco, seeking capital, generating new business opportunities, and overcoming the limits of their local economies. In contrast to this network, the Burgos network was more self-sufficient and closed, generating greater concentration and the enrichment of its community, at least while they managed to control Castilian exports (see Fig. 4). In any case, in all the communities there was a notable presence of some moneychangers who, due to their level/number of relations and their capacity for intermediation, stood out among their peers.

These communities can be well appreciated through other indicators such as modularity. In particular, the studied network presents a modularity of 0.79, detecting up to 27 different communities.[40] However, four communities represent 56% of the network. The three main communities coincide with those organized around the exchangers Diego Díaz—Sebastián Romero, Antonio de Paredes, and Bernardino de Santa María which, as we have just seen, head the relationships of their respective localities. However, a fourth community appears around the Medina

[39] Hilario Casado, 'Los negocios de la compañía Pesquera-Silos en Florencia en los inicios del siglo XVI', in: Ernesto García and Juan A. Bonachía (eds.), Hacienda, Mercado y Poder al norte de la Corona de Castilla en el tránsito del medievo a la modernidad (Valladolid, 2015), 69–98.

[40] Under the following parameters: Randomize, without edge weights—because the extraordinary relation between Antonio de Paredes and Diego Díaz influences the outcome—and resolution 1.0.

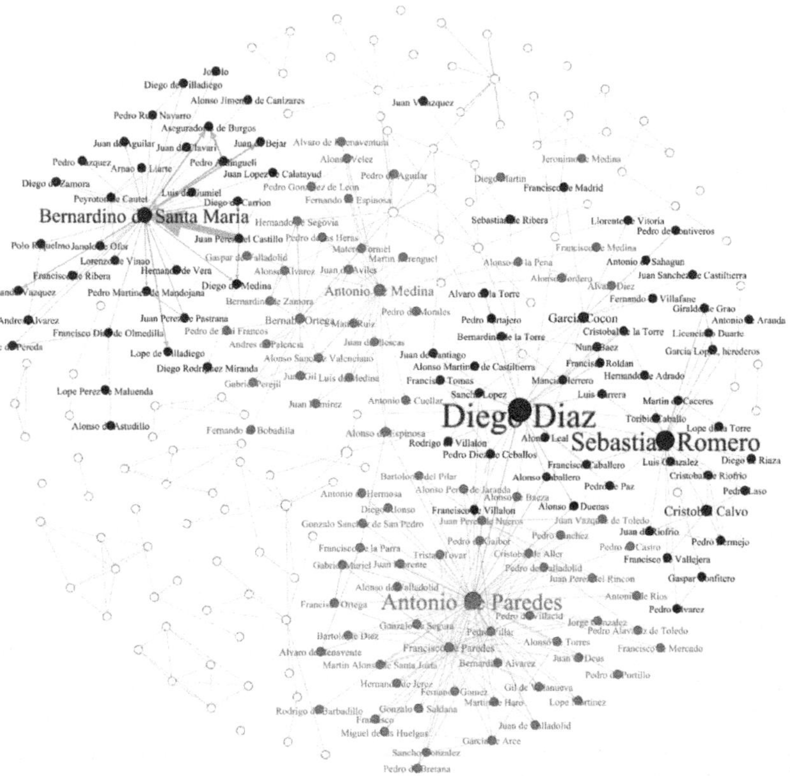

Fig. 5 Communities and modularity (1509–1520). Source: Notarial records from the Archivo Histórico Provincial de Valladolid, section *Protocolos Notariales*, numbers 1, 2, 29, 30, 32, 253, 1380/2, 4351, 4394, 6095, 6318, 7330, 7838–7840, 8433–8441, 8448, 14,065, 20,152–20,154, 20,205, collected in Carvajal et al., *Mercaderes y cambiadores*

exchanger Antonio de Medina, who does not seem to concentrate his relationships in the area around his locality (Fig. 5).

4.2 *Ego Networks*

Notary offices became ideal places to generate ego networks, networks around the moneychangers who signed obligations, or delivered and received powers of attorney. In each community that we examined in the previous point, one or two exchangers with different strategies and profiles seem to stand out.

In Medina del Campo, the moneychangers who stand out from the rest were Diego Díaz and Sebastián Romero, who carried out business in parallel with local clients but also with Genoese ones such as Cristóbal Calvo or Giraldo de Grado.[41] However, the figure that particularly emerges was Diego Díaz. His ability to network with other businessmen is clear from the documentation available on him. He was an active founder of financial companies, associating with other local moneychangers and merchants such as Antonio de Medina in 1515[42] or with the aforementioned Sebastián Romero.[43] In addition, Diego Díaz did not ignore other activities such as the buying and selling of textiles and merchandise to the Genoese and other Italians who came to the fairs. However, his role in the network is particularly marked by the relationship he maintained with the other great moneychanger of the time, the Valladolid-born Antonio de Paredes (Fig. 6).

Antonio de Paredes was an important financier in the transition between the fifteenth and sixteenth centuries. He quickly showed interest in intermediation, in the foundation of companies, and in undertaking business with other agents such as the court moneychanger Ochoa Pérez de Salinas, with whom he maintained a close relationship between 1498 and 1499 before his bankruptcy.[44] Antonio de Paredes succeeded in achieving his family becoming one of the main families in Valladolid. He was able to reach important positions in the urban government and his sons joined a position as representative in City Council. Since early sixteenth century, Antonio de Paredes expanded his business outside his native town although he continued to focus his relations and business on his neighbors, mostly merchants who negotiated in the fairs, and all kinds of personages: noblemen, clergymen, etc. For Antonio de Paredes, family was of vital importance and, as can be seen in the network, he relied on his son, Francisco de Paredes, to consolidate his bank and ensuring the

41 AHPV, Section *Protocolos Notariales*, num. 7840, 678 and 761.

42 AHPV, Section *Protocolos Notariales*, num. 8439, 379–380.

43 AHPV, Section *Protocolos Notariales*, nums. 7839, 522; 7839, 523.

44 David Carvajal, '¿Sobre la fragilidad del capital? Cambios y quiebra en Castilla (ca. 1471–1547)', in: Hilario Casado (ed.), Comercio, finanzas y fiscalidad en Castilla (siglos XV-XVI) (Valladolid, 2018), 199–216.

Fig. 6 Diego Diaz and Antonio de Paredes Egonetwork (1509–1520). Source: Notarial records from the Archivo Histórico Provincial de Valladolid, section *Protocolos Notariales*, numbers 1, 2, 29, 30, 32, 253, 1380/2, 4351, 4394, 6095, 6318, 7330, 7838–7840, 8433–8441, 8448, 14,065, 20,152–20,154, 20,205, collected in Carvajal et al., *Mercaderes y cambiadores*. Nodes: Moneychangers (Black), Merchants (Grey). Labels: Medina del Campo (Black), Valladolid (Grey)

continuity of his business.[45] He connected and had important local and regional agents as intermediaries to collect his debts, such as the merchant Pedro Villar, building a first level of relations. Moreover, beyond his local and regional contacts, Antonio de Paredes also maintained contacts with foreign merchants. He took care of his relations and diversified his business: he was dedicated to money exchange but also trading and managing the local and royal rents in Valladolid. If we observe the ego network (at two levels) of Antonio de Paredes and that of Diego Díaz, we can see that both networks are practically complementary, which allows us to establish an important group of agents closely related through these two financiers who, in turn, seems to have headed their respective communities.

[45] David Carvajal, 'Cambiadores y elites urbanas: el auge de Antonio de Paredes y su familia en Valladolid a inicios del siglo XVI', in: *Studia Histórica. Historia Moderna* 38:1 (2016), 193–222.

The third moneychanger that allows us to distinguish another strategy when generating ego networks is Bernardino de Santa María. The Burgos-born was a member and head of a Judeo-converse family linked to finance from the fifteenth century onward. Far from Medina del Campo, Bernardino de Santa María played an important role as a financier in service to the Crown, selling public debt securities and obtaining capital for the Royal Treasury, as well as managing some royal revenues in the city of Burgos. As far as his activity in Medina del Campo is concerned, we know that the obligations and letters of attorney barely show us 40% of the transactions he carried out at the fairs, according to all the data we have recorded. The other 60% of the operations were mainly linked to the payment and drawing of bills of exchange from his bank. Focusing on the first two instruments, we can see that the moneychanger was at the center of a network of Burgos merchants to whom he lent money, as was the case with the 856,059 mrs. (2,282.8 ducats) he lent in 1519 to the merchant Juan de Béjar.[46] Regarding his intermediary capacity, the moneychanger acted as a representative of great Burgos families such as the Bernuy, the Miranda, and the Melgosa when it came to paying or receiving pending debts. From his bank he paid the producers of wool which was later exported by the Burgos merchants to Flanders and Italy, developing a key role for the community he represented.

The network generated was particularly short in terms of relationships; however, it is a partial reconstruction that shows a clear specialization in its local clientele and in the generation of another parallel business. There was another large network parallel to the one shown in Fig. 7 related to bills of exchange. From his bank, Bernardino de Santa María transferred large amounts between the Castilian fairs to centers such as Lyon, Bruges, and Valencia. This network was made by members of the great Italian merchant families—Garvarín, Belache, Grimaldo, Centurión, Ardinguel, Ugoccioni—who maintained relations with the Burgos and other Castilian merchants in the context of the fairs. Bernardino de Santa María emerged in the 1520 s as one of the leading Castilian financiers and became very close to royal power,[47] and his family-owned important banks in Burgos.[48] His strategy at the fairs was different from that of Diego Díaz or Antonio de Paredes but was equally, if not more, successful.

[46] AHPV, Section *Protocolos Notariales*, num. 7840, 906.

[47] Sergio Sardone, 'Forced loans in the Spanish Empire: the first requisition of American treasures in 1523', in: *The Economic History Review* 72:1 (2019), there 69.

[48] Manuel Basas, 'Banqueros burgaleses del siglo XVI', in: *Boletín de la Institución Fernán González* 43 (1964), 314–332.

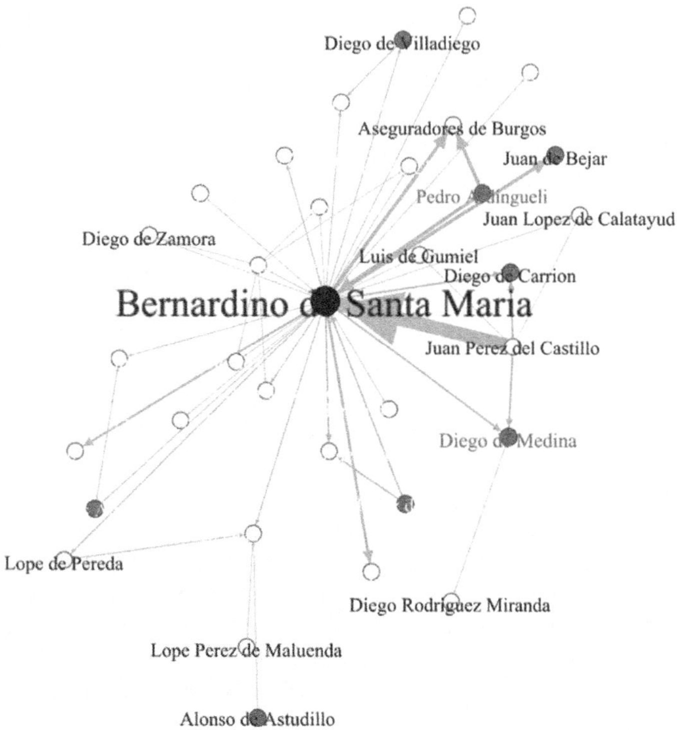

Fig. 7 Bernardino de Santa María Egonetwork (1509–1520). Source: Notarial records from the Archivo Histórico Provincial de Valladolid, section *Protocolos Notariales*, numbers 1, 2, 29, 30, 32, 253, 1380/2, 4351, 4394, 6095, 6318, 7330, 7838–7840, 8433–8441, 8448, 14,065, 20,152–20,154, 20,205, collected in Carvajal et al., *Mercaderes y cambiadores*. Nodes: Moneychangers (Black), Merchants (Grey). Labels: Burgos (Black), Medina del Campo (Grey)

5 Conclusion

The increasing financial flows and their complexity at the Castilian markets were an indicator of the progressive development of the Castilian financial system at the beginning of the sixteenth century. This phenomenon was particularly visible at the fairs like those in Medina del Campo, Medina de Rioseco, and Villalón and through the activity and action of the moneychangers.

Studying and understanding the activity of moneychangers and their relationships allow us to highlight the importance of financial intermediation and their capacity to connect economic sectors and individuals with capital needs with those who possessed it. The links between moneychangers in facilitating capital flows as creditors and intermediaries, mostly in regional markets but in peninsular and international, fostered the connection with other merchants and businessmen from the south of Castile, Aragon, Italy, Flanders, Portugal, France, etc. In fact, moneychangers such as Antonio de Paredes or Bernardino de Santa María were key connecting with the Crown and the Royal Treasury and in promoting the internationalization of the fairs thanks to their ability to connect with foreign agents, consolidating the transition from local–regional fairs to international ones.

Equally or even more important than individual action was to have solid structures or networks on which to support a fragile system, subject to the economic and financial uncertainty. Thus, the Castilian moneychangers developed important networks, as shown by their contractual relations signed in the presence of a notary, considering different strategies and interests. One of the clearest characteristics observed among the moneychangers studied is the generation of networks based on neighborhood ties. This statement is not excessively original since links such as neighborhood ties or kinship ties were common among the merchant communities but confirm the trend.[49] However, we could observe that outside their place of origin, communities seem to have developed networks depending on the nature of the trading community from which they come. For example, those from Burgos tend to create more close, cohesive, and independent networks, connected with specific Italian groups, such as the Genoese, while the moneychangers from Medina del Campo had a great capacity to connect with other Castilian and foreign communities, such as the exchangers from Segovia or those from Valladolid, also closely related. On the other hand, family relationships were important between moneychangers and some, such as Antonio de Paredes and his son Francisco de Paredes, demonstrate this.

[49] Francesca Trivellato, 'Marriage, Commercial Capital, and Business Agency: Transregional Sephardic (and Armenian) Families in the Seventeenth- and Eighteenth-Century Mediterranean', in: Chistopher H. Johnson, David W. Sabean, Simon Teuscher, Francesca Trivellato (eds.), Transregional and Transnational Families in Europe and Beyond. Experiences Since the Middle Ages (New York & Oxford, 2011), 107–130.

These closely linked businesses made it possible to consolidate the bank, expand the company, and generate new networks.

SNA, already used in other studies on businesses of the period which involved many people, makes it easier for us to identify the importance of the agents and communities through their interaction and their capacity of intermediation. The possibilities of deepening in this network through the incorporation of new relationships (weak and strong ties) will make it possible to further understand some of the internal dynamics and comprehend individual and collective strategies. Nevertheless, it is clear the role that moneychangers played as financial intermediaries between producers and consumers, buyers and sellers, creditors, and debtors, and so on, developing a fundamental activity that boosted the speed of money circulation, promoted trade, and fostered the rise of financial markets in the early modern Castile. Three elements were key to the development of the Hispanic Empire during the sixteenth century.

References

Primary Sources

Archivo Histórico Provincial de Valladolid (AHPV), section *Protocolos Notariales*, numbers 1, 2, 29, 30, 32, 253, 1380/2, 4351, 4394, 6095, 6318, 7330, 7838–7840, 8433–8441, 8448, 14065, 20152–20154, 20205.

Secondary Sources

Al-Hussein, Falah Hassan Abed. 1986. Las ferias de Medina y el comercio de la lana: 1514–1573. In *Historia de Medina del Campo y su Tierra*, edited by Eufemio Lorenzo, vol. II, 15–30. Valladolid: Ayuntamiento de Medina del Campo, Junta de Castilla y León, Diputación Provincial de Valladolid and Caja de Ahorros Provincial de Valladolid.

Arenzana, Víctor. 2019. *Los libros de actas del concejo de Valladolid (1497–1520). Estudio y descripción*. Valladolid: Ayuntamiento de Valladolid.

Asenjo, María. 1988. Participación de las mujeres en las compañías comerciales castellanas a fines de la Edad Media. Los mercaderes segovianos. In *El trabajo de las mujeres*, edited by Ángela Muñoz and Cristina Segura, 223–234. Madrid: Asociación Cultural Al-Mudayna.

Basas, Manuel. 1964. Banqueros burgaleses del siglo XVI. *Boletín de la Institución Fernán González* 43: 314–332.

Bernanke, Ben S. 1983. Nonmonetary effects of the financial crisis in the propagation of the Great Depression. *American Economic Review* 73: 257–276.

Bottin, Jacques and Calabi, Donatella (eds.). 1999. *Les étrangers dans la ville. Minorités et espace urbain du bas Moyen Âge à l'époque moderne*. Paris: Éditions de la Maison des sciences de l'homme.

Carande, Ramón. 1965. *Carlos V y sus banqueros. La vida económica en Castilla (1516–1556)*. Madrid: Sociedad de Estudios y Publicaciones.

Carvajal, David. 2011. Redes socioeconómicas y mercaderes castellanos a fines de la Edad Media e inicios de la Moderna. In *Redes sociales y económicas en el mundo bajomedieval*, edited by David Carvajal et al., 79–102. Valladolid: Castilla Ediciones.

Carvajal, David. 2014. Merchant Networks in the Cities of the Crown of Castile. In Commercial Networks and European Cities, 1400–1800, edited by Andrea Caracausi and Christoff Jeggle, 137–152. London: Pickering & Chatto.

Carvajal, David. 2015. En los precedentes de la banca castellana moderna: cambiadores al norte del Tajo a inicios del siglo XVI. In *Hacienda, Mercado y Poder al norte de la Corona de Castilla en el tránsito del medievo a la modernidad*, edited by Ernesto García and Juan A. Bonachía, 17–38. Valladolid: Castilla Ediciones.

Carvajal, David. 2016. Cambiadores y elites urbanas: El auge de Antonio de Paredes y su familia en Valladolid a inicios del siglo XVI. *Studia Histórica. Historia Moderna* 38 (1): 193–222.

Carvajal, David. 2018. ¿Sobre la fragilidad del capital? Cambios y quiebra en Castilla (ca. 1471–1547). In *Comercio, finanzas y fiscalidad en Castilla (siglos XV-XVI)*, edited by Hilario Casado, 199–216. Valladolid: Dykinson.

Carvajal, David. 2018. Ley, justicia y cambio económico en Castilla a fines de la Edad Media e inicios de la Edad Moderna. *Ricerche di Storia Economica e Sociale* 2: 35–60.

Carvajal, David. 2020. The "économie sans travail" in early modern Castile Credit and moneychangers. In *Le Droit face à l'économie sans travail, Tome II, 'L'approche internationale'*, edited by Luisa Brunori et al. 47–68. Paris: Classiques Garnier.

Carvajal, David. 2023. La banca privada castellana y el fin de una generación: diversificación, crisis de liquidez y quiebra en el cambio de Gaspar Enríquez (1531- ca. 1562). In *Finanzas y crisis financieras en la Monarquía Hispánica, siglos XVI-XVII*, edited by Ramón Lanza, 93–127. Madrid: Marcial Pons.

Carvajal, David, Mauricio Herrero, Francisco Javier Molina and Irene Ruiz. 2015. *Mercaderes y cambiadores en los protocolos notariales de la provincia de Valladolid (1486–1520)*. Valladolid: Universidad de Valladolid.

Casado, Hilario. 2000. Comercio, crédito y finanzas públicas en Castilla en la época de los Reyes Católicos. In *Dinero, moneda y crédito en la monarquía hispánica*, edited by Antonio Miguel Bernal, 135–156. Madrid: Marcial Pons.

Casado, Hilario. 2003. *El triunfo de Mercurio. La presencia Castellana en Europa (Siglos XV y XVI)*. Burgos: Caja de Ahorros del Circulo Catolico.

Casado, Hilario. 2008. Los flujos de información en las redes comerciales castellanas de los siglos XV y XVI. *Investigaciones de Historia Económica* 10: 35–68.

Casado, Hilario. 2009. Crédito y comercio en las ferias de Medina del Campo en la primera mitad del siglo XVI. In *Il mercato del crédito in Età Moderna. Reti e operatori finanziari dello spazio europeo*, edited by Elena María García and Giuseppe de Luca, 21–48. Milano: Franco Angeli.

Casado, Hilario. 2012. Crecimiento económico, redes de comercio y fiscalidad en Castilla a fines de la Edad Media. In *Los negocios del hombre. Comercio y rentas en Castilla. Siglos XV y XVI*, edited by Juan A. Bonachía and David Carvajal, 17–36. Valladolid: Castilla Ediciones.

Casado, Hilario. 2015. Los negocios de la compañía Pesquera-Silos en Florencia en los inicios del siglo XVI. In *Hacienda, Mercado y Poder al norte de la Corona de Castilla en el tránsito del medievo a la modernidad*, edited by Ernesto García and Juan Antonio Bonachía, 69–98. Valladolid: Castilla Ediciones.

de Roover, Raymond. 1948. *Money, Banking and Credit in Medieval Bruges*. Cambridge, MA: The Medieval Academy of America.

Epstein, Stephan R. 1994. Fairs, Institutional Innovation, and Economic Growth in Late Medieval Europe. *The Economic History Review* 47–3: 459–482.

Fontaine, Laurence. 2014. *Le marché. Histoire et usages d'une conquête sociale*. Paris.

Granovetter, Mark S. 1973. The Strength of Weak Ties. *American Journal of Sociology* 78–6: 1360–1380.

Hoffman, Philip. T., Giles Postel-Vinay and Jean-Laurent Rosenthal. 2000. *Priceless Markets. The Political Economy of Credit in Paris. 1660–1870*. Chicago: Chicago University Press.

Imízcoz, José M., and Andoni Artola. 2017. Redes sociales, procesos de cambio cultural y conflicto en las provincias vascas y navarra (1700–1839). *Historia Social* 89: 73–77.

Ladero Quesada, Miguel A. 1994. *Las ferias en Castilla. Siglos XII-XV*. Madrid: Comité Español de Ciencias Históricas.

Romera, Martín, and A. María. 2010. Nuevas perspectivas para el estudio de las sociedades medievales: El análisis de redes sociales. *Studia Histórica. Historia Medieval* 28: 217–239.

Ogilvie, Sheilagh. 2011. *Institutions and European Trade. Merchant Guilds, 1000–1800*. Cambridge: Cambrigde University Press.

Ortego, Pablo. 2011. Financieros y redes financieras en tiempos de Juan II: posibilidades de estudio del libro de "recepta" de 1440. In *Redes sociales y económicas en el mundo bajomedieval*, edited by David Carvajal et al., 105–129. Valladolid: Castilla Ediciones.

Padgett, John F., and Christopher K. Ansell. 1993. Robust Action and the Rise of the Medici, 1400–1434. *American Journal of Sociology* 98–6: 1259–1319.

Parker, Charles H. 2007. Introduction. Individual and Community in the Early Modern World. In *Between the Middle Ages and Modernity. Individual and Community in the Early Modern World*, edited by Charles H. Parker and Jerry H. Bentley, 1–9. Lanham: Rowman & Littlefield Publishers.

Ribeiro, Ana Sofia. 2016. *Early Modern Trading Networks in Europe. Cooperation and the Case of Simon Ruiz*. New York: Routledge.

Rubio, Juan Antonio. 2014. Andalucía durante la segunda revolución tecnológica: ciclos de inversión, sociedades mercantiles y grupos empresariales. Granada: Universidad de Granada.

Rucquoi, Adeline. 1997. *Valladolid en la Edad Media*. Valladolid: Junta de Castilla y León.

Ruiz, Felipe. 1970. La Banca en España hasta 1782. In *El Banco de España: Una historia Económica*, 1–196. Madrid: Banco de España.

Sardone, Sergio. 2019. Forced loans in the Spanish Empire: The first requisition of American treasures in 1523. *The Economic History Review* 72 (1): 57–87.

Subrahmanyam, Sanjay. 2016. *Merchant Networks in the Early Modern World*. 1st edition 1996. London and New York: Routledge.

Trivellato, Francesca. 2011. Marriage, Commercial Capital, and Business Agency: Transregional Sephardic (and Armenian) Families in the Seventeenth- and Eighteenth-Century Mediterranean. In *Transregional and Transnational Families in Europe and Beyond. Experiences Since the Middle Ages*, edited by Chistopher H. Johnson, David W. Sabean, Simon Teuscher, Francesca Trivellato, 107–130. New York & Oxford: Berghahn Books.

Yun, Bartolomé. 1987. *Sobre la transición al Capitalismo en Castilla: economía y sociedad en Tierra de Campos (15001–1830)*. Valladolid: Junta de Castilla y León.

Yun, Bartolomé. 2004. *Marte contra Minerva. El precio del Imperio Español, ca. 1450–1600*. Barcelona: Crítica.

CHAPTER 9

Moneychangers and the Local Credit Market in Late Renaissance Florence. A Social Network Analysis

Matteo Pompermaier

1 Introduction

In late medieval and early modern Europe, local money lenders played a critical role in the everyday life of people. On the one side, they sustained the lower strata, supporting poor households in their daily struggles; on the other, they supplied funds to the well-off, fostering both local and international commerce, and promoting economic development. Credit markets included several professional and non-professional lenders who worked alongside each other. Public authorities frequently regulated their activities, sometimes imposing strict conditions, as was often the case

M. Pompermaier (✉)
Università Degli Studi Di Brescia, Brescia, Italy
e-mail: matteo.pompermaier@unibs.it

E. M. Dermineur and M. Pompermaier (eds.), *Credit Networks in The Preindustrial World*, Palgrave Studies in the History of Finance,
https://doi.org/10.1007/978-3-031-67117-3_9

for Jewish moneylenders.[1] The structure of local credit markets was shaped by many variables linked to the political, economic, and social environment.

This paper studies the dense interpersonal network that linked borrowers and lenders in late Renaissance Florence. Previous research indicates that this network constituted the main access to credit available in the city at the time.[2] Various professional lenders, among which were private Christian pawnbrokers, were active in the city. However, their market share appears to have been quite limited.[3] The allocation and deployment of financial funds took place mostly via transactions that involved private individuals.

In late Renaissance Florence, lenders and borrowers were part of networks that included family members, friends, or neighbors, based on geographical, professional, and social homophily.[4] Repeated exchanges forged familiarity among individuals, creating quasi-kin relationships.[5] However, intermediaries were also active in the city and solved informational problems linking demand and offer. They matched borrowers worthy of a loan with lenders who wanted to invest their money. They were sometimes directly responsible for the repayment of the loans and were asked to settle the debt in case of default. This was the case with

[1] There are several examples that could be mentioned, see for instance B. Pullan about the Venetian Jewish community Brian S. Pullan, *La politica sociale della Repubblica di Venezia 1500- 1620*, vol. II, 'Gli ebrei veneziani e i Monti di pietà' (Rome, 1982); on the Tuscan area, see Maristella Botticini, 'A tale of 'benevolent' governments: private credit markets, public finance, and the role of Jewish money-lenders in medieval and Renaissance Italy', in: *The journal of economic history*, 60–1 (2000): 168–189.

[2] John F. Padgett and Paul D. McLean, 'Economic Credit in Renaissance Florence', in: *The Journal of Modern History* 83.1 (2011), 1–47.

[3] Elise Dermineur, and Matteo Pompermaier (forthcoming), 'Credit networks in renaissance Florence: revisiting the *catasto* of 1427', in: *Ricerche di storia economica e sociale*, VIII (2022): 89–110, https://doi.org/10.17426/R08C08, there 159.

[4] Paul D. McLean and Neha Gondal, 'The Circulation of Interpersonal Credit in Renaissance Florence', in: *European Journal of Sociology / Archives Européennes de Sociologie / Europäisches Archiv für Soziologie* 55–2 (2014): 135–176, there 157. On the topic, see Laurence Fontaine, *The Moral Economy: Poverty, Credit, and Trust in Early Modern Europe* (New York, 2014).

[5] Elise Dermineur, 'The evolution of credit networks in pre-industrial Finland', in: *Scandinavian Economic History Review* 70–1 (2022): 57–86, there 68.

guarantors (or *mallevadori*), who helped spread trust and encouraged credit transactions.[6]

This chapter delves deeper into the functioning of the interpersonal credit market in fifteenth-century Florence by investigating the roles of a specific professional category, that of moneychangers. The literature offers several examples of moneychangers who lent to family members, neighbors, or even peasants living in the Florentine countryside. It is not surprising that they were particularly active in the credit market: they were trained accountants and were among the few individuals in the city with ready cash—both gold and silver coins. The sources show that they were not only lenders, but also intermediaries and guarantors. As we will see, the moneychangers contributed to the efficiency of the market—identified as the capacity of the market to match debtors and creditors.

The paper relies on the analytical tools offered by social network analysis (SNA). By focusing on the intermediary activity of moneychangers we gain useful insights into the mechanisms of credit and intermediation in fifteenth-century Florence. The findings do not only highlight their role in matching borrowers and lenders in credit markets, but also their relevance in keeping different clusters within the network connected. Overall, this research contributes to the discussion about the structure and functioning of credit networks in preindustrial societies.

The main source for this study is the Florentine *catasto* of 1427, one of the oldest tax assessments still existing in Italy.[7] The *catasto* listed the wealth, profession, age, and marital status of almost 10,000 Florentine households. Claims and liabilities were utilized to determine the taxable net wealth, therefore each declaration also includes extensive lists of borrowers and lenders. The *catasto* is a massive source of information about the economic conditions of Florentine households. For that

[6] The literature on intermediaries is extensive. In this book, several papers focus on notarial credit and intermediation (Giuseppe De Luca and Marcella Lorenzini, 'Notary lending networks in northern Italy in the eighteenth and nineteenth centuries'; Ruben Peeters and Rogier van Kooten, 'Looking for dark matter credit: exploring notarial credit markets in Antwerp and its surroundings ca. 1835'), dialoguing particularly with existing research on France, see Philip T. Hoffman, Gilles Postel-Vinay and Jean-Laurent Rosenthal, *Dark matter credit: the development of peer-to-peer lending and banking in France* (Princeton, 2019).

[7] Archivio di Stato di Firenze (henceforth ASFi), *Catasto*, *Campioni dei cittadini*, bb. 64–85, and ASFi, *Catasto*, *Portate dei cittadini*, bb. 15–63; this research focuses on the Nicchio Gonfalone, ASFi, *Catasto*, *Portate*, bb. 17, 18_I and 18_II.

reason, the analysis limits itself to a specific part of the city of Florence, the *gonfalone* called Nicchio.[8] The chapter also relies on a judicial record produced by the *Arte del Cambio*, the guild that reunited all of moneychangers and regulated their business. This proves to be very useful in retracing qualitatively the various ways through which people lent and borrowed money in fifteenth-century Florence.

The research intersects with the literature focused on the activities of moneychangers and credit networks in preindustrial societies. This chapter aims to highlight the role of intermediaries in the local credit network from a more systematic point of view. It broadens the scope of the analysis and includes all the population residing in a specific area of the city, regardless of their social status or the value of transactions.

Previous literature focusing on credit networks in Florence mainly focused on the elites and included loans/debts of more than 10 florins.[9] Considering that the yearly average wage of an unskilled worker at the beginning of the fifteenth century was about 14 florins, ignoring all loans of less than 10 florins excludes a large part of so-called consumer credit.[10] In *gonfalone* Nicchio, about 62% of transactions were of less than 10 florins. The overall volume of these credit exchanges is surely limited if compared to the exchanges mobilized by merchant banks, but this does not reduce the significance of these transactions for a large part of the urban population.

In the next section, the paper reviews the literature on the Florentine credit market and analyses existing research on the roles of moneychangers in it. The following part introduces the data used and retraces the structure of the overall credit network investigating its main features. The fourth section focuses more closely on the moneychangers: it investigates their position in the network (i.e., their functions) and uses a multilevel algorithm to identify and study the communities that compose it. The detection and analysis of the communities in the network confirm

[8] The dataset and some of the preliminary results are drawn from a previous paper I wrote in collaboration with Elise Dermineur, which focuses on the overall structure of the local credit market in 1427 Florence; see Dermineur and Pompermaier, 'Credit networks in Renaissance Florence'.

[9] Padgett and McLean, 'Economic Credit', there 5; McLean and Gondal, 'The Circulation of Interpersonal Credit', there 144.

[10] David Herlihy and Christiane Klapisch-Zuber, *Tuscans and their Families: A Study of the Florentine Catasto of 1427* (New Haven, 1985), there 95.

the strength of professional and geographical homophily in network formation. However, it seems there is no cluster of moneychangers, who are instead an "open group", spread across the network. This particular characteristic reflects the important bridging role that moneychangers had in the Florentine credit market and the ways through which they linked various communities of the network together. The qualitative and quantitative analysis suggests the important contribution of moneychangers to the efficiency of the local credit market. They helped to overcome asymmetries of information, spreading trust, and lowering transaction costs.

2 Credit and Intermediation in Late Renaissance Florence

Preindustrial credit markets were usually much more varied than those existing in modern societies where the pre-eminence of banks over other credit institutions appears to be almost indisputable. In Renaissance Europe, several lenders operated simultaneously in the context of fragmented markets. This was the case in fifteenth-century Florence, where different kinds of lenders were supplying money to the local population.

Christian pawnbrokers were operating in the city, practicing what was perceived as a clearly usurious activity. Their activity was tolerated and regulated by the Commune, who in 1351 introduced a licensing system and imposed on them the payment of an annual fee for lending money on pledges.[11] Pawnbrokers traditionally played a significant role in preindustrial cities, especially for the lower classes. They allowed those who owned small objects of everyday use to access credit and stabilize their income.[12] However, the *catasto* disclose only limited traces of their activity, suggesting that they might have held only a marginal share of the market.

[11] Marvin B. Becker, 'Three Cases Concerning the Restitution of Usury in Florence', in: *The Journal of Economic History*, 17–3 (1957): 445–450, 446; Note that the Monte di Pietà (Municipal Pawnshop) of Florence was established only in 1495; see Carol Bresnahan Menning, *Charity and State in Late Renaissance Italy: The Monte di Pietà of Florence*, Ithaca and London, 1993.

[12] See Daniel L. Smail, 'The materiality of credit: debt collection as pawnbroking in late medieval mediterranean Europe', in: *Histoire Urbaine*, 51 (2018): 95–110; Matteo Pompermaier, 'Credit and poverty in early modern Venice', in: *Journal of Interdisciplinary History*, 52–4 (2022): 513–536.

In a previous paper, Dermineur and Pompermaier show that in the Nicchio *gonfalone*—one of the sixteen that made up Renaissance Florence—there were only a few individuals who declared to have pledges explicitly pawned at a Christian *presto* (a dozen out of about 12,000 transactions).[13] The authors point out at least two reasons that could explain why the real number of loans supplied by pawnbrokers is underestimated. First, the *catasto* could not be well-suited to record short-term loans—and pawnbroking is usually very short-term credit. Second, individuals were maybe hesitant to declare such transactions because of the social stigma connected to it. In any case, the low number of transactions suggests that pawnbrokers were not the main providers of credit for the local population.[14]

The Florentine urban credit market seems to have primarily relied on a dense network of interpersonal transactions. Indeed, credit circulated in the context of peer-to-peer relations that involved private individuals. This was true at all levels of society, and the network included both the upper and lower strata of the population. Previous research highlights that commercial credit networks among Florentine companies were indeed based on a wide range of non-economic, social relationships among the partners of these companies.[15] Padgett and Mclean stress the importance of family, friendship, geographical homophily, and *onore* (linked to public charges) as the main variables that affect the creation and development of credit networks in such a context.

Before the arrival of the Jewish moneylenders (1430s) and the establishment of the Monte di Pietà (1495), Florentines in need of funds for their own survival turned to their family and their *parentela*, to their friends and neighbors, or to the local elite and foreign lenders.[16] The

[13] See for instance Biagio di Agnolo and Cambio di Piero had a debt with the *presto* – lender – called Lioni (or Leoni) for 2.15 and 8 florins respectively. ASFi, *Catasto, Portate*, b. 17, f.º 331; ASFi, b17, f.º 438.

[14] Dermineur and Pompermaier, 'Credit networks in renaissance Florence', there 158–159.

[15] Padgett and McLean, 'Economic Credit in Renaissance Florence'.

[16] We do not know how the arrival of the Jewish moneylenders or the establishment of the municipal pawnshop affected the credit network. Jewish moneylenders were barred from living and working in Florence *intra muros* at the time of the first *catasto*, they were admitted into the city only in the 1430 s. They were nonetheless present and active throughout Tuscany. There, according to the *catasto*, Jewish moneylenders accounted for about 10% of household debts.; Botticini, 'A tale of 'benevolent' governments', there

contracting parties often knew each other: they either worked together, frequented the same places of sociability, lived in the same neighborhood, and so forth. The familiarity between individuals forged through prolonged relationships and repeated exchanges contributed to lowering asymmetries of information and promoted trust. In such a context, where endogamy and homophily were relevant in the building of credit networks, it is unclear what was the role of intermediaries.

A broad body of literature stresses the relevance of intermediaries in the economy. In particular, D. C. North highlighted the role they had in solving asymmetries of information, spreading trust, and increasing the efficiency of the market.[17] In fifteenth-century Florence, the moneychangers were among those categories who seemed to have played a relevant role in this sense. Moneychangers appear in the sources as *tavolieri, banchieri,* and *cambiavalute*, testifying about the multiple functions they were responsible for.[18] Unlike pawnbrokers, they were members of the *Arte del Cambio*, the guild that represented and coordinated all of them and regulated their business. The *Arte* was one of the most important guilds in the city: it was established at the beginning of the thirteenth century as a separate branch of the *Arte di Calimala*—the guild of the biggest merchants of the city. Its premises were not by chance located in one of the most central areas of Florence, in the *Signoria* square, under the *loggia dei Pisani*.

Defining the main functions of moneychangers is not an easy task. They were a sort of "mixed bag"—to use Richard Goldthwaite's words—"ranging from small shops to large international companies". The smaller moneychangers had little to do with banking: they usually did not accept deposits and they did not offer transfer operations to their customers. They lived off the commissions they charged for simple change operations between different currencies or between gold and silver coins. The most important moneychangers were instead involved in transfers in markets

167–174. Peer-to-peer lending markets traditionally functioned in concentric circles; see Fontaine, *The Moral Economy*, there 38.

[17] Douglass C. North, 'Transactions Cost in History', in: *The Journal of European Economic History*, 14–3 (1985): 557–576.

[18] In this paper the term banker—the literal translation of *banchiere*—is used as a synonym of moneychanger.

abroad and supplied large loans financing commerce and trade, being at the core of international networks.[19]

Many studies describe the role of the moneychangers in the credit market and the variety of forms through which they participated in it. In his research on medieval Bruges, Raymond De Roover claimed that moneychangers granted a line of credit to their customers, who were thus allowed to overdraw their accounts up to a stated limit.[20] Big international banks traded in bills of exchange, which, even if useful in extending a line of credit, were technically not loans and escaped any charge of usury (it was technically *cambium* and not *mutuum*). In both cases, it was not direct lending, and it did not imply cash transactions. However, there are also traces of more direct participation of moneychangers in the market, especially as lenders.

Richard Goldthwaite describes the activity of the banker Bindaccio di Michele de' Cerchi in the middle of the fifteenth century, highlighting his role as a lender. The ledgers of the bank record many *cose pegnate*, pawned things, in particular jewelry, that he accepted as collateral. Lending on security was, according to Goldthwaite, one of the most important activities in the early years of the bank. Cerchi also acted as guarantor and, on several occasions, promised his customers to pay the debts they had with other individuals in case of default. The amounts were as low as two florins and rarely exceeded 50 florins. His clients came from every social *milieu*, among which were artisans, bakers, notaries, weavers, etc.[21]

Charles De La Roncière retraced instead the economic activity of Lippo di Fede del Sega through the analysis of his ledgers. He had a *banco di mercato* devoted to local change, and his main activity was to convert foreign currencies and change gold and silver coins. The *banco* provided him with the liquidity he partly re-invested in his money-lending activity. In fact, he supplied small amounts, usually interest-free, to his neighbors and relatives who were part of his social network. At the same time, he lent to peasants living in the Florentine countryside. While urban loans seemed to be a means for social integration at neighborhood level,

[19] Goldthwaite, 'Local banking in renaissance Florence', there 6.

[20] Raymond De Roover, *Money, Banking and Credit in Mediaeval Bruges. Italian Merchant-Bankers, Lombards and Moneychangers. A Study in the Origin of Banking*, (Cambridge (MA), 1948,), there 294.

[21] Goldthwaite, 'Local banking in renaissance Florence', there 28.

rural loans were clearly an instrument of land expropriation aimed at broadening Lippo's real properties.[22]

The paper moves forward from these studies and analyses the intermediary roles of moneychanger from a more systemic perspective. To this end, the next section retraces and analyses the credit network in a specific area of Florence called *gonfalone* Nicchio, which will serve as case study for the analysis. It focuses on the kinds of credit relationships that linked individuals, highlighting how intermediation took place in early fifteenth-century Florence. We will then turn to graph theory to assess more in detail the positions that moneychangers occupied in the network.

3 Characteristics of the Credit Network in the *Gonfalone* Nicchio

On May 24, 1427, the commune of Florence established the first *catasto* to deal with two pressing issues: first, the city needed a tax reform to increase revenues and pay for ordinary and extraordinary expenses, especially the armed conflicts in which the city was involved. Second, the local population perceived the complicated web of forced loans (which flew into the *monte*, the public debt), *gabelle*, and other direct taxes that existed before the *catasto* as an excessive and unfair burden.[23] There was a general need for a more rational tax assessment based on the real value of assets and not on very questionable estimations, as was the case with forced loans.

The *catasto* introduced a novel way of assessing wealth. Every household provided a detailed declaration (a *portata*) outlining their real estate, livestock, cash, merchandise, and shares in the public debt. These declarations also accounted for claims and liabilities, which were utilized to

[22] 64% of loans that had real estate as collateral defaulted; see Charles M.de La Roncière, *Un Changeur Florentin du Trecento: Lippo di Fede del Sega (1285 env. – 1363 env.)* (Paris, 1973); this is something that happened also in the Venetian mainland in the fifteenth century; see Gigi Corazzol, *Fitti e livelli a grano. Un aspetto del credito rurale nel Veneto del '500* (Milan, 1979).

[23] Molho, *Florentine public finances*, there 82–83; see also Herlihy and Klapisch-Zuber, *Tuscans and their Families,* there 5.

determine the taxable net wealth.[24] The *catasto* contains interesting information about 10,000 households and more than 37,000 individuals living in Florence, and many more residing in the Florentine territories (both the *contado*, its hinterland, and the *distretto*, the other territories under the Florentine authority).[25]

This paper does not study the entire city of Florence, but only the *gonfalone* called Nicchio, one of the sixteen areas into which it was divided (in yellow in Fig. 1).[26] Nicchio was chosen for several reasons: first, it was part of the wealthy inner circle of the city but was also linked to the poor ghettoes in the south. Second, the aggregate value of both deductions and private investments (which contain debts and loans, respectively) are among the highest in the city: this suggests that the volume of credit exchanges recorded in the declarations is quite high.[27]

The analysis of the credit network is based on the lists of names of borrowers and lenders that are attached to the tax declaration of each householder living in the Nicchio *gonfalone* in 1427. In some cases, these lists can be very long, with hundreds of names of borrowers and lenders, while in others they just include a few names or even none. The number of transactions is generally correlated with several variables, like wealth, profession, and age of the householders.[28] On average, each declaration

[24] Herlihy and Klapisch-Zuber, *Tuscans and their Families,* there 93. Each family could subtract 200 florins from their total assessment for every member of the family (except for servants, apprentices, and employees), but only households who lived in Florence, see Guido Alfani and Francesco Ammannati, 'Long-term trends in economic inequality: the case of the Florentine state, c. 1300–1800', in: *Economic History Review* 70–4 (2017): 1072–1102, there 1094. A *catasto* amounted to 0.5% of an individual's net capitalization: for instance, 2 *catasti* corresponded to 1% of the total amount of net taxable assets. Between 1428 and 1433, the citizens of Florence were asked to pay 153 5/6 *catasti*, see Molho, *Florentine public finances*, there 92.

[25] Herlihy and Klapisch-Zuber, *Tuscans and Their Families*, there 56.

[26] ASFi, Catasto, Portate, bb. 17, 18I, 18II.

[27] The preliminary analysis of the *gonfalone* was based on the database developed by David Herlihy and Christiane Klapish-Zuber available at https://cds.library.brown.edu/projects/catasto/overview.html (June 2023).

[28] There is a positive but not very strong correlation between the number of transactions (both debts and credits) and the overall value of assets declared by householders (correlation = 0.44, 0.5 if we consider the number of loans, and 0.37 the number of debts).

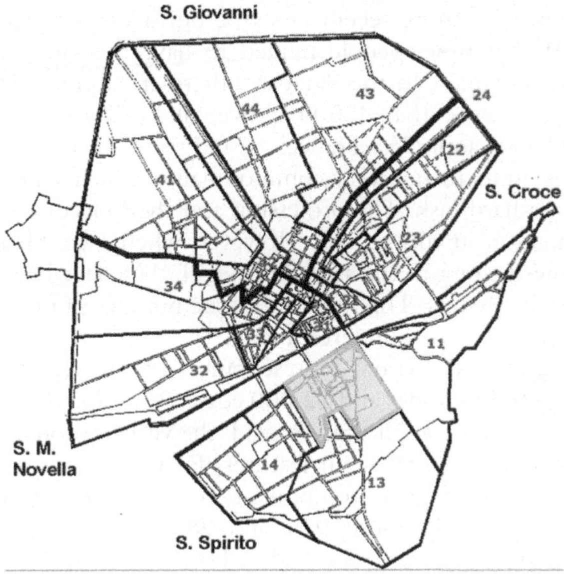

Fig. 1 Map of Florence in 1427 (based on Bonsignori 1584); S.Spirito: 11: Scala, 12: Nicchio (in yellow), 13: Sferza, 14: Drago; S.Croce: 21: Carro, 22: Bue, 23: Lion Nero, 24: Ruote; S.Maria Novella: 31: Vipera, 32: Unicorno, 33: Lion Rosso, 34:Lion Bianco; S.Giovanni: 41: Lion d'Oro, 42: Drago, 43: Chiavi, 44: Vaio; (Source: https://cds.library.brown.edu/projects/catasto/new search/1420-50_map.html

contains about 30.44 transactions or—from the perspective of the householder—28.04 claims and 10.44 debts. The average value of transactions is about 49.29 Florins, while the median value is 5.25 Florins.[29]

Individuals are listed by name, patronymic, and, in some cases, surname. Sometimes it is possible to find other pieces of information useful to identify the individuals mentioned, like for instance where they lived, their professions, nicknames, and so forth. This is extremely important for SNA, and the first step in the analysis is to identify with a certain degree of confidence all individuals in the network. This is usually

[29] Average and median values are very different because the standard deviation is high; the average and median values of loans and liabilities are 80 and 10 Florins, and 37 and 4 Florins, respectively.

not a problem with more recent datasets, but it can be problematic for historians. At that time, people tended to have the same names—and, therefore, patronymics. In the database, there are about 1,500 different first names and more than 9,500 individuals: 672 of them are called Antonio, 611 Giovanni, 355 Francesco, and so forth. In many cases, the patronymic is, in its turn, a very common name, which sometimes makes identification a hard task. The profession and their place of residence are useful information in this regard. However, when I could not establish that two names belong to the same individual, they have been considered as two different persons. This means that the number of nodes is possibly overestimated rather than underestimated.[30]

Figure 2 gives us a visual representation of the credit network. It includes about 9,500 nodes and 12,000 edges (see Table 1). Even though the structure is quite complicated to read, the visualization is very helpful and highlights at least two main features. First, there is a unique interconnected unit, called giant component, that includes almost all nodes and edges—respectively about 97% and 98% of the total. Credit was widespread and almost everyone had at least one claim or one liability; moreover, almost all households were part of a unique and interconnected ecosystem. The private credit market was the main access to credit for part of the urban population. There were just a few households that were excluded from, or that did not participate in, the credit market at all.[31]

Between 2,000 to 2,500 individuals lived in Nicchio, divided into approximately 450 households (about 5% of the city). Many of them were artisans and shopkeepers (18.44% and 11.27% respectively), but there were also noble families and individuals involved in highly qualified professions (such as notaries).[32] Wealth inequality was important,

[30] We compared my data with the database created by David Herlihy and Christiane Klapish-Zuber in order to identify even more individuals and track their declarations in the *catasto*. This reduced the problem linked to the overestimation of the number of nodes.

[31] Dermineur and Pompermaier (forthcoming), 'Credit Networks in Renaissance Florence'; widows were especially numerous among householders with few or completely without credit/debit relations.

[32] 1.4% of householders were nobles, 3.2% were employed as judges, notaries, medical doctors, and brokers; in total, 488 households lived in the Nicchio gonfalone, at least according to the 1427 catasto; the average number of individuals per household—estimated by Klapish-Zuber and Herlihy was 4.42, which means an average population of 2,200 individuals; See Herlihy and Klapisch-Zuber, *Tuscans and their Families,* there X.

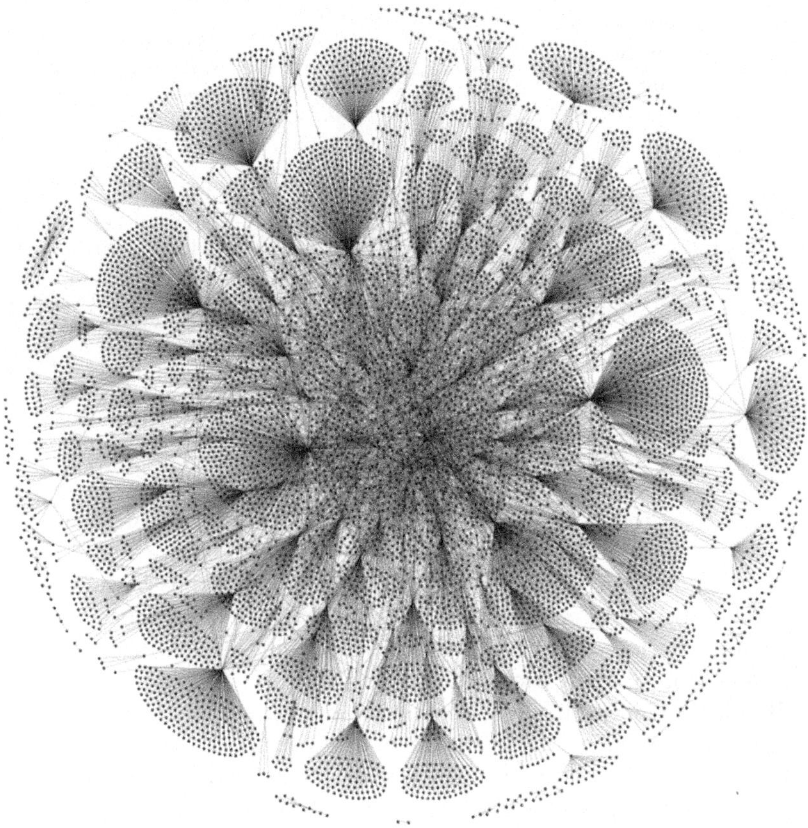

Fig. 2 Visualization of the network, Nicchio gonfalone

but still below the average of the city: 10% of the richest families in the city lived there, while 38 households (8.38% of the total) declared no assets at all.[33] Research suggests that significant inequalities usually exert a negative influence on the creation of social networks since inegalitarian

[33] Gini index in Nicchio is 0.75, and in the entire city is 0.79; the highest inequalities are in Drago (in the quarter of Santo Spirito), equal to 0.85, and the lowest in Drago (San Giovanni), 0.38. However, the value and number of deductions were so high that it is difficult to run such an analysis. For instance, the primary residence was not included in the declarations, as well as movables of everyday use (the so-called *masserizie*).

Table 1 Main characteristics of the network, Nicchio gonfalone

Measure	*Value*
Nodes	9,502
Edges	11,529
Diameter	13
Average Degree	1.213
Average path length	5.224
Size of the giant component	Nodes: 9,183 (96.64%) Edges: 11,269 (97.74%)

The database does not include any transactions that involve public institutions such as the commune of Florence and other municipalities, but only those between private individuals and private institutions (churches, monasteries, etc.). The number of nodes and edges slightly differs from Dermineur and Pompermaier (forthcoming), 'Credit Networks in Renaissance Florence' because the database is always updated as soon as new individuals are identified

societies tend to be less socially cohesive.[34] This seems not to be true in 1427 Nicchio. In the *gonfalone*, strong inequalities did not lead to the fragmentation of the social fabric. It is not among the aims of this chapter to discuss social and economic inequalities in medieval societies, but it is interesting to note that people seemed to live in different social spheres that were not mutually exclusive.

Besides visualization, there are specific measurements that can help us to identify the main characteristics of the overall credit network. The density, the number of edges in the network divided by the number of edges that could potentially exist, is very low. Compared to other social relations such as friendship, credit supply is bound to the availability of cash or to the existence of commercial transactions and, therefore, is limited. Many nodes had only a few connections, as confirmed by the relatively low average degree, the average number of links each individual had (1.213); on the other hand, there is a small group of individuals at the top of the hierarchy of the *gonfalone* featuring many connections. The network has a hierarchical structure with very few reciprocal transactions. This contributes to "provid[ing] a way to avoid self-interest and

[34] Cattell, Vicky, 'Poor people, poor places, and poor health: the mediating role of social networks and social capital', in: *Social science & medicine* 52–10 (2001): 1501–1516, there 1502.

defection or cheating", increasing the efficiency of the whole network.[35] It was a reputation-based system in which gossip spread information, and ostracism was the punishment for not adhering to a set of basic rules and social norms.

In general, the low average path length (5.224) compared to the number of nodes suggests that we are dealing with a so-called small-world network.[36] In such a structure, which characterizes many human networks, most nodes are not directly linked but can be reached from every other node with just a limited number of "steps". This means that nodes are embedded in socially close relationships. In other words, strangers are linked by a short chain of acquaintances: intermediaries were therefore important for the efficiency of the system.

4 Moneychangers in the Florentine Credit Market

4.1 A Qualitative Analysis

Figure 2 describes the high volume of transactions that involved people living in the *gonfalone* Nicchio in 1427. Despite all edges looking the same, they can represent very different credit transactions, dissimilar relationships between individuals, and various ways through which people lent and borrow money. The *catasto* usually lacks this information, and I decided to integrate it with a register produced by the *Arte del Cambio* that includes a series of 373 trials related to the period between September 3, 1409 and April 15, 1414.[37] The litigations concern various topics, and the *Arte* appears as the judiciary to which individuals turned when they had problems with moneychangers, regardless of the cause. However, most of them are linked to credit transactions.

[35] Ana S. Ribeiro, 'The Evolution of Norms in Trade and Financial Networks in the First Global Age: The Case of the Simon Ruis'z Network', in: Cátia AP Antunes and Amélia Polónia (eds.), Beyond Empires: Global self-organizing, cross-imperial networks, 1500-1800 (Leiden and Boston, 2016), 12-41, there 31.

[36] Duncan J. Watts and Steven H. Strogatz, 'Collective dynamics of 'small-world' networks', in: *Nature* 393 (1998), 440-442.

[37] ASFi, *Arte del Cambio*, b. 65; the register covers the period between the 3rd of September 1409 and the 15th of April 1414.

The analysis shows that there are four main categories of credit exchange that involved the moneychangers. First, purchases on credit or deferred payments. They were of critical importance in preindustrial societies. James Shaw and Evelyn Welch's analysis of the ledgers of a Florentine apothecary describes the daily activity of the shop between 1464 and 1568. They highlight the importance of credit in such a cashless economy. Claims and liabilities seemed to last over time, and sometimes it took many years before debts were repaid.[38] Shopkeepers' declarations in the *catasto* are filled with small debt, some of them labeled as "bad debts" or belonging to "bad borrowers". Sometimes, they can be found years later, still waiting to be closed.[39] Many of the edges we see in Fig. 2 are probably linked to the purchase of goods for personal reasons and involved small amounts, while others were maybe more substantial and were part of larger commercial transactions.

Second, individuals lent money to each other. The above-mentioned register testifies that loans were often supplied in cash, using golden and silver coins. The ease with which gold and silver coins circulate in the city and the impressive volume of transactions that emerged from the analysis of the *catasto*, suggests that this was a very dynamic credit market.[40] The third category includes the payments on behalf of others. These were direct cash payments or *giro* payments that involved at least three individuals: the banker acted usually as an agent and paid one or more creditors on behalf of one of his customers. If a client's deposit did not cover the expenses, the account balance turned negative, and the banker became a

[38] James Shaw and Evelyn Welch, *Making and Marketing of Medicine in Renaissance Florence* (Amsterdam and New York, 2011), there 84.

[39] Matteo Pompermaier, 'Dynamic Networks? Credit and Trust in Late Renaissance Florence (1427–1430)', in: Mauro Carboni, Pietro Delcorno (eds), Mobilizing Money for the Common Good. The Social Dimension of Credit (14th-19th Century) (Bologna, 2024), 149–178.

[40] It also contradicts the idea of the *strettezza del credito* (lit. Tightness of credit) and *mancamento del danaio* (lit. shortage of cash) mentioned in some documents of the 1420 s and 1430 s; A. Molho, *Florentine Public Finances in the early renaissance 1400–1433*, Cambridge (MA), 1971, pp. 155–156. However, it has not be taken for granted that what declared really happened. In a paper devoted to early modern Venice, James Shaw describes the characteristics of what he defined a baroque economy, in which there was a "discrepancy between the documentary record and the underlying practices of the informal economy", individuals describe transactions in cash that never took place in reality. See Shaw, James, 'The informal economy of credit in early modern Venice', in: *The Historical Journal* 61–3 (2018), 623–642, there 631.

creditor of his customer. According to the register, it was usually a very short-term credit, considering that four months were sufficient to proceed with legal action.

Fourth, the promises to pay. It is not always easy to clarify how promises to pay worked, nor what was the relationship between the parties involved. An example could help: Iacopo di Tommaso sued Andrea di Pierozzo Ghetti for a debt of 65 florins that he "promised us for Antonio di Bonino *pizzicagnolo*" (street food seller).[41] It is likely that Antonio di Pierozzo Ghetti acted as guarantor (the so-called *mallevatore*) of Antonio di Bonino—the street food seller—and, once clear that the latter was unable to repay his debt, he was sued by Iacopo di Tommaso, the lender. In the *catasto,* there are many cases in which guarantors (*mallevadori*) are enlisted among the debtors. This practice seemed to be quite widespread: we can imagine that creditors would turn to the courts to sue both the debtor and its guarantor in order to have more chances of getting back their money.

Florence was a rather small city, and we can suppose that information circulated easily among individuals who have repeated interactions with each other, something which reduced asymmetries in information. However, guarantors and intermediaries seemed to be important for the correct functioning of the overall credit network, supporting everyday transactions. They spread trust and gave (access to) credit to individuals who lacked it. They help to reduce transaction costs and make local exchanges more fluid. As we will see in the next section, SNA allows us to track some characteristics of the network that reflect the role of moneychangers as intermediaries.

4.2 A Social Network Analysis

As stated earlier, this paper relies on a sample of about 450 tax declarations of households residing in the *gonfalone* Nicchio in 1427. The network resulting is the sum of about 450 ego networks linked to each other through individuals who are mentioned as borrowers or/and lenders in more than one declaration. This explains the structure that the network assumes when we look at it in Fig. 2. The center of this network is highly interconnected, while the periphery looks more

[41] ASFi, *Arte del Cambio*, b. 65, f.o 4v, 10 September 1409.

modular, made by several interconnected stars, and small groups of nodes revolving around a central node, the declaration holder.

In such a network, where are the moneychangers? It is very easy to track moneychangers when they were the ones declaring taxes, simply because they stated what their job is. It is much less so when they are listed as borrowers or lenders because the profession is not always specified. To overcome this problem, we collected the names of all the members of the *Arte del Cambio* between 1400 and 1427.[42] We considered this time frame to be long enough to include all the moneychangers still alive and operating in 1427. Then, we compared this list of names with the database of borrowers and lenders in the Nicchio *gonfalone*.[43] At the end of this process, we were able to track 164 moneychangers, about 1.7% of the total sample, who were involved in about 2,000 transactions.

Moneychangers were more active than the rest of the sample, being involved on average in about 106 transactions against slightly more than 30. Also, the average and median values of loans and debts are higher, respectively 148.78 and 22.17 Florins (against 49.29 and 5.25). This is due to the fact that many moneychangers in the sample belonged to the upper classes, who are on average more active and involved in commercial transactions of a higher amount. Therefore, these numbers alone tell little about the actual involvement of moneychangers in the credit market.

Figure 3 depicts exactly the same network we see in Fig. 2, but it highlights moneychangers (larger dots) and divides the edges into two different colors according to their value (light gray and black respectively less and more than 10 Florins). This is interesting for several reasons: first, it gives us an idea of the part of the network that has been completely ignored in previous research, which did not include transactions of less than 10 florins (all the light gray area). Second, it confirms the hierarchical structure of the network, with limited reciprocity in the transactions.[44]

[42] The author thanks Claudia Tripodi for her support in the data collection.

[43] *Arte del Cambio*, b. 12, "Quaderno membranaceo contenente giuramenti per matricole e società". To identify all moneychangers living in 1427 Florence, we compared the names of all those registered at the *Arte del Cambio* with the index of the entire *catasto*, about 10,000 names. We do not know if they had a *banco* or if they were just part of the *Arte del Cambio* without running an activity, but this is the only way to identify and track all of them.

[44] The reciprocity of a directed graph can be expressed as the proportion of bidirectional edges to the overall number of edges present in the graph.

Finally, it shows the position of the moneychangers in it. Many of them are in the center where most interconnected individuals are located, and the volume and number of exchanges are higher. Others are in the peripheries, among less interconnected individuals, and are involved in smaller transactions.

Moneychangers were differently positioned in the network because they probably had different roles in the credit market. In his study on Cerchi's bank, Goldthwaite claimed that the amounts of loans provided

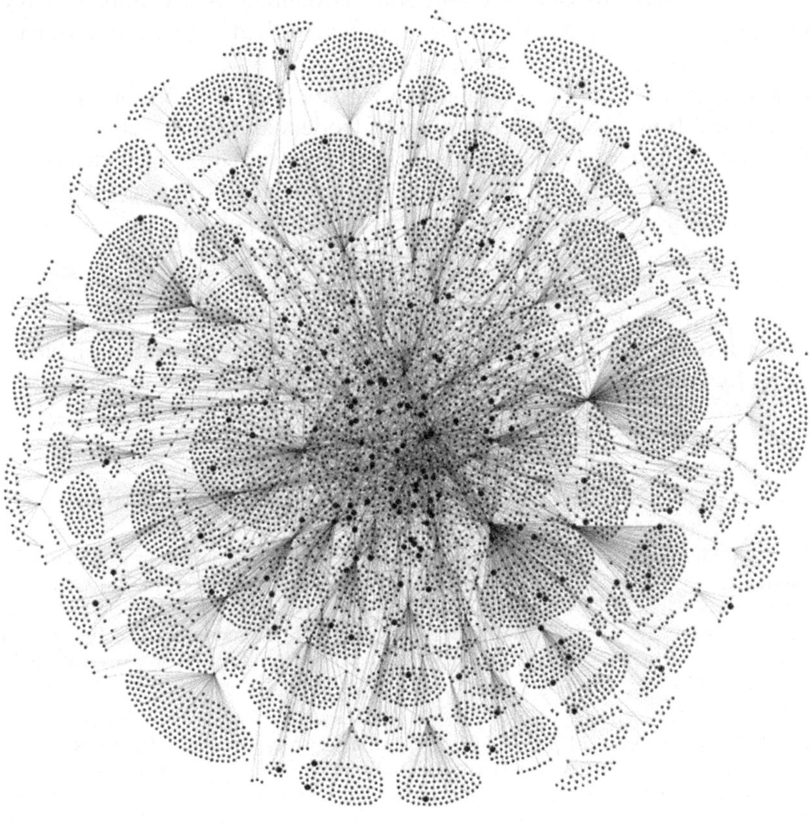

Fig. 3 Moneychangers in the network (Nicchio gonfalone); larger dots = moneychangers; the darker the color of the edge, the higher the amount

by moneychangers were directly related to the size of their banks.[45] The segmentation of the credit offer seems to be confirmed also by the fact that the personal wealth of lenders is directly proportional to the median value of the loans they supplied.[46]

Once retraced, the entire structure of the network and the position of moneychangers in it, we can move forward and focus on the analysis of the communities in the network. The visualization of the network, as powerful as it is, fails to highlight the different communities that compose it. To that end, we need to turn to the mathematical approach offered by graph theory. A community is defined as a group of actors who interact with each other more intensively than with anyone outside of the group, "to such an extent that they could be considered to be a separated entity".[47] The goal of identifying all different communities is to understand how many closed groups of lenders and borrowers are in the network and test the role of homophily in the formation of such groups. By so doing we will be able to reach two main goals: first, assess if there are communities of moneychangers; second, deepen our understanding of the structure and the functioning of the credit network.

There are several ways to identify communities, and the literature often disagrees on which one is the most appropriate.[48] In this case, we used a multilevel algorithm developed by Blondel et al. and available on the SNA software Gephi.[49] In community detection, we consider both

[45] Goldthwaite, 'Local banking in renaissance Florence', there 30.

[46] Not the average one; tested considering the declarations of 5 moneychangers with the highest degree.

[47] See Albert-László Barabasi, *Network Science*, chapter 9, available at http://networksciencebook.com/ (June 2023); for the quote, see Stephen P. Borgatti, Martin G. Everett and Jeffrey C. Johnson, *Analyzing social networks* (London, 2018), there 181; cited in Daniela Stoltenberg, Daniel Maier and Annie Waldherr, 'Community detection in civil society online networks: Theoretical guide and empirical assessment', in: *Social Networks* 59 (2019): 120–133, there 121.

[48] It depends on many variables, like data, characteristics of the network, etc. In this regard see Stoltenberg, Maier, Waldherr, 'Community detection in civil society online networks'; see also Vincent A. Traag, Ludo Waltman and Nees Jan Van Eck, 'From Louvain to Leiden: guaranteeing well-connected communities', in: *Scientific reports* 9.1 (2019): 1–12.

[49] Algorithm: Vincent D. Blondel, Jean-Loup Guillaume, Renaud Lambiotte, Etienne Lefebvre, 'Fast unfolding of communities in large networks', in: *Journal of Statistical Mechanics: Theory and Experiment* 10 (2008), P1008; find out more about Gephi here https://gephi.org/ (May 2023).

the weight of ties, as it is proportional to the quality of the relationships (i.e., the quality of credit), and the direction of the edges—even though sometimes it creates some problems such as leaving some nodes and dyads unassigned.[50]

The algorithm identifies 127 communities that include all 9,502 nodes. The average number of members per community is 74.82 and the median is 8: the smallest community includes only 2 members and the largest one 637. The first issue to solve is to unveil what are the main features that characterize these communities. At first sight, they are quite mixed, and they include individuals with different professions, coming from diverse geographical areas, and characterized by dissimilar wealth levels. However, if we deeply observe their characteristics we can notice some clear patterns. I look first for professional homophily, which suggests that individuals tend to have credit relationships with others who are employed in the same professional sector. This is usually one of the strongest patterns, and the above-mentioned literature on fifteenth-century Florence already highlighted the relevance of this phenomenon for the creation of credit networks.

The sample includes information about the professions of only a part of the nodes, around 30%. The biggest group (10.19% of the total sample) includes the manufacture and commerce of wool, silk, and linen, that we gathered in a single broad category that includes those employed in the production, retailing, and commerce of textile products. Those were the most important manufactures in late Renaissance Florence. Other categories gather artisans (crafters, 6,16%) and retailers (both food and non-food related, 2.4% and 2.7% respectively). As we saw previously, the moneychangers are only about 1,7% of the sample. The large part of nodes for which the profession is unknown invites us to be careful in interpreting the results. However, it is quite clear that certain professional groups are more represented in some communities than in others, suggesting that homophily could have a role in linking borrowers and lenders. This is far from being unexpected.

As an example, in cluster 54, in which we have 577 nodes and 651 edges, 25% of nodes are employed in textile manufacturing and commerce, especially wool. In Fig. 4, we can see the visual representation of this community. The network is composed of several small groups

[50] Stoltenberg, Maier, Waldherr, 'Community detection in civil society online networks', there 128.

of nodes, which represent the declaration holders—many of whom are employed in the textile industry—with several borrowers and lenders around them. At the center, inside the circle called "A", we notice the most central individuals in this community. Those are almost all involved in the commerce of wool or silk and have an important bridging role, connecting the different parts of the community together. There are several important individuals in this circle, like for instance Cosimo di Giovanni de' Medici, and members of families Salviati, Rondinelli, Bindi, etc. The community also includes a few moneychangers (larger dots). They contribute to connecting different parts of the network together, but their bridging role, in this case, is less important and is often redundant, since other nodes already do the same function. Therefore, professional homophily in this cluster is relevant and moneychangers have a less relevant role in such a system.

This is not the only cluster in which professional homophily is significant. Many clusters revolve around wool or silk merchants and manufacturers, which was not by chance the most relevant sector in the urban economy. In other cases, there are high percentages of nodes involved with food production and retailing, and artisans. At the same time, it is interesting to note that there are no clusters with a high percentage of moneychangers (in relative terms). Indeed, they are never more than 3–4% of nodes in each community. I can draw one interesting conclusion from this analysis: in a context in which professional homophily was relevant in community formation, no structure links all moneychangers with each other.[51] Moneychangers seem to be a sort of "open group". They are spread across the network and greatly contribute to its connectedness.

If we test the importance of homophily using the geographical origins we find similar results. The analysis suffers from a greater uncertainty, but there are communities clearly characterized by creditors and debtors residing in the same area.[52] The test is carried out with locations outside the territory that then constituted the municipality of Florence; we expect to find similar results also within Florence, but we need data from all

[51] De Roover proved that moneychangers in Bruges had accounts with each other to make transfers available in the absence of a real clearing system; see De Roover, *Money Banking and Credit in Medieval Bruges*.

[52] We selected 15 different cities and villages: Arezzo, Bologna, Brozzi, Castello Fiorentino, Certaldo, Colla, Gambassi, Pieve di Settimo, Pisa, Pistoia, Prato, Quarantola, San Casciano, San Gimignano, San Miniato.

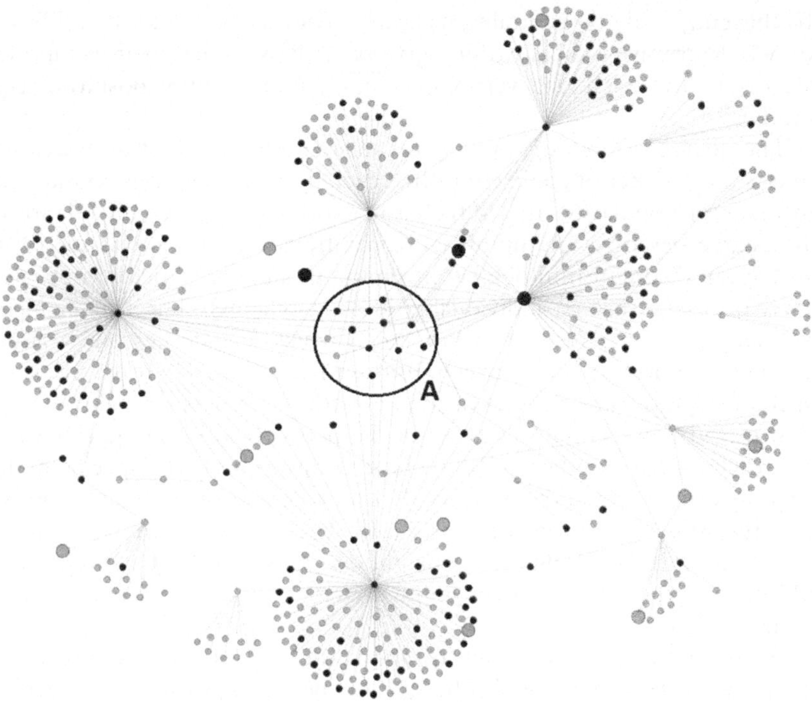

Fig. 4 Cluster 54, larger dots: moneychangers, black dots: textile, gray dots: other professions

gonfaloni to run this test thoroughly.[53] The same test based on the wealth of individuals suffers from the lack of data since we know the gross and net wealth of a limited number of nodes (10% to 20% in each community). The analysis seems to confirm the vertical structure of the network, a context characterized by mixed modules in which the well-off lent to the poor. However, these are only basic speculations.

So far, I have highlighted the structure of the network, the composition of the different clusters that compose it, and the strength of homophily in network formation. Is it possible to say something about the role of moneychangers as intermediaries? The answer is affirmative.

[53] Among others, see Padgett and McLean, 'Economic Credit in Renaissance Florence'.

To this end, I rely on centrality measures. They are the "oldest and best-known descriptive indices within network analysis … designed to capture the extent to which one vertex occupies a more central position than another".[54]

The degree of nodes is one of the most commonly used measures. It counts the number of connections that each node has, and it is considered an index of popularity. In a directed network based on credit relations, the degree describes the number of operations each node was involved in. We can distinguish in-degree, incoming money (liabilities), from out-degree, money that an individual is lending (claims). The betweenness centrality quantifies instead the extent to which a node lies on "a large number of shortest paths between various third parties".[55] It is a measure of the bridging role of nodes in the network. Closeness centrality evaluates instead how central nodes are in the network and how quickly they can reach out to all other nodes—which means how close a specific node is to any other node in the network. Finally, eigenvector centrality is probably the most interesting one, as it calculates the centrality of a node by summing the centrality of its neighbors. It is a measure of influence, which is based on the idea that central nodes are those connected to other central nodes.[56]

What do these measures tell us about the role of moneychangers in the credit market? First of all, they are on average 5.5 times more active than the rest of the nodes in the network. This is not unexpected, since it was clear from the simple comparison of the number of nodes and edges. It is more interesting to note that the betweenness centrality is on average 14 times higher in the group of moneychangers than in the rest of the sample, highlighting their importance as intermediaries. They were critical in linking different parts of the network together: they are in between different clusters, having credit relationships with individuals belonging to many of them. This is coherent with the results of the analysis of the different communities in the network. Moneychangers' closeness centrality is two times higher than that of the rest of the group, meaning that they occupy a central position in the credit network. Finally,

[54] Carter T. Butts, 'Social network analysis: A methodological introduction', in: *Asian Journal of Social Psychology*, 11–1 (2008): 13–41, there 22.

[55] Butts, 'Social network analysis', there 23.

[56] Eigenvector centrality "is a core-periphery measure, it is an index of diffusion and influence". All of that from Butts, 'Social network analysis', there 24.

the most interesting measure is eigenvector centrality, which is on average two times higher for moneychangers than for the rest of the network. This confirms their centrality in the network, and the fact that they were linked to other individuals very active in the credit market in the area.

If we compare the moneychangers to other different professional groups, the results do not change. The comparison is especially interesting with the textile manufacture and commerce, which includes many of the most wealthy and relevant individuals in fifteenth-century Florence. Again, moneychangers are at the top of the hierarchy in all centrality measures, while textile manufacturers and merchants are second in the ranking. The quantitative analysis therefore confirms what is suggested by the qualitative one.

5 Concluding Remarks

SNA "provides a powerful set of tools for describing and modelling the relational context in which behavior takes place, as well as the relational dimensions of that behavior".[57] Through SNA it was possible to retrace the main characteristics of the credit network and to delve deeper and study the communities that composed it and the nodes inside each community. The credit network in the Nicchio area includes almost all nodes and edges, meaning that credit was widespread and that almost every household living in the area was part of a unique and interconnected ecosystem. Money did not seem to be concentrated, and the credit market seemed to be quite dynamic: credit circulated widely (paper or real money) and in different ways, such as deferred payments, direct loans, book transfers, and payments on behalf of others.[58] The network has the feature of a small-world network, in which all individuals are embedded in socially close relationships and strangers are linked by short chains of acquaintances. It has low reciprocity and a hierarchical structure, which contributes to increasing its efficiency.

The identification and analysis of the communities that made up the credit network suggest the strength of professional and geographical homophily. It means that the local credit market was constituted of several

[57] Butts, 'Social network analysis', there 13.

[58] McLean and Gondal claimed that the supply of credit was rather concentrated and that there were relatively few alternatives, see McLean and Gondal, 'The circulation of interpersonal credit', there 161.

small communities characterized by common traits, more likely of professional and geographical nature. Credit flew among those individuals. Moreover, the analysis also shows the importance of intermediaries in keeping the network connected. Moneychangers played a critical bridging role, linking all the different communities together. Deals were more likely to be successful when people turned to them. Several centrality measures confirmed this hypothesis and their relevance in the credit network, especially in terms of betweenness, closeness, and eigenvector centralities. They occupied the most central positions in the network, they were the most important intermediaries, and they were connected to the most influential nodes. We tend to consider the increase in the number of intermediaries as one of the results of the progressive financialization of the credit market, but this might not be completely true. Moneychangers seemed to have contributed to the dynamism of the local credit market.

References

Primary Sources

Archivio di Stato di Firenze, Catasto, Portate, b. 17.
Archivio di Stato di Firenze, Catasto, Portate, b. 18_I.
Archivio di Stato di Firenze, Catasto, Portate, b. 18_II.
Archivio di Stato di Firenze, Arte del Cambio, b. 12.
Archivio di Stato di Firenze, Arte del Cambio, b. 65.
Printed Primary Material

Secondary Sources

Alfani, Guido, and Francesco Ammannati. 2017. Long-term trends in economic inequality: The case of the Florentine state, c. 1300–1800. *Economic History Review* 70 (4): 1072–1102.

Barabasi, Albert-László. *Network Science*. Available at http://networkscienceb ook.com/

Becker, Marvin B. 1957. Three cases concerning the restitution of usury in Florence. *The Journal of Economic History* 17 (3): 445–450.

Blondel, Vincent D., Jean-Loup. Guillaume, Renaud Lambiotte, and Etienne Lefebvre. 2008. Fast unfolding of communities in large networks. *Journal of Statistical Mechanics: Theory and Experiment* 10: P1008.

Borgatti, Stephen P., Martin G. Everett, and Jeffrey C. Johnson. 2018. *Analyzing Social Networks*. London: SAGE.

Botticini, Maristella. 2000. A tale of 'benevolent' governments: Private credit markets, public finance, and the role of Jewish money-lenders in medieval and Renaissance Italy. *The Journal of Economic History* 60 (1): 168–189.
Butts, Carter T. 2008. Social network analysis: A methodological introduction. *Asian Journal of Social Psychology* 11 (1): 13–41.
Bresnahan, Menning Carol. 1993. *Charity and State in Late Renaissance Italy: The Monte di Pietà of Florence*. Ithaca and London: Cornell University Press.
Cattell, Vicky. 2001. Poor people, poor places, and poor health: The mediating role of social networks and social capital. *Social science & medicine* 52 (10): 1501–1516.
Corazzol, Gigi. 1979. *Fitti e livelli a grano. Un aspetto del credito rurale nel Veneto del '500*. Milan: Franco Angeli.
La Roncière, Charles M. de. 1973. *Un Changeur Florentin du Trecento: Lippo di Fede del Sega (1285 env. – 1363 env.)*. Paris: SEVPEN.
De Roover, Raymond. 1948. *Money, Banking and Credit in Mediaeval Bruges. Italian Merchant-Bankers, Lombards and Moneychangers. A Study in the Origin of Banking*. Cambridge (MA): The Mediaeval Academy of America.
Dermineur, Elise and Matteo Pompermaier. 2022. Credit networks in renaissance Florence: revisiting the *catasto* of 1427. *Ricerche di storia economica e sociale*, VIII (2022): 89–110. https://doi.org/10.17426/R08C08.
Dermineur, Elise. 2022. The evolution of credit networks in pre-industrial Finland. *Scandinavian Economic History Review* 70 (1): 57–86.
Herlihy, David and Christiane Klapisch-Zuber. 1985. *Tuscans and their Families: A Study of the Florentine Catasto of 1427*. New Haven: Yale University Press.
Hoffman, Philip T., Gilles Postel-Vinay, and Jean-Laurent. Rosenthal. 2019. *Dark Matter Credit: The Development of Peer-to-Peer Lending and Banking in France*. Princeton: Princeton University Press.
McLean, Paul D., and Neha Gondal. 2014. The Circulation of Interpersonal Credit in Renaissance Florence. *European Journal of Sociology / Archives Européennes de Sociologie / Europäisches Archiv für Soziologie* 55 (2): 135–176.
Molho, A. 1971. *Florentine Public Finances in the early renaissance 1400–1433*, Cambridge, MA: Harvard University Press.
North, Douglass C. 1985. 'Transactions cost in history. *The Journal of European Economic History* 14 (3): 557–576.
Padgett, John F., and Paul D. McLean. 2011. 'Economic Credit in Renaissance Florence. *The Journal of Modern History* 83 (1): 1–47.
Pompermaier, Matteo. 2022a. 'Credit and poverty in early modern Venice. *Journal of Interdisciplinary History* 52 (4): 513–536.
Pompermaier, Matteo. 2022b. *L'Économie du 'mouchoir': crédit et microcrédit à Venise au XVIIIe siècle*. Rome: École française de Rome.
Pullan, Brian S. 1982. *La politica sociale della Repubblica di Venezia 1500- 1620*, vol. II, 'Gli ebrei veneziani e i Monti di pietà. Rome: il Veltro.

Ribeiro, Ana S. 2016. The Evolution of Norms in Trade and Financial Networks in the First Global Age: The Case of the Simon Ruis'z Network. In *Beyond Empires: Global Self-Organizing, Cross-Imperial Networks, 1500–1800*, edited by Cátia A. P. Antunes and Amélia Polónia, 12–41. Leiden and Boston: Brill.

Shaw, James and Evelyn Welch. 2011. *Making and Marketing of Medicine in Renaissance Florence.* Amsterdam and New York: Clio Medica.

Shaw, James. 2018. 'The informal economy of credit in early modern Venice. *The Historical Journal* 61–3: 623–642.

Smail, Daniel L. 2018. The materiality of credit: Debt collection as pawnbroking in late medieval Mediterranean Europe. *Histoire Urbaine* 51: 95–110.

Stoltenberg, Daniela, Daniel Maier, and Annie Waldherr. 2019. Community detection in civil society online networks: Theoretical guide and empirical assessment. *Social Networks* 59: 120–133.

Traag, Vincent A., Ludo Waltman, and Nees Jan van Eck. 2019. From Louvain to Leiden: guaranteeing well-connected communities. *Scientific Reports* 9 (1): 1–12.

Watts, Duncan J., and Steven H. Strogatz. 1998. Collective dynamics of 'small-world' networks. *Nature* 393: 440–442.

CHAPTER 10

Monetization and Relational Structures: The Diffusion of Checks in Buenos Aires During the Emergence of the Banking System

Martín L. E. Wasserman

1 Introduction

Established in 1822, the Bank of Buenos Aires was the first bank in South America. It closed with the crisis of 1826. Its emergence implied the local appearance of two new monetary tools: the bank note and the bank check.

The Bank issued bank notes as paper currency upon discounting commercial bills, and its initial metallic convertibility conferred acceptance to bank notes in commercial transactions. In turn, holders of bank accounts issued checks to release money from deposits in favor of their payees, therefore introducing the bank money (that is to say, the usage of bank accounts to make payments) for first time in local market.

This chapter delves into the initial admission process of the first bank checks, exploring the network structure employed by these instruments throughout the brief lifespan of the Bank (1822–1826). The importance

M. L. E. Wasserman (✉)
CONICET-UBA, Buenos Aires, Argentina
e-mail: mwasserman@filo.uba.ar

E. M. Dermineur and M. Pompermaier (eds.), *Credit Networks in The Preindustrial World*, Palgrave Studies in the History of Finance,
https://doi.org/10.1007/978-3-031-67117-3_10

of the acceptance relies on its role to understand the diffusion of monetary devices derived from financial innovation and the participation of economic actors in the economic institutional changes.[1]

The hypothesis guiding this chapter suggests that the main issuers of checks contributed to enhancing its acceptance in the local economy, as they gained leverage in using that means of payment. To demonstrate this hypothesis, this chapter appeals to the tools of Social Network Analysis (SNA hereafter), which allow an understanding of the relational structure of the check's flows and elucidate the position of the actors within that network.

2 Buenos Aires After the Revolution: A Critical Conjuncture

The revolutionary process that emerged in Buenos Aires since May 1810 against the Spanish crown brought about profound changes in the local monetary system. The conflicts that erupted throughout the territory of the Río de la Plata Viceroyalty affected productive activity and commercial exchanges, thereby disrupting the fiscal circulation of currency between viceregal treasuries. Consequently, interruptions in the commercial and fiscal circuits exacerbated the shortage of metallic currency in a port-town devoid of local silver or gold mines.

Given the shortage of fiscal resources and the relative inadequacy of customs collection on import taxes, the revolutionary government resorted to borrowing to finance the expenses of the armed struggle. The resulting issuance of public bonds implied in fact an expansion of currency.[2]

However, due to uncertainties regarding the government's ability to fulfill its obligations, merchants accepted those bonds at a discount from their face value when using them as means of payment in commercial transactions, sometimes losing up to 70% of their value. Conversely,

[1] Patrice Baubeau, 'Dematerialization and the Cashless Society: A Look Backward, a Look Sideward', in: Bernardo Bátiz-Lazo & Leonidas Efthymiou, L. (eds.), *The book of payments. Historical and contemporary views on the cashless society* (Palgrave Macmillan, 2016), 85–95.

[2] Alejandra Irigoin, *Finance, Politics and Economics in Buenos Aires, 1820s-1860s: the Political Economy of Currency Stabilisation*, Doctoral Thesis, London School of Economics and Political Science, 2000, 13.

the Customs treasury accepted them at their full nominal value, and merchants began paying their customs taxes using these government bonds.[3]

Monetizing public debt entailed either admitting its bonds below their face value as means of payment in the market or accepting their full value in the Customs treasury, thereby reducing the availability of resources for the government. In this situation, the government introduced some institutional changes. Since April 1814, the government allowed commercial letters as a means of payment for import taxes (better positioned in the market than their own bonds). Later, in 1818 started a process of institutional innovation to amortize the outstanding debt, establishing the South American Funds National Exchequer (*Caja Nacional de Fondos de Sud América*, hereinafter CNFSA) to take those papers in deposit, offering interest to prevent the bonds from being deposited in Custom's treasury. Yet, the interest rates did not attract the main holders of government bonds.[4]

In February 1820, the central government fell, and each of the fourteen provinces formerly belonging to that union became autonomous jurisdictions.[5] Therefore, the newly Province of Buenos Aires (headed by the namesake city) got its own legislative chamber. In 1821, it became urgent to pay off the public debt. The new legislature closed the CNFSA and established the Public Credit Office, alongside its corresponding Amortization Endowment, to purchase bonds at market prices

[3] Moutoukias shows that important commercial houses of Buenos Aires, such as Santa Coloma's one, acquired government promissory notes at low prices in the market, with discount rates that could reach 80% regards face value; Zakarias Moutoukias, 'Coacción pública e innovación. Deuda, actores y cambio institucional en el Río de la Plata (1790-1820)', in: Michel Bertrand and Zakarias Moutoukias (eds), Cambio institucional y fiscalidad. Mundo hispánico, 1760-1850 (Madrid 2018), 175-195.

[4] Martin Wasserman, 'Deuda, papeles y compromisos en la construcción del crédito público. La Caja Nacional de Fondos de Sud América (Buenos Aires, 1818–1821)', in: *Revista de Historia Económica / Journal of Iberian and Latin American Economic History*, 40:2 (2022), 371-404.

[5] Noemì Goldman, 'Argentina/Río de la Plata', in: Noemì Goldman and Javier Fernández Sebastián (eds), Diccionario político y social del mundo iberoamericano, (Madrid, 2014), 43-58, there 49; Nora B. Souto *La forma de unidad en el Río de la Plata. Soberanía y poder constituyente, 1808-1827*, Doctoral thesis, Universidad de Buenos Aires: Instituto de Historia Argentina y Americana "Dr. Emilio Ravignani", 2017, 273-275.

in exchange for new securities.[6] Nonetheless, market price of those securities fell below its nominal value once the government failed to sustain a regular payment of interests.

Addressing the scarcity of means of payment appeared to be the critical challenge for achieving financial stability.

3 The Emergence of the Banking Institution and its Instruments in Buenos Aires

The establishment of the Banco de Buenos Aires marked the most radical local monetary innovation. Founded in September 1822 as a joint-stock company, this pioneering bank was granted privileged authorization to issue paper currency. These banknotes were payable at sight to the bearer, denominated in pesos (hereinafter, $), and were convertible to metallic currency at the bank's offices, despite lacking legal tender status at the time. One paper peso equated to one silver peso, while seventeen paper pesos equated to one ounce of gold.[7] The issuance of banknotes was based on the discounting of commercial bills drawn between merchants in Buenos Aires.[8] Thus, two profound innovations occurred: the emergence of the banking institution and the introduction of its monetary instruments.

The main creditors of the public debt governed the bank, running it as its directors and main shareholders. They were mainly agrarian producers and exporters, usually associated with merchants dedicated to foreign trade funded with British capitals, or local partners of British companies established in Buenos Aires to export agrarian products from regional hinterland.[9] In this way, in order to preserve accessibility to local credit,

[6] Samuel Amaral, 'Medios de pago no metálicos en Buenos Aires a comienzos del siglo XIX. Letras de cambio y letras secas', in: *Cuadernos de Numismática y Ciencias Históricas*, 9:30 (1982), 45-55.

[7] Hereafter, amounts expressed as $ refer to nominal (paper) silver *peso* of eight *reales*, being each *peso* equivalent to a silver coin weighting 27.06 grams, made up of silver with a fineness of at least 895.8 millesimal.

[8] Octavio Garrigos, *El Banco de la provincia* (Buenos Aires, 1873); Nicolàs Casarino, *El Banco de la Provincia de Buenos Aires en su primer centenario. 1822-1922* (Buenos Aires, 1922).

[9] Some of the best acknowledge founders were Diego Brittain, Thomas Winter or Sebastián Lezica, all of them public creditors as well. See Martin Wasserman, 'Monedas de papel para una nueva soberanía. La negociación del financiamiento a la Hacienda de

the government granted the exercise of monetary power and the collection of its royalties to a group made up of some of its main local creditors. Thus, the financial bargaining between the government and its creditors found a new institutional expression in the creation of the Banco de Buenos Aires.[10]

The introduction of bank notes effectively introduced a new form of payment, helping to alleviate the shortage of metallic currency. This led to a decrease in interest rates (which previously stood at 9% or 10% per year) by enabling the monetization of commercial debts within the Buenos Aires market.[11] In addition, the banknote displaced the monetary role previously held by public debt securities, thereby aiding in the consolidation of the local debt. This marked the onset of the banking era in Río de la Plata.

However, the banknote was not the sole innovation to emerge in Buenos Aires at that time. Bank checks also made their debut as a novel form of payment within the local economy.

4 The First Bank Checks of Buenos Aires

While banknotes emerged as convertible paper currency issued by the bank as cash, checks were payment orders issued by a debtor (a holder of a current account) to the bank's accountant in favor of a creditor. By default, these checks were drawn to bearer, but the issuer could as well

Buenos Aires, entre la Revolución y el surgimiento de la banca bonaerense (1810-1826)', in: Martin Wasserman and Roberto Schmit (eds), El gobierno de la incertidumbre. La política financiera en Buenos Aires desde el Virreinato a la Confederación (Buenos Aires, 2022), 87-129.

[10] Therefore, bank notes emerged not only because of the shortage of bullion and legal tender, but because the issuance of those paper means of payment implied a potential benefit for their private issuers, and it was an incentive added to that constriction. On those constrictions specifically, see Irigoin, *Finance, Politics and Economics in Buenos Aires*, there 28; on the incentives, see Wasserman, 'Monedas de papel para una nueva soberanía'.

[11] Samuel Amaral, 'El descubrimiento de la financiación inflacionaria: Buenos Aires 1790-1830', in: *Investigaciones y Ensayos*, 37 (1988), 379-419; Carlos S.A. Segreti, *Moneda y política en la primera mitad del siglo XIX. Contribución al estudio de la historia de la moneda argentina* (Tucumán, 1975), there 141; Rafael Olarra Jiménez, *Evolución monetaria argentina* (Buenos Aires 1968), 24.

handwrite the name of a third party to identify the payee in the document. Being issued to the bearer by default (as evidenced by the printing itself), their possible circulation did not require any endorsement.[12]

The article n° 11 in the statute of the Banco de Buenos Aires allowed the bank to take deposits in current accounts, whose holders could make payments using the funds deposited by means of "letras a la vista" or *libranzas*, that is to say, checks. The initial checks introduced in Buenos Aires did not increase interest, and recipients typically redeemed them at the bank one day after issuance. This provision of security for funds, coupled with their accessibility through checks, incentivized the adoption of these instruments to facilitate transactions (Fig. 1).[13]

The bank check was an instrument equally new for the Buenos Aires market, expressing the appearance of *bank money* locally, that is to say, the use of current accounts as a means of payment.[14]

Fig. 1 Check issued by Antonio Lynch in favor of Miguel Zurro (Buenos Aires, 1825). Source: Archivo y Museo Históricos del Banco de la Provincia de Buenos Aires (hereafter, AMHBPBA), 1000-32-3. Photograph by the author

[12] To identify the payee was not mandatory and it was just an option. The printed formulary reads "pay to [*blank space*] or bearer", so even when the issuer identified a particular payee in the document, it was not necessary for her/him to personally assist to cash the check: any bearer could collect it. For instance, 1688 checks (18.71%) keep empty their blank space.

[13] Alberto De Paula, 'El Banco de Buenos Aires (1822-1826) y sus antecedentes históricos', in: Alberto De Paula and Noemì Maria Girbal-Blacha (eds), Historia del Banco de la Provincia de Buenos Aires. 1822-1997, tome I (Buenos Aires, 1997), 49.

[14] These checks are identical to the checks developed since eighteenth century in England (even when it was only around 1830 that their use reached a serious spreading

4.1 *Evolution of Bank Checks in Buenos Aires (1822–1826)*

The totality of checks preserved in the Historical Archive and Museum of the Bank of the Province of Buenos Aires (hereafter, AMHBPBA) reaches to 9018 units, issued along the BBA (from September 1822 to February 1826), mobilizing a total amount of $22,469,587.46 (Table 1).[15]

Payments with checks were not limited to high-value transactions.[16] The most frequent amount (or ***mode value***) among unitary amounts was $ 1000 (406 checks). About 90% of the documents were issued with less than $5,523.37, mobilizing 54% of the total amount transferred by checks between 1822 and 1826. Correlatively, just 10% of checks mobilized high unitary values (from $5525 to the exceptional amount of $111,204.87).

Table 2 indicates that 48.1% of checks were used within the range of $0.5 to $1,000. Within this range, the segment from $101 to $500

Table 1 General evolutions of checks at Banco de Buenos Ayres (1822–1826). Source: own elaboration on AMHBPBA, 1000–32-1; 1000–32-2; 1000–32-3. *Some checks have no date of issuing, due to the omission in the document, or due to its material deterioration

Year	*N° of checks*	*Amount ($)*	*Mean amount ($)*
1822	109	209,642.5	1,923.3
1823	1,361	2,571,475.8	1,890.7
1824	2,763	6,947,068.4	2,517.9
1825	4,003	10,736,555.8	2,682.7
1826	665	1,812,801.2	2,726.0
N/D*	117	192,043.5	1,641.4
Total	9,018	22,469,587.5	2,491.6

there), as explained by Redlich & Christman, see Fritz Reidlich and Webster M. Christman, 'Early American Checks and an Example of Their Use', in: *Business History Review*, 41:3 (1967), 285-302, 290. For this reason, they are equally similar to the checks used in the United States during the first three decades of the nineteenth century.

[15] Due to the inexistence in the archive of an account book that keeps a summary of the checks movements, it was necessary to process the information from the checks itself; taking manually from each one of the 9,018 documents the data they contain.

[16] Stephen Quinn and William Roberds, 'The Evolution of the Check as a Means of Payment: A Historical Survey' *Economic Review, Federal Reserve Bank of Atlanta*, 93:4 (2008), 1-28.

Table 2 Unitary amounts mobilized by checks. Source: Data from AMHBPBA, 1000–32-1; 1000–32-2; 1000–32-3

Unitary amount	*N° of Checks*	*Amount mobilized ($)*	*% Checks*	*% Amount mobilized*
0 a 10	18	118.5	0.2%	0.01%
11 a 100	893	64,026.5	9.9%	0.29%
101 a 500	2066	612,028.6	22.9%	2.72%
501 a 1000	1360	1,090,632.7	15.1%	4.85%
1001 a 5000	3684	9,886,095.3	40.9%	44.00%
5001 a 10,000	709	5,285,895.8	7.9%	23.53%
10,001 a 50,000	276	5,011,273.4	3.1%	22.30%
> 50,000	6	519,516.3	0.1%	2.31%
Total	9012*	22,469,587.46	100.00%	100%

accounted for 22.9% of the checks. Meanwhile, another 40% of checks were issued within the range of $1,000 to $5,000.[17]

The annual evolution of checks was closely tied to the performance of the bank's liabilities: the amounts used in cashing checks grew in correlation with the monetary emission from commercial bill discounts. However, the usage of checks exhibited a more rapid dynamic compared to the credit extended by the bank (Fig. 2).[18] Annually, the amounts paid out to cash checks represented increasing proportions of the credit lent.

In this regard, the circulation of checks expanded in line with the bank's liabilities but at a faster rate than its assets. This underlines the rapid adoption of check usage (as well as the challenges faced by the bank in capitalizing its funds at the same pace).

[17] Some prices are useful as parameters for measuring these amounts. In 1822, the daily wage of unskilled construction workers in Buenos Aires is estimated at 5 *reales* (0.625 *pesos*). For the same period, a pound of sugar in Buenos Aires equaled about 1.25 *reales* (0.15 *pesos*), a liter of wine 1.59 *reales* (0.19 *pesos*), and a pound of white bread 1 real (0.12 pesos); Julio Cesar Djenderedjian, Juan Luis Martirén, and María Inés Moraes, 'Prices and Living Standards during the Age of Revolutions: The Río de la Plata between 1772 and 1830', in: *Investigaciones de Historia Economica*, 19:2 (2023), 70–86.

[18] In this sense, the amounts paid for cashing checks in 1822 equals to 46% of the credit granted that year; in 1823, 63%; in 1824, 56%; in 1825, 87%; and in 1826, 144%.

Fig. 2 Payments for check cashing, credit granted and bank note issuance. Banco de Buenos Aires, 1822–1826 (in $). Source: data from AMHBPBA, 1000-32-1; 1000-32-2; 1000-32-3; Casarino, El Banco de la Provincia de Buenos Aires, there 18–21; De Paula, 'El Banco de Buenos Aires (1822–1826) y sus antecedentes históricos', there 56

4.2 *Purposes of Checks Issuance*

A total of 223 agents, including companies and individuals, issued 9,018 checks. Interestingly, only 21 firms, comprising 9.41% of the total, issued 75.7% of these checks (6,830) and facilitated 79% of the volume paid. In contrast, over 90% of the issuers accounted for only 24.3% of the checks, mobilizing 21% of the total amount paid.

When considering the payees of the checks, it is feasible to categorize them into four groups. First, there are checks issued to government agencies. Second, there are checks issued to the bearer, without personal identification of any payee on the document. Third, checks issued to the same bank are also common. Fourth, checks are issued to a third party, including individuals, firms, or legal entities identified in the check by the issuer (Table 3).[19]

A few issuers used checks to pay to government agencies, such as the Custom treasury (1.25% of checks, 1.23% of total amount). This implied the government's acceptance of checks drawn on bank current accounts as a means of paying fiscal obligations. Even when this use of bank checks

[19] Some 1.11% of the checks, which mobilized 0.94% of the total amount drawn, relied as illegible due to material deterioration of the documents.

Table 3 Purposes of bank checks issuing (Buenos Aires, 1822–1826). Source: Data from AMHBPBA, 1000–32-1; 1000–32-2; 1000–32-3

Purpose	*Nº Checks*	*% checks*	*Amount*	*% amount*
Means of payment to third parties	4,157	46.10%	8,926,234.3	39.73%
Payments to the bank	2,636	29.23%	9,006,626.5	40.08%
Withdrawal of cash	2,012	22.31%	4,050,173.8	18.03%
Payments to government agencies	113	1.25%	275,758.6	1.23%
Illegible	100	1.11%	210,794	0.94%
Total	**9,018**	**100%**	**22,469,587.5**	**100%**

was not representative of their usual function, it does confirm the acceptability of these instruments by the government, backing up its market admissibility.

As mentioned earlier, checks could be drawn simply to the bearer without specifying the payee's name on the document. This was often indicated by leaving the space provided for the payee's name blank or by specifying "at sight" or "at my order" (as some issuers habitually wrote). In these cases, it is possible to assume that the holders themselves used the checks as an invoice in favor of the Bank for the withdrawal of cash. This modality involved 22.31% of checks and mobilized 18.03% of the amounts drawn.

Issuers used checks to pay to the Bank itself. More than 29% of the checks were used in this way, mobilizing 40% of the total amounts drawn. In other words, depositors used papers from the bank to settle commitments with the establishment itself. Three types of said commitments are distinguishable First, the payment to the bank for the disbursements the bank previously made to third parties who cashed checks (which suggests that the issuing of checks to pay third parties could relied upon overdraft, that is, using credit granted by the bank instead of deposited savings). Second, the payment of commercial bills discounted by the Bank with still pending settlement (being the account holders the acceptors or payers of said bills). Third, the payment of shares with which the bank integrated its capital. Taking into account that the bank increasingly accepted checks for this purpose (as illustrated in the graph), and considering that checks settled the commercial bills previously discounted by the Bank, and paid for the shares commitments, therefore the institution's equity fundamentals were highly exposed.[20]

However, the main use of checks was as a means of payment to third parties, companies, or individuals identified as payees in the documents. This involved 46.10% of the checks and mobilized 39.73% of the amount drawn. The use of checks for paying daily transactions, and its acceptance by subjects without any bank account, expresses the adoption of banking instruments by the unbanked public, and the diffusion of new payment devices.[21] The following section dwells into the use that issuers gave to checks in Buenos Aires as a means of payment (that is to say, when the payee was identified in the check), in order to understand its penetration as an exchange instrument in local economic culture.

5 Check as a Means of Payment to Identified Payees

Among the 4157 checks used as a means of payment to third parties identified as payees in the check, a total of 1,305 economic actors were involved. Specifically, 118 firms issued these checks, while 1,261 payees accepted them. Even when 74 of those firms (6%) played both roles issuing as well as receiving checks, the majority of the actors involved (1,231, 94%) just played one role or another, and most of them did this as payees (1,187, 90%). Checks, therefore, had more payees than issuers, and this is a first sign of its acceptance as a means of payment.

Considering those 1,261 payees, 782 (62%) accepted checks just once, 156 (12%) twice, and 323 (26%) three or more times. Just 64 payees (5%) have accepted checks for half of the total amount mobilized, receiving 41% of the 4,157 checks. Therefore, the remaining 95% of the payees accepted the other half of the mobilized capital (receiving 59% of the checks). If this implies a relative concentration of the checks' acceptance, coherent with the commercial structure, it is relevant that 1,197 payees, who received from one to twelve checks, accepted 50% of the capital mobilized: the use of checks became widespread.

[20] Wasserman, 'Monedas de papel para una nueva soberanía'.

[21] Even when other private means of payment already existed (such as shop vouchers or tokens), and it could enhance the acceptability of another paper means (Irigoin, *Finance, Politics and Economics in Buenos Aires*, there 31), checks were issued against a bank and it was itself a very new phenomena in local economy.

Looking at the 118 issuers, 37 (31%) issued once, 10 (8%) issued twice, and 71 (61%) issued three or more times. Again, just 6 issuers (5%) mobilized 49% of the total capital amount by issuing 1,918 checks (46% of the documents), and the remaining 51% of the capital was issued by 95% of the issuers (112 firms that issued 54% of the checks). As can be seen, the issuing of checks was not only in hands of less actors than its acceptance, but it was as well more concentrated since the majority of issuers used them frequently (Fig. 3).

When examining the distribution between payees and issuers, the annual evolution shows an increase in both the volume of payees and their acceptance of checks. This trend persisted over the years, except for the critical first and a half month of 1826, immediately before the closure of the establishment. Driven by payees who accepted checks at least once a year, the acceptance of checks increased annually. Furthermore, 43% of payees accepted more checks in 1825 than in 1823, indicating an iterative process leading to an increasing acceptance of checks.[22]

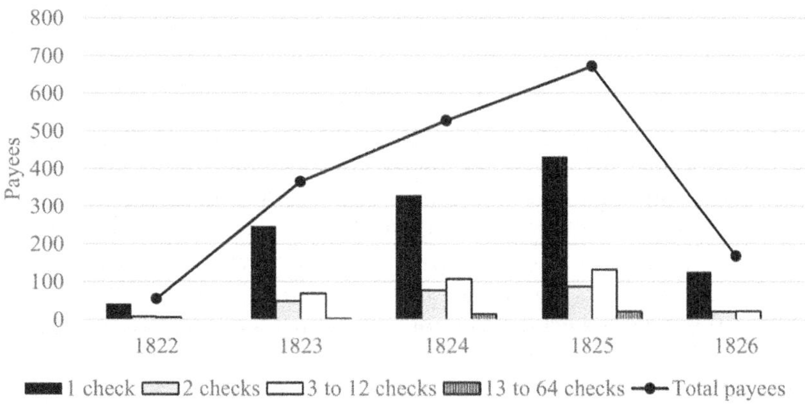

Fig. 3 Frequency of check acceptance.. Buenos Aires, 1822–1826. Source: Data from AMHBPBA, 1000-32-1; 1000-32-2; 1000-32-3

[22] In terms of annual evolution, 30.7% of the payees accepted more checks in 1824 than in 1823; and 37.7% increased the number of checks admitted between 1825 and 1824.

In other words, checks gained acceptability as a means of payments since the establishment of the Bank itself. Main issuers could have had some incidence in this dynamic diffusion.

6 A Network of Checks for Payments

The network that emerged from the circulation of checks delivered to identify payees allows an interpretation of the role of the main issuers in its dissemination. By focusing on them, we can elucidate their contribution to the growing local acceptance of checks (Fig. 4).

Circumscribing the observation to the checks that explicitly mention the payees, the network is built taking economic actors as *nodes* (1,305 issuers and payees) and modeling the links between issuers and payees as *directed edges* from the former to the latter (edges weighted by the frequency of checks delivered into the same link, and amounts accumulated). Therefore, the directed graph resulting since September 1822 to February 1826 (when the Bank closed) accumulated 2,208 edges within which the 4,157 payments took place, as shown in Fig. 4.[23]

Focusing on the main issuers, three firms accumulated the issuing of 33% of the total checks to pay identified payees. Those firms were Bertram, Armstrong & Co., Stewart McCall & Co., and Guillermo Ford & Co., three firms established in Buenos Aires and dedicated to the Atlantic trading as importers, exporters, and consignees.

Considering the checks issued as means of payment in favor of an identified payee, Bertram, Armstrong & Co. (hereafter referred to as BACo) issued 514 checks (and received 71 as payee), Stewart McCall & Co. (hereafter referred to as SMCo) issued 432 checks (and accepted 29), and Guillermo Ford & Co. (hereafter referred to as GFCo) issued 444 checks (accepting 15).[24] This statistical ranking finds direct expression in the network structure through the out-degree measure accumulated by each firm between 1822 and 1826; in other words, the number of adjacent nodes (payees) to which the firms directly delivered their issued checks at

[23] The overall directed network reports a density of 0.003 and a diameter of 7, while the average weighted degree is 2.229.

[24] The fourth issuer firm follows them very distantly (Enrique Thiessen, with 204 checks issued and 10 accepted), as well as the fifth (Winter, Brittain and Co., with 166 checks issued and 56 accepted).

Fig. 4 Bank checks' flow network. Buenos Aires, 1822–1826. Source: data from AMHBPBA, 1000-32-1; 1000-32-2; 1000-32-3. Notes: Out-degree values define the size of nodes. References: Main issuers are indicated in the graph as 1) Bertram Armstrong & Co.; 2) Stewart, McCall & Co.; 3) Guillermo Ford & Co

least once. BACo reached an out-degree of 232 adjacent receiver nodes, SMCo reached 227, and GFCo reached 200 (Fig. 5).[25]

[25] No other node in the network reaches an *out-degree* value of 200: for instance, GFCo is just followed by Juan Parish Robertson & Co, with an *out-degree* level of 103.

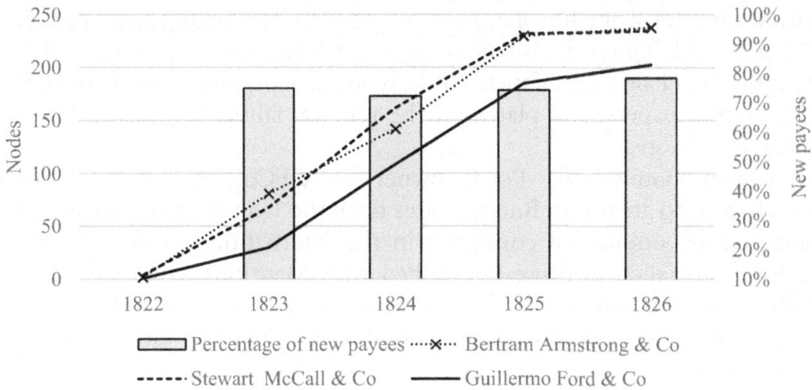

Fig. 5 Evolution of nodes in checks' ego-networks. Buenos Aires, 1822–1826. Source: data from AMHBPBA, 1000-32-1; 1000-32-2; 1000-32-3

BACo was a firm dedicated to foreign commerce, established by Thomas and John Armstrong (Irish brothers settled in Buenos Aires since 1817) with Francis George Bertram.[26] The company had an important warehouse in downtown, and developed a dynamic Atlantic commerce with Europe, receiving frequently ships with imports consigned to the firm, and dispatching freights with merchandise and passengers.[27] These British merchants achieved to integrate the local society, by means of marriages with daughters of local commercial antique families and by the establishment of sociability circles.[28]

SMCo was a merchant consignee firm established in Buenos Aires with strong commercial links with the United States and Europe. It exported leather to New York and Gibraltar, as well as jerk meat to Saint Thomas, importing flour, tea, tobacco and codfish from North America, and

[26] Alina Silveira, 'Comerciantes británicos en el Rio de la Plata. En torno a la construcción de una comunidad mercantil (1810-1860)', in: *Anuario del Centro de Estudios Históricos Prof. Carlos S. A. Segreti* 15:5 (2015), 265-285. See as well: https://www.lieber.com.ar/familia/arm.html.

[27] Jean J.M. Blondel, *Almanaque político y de comercio de la Ciudad de Buenos Ayres para el año de 1826* (Buenos Aires, 1825). For instance, see *Gazeta de Buenos Aires* (hereafter, GBA), 46, March 14, 1821, 212, among other similar announces.

[28] Silveira, 'Comerciantes británicos en el Rio de la Plata'.

various articles from Europe, such as paper.[29] The strong links between the firm and Banco de Buenos Ayres led SMCo to negotiate in 1825 with the firm Fairman, Draper, Underwood & Co., from Philadelphia, the lithography, papers, and plates for the renewal fabrication of the Buenos Aires' bank notes.[30]

William (Guillermo) Ford, owner of GFCo, was an important merchant who arrived in Buenos Aires from the United States, whose firm operated as commercial consignee in the international trade with large connections (such as those established with Mauritius to import pepper among other merchandise).[31] As it happened with other merchants since colonial era in Buenos Aires, his businesses were involved into accusations of fraud.[32]

None of them belonged personally to the Bank's directory during its lifespan (1822–1826) and neither were Government's creditors, but Francis Bertram, Thomas Armstrong, and SMCo were foundational shareholders of the Banco de Buenos Aires and belonged to the list of main operators of the bank (that is to say, those actors who credited more than $100,000 from the bank).[33]

7 The Development of a Network for the Check's Acceptance

Studying the check's information through the lens of SNA allows a deeper interpretation of the role those three main issuers had in the diffusion of bank checks as means of payments in the local economy. The evolution of

[29] GBA, 40, January 31, 1821; 43, February 21, 1821; 44, February 28, 1821; 47, March 21, 1821.

[30] Fernando Perticone, *Historia de nuestros primeros bancos. Del billete de banco al papel moneda* (Buenos Aires, 2022), 96.

[31] GBA, 5, May 31, 1820; 55, May 16, 1821.

[32] John Murray Forbes, *Once años en Buenos Aires. 1820-1831* (Buenos Aires, 1956), 183.

[33] AMHBPBA, 001-1-1, Actas de Directorio, Sección Comercial, Libro N° 1. In turn, SMCo, Francis Bertram and William Ford belonged: between 1822 and 1826, BACo reimbursed the bank with $969,500 due to credits previously granted, GFCo reimbursed $765,000 and SMCo did so for $664,000. Samuel Amaral, 'Comercio y Crédito en Buenos Aires, 1822-1826', in: *Siglo XIX*, 5:9 (1990), 105-121, 155-156. In the three cases, their amounts exceed the mean amount among the segment of main operators (those with credit movements over $100,000).

the three main issuers' ego-networks, the internal integration of each one, the shared payees among them, and the relational position that allowed the main issuers to integrate those ego-networks into a broader web of acceptance suggest their role in encouraging the acceptance of checks.

As shown in the annual growth experienced by the check network of each main issuer, checks increased rapidly their acceptance as a payment instrument. Between 1822 and 1826, the checks networks developed around each one of these main firms (*ego-networks*) show a visible growing acceptance of their checks: each firm increased annually the number of counterparts with whom they transacted by means of checks. As shown in Fig. 5, even if a percentage of those counterparts admitted checks frequently (on average, 25% of the payees that received checks from these three firms did it more than once a year), a major part of the payees (75% on average) did so for the first time, adopting this newly means of payment among their assets.[34]

Hence, the expansion of the check networks of each firm was spearheaded by new acceptors, resulting in an annual increase in the proportion of providers and creditors who accepted checks from each of those three firms. In simpler terms, checks were increasingly embraced within the local economy.

Given that this observation centers on the checks used by the three main firms to settle debts with identified payees, their identities indicate that they likely comprised daily providers, shopkeepers, or local sellers. These individuals typically supplied each firm with the necessary services or products to sustain their operations. Being those main issuers importers and exporters, their payees used to be as well ship captains arriving at (and departing from) the port of Buenos Aires with their freights, who accepted checks for the shipping services provided. Local merchants and firms were too payees of those three main check's issuers. This suggest that the check was firstly introduced as a new means of payment among a preexisting network of providers and creditors, who already transacted with each firm before the appearance of this instrument.

In other words, those three main issuers started using checks among their respective preexisting networks of business. A relational analysis

[34] In 1823, 75% of payees did not accepted checks more than once, being the first time in admitting that means of payment. Even when in 1824 the percentage of new acceptors was 72% of a growth network, the inclusion of new payees continued increasing up to 1826: 74.3 in 1825 and 78.4% in 1826.

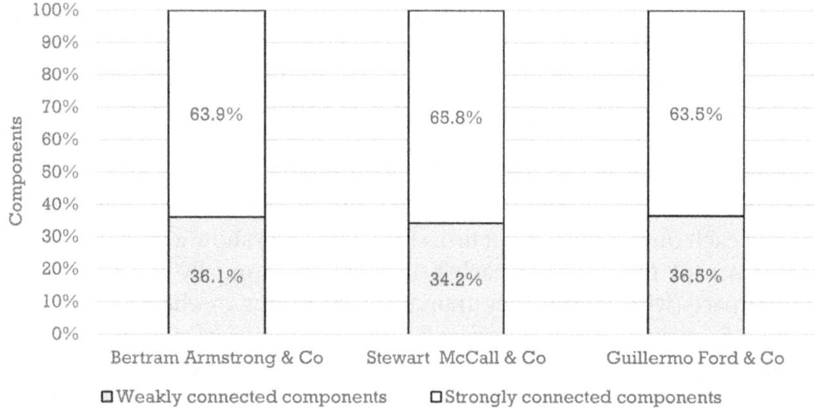

Fig. 6 Quality of components connectivity inside each checks' ego-network. Buenos Aires, 1822–1826. Source: data from AMHBPBA, 1000-32-1; 1000-32-2; 1000-32-3. Note: the algorithm applied to calculate connected components is taken from Robert Tarjan, 'Depth-First Search and Linear Graph Algorithms', in: SIAM Journal on Computing, 1:2 (1972), 146–160, and ran on Gephi 0.9.2

shows, in fact, that each *ego-network* had a high internal connectivity, that is to say, a strong internal connection that potentially allowed the rest of the nodes to be in contact with relative independence of the *ego-node* (the main issuer firm).

The *strongly connected components* consist in a SNA variable that indicates groups of nodes with high connectivity inside a network. As shown in Graph 10, each *ego-network* had a high internal proportion of strongly connected components: on average, 64.4% of its internal components were solidly interconnected (Fig. 6). Being each check *ego-network* mainly a web of preexisting links, it is not surprising to note that those networks were communities strongly connected. The *weakly connected components* expresses, therefore, the newly checks acceptors annually incorporated, less connected than those payees who already participated in the business web of each firm. Therefore, checks had the acceptance of the traditional providers and creditors of each firm, due to an already acknowledgment of the issuer and to the preexistence of its providers' network (Fig. 7).[35]

[35] Consisting in preexisting networks of creditors already transacting with each firm, the acknowledgment of the counterparts could imply reputational constraints, which in

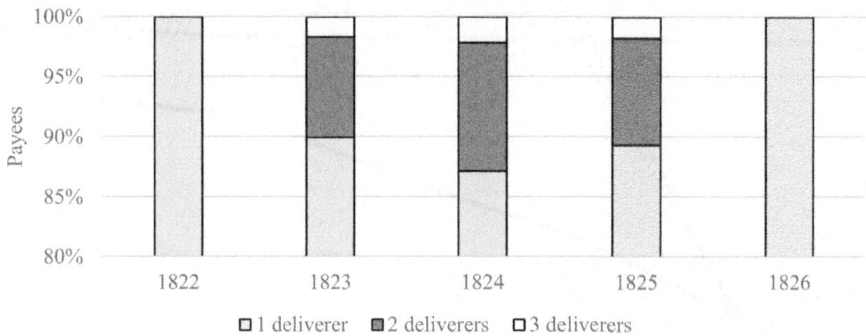

Fig. 7 Shared payees between BACo, SMCo and GFCo. Buenos Aires, 1822–1826. Source: Data from AMHBPBA, 1000-32-1; 1000-32-2; 1000-32-3

However, bank check achieved acceptance in local economy because it transcended the exclusive circulation among each firm *ego-network* nodes, gaining the acceptance from new payees.

This has its first expression in the interconnection between those ego-networks. Within the world of 538 payees who received checks issued by those three firms, 81.8% of them (440) have accepted checks solely from one of the three firms, thereby exclusively belonging to the ego-network of that deliverer. Nevertheless, the three firms shared the remainder 18% payees (98): 13.6% of those payees received checks from two of those firms, and 4.6% accepted checks from the three. The evolution of those shared payees among those main check's issuers (Fig. 7) shows an increasing acceptation since 1823 (in September 1822, when the bank was established, there were no shared payees, in the same way of the two first months of 1826 –when the crisis imposed the closure of the bank).

In this sense, the increasing juxtaposition of more than one issuer on the same payee indicates an increasing acceptance of that means of payment by that payee. Therefore, an increasing margin of shared payees suggests the growing interconnection between those main issuer's check networks.

Thus, the firms increasingly used checks to pay shared providers and creditors, and each firm accepted as well checks from agents belonging

turn increased the cost of defaulting (enhancing the acceptance of checks as means to settle the firm's commitments).

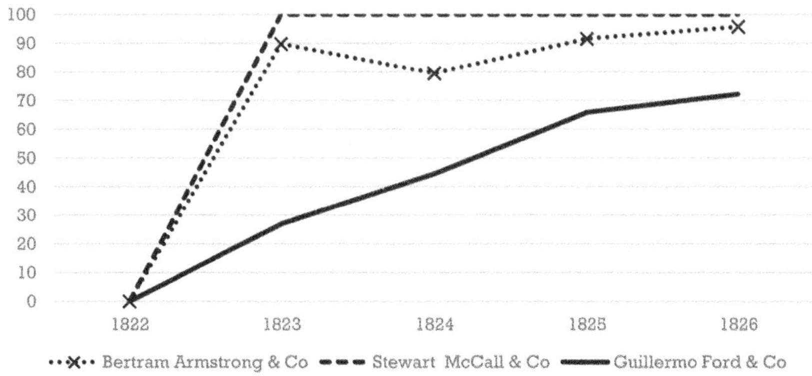

Fig. 8 Betweenness centrality evolution among the overall check's network. Buenos Aires, 1822–1826. Source: data from AMHBPBA, 1000-32-1; 1000-32-2; 1000-32-3. Note: 100 equals maximum betweenness centrality value in each year, being 1822 = 12; 1823 = 2,025.5; 1824 = 6,640.1; 1825 = 21,465.6 and 1826 = 20,966.7

to other firms' networks. The growing *betweenness centrality* achieved by the three firms over the whole network expresses that integration.

SNA allows a deeper interpretation of this trend, suggesting that those three main issuers had themselves a key role to integrate their respective *ego-networks* into a broader web of check's acceptance, contributing to explain the growing admission of the checks as means of payment.

The *betweenness centrality* is a structural variable that allows knowing the ability of a node to put in contact other nodes lacking mutual adjacency (that is to say, without immediate contact in the network). In this case, the betweenness centrality reached by an actor serves to know the ability of this actor to position himself as a mediator in the distribution of checks among the whole check's network.[36]

[36] John Scott, *Social Network Analysis. A Handbook* (London-Thousand Oaks-New Delhi, 1992), 86. Betweenness centrality allows to identify the importance of a node according to its ability to put other nodes in contact, as a function of its position in the network; in this sense, such ability depends on the positioning of the node in the geodesic path (the shortest way) between those nodes connected. In this sense, the value of betweenness centrality of an actor depends on his or her participation in defined quantities of geodesic paths linking no-adjacent nodes over the network, and therefore increasing the dependence of nodes regards the intermediator, who fills a *structural hole*. See Ronald

It is important to note that only a tiny proportion of nodes involved in the overall checks network registered positive intermediation values (expressed in the betweenness centrality): on average, just 5.7% of nodes reports positive values of betweenness centrality each year.[37]

BACo, SMCo, and GFCo belonged to that little reticle of nodes with positive betweenness centrality values. Excepting the first months of functioning of the bank (the last four months of 1822), during the following years these firms gained positions as intermediaries into the whole check network (Fig. 8).

The algorithm applied to calculate betweenness centrality is taken from Brandes Ulrik, 'A Faster Algorithm for Betweenness Centrality', in: *Journal of Mathematical Sociology*, 25:2 (2001):, 163–177, and ran on *Gephi 0.9.2*. See Bastian Mathieu, Sebastien Heymann, and Mathieu Jacomy, 'Gephi: an open source software for exploring and manipulating networks', in: *International AAAI Conference on Weblogs and Social Media*, 3:1 (2009), 361–362.

The high betweenness centrality of these three firms suggests that they were positioned in such a way that one firm could enhance their own providers to accept other main firms' checks, to the extent that their own issued checks could gain the acceptance of other firms' providers. In other terms, ego-networks were linked through the relational position reached by the main check issuers. Therefore, the high betweenness centrality of those main issuers suggests that they contribute to integrate their ego-networks into a broader one.

In this sense, the main issuers of checks not only achieved to use their checks as a means of payment inside their respective providers and creditors ego-networks, but they also accomplish to link their ego-networks, integrating them as a broader interconnected circuit in which checks were admitted.

S. Burt, 'The Social Capital of Structural Holes', in: Mauro Guillén, Randall Collins, Paula England, and Marshall Meyer (eds), The New Economic Sociology. Developments in an Emerging Field (New York, 2002), 201-247.

[37] In 1822, just 6.5% of the nodes belonging to the overall check's network reported positive betweenness centrality values. The following years expressed similar values: 5.4% (1823), 5.7% (1824), 5.6% (1825) y 5.4% (1826).

8 Overdraft: The Stimulus for Developing an Acceptance Environment

Building an environment of checks' acceptance was consistent with the use of those checks to pay the firm's own commitments. The reason why those main firms were interested in using checks and enhancing its acceptance relied on the leverage provided by the Bank.

Ratio between the annual average balance of each firm (recorded in the bank account ledger), and the annual amount issued by those firms through the delivery of checks in favor of third parties, shows the average percentage the bank paid on those checks as annual overdraft (Fig. 9).

The average annual leverage of BACo between 1822 and 1826 reached 0.53% (ranging between 0.1% and 0.8% throughout the period), while the average overdraft of SMCo was 6.03% (starting with 0.7% and ending with 21.5%), and the average annual leverage of GFCo was 3.8% (with ranges between 0.7 and 8.9% annually).[38]

In other words, paying with checks implied settling commitments not just with the savings the firms had in their bank accounts, but with the credit the bank granted to the issuing firms: the bank partially

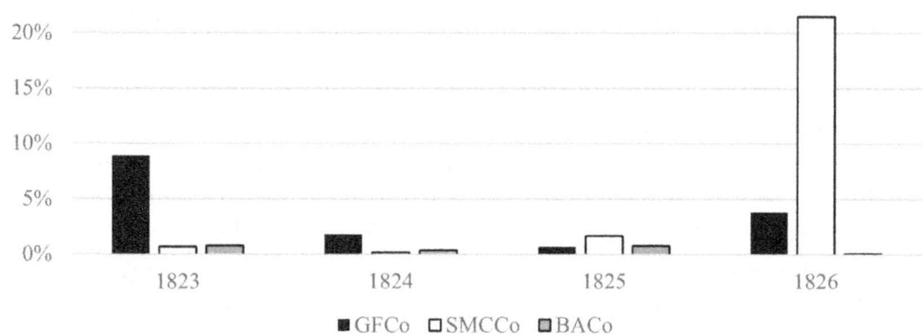

Fig. 9 Annual average leverage granted to the three main check's issuers at Banco de Buenos Aires (1823–1826). Source: Data from AMHBPBA, 1000-1-1, Ledger; 1000-32-1; 1000-32-2; 1000-32-3. Annual average leverage of each firm is calculated as the ratio between annual average firm balance and annual amount delivered by the Bank to third payees through means of checks

[38] Considering that this calculation only computes annual averages, future research on shorter periods will demonstrate that overdrafts could be greater when computing it in one month or one week.

assumed the settlement of the firm's commitments. Overdraft incentivized the usage of checks, and this was the main stimulus to enhance check acceptance as a means of payment in the local economy.

9 Conclusion

The Bank's pillars were weak. Shareholders had funded half of the capital integration not with cash, but with credit provided by the Bank itself.[39] In fact, those checks paying commitments to the Bank were partly applied to pay dues of the share integration. Therefore, the bank own papers made up a large part of its capital, and it conferred a feeble institutional base.

This institutional weakness became evident with the war declaration against Brazil in December 1825. The already scarce bank's metallic reserves experienced a growing demand both from the government and from the public, weakening even more the collateral of bank notes. In January 1826, Buenos Aires' parliament authorized the inconvertibility of bank notes, and four months later acquired legal tender, while closing the Bank replacing it by a new entity, the Banco Nacional. The rapid depreciation of the bank notes became inevitable.[40]

Despite its short lifespan, the Banco de Buenos Aires enabled the appearance of new means of payment for the local economy. Besides the bank notes, bank checks gained acceptance among the city economic actors, and beyond bank users. In fact, the issuance of checks grew faster than the credit lent by the Bank, and the issuers increasingly used these instruments to pay daily transactions using their deposits in account. Checks widespread among payees that accepted these documents to settle payments with an increasingly frequency.

The network deployed by the check flows showed three outstanding issuers: Bertram, Armstrong & Co., Stewart McCall & Co., and Guillermo Ford & Co., international British traders established in Buenos

[39] *El Argos de Buenos Aires*, 104, December 18, 1824, p. 5; Agustìn De Vedia, *El Banco Nacional. Historia Financiera de la Republica Argentina* (Buenos Aires, 1890), there 71; Miron Burgin, *Aspectos economicos del federalismo argentino* (Buenos Aires, 1969), there 91; Horacio J. Cuccorese, *Historia del Banco de la Provincia de Buenos Aires* (Buenos Aires, 1972), 52; Perticone, *Historia de nuestros primeros bancos*, 99-100); Wasserman, 'Monedas de papel para una nueva soberanía'.

[40] On the evolution of the currency depreciation since the establishment of the inconvertible system in Buenos Aires at 1826, see Irigoin, *Finance, Politics and Economics in Buenos Aires*.

Aires with a remarkable issuance of checks over the total. Focusing on their dynamics, their respective networks of checks admittance grew, incorporating to this way of payment a growing portfolio of their commercial providers and creditors.

The networks of these firms developed two attributes: structures with strongly connected components and interconnections between those structures. The first feature implied that the checks of one firm circulated among a network with solid internal connections (built on preexistent webs of providers and creditors of the firm). The second feature implied the interconnection between those firms' network, resulting not only from shared payees but, primarily, from the intermediation exercised by each firm over the whole network of checks.

Since the usage of checks implied a leverage provided by the Bank as overdraft, those main issuers had obvious interest in reaching the diffusion and acceptance of this instrument. By using checks, the Bank could assume the settlement of their businesses' commitments, at least partially.

In this sense, those three main issuers contributed to create interconnected networks, among which the checks found a space of circulation and increasing admission as means of payment. Bertram, Armstrong & Co., Stewart McCall & Co., and Guillermo Ford & Co. not only constituted the main issuers of checks: they were as well the main diffusor of its usage as a means of payment, configuring the relational infrastructure necessary for the admission of this device in the local society. Those firms shaped, in this way, the relational infrastructure for the financial institution changed.

References

Primary Sources

Archive and Museum of the Bank of the Province of Buenos Aires, 1000–32–1; 1000–32–2; 1000–32–3

Printed Primary Material

Blondel Jean J.M., *Almanaque político y de comercio de la Ciudad de Buenos Ayres para el año de 1826* (Buenos Aires, 1825).

De Vedia Agustìn, *El Banco Nacional. Historia Financiera de la Republica Argentina* (Buenos Aires, 1890).

Garrigos Octavio, *El Banco de la provincia* (Buenos Aires, 1873).

Secondary Material

Amaral, Samuel. 1990. Comercio y Crédito en Buenos Aires, 1822–1826. *Siglo XIX* 5 (9): 105–121.

Amaral, Samuel. 1988. El descubrimiento de la financiación inflacionaria: Buenos Aires 1790–1830. *Investigaciones y Ensayos* 37: 379–419.

Amaral, Samuel. 1982. Medios de pago no metálicos en Buenos Aires a comienzos del siglo XIX. Letras de cambio y letras secas. *Cuadernos de Numismática y Ciencias Históricas* 9 (30): 45–55.

Bastian, Mathieu, Sebastien Heymann, and Mathieu Jacomy. 2009. Gephi: An open source software for exploring and manipulating networks. *International AAAI Conference on Weblogs and Social Media* 3 (1): 361–362.

Baubeau, Patrice. 2016. Dematerialization and the Cashless Society: A Look Backward, a Look Sideward. In *The Book of Payments. Historical and Contemporary Views on the Cashless Society*, edited by Bernardo Bátiz-Lazo & Leonidas Efthymiou, L., 85–95. Palgrave Macmillan.

Brandes, Ulrik. 2001. A Faster Algorithm for Betweenness Centrality. *Journal of Mathematical Sociology* 25 (2): 163–177.

Burgin, Miron. 1969. *Aspectos economicos del federalismo argentino*. Buenos Aires: Librería Hachette.

Burt, Ronald S. 2002. The Social Capital of Structural Holes. In *The New Economic Sociology. Developments in an Emerging Field*, edited by Mauro Guillén, Randall Collins, Paula England, and Marshall Meyer, 201–247. New York: Russell Sage Foundation.

Casarino, Nicolàs. 1922. *El Banco de la Provincia de Buenos Aires en su primer centenario. 1822–1922*. Buenos Aires: Talleres S. A. Casa Jacobo Peuser.

Cuccorese, Horacio J. 1972. *Historia del Banco de la Provincia de Buenos Aires*. Buenos Aires: BPBA.

De Paula, Alberto. 1997. El Banco de Buenos Aires (1822–1826) y sus antecedentes históricos. In *Historia del Banco de la Provincia de Buenos Aires. 1822–1997, tome I*, edited by Alberto De Paula and Noemì Maria Girbal-Blacha. Buenos Aires: Ediciones Macchi - BPBA.

Djenderedjian, Julio Cesar, Juan Luis Martirén, and María Inés. Moraes. 2023. Prices and Living Standards during the Age of Revolutions: The Río de la Plata between 1772 and 1830. *Investigaciones de Historia Economica* 19 (2): 70–86.

Fernando, Perticone. 2022. *Historia de nuestros primeros bancos. Del billete de banco al papel moneda*. Buenos Aires: Centro Numismático de Buenos Aires.

Goldman, Noemì. 2014. Argentina/Río de la Plata. In *Diccionario político y social del mundo iberoamericano, tome II*, edited by Noemì Goldman and

Javier Fernández Sebastián, 43–58. Madrid: Centro de Estudios Políticos y Constitucionales.

Irigoin, Alejandra. 2000. Finance, Politics and Economics in Buenos Aires, 1820s-1860s: The Political Economy of Currency Stabilisation. Doctoral Thesis, London School of Economics and Political Science.

Moutoukias, Zakarias. 2018. Coacción pública e innovación. Deuda, actores y cambio institucional en el Río de la Plata (1790–1820). In *Cambio institucional y fiscalidad. Mundo hispánico, 1760–1850*, edited by Michel Bertrand and Zakarias Moutoukias, 175–195. Madrid: Casa de Velázquez.

Murray, Forbes John. 1956. *Once años en Buenos Aires. 1820–1831*. Buenos Aires: Emecé.

Olarra, Jiménez Rafael. 1968. *Evolución monetaria argentina*. Buenos Aires: Eudeba.

Quinn, Stephen, and William Roberds. 2008. The Evolution of the Check as a Means of Payment: A Historical Survey. *Economic Review, Federal Reserve Bank of Atlanta* 93 (4): 1–28.

Reidlich, Fritz, and Webster M. Christman. 1967. Early American Checks and an Example of Their Use. *Business History Review* 41 (3): 285–302.

Scott, John. 1992. *Social Network Analysis. A Handbook*. London-Thousand Oaks-New Delhi.

Segreti, Carlos S.A. 1975. *Moneda y política en la primera mitad del siglo XIX. Contribución al estudio de la historia de la moneda argentina*. Tucumán: Fundación Banco Comercial del Norte.

Silveira, Alina. 2015. Comerciantes británicos en el Rio de la Plata. En torno a la construcción de una comunidad mercantil (1810–1860). *Anuario del Centro de Estudios Históricos Prof. Carlos S. A. Segreti* 15 (5): 265–285.

Souto, Nora B. 2017. *La forma de unidad en el Río de la Plata. Soberanía y poder constituyente, 1808–1827*. Doctoral thesis, Universidad de Buenos Aires: Instituto de Historia Argentina y Americana "Dr. Emilio Ravignani".

Tarjan, Robert. 1972. Depth-First Search and Linear Graph Algorithms. *SIAM Journal on Computing* 1 (2): 146–160.

Wasserman, Martin. 2022a. Deuda, papeles y compromisos en la construcción del crédito público. La Caja Nacional de Fondos de Sud América (Buenos Aires, 1818–1821). *Revista de Historia Económica / Journal of Iberian and Latin American Economic History*, 40:2, 371–404, Cambridge University Press.

Wasserman, Martin. 2022b. Monedas de papel para una nueva soberanía. La negociación del financiamiento a la Hacienda de Buenos Aires, entre la Revolución y el surgimiento de la banca bonaerense (1810–1826). In *El gobierno de la incertidumbre. La política financiera en Buenos Aires desde el Virreinato a la Confederación*, edited by Martin Wasserman and Roberto Schmit, 87–129. Buenos Aires: Prometeo.

CHAPTER 11

Notary Lending Networks in Northern Italy in the Eighteenth and Nineteenth Centuries

Giuseppe De Luca and Marcella Lorenzini

1 Introduction

In the expansive phase of the 'long sixteenth century', the credit system developed similar structures across northern Italy, albeit varying in terms of proportions and coverage. Next to the steady growth of formal financial institutions such as public banks, Monti di Pietà, private banks, and moneychangers the informal level of the money market was also ballooning. Networks that linked religious and private bodies, urban and rural populations, specialized and non-specialized operators in a large mass of credit transactions developed an increasingly ramified and capillary geography. In Milan, Genoa, Florence, Bologna, and smaller towns,

G. De Luca · M. Lorenzini (✉)
Università degli Studi di Milano, Milan, Italy
e-mail: marcella.lorenzini@unimi.it

G. De Luca
e-mail: giuseppe.deluca@unimi.it

G. De Luca
Università degli Studi di Milano, Milan, Italy

E. M. Dermineur and M. Pompermaier (eds.), *Credit Networks in The Preindustrial World*, Palgrave Studies in the History of Finance,
https://doi.org/10.1007/978-3-031-67117-3_11

formal and informal circuits functionally intertwined, matching supply to demand for capital, playing a decisive role in both production, political, and social dynamics.[1]

Within these networks, notaries performed their traditional role as certifiers of transactions, their services ensuring public faith in deeds and possible legal enforcement. The information that led to the stipulation of credit contracts, such as the knowledge relationship matching contracting parties to capital supply/demand, stemmed from the institutional nature of the credit organization and the inherent functions of its actors. When, from the mid-seventeenth century onward, the urban cycles of the northern regions of the peninsula gradually lost momentum and the center of gravity of regional economies shifted from city manufacturing hubs to the production of semi-finished goods and raw materials in the countryside, the notaries became the protagonists of a credit market increasingly freed from its previous masters.

The economic downturn then pruned back the diversified credit landscape. The new production balance, based on the export of semi-finished silk products against the import of finished goods, no longer supported the rich retail structure of the Renaissance world; a marked polarization of roles began to characterize the eighteenth-century recovery in these regional areas, and entrepreneurs in both business and finance were concentrated at either end of the size scale. In the middle, between small consumer credit and super-specialized credit for international payments, lay the bulk of the capital market, where supply appeared to be dominated by a mass of people who were distant from the professionals and where information flows were conveyed by the action of notaries.

[1] On the co-essential nature of credit networks with some traits typical of Ancien Régime economies, see Jean Louis Gaulin and François Menant, 'Crédit rural et Endettement Paysan dans l'Italie communale', in: Maurice Berthe (ed), Endettement Paysan et Crédit Rural dans l'Europe médiévale et moderne (Toulose, 1998), there 36; Renata Ago, *Economia barocca. Roma nel Seicento* (Roma, 1998); Massimo Fornasari, 'Istituzioni, professionisti, privati: le reti di credito nella Bologna moderna', in: Adriano Prosperi and Paolo Prodi (eds), *Storia di Bologna*, tome III, 'Bologna nell'età moderna' (Bologna, 2008), 791–855; Giuseppe Felloni, 'Dall'Italia all'Europa: il primato della finanza italiana dal Medioevo alla prima età moderna', in: A Alberto Cova et al. (eds), *Storia d'Italia*, Annali 23, 'La Banca' (Torino, 2008), 93–149; Giuseppe De Luca and Angelo Moioli, 'Il potere del credito. Reti e istituzioni in Italia centro-settentrionale fra età moderna e decenni preunitari', in: Alberto Cova et al. (eds), *Storia d'Italia*, Annali 23, 'La Banca' (Torino, 2008), 212–255.

If credit networks had essentially been characterized by personal relationships, they now consisted of ties between borrowers and lenders who did not know each other but were put in contact thanks to the (non-institutional) match-making action of notaries. Whereas in the seventeenth century the main novelty of the credit market in Central-Northern Italy had been represented, on the supply side, by the massive intervention of a wide range of heterogeneous institutions, such as congregations and religious bodies, pious institutions and lay confraternities, between the end of the seventeenth and the beginning of the eighteenth century, it was the aggregate activity of these *sui generis* brokers that built an efficient capital market capable of fostering progress in the real economy.

The branch of studies that drew attention almost 30 years ago to the credit function of these operators (the notaries), who had hitherto been considered by economic historians almost only as 'producers' of sources, has gradually extended. From the seminal analysis of Paris between the eighteenth and nineteenth centuries it widened to many other contexts of Europe and beyond, also to South America.[2] More recently, notarial records have offered an interesting dataset on which to fund a new social comparative history.[3]

The analysis of notarized credit networks in some northern Italian settings aims to contribute to the overall results of this line of research not only by providing some confirmations, from the study of large Italian cities such as Milan, but also by bringing some new results related to the purposes of debts and to the use of capital mobilized by notarial networks.

2 The Data

Our methodological framework combines a longitudinal with a horizontal approach. As regards the longitudinal perspective we collected lending contracts drawn up by the most important notaries of three

[2] Philip T. Hoffman, Gilles Postel-Vinay, Jean-Laurent Rosenthal, *Priceless Markets. The Political Economy of Credit in Paris, 1660–1870* (Chicago, 2000); Juliette Levy, *The Making of a Market: Credit, Henequen, and Notaries in Yucatan, 1850 1900* (University Park, PA, 2012), Martin Wasserman, 'Diseño institucional, prácticas y crédito notarial en Buenos Aires durante la primera mitad del siglo XVII', in: *Investigaciones de Historia Económica - Economic History Research*, 10:1 (2014), 1–12.

[3] Claire Lemercier, Francesca Trivellato, '1751 and Thereabout: A Quantitative and Comparative Approach to Notarial Records', in: *Social Science History*, 46 (2022), 555–583.

different-sized cities—Milan, Pavia, and Imperia—from the eighteenth to the nineteenth century. As regards the horizontal perspective, we gathered all loan contracts of larger and smaller cities—Milan, Trento, and Rovereto—in some benchmark years. On the whole we sampled 8,700 loan contracts.[4] Lien registers not available, and neither notarial index registers, the collection implied the selection of debt/credit contracts among all types of deeds contained in notarial protocols.

A significant volume of capital was mobilized by notarial credit networks. In 1784 four of the biggest notaries of Milan were able to circulate 3% of State tax revenues, which amounted to 19,663,229 Milanese lire.[5] In 1840 the entire group of notaries mobilized 10,648,000 Milanese lire, amounting to 17% of State revenues (62,539,000 Milanese lire)[6] or 71% of the 1829 balance of trade (14,979,172 Milanese lire).[7]

Milan was one of the most financially and economically prosperous cities on the Italian peninsula, with a growing population that reached 130,000 inhabitants in the 1780s.[8] Its geographical position, at the crossroads of central Italy and northern European countries, made it an important international trade hub. However, if we consider other smaller

[4] This is a selection of a broader sample comprising over 30,000 contracts.

[5] The notaries were Carlo Giuseppe Aureggi, Archivio di Stato di Milano (hereafter ASMI), Rubrica notarile (hereafter Rn.), 311; Carlo Ambrogio Coquio, ASMI, Rn. 1712; Giovanni Agostino Gariboldi, ASMI, Rn. 2326; Marco Antonio Pizzagalli, ASMI, Rn. 3775. For the State revenues see Marco Bianchi, 'Le entrate e le spese dell'amministrazione centrale e delle province dello Stato di Milano nella seconda metà del Settecento', in: *Archivio Storico* Lombardo, 10:4 (1978), 174-196, there 188.

[6] The amount of capital flow drawn up by notaries was more precisely 12,100,050 Austrian lire (Giuseppe De Luca, 'Informal Credit and Economic Modernization in Milan (1802-1840)', in: *The Journal of European Economic History*, 52 (2013), 211-234, there 225). One Milanese lire was worth 0.88 Austrian lire (Rupert Pichler, *L'economia lombarda e l'Austria: politica commerciale e sviluppo industriale 1815-1859* (Milan, 2001), there 10). The revenues of Lombardy in 1840 amounted to 23,689,000 Florins or 62,539,000 Milanese lire (Uggé Albino, 'Le entrate del Regno lombardo-veneto dal 1840 al 1864', in: *Archivio economico dell'unificazione italiana*, 1 (1956), 1-15, there 9). In 1840 the population of Milan represented 5.8% of the entire population of Lombardy (148,434 inhabitants out of 2,516,000) (Mario Romani, *Aspetti e problemi di storia economica lombarda nei secoli XVIII e XIX* (Milan, 1977), there 317-318). One florin was worth 3 Milanese lire.

[7] Pichler, *L'economia lombarda e l'Austria*, there 112.

[8] Romani, *Aspetti e problemi di storia economica lombarda*; Luciano Segre, 'Bonifica e irrigazione in Lombardia nel secolo XIX: lo schema di base', in: *Rivista di Storia dell'Agricoltura*, 32:1 (1992), 174–181, there 184.

cities and towns, notarized loans covered a share of credit transactions comparable to that in Milan. In late-seventeenth-century Verona (32,000 inhabitants), which was still recovering from the plague of the 1630s,[9] the sixty 'active' notaries drew up credit contracts amounting to 372,000 Venetian lire per year, which was close to one-fourth of the revenues of the Camera Fiscale (taxation), equal to 1,539,088 Venetian lire.[10] In one of the most thriving manufacturing towns of South Tyrol, Rovereto, notarized loans in the mid-eighteenth century totaled 406,000 Venetian lire, more than three times the city's revenues of 123,000 Venetian lire.[11]

Our study shows that the larger the city the smaller the ratio of notaries to inhabitants. In Milan in 1825 there were forty-five 'active' notaries[12] and a population of 126,000,[13] which means one notary per 2,800 inhabitants. In Paris in 1790, there were 114 notaries per 524,000 inhabitants, or one notary per 4,596 individuals.[14] In the smaller city of Trento (1780) the proportion was one notary per 257 citizens, similar to the ratio of Rovereto: one notary per 280 inhabitants.[15] The size of the city and

[9] Verona was one of the cities in northern Italy most severely affected by the plague. A 'typical English epidemic had mortality rates of 100–120 per thousand, as opposed to Italy where the most common rate was 300–400 per thousand, with peaks of 500–600 per thousand. [...] The mortality rate was 330 per thousand in Venice, 443 per thousand in Piacenza, *615 per thousand in Verona in 1629–1630* [Italics ours], 490 per thousand in Genoa, and 500 per thousand in Naples in 1656 – 1657'. Guido Alfani, 'Plague in seventeenth-century Europe and the decline of Italy: an epidemiological hypothesis', in: *European Review of Economic History*, 17 (2013), 408-430, there 417, 425.

[10] This is the average calculated on four benchmark years: 1676, 1681, 1686, 1691.

[11] Marcella Lorenzini, 'Borrowing and lending money in Alpine areas during the eighteenth century: Trento and Rovereto compared', in Marcella Lorenzini, Cinzia. Lorandini and D'Maris Coffman (eds), *Financing in Europe: Evolution, coexistence and complementarity of lending practices from the Middle Ages to Modern Times* (New York, 2018), 105–132, there 109; Andrea Bonoldi, *La fiera e il dazio: economia e politica commerciale nel Tirolo del secondo Settecento* (Trento, 1999), there 67.

[12] De Luca, 'Informal Credit and Economic Modernization in Milan', there 225.

[13] Romani, *Aspetti e problemi di storia economica lombarda*, there 316.

[14] Hoffman, Postel-Vinay, Rosenthal, *Priceless Markets*, there 27.

[15] Lorenzini, 'Borrowing and lending money in Alpine areas', there 105-132. Although it had half the population of Trento, Rovereto under the Habsburg Monarchy had a much livelier credit market due to its high silk production. The total capital mobilised by Rovereto's notaries (400,000 Venetian lire per year) was three times as much as Trento's (Lorenzini, 'Borrowing and lending money in Alpine areas', there 109). One florin was worth 5 Venetian lire.

the number of notaries had distinct outcomes on the distribution of credit and wealth. Countries with smaller cities, such as Italy, Germany, and the Netherlands, allowed greater democratization of wealth and credit: 'a far more egalitarian urban network, with a large number of medium-sized cities'. Conversely, in states where the largest cities tended to dominate the others, credit tended to benefit the most affluent: 'The size of a dominant large city means that credit transactions are frequent, but since big cities usually have skewed wealth distributions, loans tend to be large, but fewer overall, because many borrowers lack collateral. The result, typically, is a capital market that services the elite'.[16] Accordingly, our data demonstrate that while in Milan in the early nineteenth century (1825) the average loan was 13,000 lire, in smaller centers it was much lower. In Imperia (Liguria) 75% of loans were below 1,000 new Piedmont lire, while 22% were in the 1,000–3,000 lire range.

3 The Emergence of Credit Networks Brokered by Notaries

From mid-eighteenth century onward, transactions involving non-specialized operators (namely private individuals or subjects that transcended their own institutional spheres) constituted, in most situations, the bulk of the credit market. According to a memoir by Francesco Gianni, by 1774 in Tuscany, the religious institutions had completely abandoned their poor-relief functions in order to intervene freely on the capital market, while the Monte di Pietà of Faenza—to give but one example—handed out the money received from the State or from donations, not in pawn loans (as established by the statutes) but by disbursing *censi* and mortgages to small landowners, artisans, and shopkeepers at market prices.[17]

[16] Hoffman Philip T., Gilles Postel-Vinay, Jean-Laurent Rosenthal, *Dark Matter Credit: The Development of Peer-to-Peer Lending and Banking in France* (Princeton and Oxford, 2019), there 233.

[17] Giovannini Carla, *La presenza e l'attività del Monte nei secoli XVII e XVIII*, in Giuseppe Adani (ed), *Il Sacro Monte di Pietà di Faenza. Cinque secoli di storia e società 1491–1991* (Faenza, 1990); Recent historiography on pawnbanks, which had often been victim of excesses, simplifications, and superficial judgements, and harshly stigmatised by Oscar Nuccio (Nuccio Oscar, 'Chiesa e denaro dal XVI al XVIII secolo', in: Ugo Dovere (ed), *Chiesa e denaro tra Cinquecento e Settecento. Possesso, uso, imagine* (Cinisello Balsamo, 2004), 11–85), has brought to light numerous, solidly documented examples of behaviour

With the issuance of *Vix pervenit* in 1745 and the publication the year after of *Dell'impiego del denaro* by Scipione Maffei, the question of the legitimacy of interest-bearing loans obtained positive reactions, attenuating and almost annulling the religious deterrence toward the trade of money.[18] This widespread moral emancipation was significantly matched by the progressive formal definition of the loan instrument, which in those very years began to assert itself in the Ambrosian notarial protocols in place of the dissimulating *reorganiza, reorganizat, consensus prestitus*, and which became increasingly prevalent in the notaries' work, as Tables 1 and 2 show. Since the late 1770s, monetary stability linked to the 1778 reform[19] and the upward trend of the interest rate[20] made investments in the local capital market particularly attractive; in the same period, more than 28 million Milanese lire in cash were reimbursed to the holders of *regalia* (i.e., the taxes that had been granted or sold in the Spanish era and beyond), thus fueling an enormous flow of additional liquidity that greatly expanded—as Pietro Verri also testified—the credit supply of private individuals.[21]

During the second half of the century, in an expansive phase of the economy in northern Italy (largely due to the reorganization of public

similar to that of Faenza's pawnshop, see Montanari Daniele (ed), *Monti di Pietà e presenza ebraica in Italia (secoli XV-XVIII)* (Roma, 1999).

[18] Vismara Paola, *Questioni di interesse. La Chiesa e il denaro inn età moderna* (Milano 2009), there 107; Pecorari Paolo, 'Orientamenti della cultura cattolica sul prestito a interesse nel secolo XIX', in: *Chiesa, usura e debito estero. Supplemento a «Scienze sociali e dottrina sociale della Chiesa,* 2 (1998), 85–87.

[19] Tucci Ugo, 'Monete e riforme monetarie nell'Italia del Settecento', in: *Rivista storica italiana*, 93:1, (1986), 78–119; Gianelli Giulio, 'La riforma monetaria di Maria Teresa', in: Giovanni Gorini (ed), *La Zecca di Milano* (Milano, 1984).

[20] See Kaunitz's letter of early 1785 to Wilzeck and the assertions by the cameral magistrate, who stated during the council meeting of 7 October 1785 that the interest rate on cash loans had risen on average from 3.5 to 5% (De Maddalena Aldo, *Prezzi e mercedi a Milano dal 1701 al 1860* (Milano, 1974), there 195).

[21] Zaninelli, 'Un capitolo centrale del riordino dei tributi indiretti dello Stato di Milano nella seconda metà del '700: la "redenzione delle regalie"', in: *Studi in onore di Antonio Petino*, tome I, 'Momenti e problem di storia economica' (1986), there 334 That the effect of these repayments on credit supply, interest rates, and money circulation was very substantial is also affirmed by Pietro Verri; see his letter of 5 July 1769 to his brother Alessandro, in Greppi Emanuele, Alessando Giulini (eds), *Carteggio di Pietro e Alessandro Verri* (Milano, 1923), there 346; quoted also in Bruno Caizzi, *Industria, commercio e banca in Lombardia nel XVIII secolo* (Milano, 1986), there 200.

Table 1 Mortgage contracts of Milanese notary Carlo Giuseppe Aureggi (1751–1785). Source: ASMI, notary C. G. Aureggi, Rn. 311

Years	*Contracts*	*Loan contracts*	*% loan contracts*
1751–1755	47	16	34.04
1755–1760	98	30	30.61
1760–1765	115	28	24.34
1765–1770	137	54	39.41
1770–1775	96	29	30.20
1775–1780	82	32	39.02
1780–1785	73	34	47.22

Table 2 Mortgage contracts of Milanese notary Marco Antonio Pizzigalli (1751–1785). Source: ASMI, notary M.A.Pizzigalli, Rn. 3775

Years	*Contracts*	*Loan contracts*	*% loan contracts*
1751–1755	55	8	14.54
1755–1760	113	28	24.77
1760–1765	114	30	26.31
1765–1770	166	38	22.81
1770–1775	221	53	23.98
1775–1780	106	65	61.31
1780–1785	205	65	31.70

finance and the Enlightenment reforms in favor of agriculture, trade, and manufacturing), peer-to-peer relations between those who had capital and those who needed it, together with those who professionally traded in money and those who used its circuits, became the main channel through which information on the availability of money, its price, and the reliability of the various parties circulated. At the center of these credit networks were the notaries who performed the fundamental function of effective transmission of information between the parties; even if some notaries did not disdain the role of lenders of capital themselves, their strategic and crucial role consisted precisely in being privileged centers of reliable information for loans granted or requested by non-specialized subjects.

In pre-modern societies as today, information is at the heart of the financial sector. Only if it flows easily and reliably can a credit system work and improve. It was information, rather than prices (interest rates), that determined the allocation of capital and, as a consequence, set the rules.[22] While registering contracts, notaries collected a great deal of information about their clients, ranging from their level of wealth, state of indebtedness, and financial means to their level of trustworthiness; they knew whether their clients had cash to lend, if they had recently sold or bought properties, if they were reliable business partners and prompt payers, or if they were close to bankruptcy and needed to sell their assets quickly. The willingness to pay a higher interest rate for a debt was a necessary yet not sufficient condition for obtaining the loan.[23] Notaries screened this information and channeled it into the credit circuits, ably matching lenders and borrowers.[24] Most significantly, this information bears no cost for either the creditor or the debtor, unlike in the case of *sensali* (specialized matchmakers). The notaries found their microeconomic incentives—in the careful management of these reputational mechanisms—only in terms of keeping and increasing their clientele, as they were only paid for the stipulation of the deed. The more satisfied a lender was with the loan granted (in terms of payment and punctuality of interest and the repayment of the principal), the more likely he/she would be to return to the same notary. Similarly, borrowers who had managed to find the capital they sought would turn to the notary who had been able to put them in contact with appropriate lenders. Safeguarding the reliability of this market produced increasing returns for the notary. In Milan, the clear evidence of the establishment of these dynamics and of the intermediary function performed by the notary is the letter by Giovanni Filippo Visconti to Giuseppe Macchi, who worked as a notary in the city during the second half of the eighteenth century. On 1 June 1778, the young count addressed Macchi begging him to 'procure [for Visconti] a loan, if possible, of two thousand gigliati'.[25] The case of the notary Ignazio Baroggi and the loan he procured for Gaetano

[22] Hoffman, Postel-Vinay, Rosenthal, *Priceless Markets*.

[23] Hoffman, Postel-Vinay, Rosenthal, *Priceless Markets*, there 43.

[24] Hoffman Philip T., Gilles Postel-Vinay, Jean-Laurent Rosenthal, 'What do Notaries do? Overcoming Asymmetric Information in Financial Markets: The Case of Paris, 1751', in: *Journal of Institutional and Theoretical Economics*, 154:3 (1998), there 499-530; Insolvent debtors were not rare, but in those cases notaries were able to find new investors willing to finance them. Differently, since most loans were backed by collateral, lenders would become owners of the asset, usually a plot of land, a house, a mill, etc.

[25] A gigliato was a pure silver coin weighing 4 grams.

Battaglia in 1802 is also compelling to prove the match-maker role of these Milanese professionals. In order to fulfill the request of Battaglia, who was a Napoleonic colonel and majority partner in his father's firm, for 15,000 lire to finance his leather trade, the notary drew up a three-year loan contract at 5.5% interest with some of his clients 'who had capital at their disposal', namely the engineer Giovanni Cogliati of Milan, Onofrio Carnocino of Cremona, and Antonia Fumagalli, widow of Fortunato Radice, to whom he represented Battaglia as coming from a family of 'highly esteemed merchants'.[26]

The costs of raising and allocating capital were thus absorbed by the network of relations centered on notaries. The reputational and fiduciary dynamics of which they were protagonists thus significantly reduced the risks associated with information asymmetries (mitigating the distortions of moral hazard and adverse selection) with the result of making loans between private individuals increasingly reliable, attractive, and abundant. Italian notaries did not specialize in any one type of contract, e.g., wills, sales, dowries, or loans. Their status depended instead on the size of their studios. There were notaries whose clientele included the wealthiest and most important urban institutions and who thus brokered the highest sums; having a large clientele meant having more information and managing bigger capital flows. For example, Giovanni Agostino Gariboldi's network was populated mainly by the local élite (dukes, princes, marquises, counts), and religious institutions (convents and monasteries), while Marco Antonio Pizzigalli and Carlo Giuseppe Aureggi mainly served merchants and partnerships. Wealthy households, professionals, and municipal institutions all used to rely on their own *notaio di fiducia* (trusted notary), whose archives contained all the documents relating to his clients' assets, property transfers, and financial activities. While defining the terms of the contract, notaries from Pavia used to specify that the debtor was 'a person I know' (*persona da me conosciuta*), or 'most worthy person' (*persona di grande affidabilità*) to underscore good faith and ensure the absence of risk.

Thus, through solid and prolonged scrutiny and an information set that covered the entire economic life of their clients, the notaries were able to sustain a market in which a separating equilibrium could be achieved. In this market, high-risk agents could find lenders willing to

[26] ASMi, Rn. 49,730, 05/06/1802.

loan them capital, charging them a higher interest rate, and low-risk borrowers could find less costly options leveraging their reliability as debtors. The capital market thus prevented the exclusion of operators who could not offer the real property in guarantee but staked the success of their more innovative ventures on their motivation, entrepreneurial spirit, and business acumen. This was the case of the credit network centered around the notary Carlo Ambrogio Coquio. Thanks to him, Francesco Sala, a diamond and jewelry dealer, provided a total of 278,241 lire in loans spread over fifteen deeds. While some agreements stipulated gradual repayment—such as the payment for jewelry worth 77,500 lire sold to Prince Alberigo di Barbiano Belgioioso d'Este[27]—others regarded single large sums, like the 2,000 gigliati (33,500 lire) lent to Giovanni Andrea Valle, major of Cremona.[28] The major had permission from the Imperial Court of Vienna to seek funds to build a postal road connecting Cremona to Mantua. The loan expired after 6 years at a modest rate of 4.25%.[29] Francesco Sala also lent 200 gigliati to Carlo Maggioni, owner of a fabric shop (*teleria*), in a 3-year loan (credit transfer) at 4.5%.[30] Another credit involved 24,500 lire at 4.5% for 1 year to the count Carlo Pertusati, General Vice Superintendent of Finance from Milan, who needed the sum to buy a noble dwelling (*casa da nobile*).[31] Carlo Giuseppe Bossi borrowed 10,291 lire to pay off the house and two workshops he had purchased from the Ospedale Maggiore in 1774.[32] Within this notarial credit market, the Grianta brothers, tax farmers, were leading players.[33] Tommaso, Carlo, and Giuseppe Brentano supplied a total of 5,561,575 lire in 19 transactions through the notary Carlo Giuseppe Aureggi. The latter was also the notary for the Venini brothers, likewise wealthy tax contractors who issued credit for 231,122 lire distributed in 12 transactions.

[27] ASMI, notary C.A. Coquio, Rn. 1712, 10/12/1788; 2/9/1790.

[28] The value of gigliati underwent frequent variations. The figures here are drawn from Aldo De Maddalena, *Prezzi e mercedi a Milano dal 1701 al 1860* (Milano, 1974), there 421.

[29] ASMI, notary C.A. Coquio, Rn. 1712, 24/5/1780.

[30] ASMI, notary C.A. Coquio, Rn. 1712,19/12/1781.

[31] ASMI, notary C.A. Coquio, Rn. 1712, 9/5/1781.

[32] ASMI, notary C.A. Coquio, Rn. 1712, 9/7/1780.

[33] Bruno Caizzi, *Industria, commercio e banca in Lombardia*, there 159.

Good creditors (i.e., operators who lent money to different good debtors) and good debtors (i.e., operators who received multiple loans from different good creditors) populated the market intermediated by notaries, as shown by the network analysis of the longitudinal activity of the four main city notaries during the second half of the eighteenth century.[34] For each notarized loan of this sample, we took into account the date, loan amount, interest rate, debtor(s) and creditor(s), and notary and defined a one-mode directed network:

- $\mathcal{G}(\mathcal{A}, \mathcal{L})$, with $\mathcal{A} = (a_1, \cdots a_n)$ the set of debtor(s) and creditor(s), and $\mathcal{L} \subseteq \mathcal{A} \times \mathcal{A}$ the links (a_i, a_j) an ordered couple denoting the a_i as creditor and a_j as debtor, i.e., each loan is an arch in the network;
- Loan amount, interest rate, notary, and motivation can be considered attributes of the links (not fully exploited in this analysis).

For each network we compute actor degree centrality: in-degree (received loans), out-degree (given loans), total degree; and hub and authorities scores. Given the graph $\mathcal{G}(\mathcal{A}, \mathcal{L})$ and the corresponding adjacency matrix **A** the hub and authority score are related to the eigenvector of the matrix **A.** Hyperlink-Induced Topic Search (HITS) algorithm is used to estimate these scores.[35] Namely, the authority scores are determined by the entries of the dominant eigenvector of the matrix $\mathbf{A}^T\mathbf{A}$, i.e., the authority matrix; the hub scores are determined by the entries of the dominant eigenvector of the matrix $\mathbf{AA}^T$, , i.e., the hub matrix. In our case authorities are good debtors, i.e., they receive multiple loans from different good creditors, hubs are good creditors, i.e., they lend money to different good debtors (Figs. 1, 2).[36]

Regarding interest rate, compared to the previous century, they tended to decrease in the second half of the eighteenth century also as a result of the increase in the supply of money brought about by the redeeming of public debt by the State of Milan. The most frequent interest rates ranged

[34] See footnote 4.

[35] Jon M. Kleinberg, 'Hubs, authorities, and communities', in: *ACM Computing Surveys*, 31:4 (1999), 1–3; Michele Benzi, Ernesto Estrada, and Christine Klymko, 'Ranking hubs and authorities using matrix functions', in: *Linear Algebra and its Applications,* 438:5 (2013), 2447–2474.

[36] We are debtors and grateful to Giancarlo Ragozini of the Università degli Studi di Napoli Federico II for the network analysis of the sample and for creating the graphs.

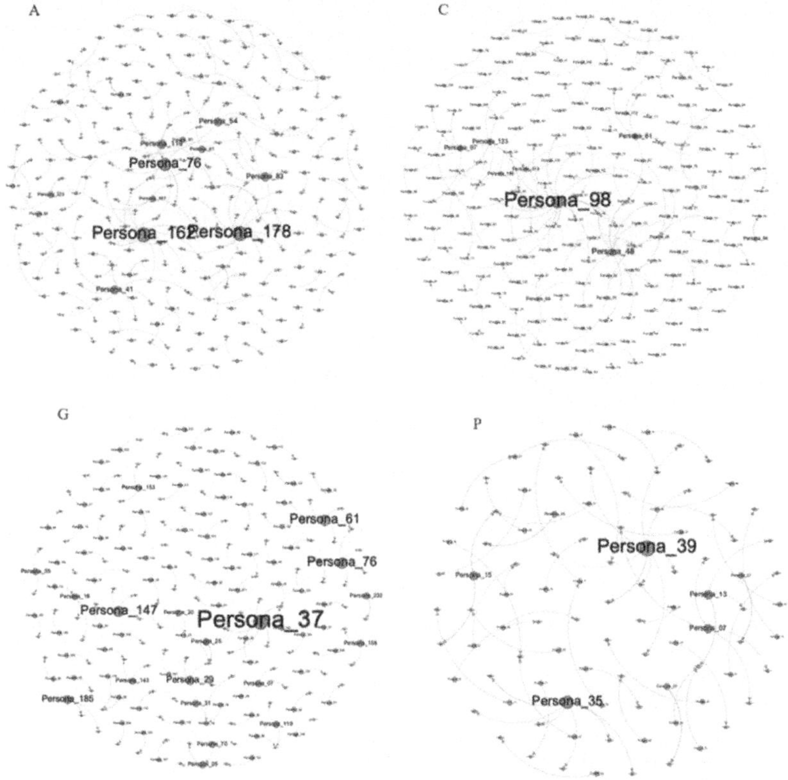

Fig. 1 Hubs and out-degree in Aureggi (A), Coquio (C), Gariboldi (G) and Pizzigalli (P) networks

from 3.75 to 4.75%, while the span was 3 to 6%. There was no correlation between amount, duration, and interest rate, although for the higher amounts the interest tended to be lower. For instance, Giovan Battista Cattaneo lent 2,158 lire to Domenico Rocca at 6%[37] while Giuseppe Maria Zaccaria was willing to lend 106,500 lire (6,000 gigliati) at 4%

[37] ASMI, notary M.A. Pizzigalli, Rn. 3775, 15/09/1767. The purpose of the debt was to pay off the balance.

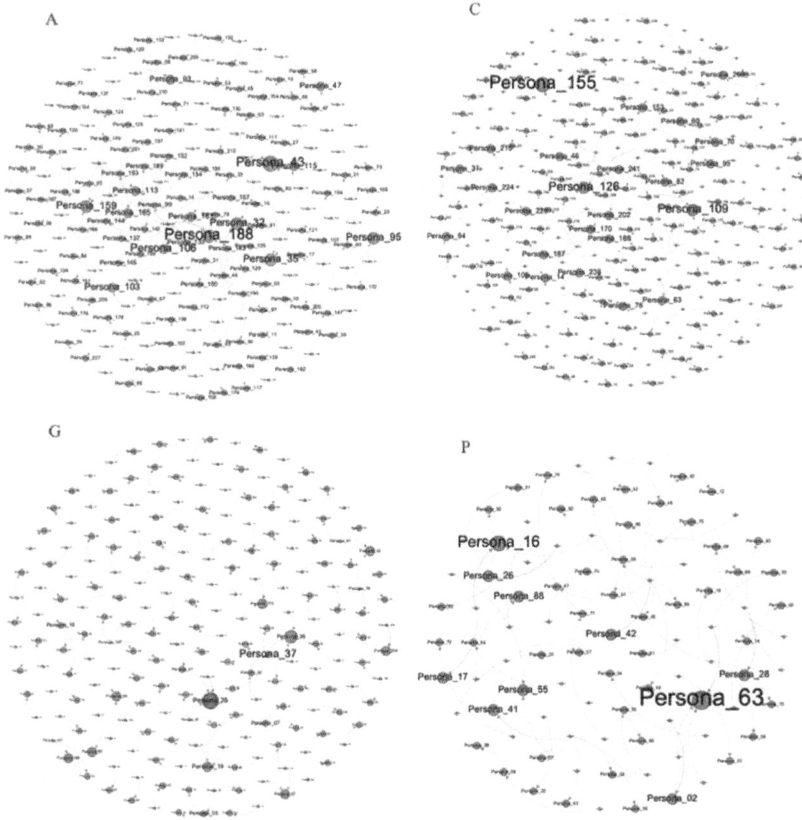

Fig. 2 Authorities and in degree in Aureggi (A), Coquio (C), Gariboldi (G), and Pizzigalli (P) networks

to the count Antonio Greppi.[38] It was the reputational factor of the debtor assessed by the notary that determined the price variations. With the decree of October 1807, as set forth in the Napoleonic Civil Code,

[38] ASMI, notary C.A. Coquio, Rn. 1712, 15/05/1779. As stated, this cannot be considered the rule. Greppi was one of the most prominent tax farmers and richest people in Milan.

the legal interest rate was fixed at 5% for civil uses and at 6% for commercial ventures.[39] However, during the first half of the nineteenth-century rates varied from 4 to 5%.

3.1 Lenders and Cash Pooling

In credit networks, the pool of lenders comprised men and women from different professions and of different socio-economic status. In Milan the duke Giovanni Galeazzo Serbelloni lent 193,000 lire in just six transactions.[40] Prince Don Antonio Maria di Barbiano di Belgioioso borrowed 62,000 lire at a relatively low interest rate, 3.75% (1776), for 6 years.[41] Another 45,000 lire were supplied to the countess Maria Olgiati Pertusati, at 3.5% for 5 years, and 15,000 lire to Monsignor Michele Daverio at an even lower interest rate of 3% for 4 years.[42]

The marquis Carlo Camillo Carcano lent even larger sums to a wider range of borrowers. His wealth was accumulated through trade and business, he became soon a protagonist in the private credit market as evidenced by the numerous transactions he ran. On the whole the marquis supplied 1,444,000 lire in 123 deeds, an average of almost 12,000 lire per deed, charging interest rates that spanned from 3.75 to 5%.[43] He also provided significant sums in a single transaction, such as the 196,000 lire at 3.75% that he supplied in 1782 to the heirs of the marquis Antonio Menafogli[44]; he lent another 47,450 lire at 4% to the count Aloisio Ignazio Belloni. Carcano's borrowers were not only his peers but also people from emerging professions at higher interests, such as the lawyer

[39] Robert Bigo, *Les banques françaises au cours du XIXe siècle* (Paris, 1947), there 48; ASMI, Giustizia civile pm, cart. 40.

[40] The Duke Serbelloni was 'Chamberlain of SMI, member of the 60 decurions and executor of the orders of the city of Milan, superintendent general of the militia, Marquis of Incisa', see Levati, *La nobiltà del lavoro, Negozianti e banchieri a Milano tra Ancien Régime e Restaurazione* (Milano, 1997), there 220.

[41] ASMI, notary G.A. Gariboldi, Rn. 2326, 29/04/1776,

[42] The duke also raised considerable sums from the private money market, borrowing almost 100,000 lire over 10 years (1785-1796) from different lenders: marquis (Trotti), counts (Sormani), cardinals, and also monasteries.

[43] Contracts were always drawn up by the same notary, Gariboldi: ASMI, notary, G. A. Gariboldi, Rn. 2326.

[44] It was a credit transfer (*cessione di credito*).

Giuseppe Soardi, to whom he gave 1,000 imperial lire at 4.5%,[45] or another 1,000 lire to the physician Carlo Recalcati at 5%.[46]

At the same time, the pool of lenders was being enriched by members of new professions, who together with artisans, accountants, and clerks represented an increasingly bourgeois society, in which work and wealth defined a new scale of values.[47] Their accumulated earnings and capital poured continuously into the informal market centered around notaries. In 1825, the architect Luigi Canonica and the lawyer Giovanni Orleri lent 70,000 lire to the merchant Giuseppe Zanella for 3 years at 4.5%,[48] while the engineer Francesco Belotti granted three loans totaling 7,500, at 5% and with a three-year term.[49] That same year, the town clerk accountant Carlo Ferraboschi lent 4,500 lire to the surgeon Francesco Campaniga[50] and the physician Bernardino Grassi granted a ten-year loan of 10,000 lire to Pietro Patrizio.[51]

Women—chiefly widows over the period considered—were also frequent lenders. They were often active in notaries' networks, supplying large amounts overall. The widow Paola Tartara issued a total credit of 232,873 Milanese lire in ten transactions at an interest rate that ranged from 3.5 to 5%.[52] Her preference for gigliati or zecchini (gold currencies) as transaction currency is probably due to the fact that they were less subject to devaluation. On the other hand, the countess Maria Olgiati Perusati borrowed 45,000 Milanese lire from the Duke Gian Galeazzo Visconti at 3.5% for 5 years, in order to pay her sister's dowry.[53] The countess Aurelia Gonzaga, Visconti's widow, manager of her children's estates, in just two transactions supplied loans totaling 100,000 lire at 4.5%. Rosa Sturioni in Galbiati, transacting on behalf of her children, supplied 99,931.50 lire in 12 loans at an interest rate of 4%. To give an idea of the magnitude of this sum, a bricklayer's income was 1.46 lire per

[45] ASMI, notary G.A. Gariboldi, Rn. 2326, 4/3/1771.

[46] ASMI, notary G.A. Gariboldi, Rn. 2326, 18/5/1771.

[47] Levati, *La nobiltà del lavoro.*

[48] ASMI, notary I. Baroggi, Rn. 49789, 04/10/ 1825.

[49] ASMI, notary I. Baroggi, Rn. 49789, 04/10/ 1825.

[50] ASMI, notary B. Pozzi, Rn. 475, 07/11/1825.

[51] ASMI, notary G. Arpegiani, Rn. 50096, 02/03/1825.

[52] ASMI, notary G. A. Gariboldi, Rn. 2326, 10/06/1779.

[53] ASMI, notary G.A. Gariboldi, Rn. 2326, 10/06/1779.

day, and 1 *moggio* of wheat (approx. 146 liters) cost 32.10 lire,[54] which means it was enough to pay the former for more than 185 years of work or to buy nearly 12,000 bushels of wheat.

As the population grew, notaries' credit network expanded, engaging individuals who lived in distant parts of the city or in other towns. In notarized mortgage contracts in Milan, people from San Babila signed the agreement with others from San Pietro; or from San Nazzaro Maggiore with others from San Salvatore, Sant'Eufemia, Morbegno, Sant'Ambrogio, San Michele, or San Bartolomeo.

The case of Giuseppe Alberti, as Fig. 3 shows, is an example of the wide credit network centered on notaries.

As the network broadened, people coming from other towns such as Como, Pavia, Lodi, or Novara began to be involved in loans. Luigi Petazzi, royal feudal lord of Conterico in the province of Lodi, lent the large sum of 60,000 lire to the marquis Pietro Antonio Natta, royal feudal lord from Novara (50 km from Milan).[55] Giuseppe Maria Villa from San Bartolomeo, who had to extinguish his father's debt with the countess Francesca Bonenzia (dated in 1743) signed for a debt of 600 zecchini with Carlo Francesco Campini from Monza.[56] In 1830 the widow Marianna Linati of Milan lent 2,900 lire at 5% to two brothers from Saronno, both of them butchers.[57]

Alongside the elite, religious bodies played a key role in the early-modern lending market. They participated almost exclusively as suppliers of capital and very rarely as borrowers. Their wealth came from donations, bequests, and charity, and also from a parsimonious conduct, contrasting with the dissipative behavior that characterized some aristocratic households.[58] Most convents and monasteries had been founded in Medieval times, but their centrality in the credit market emerged in the sixteenth century, when the position of the Church on usury started to soften, legitimizing interest-bearing loans, albeit under strict terms.[59] Regular Orders

[54] De Maddalena, *Prezzi e mercedi a Milano*, there 379.

[55] ASMI, notary C.G. Aureggi, Rn. 311, 17/03/1789.

[56] ASMI, notary, G.A. Gariboldi, Rn. 2326, 16/03/1765.

[57] ASMI, notary, L. Clerici, Rn. 295, 17/06/1830.

[58] Fiorenzo Landi, *Storia economica del clero in Europa. Secoli XV-XIX* (Roma 2005).

[59] The reference is in particular to the publication of the *Bulla Plana* in 1569, after which the *census consignativus* rapidly spread, becoming the leading financial instrument

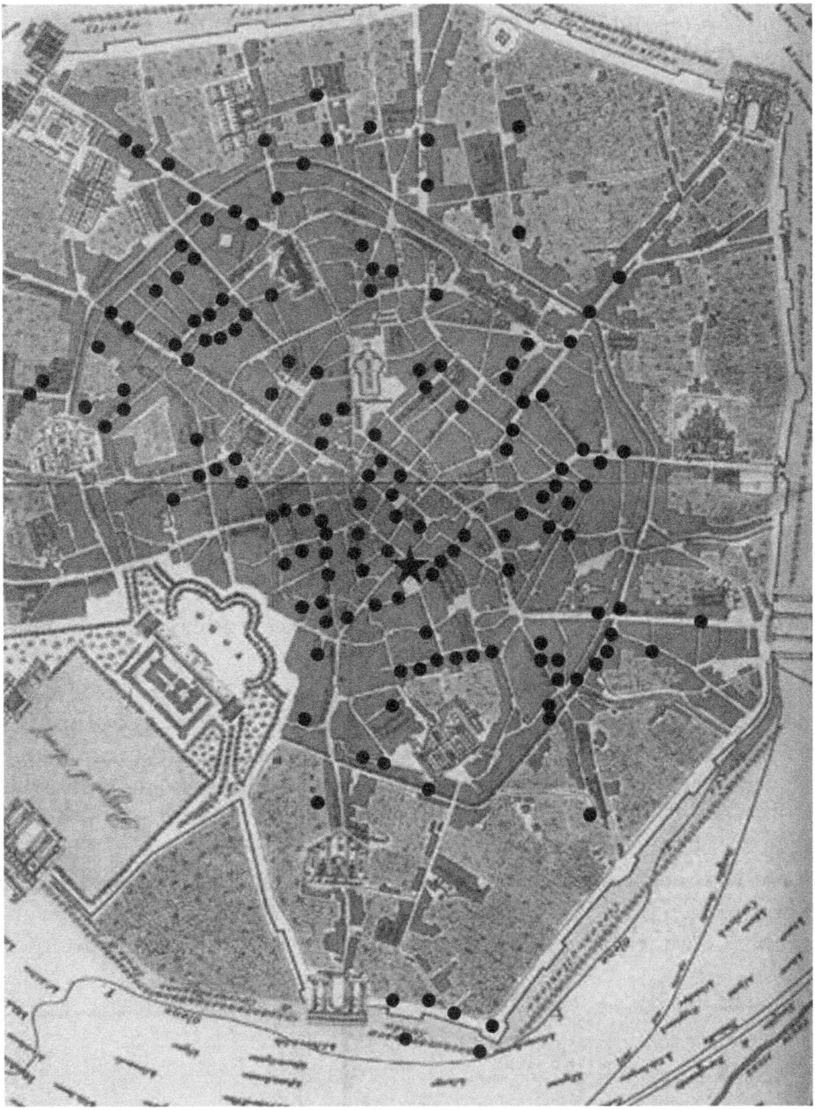

Fig. 3 The star pinpoints the notary's office in via Santa Maria Fulcorina in Milan centre. The black dots locate the place of residence of debtors and creditors. Archivio di Stato di Milano, notary Giuseppe Alberti, Notarile, Ultimi versamenti, folders 766–794 (1860–1865) Milan's map is the Nuovo Panorama Geometrico Orografico Pittoresco di Milano Ideato Disegnato ed Inciso da Leoni Zucoli e dal medesimo pubblicato nel 1844, in Civica Raccolta Stampe Achille Bertarelli", Castello Sforzesco, Milano

underwent a process that may be defined as a heterogenesis of ends: alongside their primary spiritual mission, they started a credit activity (*censi, fitti, livelli*) that progressively developed and increased. In Milan, the Monastero di St. Caterina Braidense, Monastero di St. Agostino e Pietro Martire, Convento Santa Maria dei Servi, Monastero di St. Vittore, Monastero di St. Celso, and the Collegio Santa Ursula di Monza supplied in total 258,064 lire, with an average of 10,320 lire per transaction. Acting as creditors, religious bodies thus entered into competition with professional lenders. However, their activity differed from that of the latter because they put no pressure on the debtor to repay the capital; their priority was, in effect, to generate a continuing revenue stream. The Church circles and the city elite enjoyed a strong relationship since the borrowers were usually members of the aristocracy who had daughters or cadets in convents, monasteries, or abbeys. This alliance also influenced the price of money, with these institutions charging lower interest rates for higher sums. The Monastero San Vittore di Meda lent 22,000 lire to Bianca Maria Sforza, marquise of Caravaggio, charging a 3.5% interest rate to be paid off in 10 years.[60] The Monastero San Celso lent 266 gigliati (4,671 lire) to the counts and brothers Scotti, charging an interest rate of 4% for 4 years.[61] In the mid-nineteenth century, the Church still represented golden coffers whence governments could draw capital in times of financial strain. Their capital covered 31% of the total flow in Milan, and an even greater proportion in other cities.

One of the main innovations of the nineteenth century regarded the techniques used by notaries to overcome the limit represented by the capacity of individual borrowers. More precisely, notaries began to leverage the method of cash pooling, which enabled them to collect large sums by bundling together different lenders (who had no relationship to one another) and to avoid multiple loan deeds. All the creditors shared the same risk and the same profits, issuing their portion of capital to one

for collateral-backed loans. See Luigi Alonzi, *Economia e finanza nell'Italia moderna. Rendite e forme di censo (secoli XV-XX)*, (Roma, 2012); Giuseppe De Luca and Marcella Lorenzini, 'Not only land: mortgage credit in central-northern Italy in the sixteenth and seventeenth centuries', in: Chris Briggs and Jaco Zuijderduijn (eds), Land and credit: mortgages in the medieval and early modern European countryside (Cham, 2018): 181-204.

[60] ASMI, notary G.A. Gariboldi, Rn. 2326, 01/02/1775.

[61] ASMI, notary G.A. Gariboldi, Rn. 2326, 11/02/1778.

single borrower. In this way, in 1825 the notary Sormani procured a loan of 50,000 lire for engineer Giuseppe Albini and his brothers by combining funds from the widow Caterina Sanchioli with those of the priest Scavenizza Visconti.[62] Francesco Viscontini obtained a loan of 16,000 lire at 4% interest from two creditors, Vedani and Piazza (contributing 4,000, and 12,000 lire, respectively).[63] As we have seen, the Milanese notary Ignazio Baroggi gathered together some of his clients 'who had capital on hand', an engineer, Giovanni Cogliati of Milan, Onofrio Camocino from Cremona, and Antonia Fumagalli, the widow of Fortunato Radice, giving the lenders assurances about the Battaglia family, who were well-respected merchants.[64]

But the real specialist in this technique was the notary Achille Marocco. Between 1844 and 1848, he drafted an impressive series of loans in which the lending party was always two or more people (shopkeepers, silk merchants, and accountants and very often widows), who 'jointly subsidized by way of an interest-bearing loan'.[65] The credit pooling method developed and spread to other cities. In nearby Pavia the notary Luigi Vecchio grouped together nine creditors, all individuals who were unrelated to each other, hence: Carolina Ferrara, Ludovico Albani, Angelo and Alberto Morandotti, Bartolomeo Polloni, Luigi Spagnuoli, Ferdinando Granellini, Giuseppe Francesi, and Giovanni Bottiglia Vigo, who lent a total of 22,250 lire to Luigi Pietrasanta.[66]

3.2 *Reasons for Loan and Evolving Collateral*

Another element that helped to expand the peer-to-peer market in the 1800s was the collateral that progressively shifted from immovable (real estate) to movable assets (capitals, tolls, duties, the rights of perceiving thites' revenues). Whereas the first modern banks, such as the Cassa di

[62] ASMi, notary F. Sormani, Rn. 50236, 11/11/1825.

[63] ASMI, deed of 17/06/1835.

[64] ASMI, notary I. Battaglia, Rn. 49,730, 05/01/1802.

[65] See by way of example deeds no. 925 of 24/09/1844 (cart. 876), no. 991 of 26/02/1845 (cart. 877), no. 1090 of 23/09/1845 (cart. 878), no. 1145 of 10/01/1846 (cart. 879), no. 1148 of 19/01/1846 (cart. 879), no. 1201 of 05/06/1846 (cart. 879), no. 1336 of 01/04/1847 (cart. 881), no. 1452 of 13/01/1848 (cart. 882), ASMI, notary A. Marocco.

[66] Archivio di Stato di Pavia, notary L. Vecchio, Rn. 4961/7035, 15/11/1880.

Risparmio (Savings Bank) of Milan (founded in 1823), accepted only real estate assets, the possibility of using annuities from capital, *censi*, and other income as forms of collateral made the informal credit market particularly accessible, liquid, and attractive. In 1830 Carl'Antonio Crippa obtained 5,000 lire from Pietro Ferrandi using as collateral a claim he had on Ferdinando Gallavresi,[67] while in 1843 Pietro Manzoni, the eldest son of the author of *I promessi sposi* (*The Betrothed*), borrowed 5,000 lire from Matilde Arnaboldi as security for a debt that his father owed her.[68] In 1849, the Laurin brothers obtained 365 gold pieces at 5% by using as collateral a credit of 20,000 lire to Luigi Brunetti's wife, and Carolina Bernasconi received 3,300 lire by pledging a three-year loan she had granted the year before.[69] As we may deduce from the latter, the mortgages to private individuals brokered via a notary's network could be used as collateral for loans, preventing the creditor in need from having only one means of obtaining further capital, i.e., collection of active loans; credit thus became a matrix of other credit, ending up acting as a multiplier of the resources available to the economy.

At the same time, it was a very liquid market and if the lender wanted or needed to repay the loan, it was not difficult for the notary to find someone to take it over (to buy the credit), as in the case of the loan of 30,000 lire at 4.25% that Paolo Sessa of Rovagliola, from Arzago, had taken out with Regina Niada Milani of Vaprio and which was subrogated to Giuseppa Arnaboldi on 15 April 1839.[70]

The analysis of the motivations underlying debts shows some elements of continuity with the past and others marking a break and opening the way to a new modern age. In the preindustrial era a large proportion of mortgages were taken out in order to extinguish old debts, for *urgentissimi bisogni* (urgent needs), for paying taxes, house maintenance, purchasing plots of land, or buying working tools or draught and pack animals. In periods of economic expansion, individuals borrowed funds to open new shops, create factories, start a new business or enlarge an existing one, or establish new partnerships. Often families went into debt in order to provide a dowry for a daughter who was going to get married

[67] ASMI, notary A. Finalli, Rn. 50392, 16/08/1830.

[68] ASMI, notary A. Marocco, Rn. 873, 24/06/1843.

[69] ASMI, notary A. Marocco, Rn. 884, 08/03/1849.

[70] ASMI, notary A. Marocco, Rn. 866, 15/04/1839.

or enter a convent.[71] The dowry could be part in cash and part in real estate and attracted the attention of families for its economic, social, and political implications. It stopped being considered as the mere transfer of property from one household to another and began to be seen as a vehicle by which to climb the social ladder, create businesses, and forge political alliances. 'A good marriage could guarantee not only liquidity to invest in partnerships and businesses, but also access to a system of social relationships that often, more than others, determined successful dealings'.[72] As well documented in wills, dowries had become larger and larger since the sixteenth century. Though the Republic of Venice issued sumptuary laws that fixed a maximum amount for dowries, the dowry inflationary trend continued to increase in the following centuries.[73] The accelerated inflation that occurred in the nineteenth century was only partially attributable to currency inflation (the lira), being mainly due, in effect, to the rising amounts allocated to a daughter's assets. In addition, the introduction of the Civil Code (1806) established that women could obtain a share of the inheritance, which had to be proportional to the entire family estate. Dowries between 1801 and 1820 were often in excess of 100,000 lire, as in the case of Sidonia Montorfano. When she married Cristoforo Busti, son of the famous banker Giulio Cesare Busti, she held a dowry of 105,000 lire. Thanks to the sums they enjoyed from dowries,

[71] On the function of the dowry in defining the social, economic, and financial position of women see, among others: Paola Lanaro and Gian Maria Varanini, 'Funzioni economiche della dote nell'Italia centro-settentrionale (tardo medioevo/inizio età moderna)', in: Simona Cavaciocchi (ed), *La famiglia nell'economia europea, secc. XIII – XVIII* (Florence, 2009), 81–102; Anna Bellavitis, 'Dare credito, fiducia e responsabilità alle donne (Venezia, secolo XVI)' in: Giovanna Petti Balbi and Paola Guglielmotti (eds), Dare credito alle donne. Presenze femminili nell'economia tra medioevo ed età moderna (Asti, 2012), 259–267; James Shaw, 'Women, credit and dowry in early modern Italy', in Elise Dermineur (ed), *Women and credit in preindustrial Europe* (Turnhout 2018), 173–202; Stefania Licini, 'Assessing female wealth in nineteenth century Milan, Italy', in: *Accounting History* 16:1 (2011), 35–54; Elise Dermineur, 'Single Women and the Rural Credit Market in Eighteenth-Century France', in: *Journal of Social History*, 48:1 (2014), 175–199; Elise Dermineur, 'Peer-to-peer lending in pre-industrial France', in: *Financial History Review*, 26:3 (2019), 359–388; Marcella Lorenzini, 'The Other Side of Banking. Private Lending and the Role of Women in Early Modern Italy', in: Stephan Nicolussi-Köhler (ed), *Change and Transformation of Premodern Credit Markets. The importance of Small-Scale Credits,* (Heidelberg, 2021), 177–197.

[72] Levati, *La nobiltà del lavoro*, there 111.

[73] Lanaro and Varanini, 'Funzioni economiche della dote nell'Italia centro-settentrionale.

the Milanese were among the wealthiest families in Lombardy, reaching levels comparable to those of landed aristocrats.[74]

The purposes underlying debts reveal much about the new streams of investment. In the early nineteenth century the invested capital moved toward the silk industry. It was a sector increasingly expanding as a consequence of the rising domestic demand—partly driven by population growth—and expanding foreign demand. The principal exports were raw and spun silk, whose volumes grew more than threefold from 1825 (415,000 libbre) to 1846 (1,412,000 libbre).[75] This demand provided a strong stimulus to manufacturing, technological development, and organizational and entrepreneurial capacities.[76] A specific bank was founded to support and finance the silk industry and silk trade, the Monte Sete (bank for silk producers, 1781–1796). The aim was to free producers from their dependence on spinners, who speculated on cocoon prices (which were unknown at the time of sale) and the final price of silk yarn. Loans were invested in raw and spun silk. Between 1781 and 1782 Monte Sete supplied credit of 1,464,234 lire, of which only a part, 928,477 lire, was repaid. Monte Santa Teresa, a pawn bank created under Maria Theresa of Austria, could not insulate against uncertainties or dampen the cyclical ups and downs of that market, which produced drastic effects for Monte Sete. The silk bank's turnover in effect began to evaporate in the last decade of its life, with the arrival of Napoleon's troops putting the final nail in its coffin.[77] Due to the high price fluctuations, the bank had exposures that remained unsolved and the financial support from Monte Santa Teresa was not enough to save it. The strict conditions on Monte Sete loans certainly did not play in its favor: they were short-term, charged at a 4.5% interest rate, and collateralized by national silk products. It was not rare then for tradesmen to turn to the private capital market to borrow or lend extra money at different terms (rates, guarantees, and deadlines). Debts were contracted to pay for merchandise, create partnerships, or open shops or factories. The numerous transactions and the

[74] Levati, *La nobiltà del lavoro*, there 92–99.

[75] One libbra was equal to 0.327 kg. Data refer to exports to London and Lyon. But foreign markets also included Austria (Wien), Germany, Switzerland, and Russia (Romani, *Aspetti e problemi di storia economica lombarda,* there 301).

[76] Giandomenico Piluso, *L'arte dei banchieri. Moneta e credito a Milano da Napoleone all'Unità*, (Milan, 1999), there 32–33.

[77] Caizzi, *Industria, commercio e banca in Lombardia*, there 185–189.

sums linked to silk manufacturing and trade show the territory that this sector was gaining within the economic system.[78] Capital raised on the informal market implied a long-term expiry and interest rates with a wider range, from 4 to 6%. A great growth spurt was witnessed in the 1760s, with the production of mulberry leaves increasing by 60 or 70%. Likewise, the manufacturing sector was expanding, attracting investments to upgrade existing plants and machinery. Money borrowed through notarized loans was in effect used to finance fixed capital. Marco Antonio Chiappone asked for 400 gigliati to establish a silk works in Civate Pieve of Oggiono, part of the Duchy of Milan.[79] Dario G. Botta and his son borrowed 2,000 lire from Romolo Frontino to expand their drapery shop on the Dom square. It was a short-term (1-year) loan at 4.5% interest.[80] At the same time Pietro Lanelli received 2,600 lire from Felice Bonanone at 5% to finance a shop in Gessate. Payment had to be made at the fairs of Bergamo.[81] The Redaelli brothers obtained a loan of 7,050 lire to fund their silk shop in Pieve d'Oggiono. The credit was supplied by Giovan Battista Pasta at 4%, which was a good rate.[82]

Capital raised on the private credit market turned out to be fundamental for the establishment of new partnerships. The Caldaras, for example, took out debt of 14,000 lire from the Venini brothers, prominent and wealthy tax farmers from Milan, in order to establish a partnership with their brother-in-law, Flaminio Prina.[83] Their plan was to build a yarn mill for a silk shop. They received the sum at 5% with a 5-year deadline.[84] On the other hand, Giovanni Domenico and Carlo, Grazia, and Antonio Francesco Rognoni borrowed 600 gigliati (10,410 lire) to pay a partnership share in a store with the Rava brothers.[85] They received the sum from the tax farmer Antonio Greppi at an advantageous rate of 3.75%

[78] Angelo Moioli, 'Il commercio serico lombardo nella prima metà dell'Ottocento', in: Simona Cavaciocchi (Ed), La seta in Europa sec. XII-XX (Florence, 1993), 723–739.

[79] ASMI, notary M. A. Pizzigalli, Rn. 3775, 23/04/1771.

[80] ASMI, notary G. Aureggi, Rn. 311, 10/12/1753.

[81] ASMI, notary G. Aureggi, Rn. 311, 23/09/1769.

[82] ASMI, notary M. A. Pizzigalli, Rn. 3775, 13/03/1778.

[83] Caizzi, *Industria, commercio e banca in Lombardia*, there 159.

[84] ASMI, notary G. Aureggi, Rn. 311, 04/01/1791.

[85] ASMI, notary G.A. Gariboldi, Rn. 2326, 17/03/1777.

for 4 years.[86] Tax farmers were crucial figures in the lending market, as the income from their activity was largely reinvested in the credit circuits. According to the ledgers we have consulted, they boasted significant surpluses, reaching 600,000 lire in the mid-eighteenth century.[87] Less attracted to investments in land or public bonds, they preferred to employ their liquidity in financial activities, especially interest-bearing loans to dukes, princes, and governors, such as the Duke of Mantua or Prince Kaunitz.[88]

Merchants took out loans to pay outstanding debts and thus avoid bankruptcy or failure. One of the main features characterizing the notarized market was its resilience, which derived from the service provided by notaries, who were able to meet the demand and supply of money also in case of insolvency. By drawing on his familiarity with his clientele, he knew which debtors were trustworthy—even in the event that they were unable to pay back the money at the deadline, he knew they could be trusted to pay in the end—and was able to select financiers willing to supply credit to them. Francesco Butti, for instance, borrowed 500 zecchini at 4% with a 3-year term to 'pay credit to the business Giovan Battista Barca and Angiolo Carrara and Company'. The de Capitani brothers, silk spinners, asked for 2,000 imperial lire from Giovan Battista Cattaneo, (*pubblico negoziante*), which they obtained at 6%; during the time of the contract, debtors were also obliged to process Cattaneo's raw silk.[89]

The expansive trend in silk manufacturing and trade is reflected in the numerous loans to purchase merchandise. Carlo Maggini borrowed money to buy 'supplies for his clothing and lace shop'.[90] He obtained 12,000 lire for 3 years at 4% from Camillo Carcano. Carlo Brentani needed a much higher amount, 30,000 lire, to pay off the goods he had purchased in Caltingnana agri Novarese,[91] while Carlo Martini borrowed

[86] Caizzi, *Industria, commercio e banca in Lombardia*, there 162.

[87] Lombard tax farm profits came from the taxes on salt, tobacco, gunpowder, saltpetre, and merchandise, and tolls from Lodi and Cremona, Caizzi, *Industria, commercio e banca in Lombardia*, there 163.

[88] Caizzi, *Industria, commercio e banca in Lombardia*, there 163.

[89] ASMI, notary M.A. Pizzigalli, Rn. 3775, 13/03/1778.

[90] ASMI, notary G.A. Gariboldi, Rn. 2326, 30/07/1771.

[91] ASMI, Notary G.A. Gariboldi, Rn. 2326, 09/09/1756.

21,350 lire from Giuseppe Marini to purchase silk for commercial purposes.[92]

Loans often took the form of deferred payments, sometimes interest-free. The possibility to enjoy cash advances shows the compensative action played by the informal money market, which, via the intermediation of notaries, could limit risks and transaction costs. For example, the Rougier and Carlo Francesco Volpino partnerships obtained silk for the amount of 3,012 lire, charging no interest, from Francesco Vergani.[93] In 1782, the latter provided a loan of 7,140 lire also to two partnerships, Giacomo Biffi and Albuzio, who had bought 340 libbre of silk from Cattaneo (one of the biggest silk producers in Milan) that they had to repay in two instalments at zero interest.[94] Bartolomeo Aureggi needed money to cover costs in his silk hosiery shop in Bellagio. His financier was Bernardo Monti, who lent him 375 gigliati (6,094 lire) for 4 years at the relatively low interest rate of 4%.[95]

Along with silk, the cotton industry also started to develop throughout the eighteenth century. A number of major loans were drawn up in notarized contracts to modernize this emerging sector. Pioneers of the innovations in this field were the Kramers. The family was originally native to Essenheim, near Frankfurt, with which Milan had important commercial relations. They arrived in Milan at the end of the eighteenth century and took over management of the 'Rho Brothers' partnership, which operated in the spinning and weaving processes of silk manufacturing. The family soon distinguished itself within the city's business community and began to branch out, initiating business ventures in different fields, from silk manufacturing to insurance, from contracts for military barrack sewage management to fertilizer marketing.[96] However, it was the cotton industry where they made their fortune, pioneering important innovations such as process mechanization.[97] They had a great impact on the social and economic life of Milan, promoting initiatives that were crucial

92 ASMI, Notary, Giusti, Rn. 49.661, 14/11/1840.

93 ASMI, Notary M.A. Pizzigalli, Rn. 3775, 21/03/1782.

94 ASMI, Notary M.A. Pizzigalli, Rn. 3775, 10/04/1782.

95 ASMI, Notary G. Aureggi, Rn. 311, 15/01/1772 (1 gigliato equalled 16.25 lire).

96 Levati, *La nobiltà del lavoro*, there 223.

97 Romani, *Aspetti e problemi di storia economica lombarda nei secoli XVIII e XIX*, there 244–245.

to its future economic development.[98] Their notary-mediated transactions were associated with a quest for financing, turning to the private capital market to raise money. In 1835 they borrowed 26,500 lire from Michele Begtheden and Vincenzo Ferrario (who supplied 15,000 and 11,500 lire, respectively).[99] Two days later (4 September) they received another loan from Antonio Arena, who supplied another significant sum of 20,000 lire.[100] Some months later (14 November) another 30,000 lire were loaned to them by Antonio Cagnola.[101]

Although they were in a declining phase, other manufacturing sectors still received funds, particularly woolen and linen manufacturing. Mr and Mrs Guaita turned to the count Stefano San Giuliani—outside of the specialized merchant circuit—for a sum of 60,000 lire that they obtained at 4.75% for 3 years. As collateral, the couple mortgaged their woolen mill in Como along with their partnership in Amsterdam.[102] Clara Clerici and her husband Giovanni Battista Ballioni obtained a loan of 2,000 lire to set up a linen, wool, and silk spinning mill in the village of Luino.[103] The couple obtained the financing from Count Crivelli's widow, Carlotta Pickler.

As regard the mining sector, in the eighteenth century it entered a declining phase due to resource depletion and outdated organization. No significant technological progress was introduced and the transformations that took place in the 1760s mainly regarded management structure, rather than effective economic or technical innovations.[104] However, some mining centers were still alive in the eighteenth century and required financing. In 1757, the Rabaglietti brothers, who leased a mine in Val Anzasca on Lago Maggiore, were looking for money to pay rent and turned to the count Federico Borromeo for a loan of 270 gigliati.[105]

[98] Levati, *La nobiltà del lavoro*, there 65.

[99] ASMI, Rn. 3513, 2/09/1835.

[100] ASMI, Rn. 3516, 4/09/1835.

[101] ASMI, Rn.3529, 14/11/1835.

[102] ASMI, notary M.A. Pizzigalli, Rn. 3775ASMI, notary M.A. Pizzigalli, Rn. 3775.

[103] ASMI, notary G. A. Gariboldi, Rn. 2326, 24/01/1784.

[104] Caizzi, *Industria, commercio e banca in Lombardia*, there 124–131.

[105] ASMI, notary G.A. Gariboldi, Rn. 2326, 10/05/1757.

The eighteenth and nineteenth centuries were marked by the growth of transportation infrastructure, especially roads and canals. Its increasing importance is reflected in the requests for money for maintaining and repairing old routes or creating new stretches of road connecting city and countryside, or building postal roads, as in the case of the 2,000 gigliati (33,500 lire) sought by the mayor of Cremona. The road would link Cremona to Mantua and had been authorization by the Habsburg government.[106] The transportation infrastructure improved particularly by the development of canals, and Lombardy pioneered new and advanced technologies. Lombardy had a long tradition of using canals for trade and agriculture: The oldest canals of Europe were the *Navigli*, which were built in here in the Middle Ages, to foster commerce and agriculture.[107] But the real boom of water communication routes took place in the nineteenth century, both for transportation and irrigation.[108] Lombardy's broad plains and rich hydrographic network presented an ideal environment from a morphological viewpoint. One of the most important irrigation canals was the Lorini-Marocco that started to be built in 1806 and finished in 1817.[109] While the main waterways were usually supported and managed by the State, minor and secondary canals were financed and administrated by private individuals organized into

[106] ASMI, notary C.A. Coquio, Rn. 1712, 24/05/1780.

[107] This canal network was funded mainly by the municipalities and by the nobility: Visconti, Sforza, Pallavicini, and Maggi. For the Navigli canals see also, Stefano Jacini, *La proprietà fondiaria e le popolazioni agricole in Lombardia* (Milano, 1854).

[108] See Bruschetti Giuseppe, *Storia dei progetti e delle opere per l'irrigazione del milanese* (Lugano, 1834); Carlo Cattaneo, *Notizie Naturali e Civili sulla Lombardia* (Milano 1844); Giulio Cesare Zimolo, 'Canali e navigazione interna nell'età moderna', in: *Storia di Milano*, 24 (1960); Gabriele Pagani, *Storie d'acqua. Contado di Milano: dalla formazione della pianura alla civiltà dei fontanili e dei navigli Lombardi* (Milano, 2017).

[109] The 'canal fever' (1844-1855) that was sweeping over England and the United States also arrived in Lombardy, whose canals irrigated 427,200 hectares. The most remarkable waterway of Lombardy was the Cavour Canal (1840-1863). It was built under Camillo Benso count di Cavour, Minister of Agriculture and then of Finance, and financed with private capital. For that purpose Cavour created the first irrigation partnership, which was an 'association of the owners of land irrigated with public waters, to whom exclusive rental rights to these waters was to be granted'. The Cavour canal (83 km long) was built as a deviation from the Po River, in order to improve land cultivation, especially of rice (Segre, 'Bonifica e irrigazione in Lombardia nel secolo XIX').

partnerships, as was the case of Lorini-Marocco.[110] In 1806 a partnership was created by Francesco Zaccaria Lorini, by the lawyer Carlo Marocco, and the Balabio and Besana partnership, which was one of the most prominent merchant banks (originally silk merchants) in Milan at the turn of the nineteenth century.[111] Ignazio Besana, representing his brothers in the Balabio and Besana partnership, borrowed 30,000 lire from Giovanni Battista Camagni necessary to cover the costs of digging and operating the canal. The loan was issued at a 5.5% interest rate for 5 years.[112] Numerous other credit transactions were drawn up by the notaries Sacchi and Gianorini for the construction of the canal.[113] The total cost amounted to 4 million lire. It was 80 km long with another 193 km of feeder canals and provided irrigation to 6,666 hectares of rice and flax (linen) fields. Other zones were devoted to pastures and cattle raising, notably associated with the region's dairy farms. The canal crossed through the countryside around Milan, Lodi, and Pavia.[114]

4 Concluding Remarks

Large, bustling private capital networks centered on notaries emerged during the second half of the eighteenth century in northern Italy, from Lombardy to Veneto and from Liguria to Trentino. Incomes, annuities, savings, cash flows, and civilian or monastic dowries began to fuel a complex, well developed network of money exchange centering around notaries. Notaries were crucial actors within this market as they acted 'informally' as financial intermediaries, matching those seeking capital with those looking for investments. The great store of information they collected and consulted during their regular activities reduced transaction

[110] Gandolfi Claudio, 'Acqua e irrigazione per nutrire il pianeta. la realtà della pianura padana lombarda', in: *Istituto Lombardo, Accademia di Scienze e Lettere - Incontri di Studio* (2017), 51-66, there 62. For methods of financing infrastructure from ancient Rome to modern times, see Giuseppe De Luca and Marcella Lorenzini, 'A taxonomy of infrastructure financing in Europe on the long run (12th-18th century)', in: *Entreprises et histoire*, 70:1 (2013), 10-36.

[111] Levati, *La nobiltà del lavoro*, there 219–222.

[112] ASMI, notary G. Sacchi, Rn. 543, deed of 08/05/1807.

[113] ASMI, notary G. Gianorini, Rn. 49.205, 49.206, 49.207, 49.208; notary G. Sacchi, Rn. 542, 543, 544, 545, 546, 547, 548, 549, 550, 551, 552, 553, 554, 555.

[114] Bruschetti, *Storia dei progetti e delle opere per l'irrigazione del milanese*, there 323.

costs, such as adverse selection, preventing the market from failing and helping to expand it.

The networks penetrated like fine capillaries through society. The thousands of large and mid-sized transactions made this market the 'dark matter' of financial systems, i.e., the bulk of capital markets (Hoffman et al. 2019). In northern Italian regions, both in towns and metropolises, the sums mobilized in these informal credit networks reached significant amounts. In Rovereto, for instance, during the economic boom of the eighteenth century, the private capital market amounted to four times the revenues from tolls. In 1840 Milan, it was over 17% of total State revenues (10,648,000 Milanese lire). Here, almost one fifth of the families had turned to the credit services offered by notaries, who relied on consolidated information rather than generic mortgage guarantees.

Thanks to a massive scrutiny and a longitudinal information set about their clients, notaries were able to sustain a market in which a separating equilibrium could be achieved. High-risk agents could find creditors willing to lend them capital, charging a higher interest rate, and low-risk debtors could find less costly options leveraging their reliability as debtors. The capital market thus prevented the exclusion of operators who could not offer real estate in guarantee but staked the success of their more innovative ventures on their motivation, entrepreneurial spirit, and business acumen. Medium- and long-term capital was mobilized to finance the more modern entrepreneurial initiatives that were animating the local economic environment and that could not find support from the *casse di risparmio* (savings banks). These institutions, which did not have the same extensive social knowledge network, relied on the scrupulous assessment of the value of mortgaged assets and thus ended up granting loans only to aristocratic families or municipalities. The relationship between banks and notaries' credit activity was not one of exclusion, but rather of coexistence, complementarity, and later hybridization.

The effectiveness of the credit system rested on a thick and articulated credit network, which was elastic and, thanks to the decisive role of notaries, offered increasing returns on the accumulation and distribution of information, establishing a process of path-dependence that highly influenced the formation of Italy's post-unification 'financial identity'. In the middle of the nineteenth century, when Vienna asked for a voluntary loan from the ecclesiastical bodies of Lombardy-Venetia (after realizing that religious bodies and other similar institutions were endowed with 'the most conspicuous capital') it turned out that in Brescia the sum invested by these institutions in mortgage loans was over 9 million Austrian lire, complemented by over 23 million from private individuals. The competition within this effervescent mortgage business—centered on notarial credit networks, which put the forced savings of convent dowries or charitable endowments back into circulation—hindered formal lending institutions, like modern banks, from gaining a favorable position in the private lending market.

References

Primary Sources

Archivio dell'Ospedale Maggiore, Milano, Causa Pia Macchi, Macchi 41, 1 giugno 1778.

Archivio di Stato di Milano, Rubrica notarile (Rn.): Rn. 1712; Rn. 3775; Rn. 2326; Rn. 2326; Rn. 3775; Rn. 49789; Rn. 475; Rn. 50096; Rn. 311; Rn. 295; Rn. 50236; Rn. 49730; Rn. 50392; Rn. 873; Rn. 884; Rn.866; Rn. 48944; Rn. 49.661; Rn. 3513; Rn. 3516; Rn.3529 Rn. 542; Rn. 543; Rn. 544, Rn. 545, Rn. 546, Rn. 547, Rn. 548, Rn. 549, Rn. 550, Rn. 551, Rn. 552, Rn. 553, Rn. 554, Rn. 555, Rn. 49.205; Rn. 49.206; Rn. 49.207; Rn. 49.208; Rn. 542, 543;

Archivio di Stato di Pavia, deed: n. 4961/7035; 925; n. 991; n. 1090; n. 1145; n. 1148; n. 1201; n. 1336; n. 1452.

Printed Primary Material

Bruschetti Giuseppe, *Storia dei progetti e delle opere per l'irrigazione del milanese* (Lugano, 1834).

Cattaneo Carlo, *Notizie Naturali e Civili sulla Lombardia* (Milano 1844).

Jacini Stefano, *La proprietà fondiaria e le popolazioni agricole in Lombardia* (Milano, 1854).

Secondary Sources

Ago, Renata. 1998. *Economia barocca. Roma nel Seicento*, Donzelli, Rome.

Alfani, Guido. 2013. Plague in seventeenth-century Europe and the decline of Italy: An epidemiological hypothesis. *European Review of Economic History* 17: 408–430.

Alonzi, Luigi. 2012. Economia e finanza nell'Italia moderna. Rendite e forme di censo (secoli XV-XX), Carocci, Rome.

Bellavitis, Anna. 2012. Dare credito, fiducia e responsabilità alle donne (Venezia, secolo XVI). In *Dare credito alle donne. Presenze femminili nell'economia tra medioevo ed età moderna*, edited by Giovanna Petti Balbi and Paola Guglielmotti, 259–267, Centro Studi Renato Bordone sui Lombardi, Asti.

Benzi, Michele, Ernesto Estrada, and Christine Klymko. 2013. Ranking hubs and authorities using matrix functions. *Linear Algebra and its Applications* 438 (5): 2447–2474.

Bertini, Fabio. 1989. *Nobiltà e finanza tra '700 e '800. Debito e affari a Firenze nell'età napoleonica*, Centro Editoriale Toscano, Firenze.

Bianchi, Marco. 1978. Le entrate e le spese dell'amministrazione centrale e delle province dello Stato di Milano nella seconda metà del Settecento. *Archivio Storico Lombardo* 10 (4): 174–196.

Bigo, Robert. 1947. *Les banques françaises au cours du XIXe siècle*, Libraire du Recueil Sirey, Paris.

Bonoldi, Andrea. 1999. *La fiera e il dazio: economia e politica commerciale nel Tirolo del secondo Settecento*, Società Studi Trentini, Trento.

Borelli, Giorgio. 1983. Teoria e prassi dell'attività di prestito nei domini della Repubblica veneta al cadere del Settecento. *Economia e storia* 3: 377–387.

Caizzi, Bruno. 1986. *Industria, commercio e banca in Lombardia nel XVIII secolo*, Banca Commerciale Italiana, Milano.

De Luca, Giuseppe and Angelo Moioli. 2008. Il potere del credito. Reti e istituzioni in Italia centro-settentrionale fra età moderna e decenni preunitari. In *Storia d'Italia*, Annali 23, 'La Banca', edited by Alberto Cova, Salvatore La Francesca, Angelo Moioli, Claudio Bermond, 212–255, Einaudi, Torino.

De Luca, Giuseppe, and Marcella Lorenzini. 2013. A taxonomy of infrastructure financing in Europe on the long run (12th-18th century). *Entreprises et histoire* 70 (1): 10–36.

De Luca, Giuseppe and Marcella Lorenzini. 2018. Not only land: mortgage credit in central-northern Italy in the sixteenth and seventeenth centuries. In *Land and Credit: Mortgages in the Medieval and Early Modern European Countryside*, edited by Chris Briggs and Jaco Zuijderduijn, 181–204, Palgrave, Cham.

De Luca, Giuseppe. 2013. Informal Credit and Economic Modernization in Milan (1802–1840). *The Journal of European Economic History* 52: 211–234.

De Maddalena, Aldo. 1974. *Prezzi e mercedi a Milano dal 1701 al 1860*, Banca Commerciale Italiana, Milano.

Dermineur, Elise. 2019. Peer-to-peer lending in pre-industrial France. *Financial History Review* 26 (3): 359–388.

Dermineur, Elise. 2014. Single Women and the Rural Credit Market in Eighteenth-Century France. *Journal of Social History* 48 (1): 175–199.

Dermineur, Elise. 2009. Female Peasants, Patriarchy and the Credit Market in Eighteenth-Century France. *Proceedings of the Western Society for French History* 37: 61–84.

Fantini, Ilenia. 2019. Notai e reti creditizie a Forlì nel primo Ottocento. *Romagna, arte e storia* 113: 61–84.

Felloni, Giuseppe. 2008. Dall'Italia all'Europa: il primato della finanza italiana dal Medioevo alla prima età moderna. In *Storia d'Italia*, Annali 23, 'La Banca', edited by Alberto Cova, Salvatore La Francesca, Angelo Moioli, and Claudio Bermond, 93–149, Einaudi, Torino.

Fornasari, Massimo. 2008. Istituzioni, professionisti, privati: le reti di credito nella Bologna moderna. In *Storia di Bologna, tome III, 'Bologna nell'età moderna'*, edited by Adriano Prosperi and Paolo Prodi, 791–855, Bononia University Press, Bologna.

Gandolfi, Claudio. 2017. Acqua e irrigazione per nutrire il pianeta. la realtà della pianura padana lombarda. In *Istituto Lombardo, Accademia di Scienze e Lettere - Incontri di Studio*, 51–66.

Gaulin, Jean Louis and François Menant. 1998. Crédit rural et Endettement Paysan dans l'Italie communale. In *Endettement Paysan et Crédit Rural dans l'Europe médiévale et moderne*, edited by Maurice Berthe, 1–22, Presses Universitaires du Midi, Toulose.

Gianelli, Giulio. 1984. La riforma monetaria di Maria Teresa. In *La Zecca di Milano*, edited by Giovanni Gorini, Società Numismatica Italiana, Milano.

Giovannini, Carla. 1990. *La presenza e l'attività del Monte nei secoli XVII e XVIII*. In *Il Sacro Monte di Pietà di Faenza. Cinque secoli di storia e società 1491–1991*, edited by Giuseppe Adani, Banca del Monte e Cassa di Risparmio, Faenza.

Greppi, Emanuele, Alessando Giulini (eds). 1923. *Carteggio di Pietro e Alessandro Verri*, Cogliati, Milano.

Hoffman, Philip T., Gilles Postel-Vinay, and Jean-Laurent. Rosenthal. 1998. What do Notaries do? Overcoming Asymmetric Information in Financial Markets: The Case of Paris, 1751. *Journal of Institutional and Theoretical Economics* 154 (3): 499–530.

Hoffman, Philip T., Gilles Postel-Vinay, Jean-Laurent Rosenthal. 2019. *Dark Matter Credit: The Development of Peer-to-Peer Lending and Banking in France*, Princeton University Press, Princeton and Oxford.

Hoffman, Philip T., Gilles Postel-Vinay, Jean-Laurent Rosenthal. 2000. *Priceless Markets. The Political Economy of Credit in Paris, 1660–1870*, University of Chicago Press, Chicago.

Kleinberg, Jon M. 1999. Hubs, authorities, and communities. *ACM Computing Surveys* 31 (4): 1–3.

Lanaro, Paola, Gian Maria Varanini. 2009. Funzioni economiche della dote nell'Italia centro-settentrionale (tardo medioevo/inizio età moderna). In

La famiglia nell'economia europea, secc. XIII – XVIII, edited by Simona Cavaciocchi, 81–102, Firenze University Press, Florence.

Landi, Fiorenzo. 2005. *Storia economica del clero in Europa. Secoli XV-XIX*, Carocci, Roma.

Lemercier, Claire, and Francesca Trivellato. 2022. 1751 and Thereabout: A Quantitative and Comparative Approach to Notarial Records. *Social Science History* 46: 555–583.

Levati, Stefano. 1997. *La nobiltà del lavoro. Negozianti e banchieri a Milano tra Ancien Régime e Restaurazione*, FrancoAngeli, Milano.

Levy, Juliette. 2012. *The Making of a Market: Credit, Henequen, and Notaries in Yucatan, 1850–1900*, Penn State University Press, University Park, PA.

Licini, Stefania. 2011. Assessing female wealth in nineteenth century Milan, Italy. *Accounting History* 16 (1): 35–54.

Lorenzini, Marcella. 2018. Borrowing and lending money in Alpine areas during the eighteenth century: Trento and Rovereto compared. In *Financing in Europe: Evolution, coexistence and complementarity of lending practices from the Middle Ages to Modern Times*, edited by Marcella Lorenzini, Cinzia Lorandini and D'Maris Coffman, 105–132, Palgrave, New York.

Lorenzini, Marcella. 2021. The Other Side of Banking. Private Lending and the Role of Women in Early Modern Italy. In *Change and Transformation of Premodern Credit Markets. The Importance of Small-Scale Credits*, edited by Stephan Nicolussi-Köhler, 177–197, Heidelberg University Publishing, Heidelberg.

Lorenzini, Marcella. 2016. *Credito e notai.* Capitali per l'economia veronese del secondo Seicento, Il Mulino, Bologna.

Moioli, Angelo. 1993. Il commercio serico lombardo nella prima metà dell'Ottocento. In *La seta in Europa sec.* XII-XX, edited by Simona Cavaciocchi, 723–739, Le Monnier, Florence.

Montanari, Daniele (ed.). 1999. *Monti di Pietà e presenza ebraica in Italia (secoli XV-XVIII)*, Bulzoni, Roma.

Nuccio ,Oscar. 2004. Chiesa e denaro dal XVI al XVIII secolo. In *Chiesa e denaro tra Cinquecento e Settecento. Possesso, uso, imagine*, edited by Ugo Dovere, 11–85, San Paolo Edizioni, Cinisello Balsamo.

Pagani, Gabriele. 2017. *Storie d'acqua. Contado di Milano: dalla formazione della pianura alla civiltà dei fontanili e dei navigli Lombardi*, Pagani Edlin, Milano.

Pecorari, Paolo. 1998. Orientamenti della cultura cattolica sul prestito a interesse nel secolo XIX. *Chiesa, usura e debito estero. Supplemento a «Scienze sociali e dottrina sociale della Chiesa*, 2, 85–87.

Pichler, Rupert. 2001. *L'economia lombarda e l'Austria: politica commerciale e sviluppo industriale 1815–1859*, FrancoAngeli, Milan.

Piluso, Giandomenico. 1999. *L'arte dei banchieri. Moneta e credito a Milano da Napoleone all'Unità*, FrancoAngeli, Milan.

Pompermaier, Matteo. 2022. *L'économie du 'mouchoir': crédit et microcrédit à Venise au XVIIIe siècle*, Collection de l'École française de Rome, Rome.

Romani, Mario. 1977. *Aspetti e problemi di storia economica lombarda nei secoli XVIII e XIX*, Vita e Pensiero, Milan.

Segre, Luciano. 1992. Bonifica e irrigazione in Lombardia nel secolo XIX: Lo schema di base. *Rivista di Storia dell'Agricoltura* 32 (1): 174–181.

Shaw, James. 2018. Women, credit and dowry in early modern Italy. In *Women and Credit in Preindustrial Europe*, edited by Elise Dermineur, 173–202, Brepols, Turnhout.

Tucci, Ugo. 1986. Monete e riforme monetarie nell'Italia del Settecento. *Rivista storica italiana* 93 (1): 78–119.

Uggé, Albino. 1956. Le entrate del Regno lombardo-veneto dal 1840 al 1864. *Archivio economico dell'unificazione italiana* 1: 1–15.

Vismara, Paola. 2009. *Questioni di interesse. La Chiesa e il denaro inn età moderna*, Mondadori, Milano.

Wasserman, Martin. 2014. 'Diseño institucional, prácticas y crédito notarial en Buenos Aires durante la primera mitad del siglo XVII. *Investigaciones de Historia Económica - Economic History Research* 10 (1): 1–12.

Zaninelli, S. 1986. Un capitolo centrale del riordino dei tributi indiretti dello Stato di Milano nella seconda metà del '700: la "redenzione delle regalie". In *Studi in onore di Antonio Petino*, tome I, 'Momenti e problem di storia economica.

Zimolo, Giulio Cesare. 1960. Canali e navigazione interna nell'età moderna. *Storia di Milano*, 24.

CHAPTER 12

Looking for Dark Matter Credit: Exploring Notarial Credit Markets in Antwerp and Its Surroundings ca. 1835

Ruben Peeters and Rogier van Kooten

1 Introduction

Until the twentieth century, notarial credit markets provided large amounts of investment capital to firms and households. However, there seem to have been major differences in the importance of these markets

R. Peeters (✉) · R. van Kooten
University of Antwerp, Antwerp, Belgium
e-mail: Ruben.Peeters@uantwerpen.be

R. van Kooten
Utrecht University, Utrecht, The Netherlands

E. M. Dermineur and M. Pompermaier (eds.), *Credit Networks in The Preindustrial World*, Palgrave Studies in the History of Finance,
https://doi.org/10.1007/978-3-031-67117-3_12

across time periods and geographical.[1] Recently, Lemercier and Trivellato demonstrated that the amount and proportion of notarial credit registration strongly differed between cities in France and Italy in the eighteenth century.[2] In France, notarial credit was extremely important, dominating the mortgage credit market until the end of the nineteenth century.[3] In the Low Countries, notarial credit markets at the end of the eighteenth century were smaller yet economically relevant and remained widely present well into the twentieth century.[4]

Apart from France we know little about the structure, functioning, and flows of notarial credit, let alone being able to document historical evolutions and geographical differences. Especially in the Low Countries, we have a clear knowledge gap about the (dis)continuities of notarial credit markets between the end of the early modern era and the start of the twentieth century.[5] Therefore, by selecting a well-documented Low Countries case study, Antwerp and its surroundings in the nineteenth century, the knife cuts both ways.

[1] Chris Briggs and Jaco Zuijderduijn (eds.), *Land and Credit* (Springer International Publishing, 2018); Luis Zegarra, 'Information Asymmetries, Personal Connections and Private Credit. Evidence from Lima, Peru, 1825–1865', in: *Economic History Society Working Papers* (2018); Juliette Levy, *The Making of a Market: Credit, Henequen, and Notaries in Yucatán, 1850–1900* (Penn State University Press, 2012).

[2] Claire Lemercier and Francesca Trivellato, '1751 and Thereabout: A Quantitative and Comparative Approach to Notarial Records' in: *Social Science History* 46:3 (2022), 555–583, https://doi.org/10.1017/ssh.2022.8.

[3] Philip T. Hoffman, Gilles Postel-Vinay and Jean-Laurent Rosenthal, *Priceless Markets: The Political Economy of Credit in Paris, 1660–1870* (The University of Chicago Press, 2001); Philip T Hoffman, Gilles Postel-Vinay and Jean-Laurent Rosenthal, *Dark Matter Credit: The Development of Peer-to-Peer Lending and Banking in France* (Princeton University Press, 2019).

[4] Oscar Gelderblom, Mark Hup, and Joost Jonker, 'Public Functions, Private Markets: Credit Registration by Aldermen and Notaries in the Low Countries, 1500–1800', in: Marcella Lorenzini, Cinzia Lorandini, and D'Maris Coffman (eds.), *Financing in Europe. Evolution, Coexistence and Complementarity of Lending Practices from the Middle Ages to Modern Time* (Palgrave Macmillan, 2018), 163–94; Oscar Gelderblom et al., 'Exploring Modern Bank Penetration: Evidence from the Early 20th-Century Netherlands', in: *Economic History Review* 76 (2023): 892–916.

[5] Gelderblom, Hup, and Jonker, 'Public Functions, Private Markets'; Gelderblom et al., 'Exploring Modern Bank Penetration: Evidence from the Early 20th-Century Netherlands'; Fred Stevens, *Revolutie en notariaat: Antwerpen 1794–1814* (Koninklijke Van Gorcum bv, 1994).

According to Hoffman, Postel-Vinay and Rosenthal one of the major historiographical gaps to be filled is the explanation of the wide variation of credit markets in size, both in frequency of lending and the loan amounts, and its evolution in time and space.[6] Apart from a relationship between size of the market, population density, and wealth, they hypothesize a strong effect of the *distribution* of wealth within the population on market participation. Wealthy people usually had more property (movable and immovable) that could serve as collateral and therefore a much stronger position on the credit market. In very unequal societies, the elite domination would barely leave room for the participation of other social groups (laboring and middle classes) or demand from the (rural) surroundings. It would lead to strong competition between wealthy members of the elite with relatively few loans but of very large sums. This would also mean that the opposite is true in more egalitarian societies: the market share of non-elite social groups should be bigger, its spatial reach larger, and loan amounts on average should be smaller. Our research aims to contribute to answering the question of how inequality in income and especially in wealth relate to the size and social and geographical structure of credit markets. In the current chapter, we analyze the Antwerp notarial credit market around 1835 as a starting point of a longer-term case study that will, in the end, encompass the entire nineteenth century, different types of credit and different geographical scales. Where possible we compare our results with the outcome of other research, especially with France and elsewhere in the Low Countries.

In 1835, Belgium was a new nation state whose independence was still being contested. Antwerp, which was a medium-size and impoverished textile-based industrial city in 1800, would grow into one of Europe's largest ports already by 1840 and would continue to grow rapidly until the end of the century.[7] Antwerp at that time, embodied both premodern and modern characteristics. On the one hand, there was continuity from the eighteenth century, after all, notaries continued to exist. On the other hand, the French revolutionary regime had left its mark by institutional reorganization of the notarial profession and the abolishment of

[6] Hoffman, Postel-Vinay, and Rosenthal, *Dark Matter Credit*, there 232–233.

[7] Catharina Lis, *Social Change and the Laboring Poor: Antwerp, 1770–1860* (Yale University Press, 1986); Anne Winter, *Migrants and Urban Change: Newcomers to Antwerp, 1760–1860*, (Pickering & Chatto, 2009).

the alderman's bench. Notaries were solely at the center of (mortgage) credit registration.[8] At the same time, despite its sixteenth-century fortification and largely unchanged rural surroundings in 1835, the city was undergoing significant political, economic, and social changes. Antwerp during the nineteenth century was experiencing an economic, commercial, and financial push with the establishment of new banks that may have made notarial credit redundant earlier than in France. This push had severe social consequences, particularly concerning the labor market and employment.[9] Several authors have claimed that the rapid urbanization leads to equally rapid rising inequality, residential segregation, and poverty. At the same time, Antwerp's rural hinterland, which was mostly unaltered since the early modern period, experienced a large outflow of migrants to the city from the 1820s and 30s on.[10] Following Hoffman et al., rapid urbanization and strong demographic growth may have caused steep rising social inequality, a more dominant position of elites on notarial credit markets at the expense of other social groups and less hinterland interaction.

In 1835, there was a clear demographic urban–rural divide.[11] The city of Antwerp with its 77,000 inhabitants served as the focal point for the region. The surrounding villages, on the other hand, in majority had populations between 1,000 and 2,000 residents. Second-tier urban centers of Mechelen, Lier, and Turnhout with around 15,000 inhabitants each were located 15 to 40 kilometers away. Our data allow us to compare Antwerp and rural notarial credit networks, their size, interest rates, major participants, and also unravel their interactions.

[8] Stevens, *Revolutie en notariaat.*

[9] Lis, *Social Change and the Laboring Poor.*; Winter, *Migrants and Urban Change.*

[10] Winter, *Migrants and Urban Change.*

[11] We define 'rural' as all municipalities not being Antwerp within the NOTANT dataset. Most rural municipalities in the NOTANT dataset typically have between 1000 and 2000 inhabitants (village and surrounding countryside). Municipalities of second-tier centers Mechelen, Lier and Turnhout were not included in the NOTANT dataset. We realize that this classification is subjective and may be somewhat biased by the relatively high population density and level of urbanization in the Low Countries. In other countries or regions places with 1000 to 2000 inhabitants may be called 'towns' and not considered rural.

This contribution discusses the results for the starting point and first sample period of our research period: 1833–1837.[12] Section 2 presents our dataset. We then estimate the size of the market and analyze if there were differences between Antwerp and rural markets in terms of size, types of loans and conditions (Sect. 3). In Sect. 4 we discuss the social and spatial composition of debtors and creditors participating in these markets and in Sect. 5 we reconstruct and analyze the flows of credit within the city of Antwerp and between different localities using proximity and social network analysis. Finally, we look at how notaries were positioned in these intermunicipal networks (Sect. 6).

2 The Dataset

We use a newly constructed dataset of summaries of notarized deeds, gathered by the National Archive of Belgium (hereafter NOTANT dataset) and supplemented with extra information from the original deeds as well as extra selected notarial deeds gathered by our research team (hereafter ANCRED dataset).[13] Notarial registration has a long history in Western Europe and large groups of people used them for various purposes including land transactions and credit registration.[14] Our dataset captures around 40% of total notary registration in the province of Antwerp with near complete records of municipalities surrounding Antwerp, around a quarter of the Antwerp market, but none of the second-tier cities. Figure 1 shows where notaries resided in this period (gray or shaded areas), while the dots indicate those notaries included in the NOTANT dataset.

Between 1833 and 1837, the NOTANT dataset of notarial summaries lists 18,022 notarial registrations by 42 notaries in Antwerp and its surroundings. Of those contracts, 1,192 were credit transactions registered by 40 notaries (Appendix A.1). Two notaries did not register any credit transactions during this period. Since there was only one Antwerp

[12] The whole research period spans 1830–1900. We are preparing three more sample periods: 1846–1850, 1868–1872 and 1896–1900.

[13] More information about the project: https://search.arch.be/nl/zoeken-naar-personen/projecten/10-notant-nl.

[14] Briggs and Zuijderduijn, *Land and Credit*; Hoffman, Postel-Vinay, and Rosenthal, *Priceless Markets*; Hoffman, Postel-Vinay, and Rosenthal, *Dark Matter Credit*; Lemercier and Trivellato, '1751 and Thereabout'.

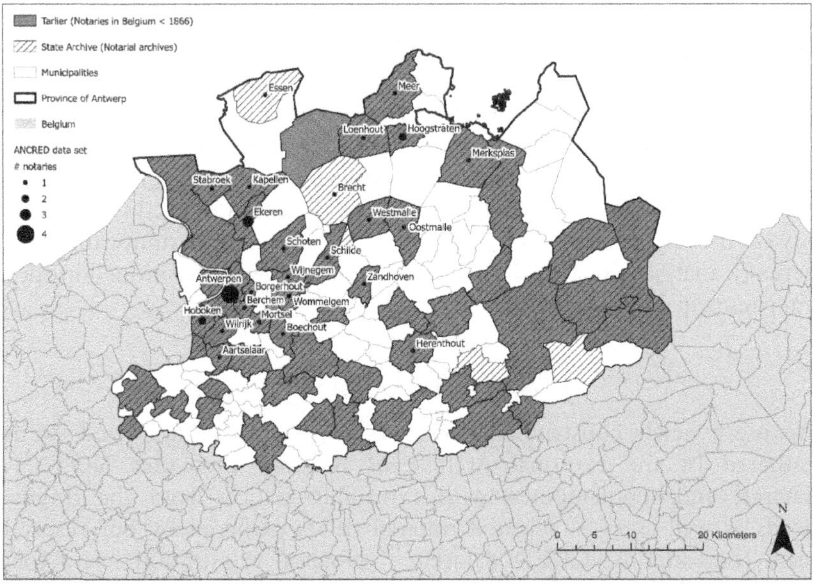

Fig. 1 Locations of notaries in the province of Antwerp and coverage in NOTANT, 1833–1837. Sources: Tarlier H., *Liste Alphabetique*, NOTANT

notary in the set, we gathered another 710 credit contracts from three additional Antwerp notaries. We transcribed all credit contracts from the archive into the ANCRED dataset. We have information on the type, size, price, and maturity of the loan, together with the name, profession, municipality of residence, and sex of the contractors. For those residing in Antwerp, we connected their names to the 1838 Ratinckx address book and real estate tax ledger for the city of Antwerp in 1834 to obtain professions, addresses, and estimates of the cadastral income of the real estate they inhabited. This allowed us to compose social and spatial profiles of the relevant Antwerp households. The source material thus made it possible to adopt both a regional (across-municipalities) and an intra-urban (within the city of Antwerp) perspective.

The NOTANT dataset allows us to go beyond cities and compare the registration practices of notaries in Antwerp and surrounding rural municipalities in 1835. Appendix A.1 shows that Antwerp and rural notaries registered different types of deeds. Sales of movables (mostly agricultural produce), registrations of wills, and allocations of property were more common with village notaries, while Antwerp notaries registered more cancelations of mortgages, powers of attorney, discharges, and copies of deeds. Both Antwerp and rural notaries registered credit contracts (including obligations, mortgages, and annuities), probates, public auctions, rental contracts, and sales of real estate in equal measure. Credit contracts and annuities together made up around 15% of notaries' total number of deeds, making it one of the most important types of activities for notaries.

3 Market Overview

Before we explore market participants and Antwerp—rural interaction, we discuss the macro characteristics of the notarial credit market in the Antwerp region and, where possible, compare these with France in the same period. We collected the deeds of credit transactions and gathered information on the loan sizes, maturities, interest rates, repayment conditions, and socio-geographic information about the contracting parties in our dataset. On the basis of this set, we estimated the size of the credit market between 1833 and 1837 (Table 1).

Consistent with what Hoffman et al. observed for France, the urban credit market was thicker than the rural one. The average amount of new credit registered through Antwerp notaries was much larger than through rural ones, even though there were around five rural notaries for every Antwerp one. On the other hand, the number of new loans per 100 inhabitants was only slightly higher in Antwerp. The average loan size registered by Antwerp notaries was twice that of loans in the countryside. Antwerp notaries thus registered fewer more loans but for larger amounts. Antwerp notaries also registered more loans per notary: on average one credit contract every 17 days compared to less than one contract per two months in the countryside. Nonetheless, the yearly amounts mobilized through Antwerp notaries appear rather small, around 3.4 million Belgian Francs annually. In comparison, the *Banque d'Anvers*, an offshoot of the Société Générale and the most important universal bank in Antwerp, provided 10 to 20 million francs in advances annually and an additional 5 million francs in 1834 through bill discounting and even 25 million

Table 1 Credit market estimate by rural and Antwerp notaries 1833–1837

	Rural Notaries	*Antwerp Notaries*
Average new loans per year (million BEF)[a]	0.24	3.41
Average credit stock (million BEF)	2.70	39.53
Credit stock as percent of provincial GDP	2.5%	36.8%
Yearly Number of Loans	148	355
Mean new loan size[b]	1,580	2,859
Nr of new loans per 100 inh. per year (extrapol)	0.31	0.46
Average nr of loans per notary per year	5.36	21.8

Sources: ANCRED, Tarlier H., *Liste Alphabetique*, Population data for extrapolations from LOKSTAT (UGent)

Note: Weighting happened on the level of the notary. Based on H. Tarlier H., *Liste Alphabetique*, *Liste alphabétique des notaires de Belgique depuis l'origine du notariat jusqu'en juillet 1864: supplém. jusqu'au 31 Décembre 1865* (Tarlier H. 1865), we know exactly how many notaries we are covering per municipality. Based on this we extrapolate the number of contracts and values

[a]The silver weight (and value) of the Belgian Franc was set to equal the French Franc by the law of 2 June 1832. See: Pierre Pringels, 'Le Franc Belge 1832–2001 Histoire et évolution des monnaies. Taux de change des valeurs européennes en 1832', *Annales du Cercle archéologique d'Enghien* 35 (2001), 143–182. The 1:1 exchange rate would continue until the dissolution of the Latin Monetary Union. Our BEF estimates are thus directly comparable to French values

[b]The annual wage of a rural worker around 1835 was approximately 300 BEF, of an industrial worker around 600 BEF and a public servant earned more or less 1350 BEF. See: Yves Segers, *Economische groei en levensstandaard. Particuliere consumptie en voedselgebruik in België, 1800–1913* (Leuven University Press, 2003)

francs in 1836 and 1837.[15] While substantial, bank credit showed large swings from year to year due to fluctuations in the underlying commercial transactions.

Bank credit was mostly short-term, with the standard bill of exchange maturing at around 100 days.[16] Given the short-term nature of these loans and the mechanics of calculating the stock of loans, the total outstanding amount of credit can be estimated to be around a quarter of the total yearly amount.[17] In 1833–1834 this was 2.3 to 4.8 million

[15] Karel Veraghtert, 'De Antwerpse Bankwereld en de Expansie van de Haven, 1820–1850', in: *Bank- en Financiewezen* 8, 9 (1980).

[16] B.S. Chlepner, *Belgian Banking and Banking Theory* (Brookings Institute, 1943), there 30.

[17] Following Hoffman, Postel-Vinay, and Rosenthal, *Dark Matter Credit*. We calculate the outstanding stock of loans by multiplying the value of the loan with its maturity. Because most bank debt had maturities of less than one year (promissory notes, bills of

francs, and even rose to around 12 million in 1835. Between 1833 and 1837, the average stock of bank credit by the *Banque d'Anvers* was 6.8 million francs. Conversely, we estimate the stock of outstanding notarial loans to have been six times larger at around 39.5 million BEF or nearly 37% of provincial GDP.[18] The outstanding amount of credit in Antwerp is notably higher than the estimate for France in 1840 where notarized debt to GDP stood at almost 30%.[19]

The credit transactions drawn up by notaries consist nearly exclusively of obligations (86% of total) and declarations of debt (12.5% of total). The median obligation and declaration of debt looked very similar in Antwerp and rural markets: a ten-year loan at 4.5% annually.

Underlying the median, the loans registered by Antwerp and rural notaries varied in price and maturity (Figs. 2 and 3). The maturities in rural contracts were much more diverse, ranging from a few months to 60 years, while Antwerp loans were mostly ten-year contracts or shorter.

Rural and Antwerp loans came roughly at three prices, costing 4, 4.5 or 5%, with some exceptions costing less, while Antwerp contracts had almost no deviation from the norm (Fig. 3). This seems to have been common in other places as well. Mortgages in the arrondissement of Leuven in 1848 cost 4, 4.5, or 5%, with the majority at 5%.[20] The

exchange, and advances), the stock of debt must have been lower than the amount of new loans. In the case of notarial debt contracts, where we do not have the maturity, we multiply them by one to come up with a conservative estimate of the total stock.

[18] Hoffman, Postel-Vinay, and Rosenthal, *Dark Matter Credit* provide point estimates of the notarial credit market in France, extrapolating the loan stock from single years. This is based on the assumption that the credit market is in equilibrium. We opt for the average of our sample period. This makes our estimates for stock more robust to outlier years, as the early 1830s saw some turbulence with the Belgian independence, revival of the Antwerp port and economic crisis of 1838.

[19] Philip T. Hoffman, Gilles Postel-Vinay, and Jean Laurent Rosenthal, 'Entry, Information, and Financial Development: A Century of Competition between French Banks and Notaries', in: *Explorations in Economic History* 55:1 (2015), there 3; Hoffman, Postel-Vinay, and Rosenthal, *Dark Matter Credit* hypothesize that the French Revolution and inflationary period greatly reduced the stock of credit. Data on the number of credit contracts in Antwerp between 1785 and 1814 indicate that Belgian notarial markets were as severely, if not more severely hit by the turmoil of the French and Brabant/Liege revolutions, and French occupation, but also recovered quickly. See: NOTANT and Stevens, *Revolutie en Notariaat*.

[20] Pierre Têcheur, 'Le crédit immobilier en Belgique de 1802 à 1954', in: *Bulletin de l'Institut de recherches économiques et sociales* 23:2 (1957), there 107, https://doi.org/10.1017/S1373971900010234.

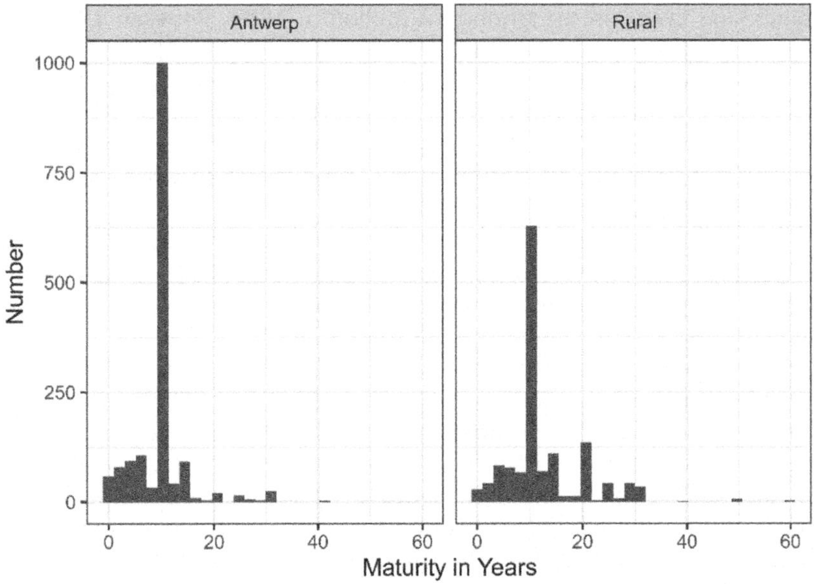

Fig. 2 Maturity of credit contracts by Antwerp and rural notaries, 1833–1837 (Source ANCRED)

trimodal distribution of prices contrasts with the single price (5%) market that Hoffman et al. encountered in France in the same period. They explained the existence of a single price through incentives for notaries to not differentiate between their referrals and thus mix excellent and good debtors. Otherwise, creditors would prefer to only contract with excellent debtors and not with good debtors for a slightly higher return but also higher risk. In the long term this would cost the notary business as the overall number of referrals and resulting contracts would go down.[21] It was the introduction of the *Hypothèque* (Mortgage) Registers in France which made knowledge on existing mortgages and property registration much more easily accessible since the 1880s, combined with

[21] For a full explanation of the model and the reasoning see Hoffman, Postel-Vinay, and Rosenthal, *Dark Matter Credit*, there 197–204.

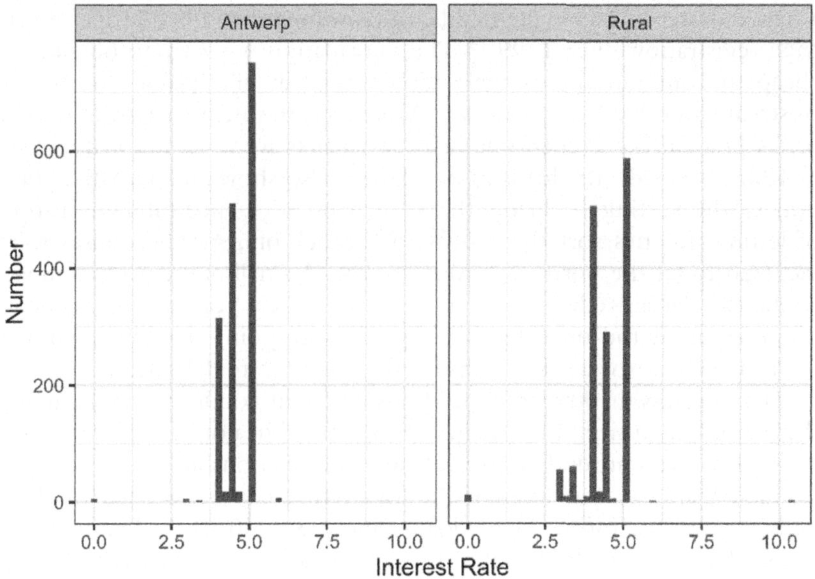

Fig. 3 Interest rates in credit contracts by Antwerp and rural notaries, 1833–1837 (Source ANCRED)

the introduction of the *Crédit Foncier* in 1852 that increased the competition between creditors and allowed excellent debtors to cheaply prove their worth. As a result, the equilibrium unraveled.[22]

Data for Leuven shows that a 5% single price market for mortgages existed in 1822 but had dissolved by 1848 into a triple price market (4, 4.5, and 5%) which persisted until 1888.[23] We do not have data for 1822 for Antwerp, but given the similar political and institutional history, Antwerp most likely followed the same pattern. Nonetheless, the hypotheses posited for the breakdown of the single price equilibrium in France are only partially supported by our Antwerp data. Belgium finished

[22] Hoffman, Postel-Vinay, and Rosenthal, *Dark Matter Credit*, there 208.

[23] Têcheur, 'Le crédit immobilier', there 107.

a new cadaster in 1835 (the middle of our sample) and had proper mortgage registration since 1799.[24] The information was easy to obtain and cheap to communicate as the region was easily traversable due to the Austrian stone roads and canals.[25] Moreover, the Belgian *Crédit Foncier* banks predate the French one, and two banks were operational already in 1835.[26] Finally, the loans in our dataset also show an alternative solution to the sorting problems the French notaries encountered. Instead of letting notaries sort the quality of the debtors, specific clauses were included to let the borrower reveal its type. A small number of contracts contained clauses reducing the interest rates in case of prompt payment, often lowering the price by half a percentage point. Perhaps contracts with such clauses were drawn up for the second-rate debtors.

In a priceless market, creditors adjusted credit conditions by changing the maturity and size of the loan.[27] This seemed to not have played much in rural markets around Antwerp where the relationship between maturity and loan size was limited. But Antwerp creditors seemed to allow higher maturities for very large loans (above 30,000 BEF). Figure 4 also shows that loans made through Antwerp notaries were relatively shorter. Most likely this is related to the higher wages and earnings potential of city dwellers. However, Antwerp was no single price market and creditors adjusted prices to loan values and maturities. Loans with higher maturities, which were mostly very large loans, were cheaper on average (Fig. 5). For rural loans there does not seem to be a relationship between prices and maturities, but overall, the interest rates in the city were higher than in rural markets.

4 Market Participants

Now that we have presented the macro characteristics of the Antwerp notarial credit markets, we turn to its key players: the credit contractors. Who were the debtors and creditors in the notarial credit market and how

[24] Pieter De Reu, *Kopen en verkopen van vastgoed (1795 tot heden)*, *Zoekwijzers*, vol. 37 (Algemeen Rijksarchief, 2012), http://hdl.handle.net/1854/LU-3071901.

[25] Bruno Blondé, 'At the Cradle of the Transport Revolution? Paved Roads, Traffic Flows and Economic Development in Eighteenth-Century Brabant', in: *The Journal of Transport History* 31:1 (2010): 89–111, https://doi.org/10.7227/TJTH.31.1.6.

[26] E. Royer, *Des institutions de Crédit foncier en Allemagne et en Belgique* (Paris, 1845).

[27] Hoffman, Postel-Vinay, and Rosenthal, *Dark Matter Credit*.

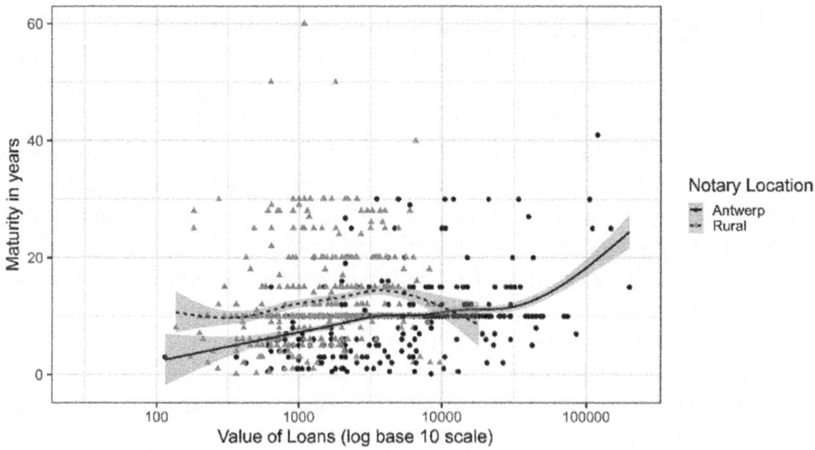

Fig. 4 Smooth estimation loan size vs maturity (Source ANCRED)

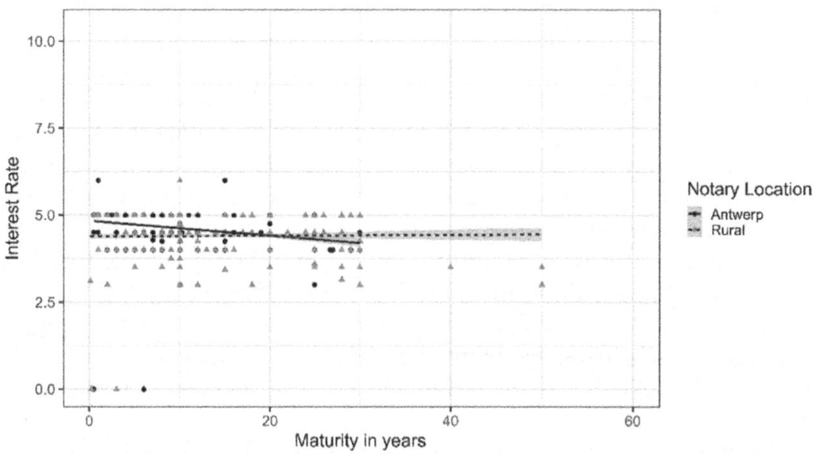

Fig. 5 Interest rate and maturity in years, loans by Antwerp and rural notaries (Source ANCRED)

did this relate to overall social and professional structures? What were the major differences between contractors in Antwerp and in the rural municipalities? To what extent was market participation in the 1830s a continuation of or break with the early modern period?

Our 1833–1837 ANCRED dataset contains summaries of 1,776 credit contracts of which 1,642 contracts involving 4,630 persons could be traced in the archive. To reconstruct social profiles in the rural market, we had to rely on occupations mentioned in the credit contracts. In the urban market, we were able to combine contractors with the cadastral income of their homes and enrich or complete occupational information with information from the 1838 Ratinckx address book (cfr. infra). The credit contracts and Ratinckx gave us the professions of 2,778 persons in total. In 2,311 cases (1,225 rural, 1,058 from Antwerp and 28 from other cities) debtor and creditor roles were clearly mentioned in the contracts. Occupations were divided into 20 sectors and 8 categories to allow for systematic comparison both within this and with earlier studies.

The rural market was, not surprisingly, dominated by creditors and debtors from the agricultural sector (almost 43% of all debtors and 24% as creditors) followed at some distance by landowners/rentiers (26% of the creditors) and occupations in the food and hospitality sector (15% debtors and 11% creditors) with a prominent role for innkeepers as creditors. Surprisingly, creditors from the financial and legal sectors were also relatively well represented (12% as creditors) in these rural networks. We found several rural notaries among them who were active on the credit market, mostly as creditors, but never officially acting for their own professional account providing direct debit or using their own office, which must have been prohibited by law. In all cases they used colleagues to notarize their loans, enabling themselves to participate in the credit market and possibly taking advantage of their beneficial information position.

The inner-city market was serviced by 16 notaries of which four were included in our sample. Apart from these 16 Antwerp notaries, some rural notaries drew up contracts with urban dwellers, but usually only when also rural contractors were involved. Between 1833 and 1837 they all together drew up 681 contracts that had at least one creditor or debtor based in Antwerp. 1,633 Antwerp contractors out of a total of ca. 4,630 (Antwerp and rural combined) appeared, sometimes more than once, in these contracts. Of those 1,633 contractors, we were able to match 1,456 names (in 641 contracts) with the primitive cadaster and Ratinckx address book using HGIS. In 1,027 cases creditor and debtor roles were clear. This enabled us to reconstruct professional and social class profiles (Tables 2 and 3, Appendix A.2 and A.3) and put creditors and debtors on the map (Fig. 6).

The inner-city credit network was strongly dominated by rentiers, financial specialists, wholesalers, manufacturers, and company directors (Appendix A.2 and A.3). Together they made up 66% of the creditors and 37% of the debtors. Not surprisingly, these groups, especially the rentiers, belonged to the wealthiest households in Antwerp. Within the

Table 2 Notarial credit and social class

Social class[a] (Cad. inc. BEF)	*Antwerp*		*Credit contractors*			
			Debtors		*Creditors*	
	N	*%*	*N*	*%*	*N*	*%*
Very poor < 88	2,736	26[a]	86	13[b]	40	7[c]
Poor 88–176	2,331	22[a]	97	15[b]	34	6[c]
Middle class 176–352	2,770	27[a]	207	31[b]	146	25[a]
Upper middle class 352–703	1,629	16[a]	148	22[b]	129	22[b]
Rich 703 >	943	9[a]	124	19[b]	243[c]	41[c]
Total	10,409	100	662	100	592	100

(Source ANCRED / GIStorical Antwerp-1830)

Note: Values in the same row and sub table not sharing the same subscript are significantly different at $p < 0.05$ in the two-sided test of equality for column proportions. There is a levelling bias in the total Antwerp figures because in poor quarters, houses were often inhabited by multiple households. The Antwerp Cadaster had 275 non-taxed plots. 7 contractors were connected with these plots. All were excluded from the analysis. Analysis based on contracts where creditors and debtors were clearly specified including contractors without profession

[a]Cadastral income in median classes: very poor: < ½ median, poor: ½ median–median, middle class: median-2 times median, rich: 2 times median-4 times median, very rich: > 4 times median. For more information on this classification see: Johan Dambruyne, *Corporatieve middengroepen. Aspiraties, relaties en transformaties in de 16de–eeuwse Gentse ambachtswereld*, Verhandelingen der Maatschappij voor Geschiedenis en Oudheidkunde te Gent, dl. 28, (Academia Press, 2002); Rogier van Kooten, 'Levelling Through Space? The Redistributive Capacity of Demographic Decline in Antwerp's Darkest Hour (1584–1586)', in: Bruno Blondé, Sam Geens, Hilde Greefs et al. (eds.), *Inequality and the City in the Low Countries (1200–2020)*, Studies in European Urban History (1100–1800), 50, (Brepols, 2020), https://doi.org/10.1484/M.SEUH-EB.5.119604

Table 3 Notarial credit and professional groups in Antwerp, seventeenth-nineteenth century

	Debtors				*Creditors*			
	1660–1780		*1833–1837*		*1660–1780*		*1833–1837*	
	N	*%*	*N*	*%*	*N*	*%*	*N*	*%*
Nobles and Officers	33	6_a	1	0_b	18	4_a	4	1_b
Clergy	36	6_a	1	0_b	119	24_a	10	2_b
Merchants and Bourgeois	101	18_a	214	45_b	156	31_a	330	60_b
Artisans and Masters	163	29_a	159	33_a	86	17_a	63	12_b
Professions and Services	137	24_a	93	19_a	106	21_a	136	25_a
Rural	93	17_a	6	1_b	12	2_a	0	0^1
Laborers	0	0^1	7	2_a	0	0^1	3	1_a
Total	563	100	481	100	497	100	546	100

(Source ANCRED/EURY/VIDI database / GIStorical Antwerp-1830/1838)
Note: Values in the same row and sub table not sharing the same subscript are significantly different at $p < 0.05$ in the two-sided test of equality for column proportions

Antwerp market these groups were also strongly overrepresented among the credit contractors compared to the overall professional structure: rentiers: 9% overall, financial specialists: less than 2% and wholesalers and manufacturers: 11% overall. As expected, agricultural professions (some horticulturists in the rural fringe) were hardly involved in inner-city credit relations and in case they were, it was predominantly as debtors.

On the other hand, although wholesalers, manufacturers, financial specialists, and rentiers dominated the credit market, the many different other occupational categories almost hid the relative importance of typical middle-class professions: retailers, specialized craftworkers, and professions in food and hospitality (e.g. bakers, butchers, innkeepers, etc.). Taken together these five professional groups represented more than 40% of all debtors and 18% of all creditors. They were therefore significant players in an otherwise very unequal city. Using a more aggregate professional classification by Gelderblom, Hup, and Jonker

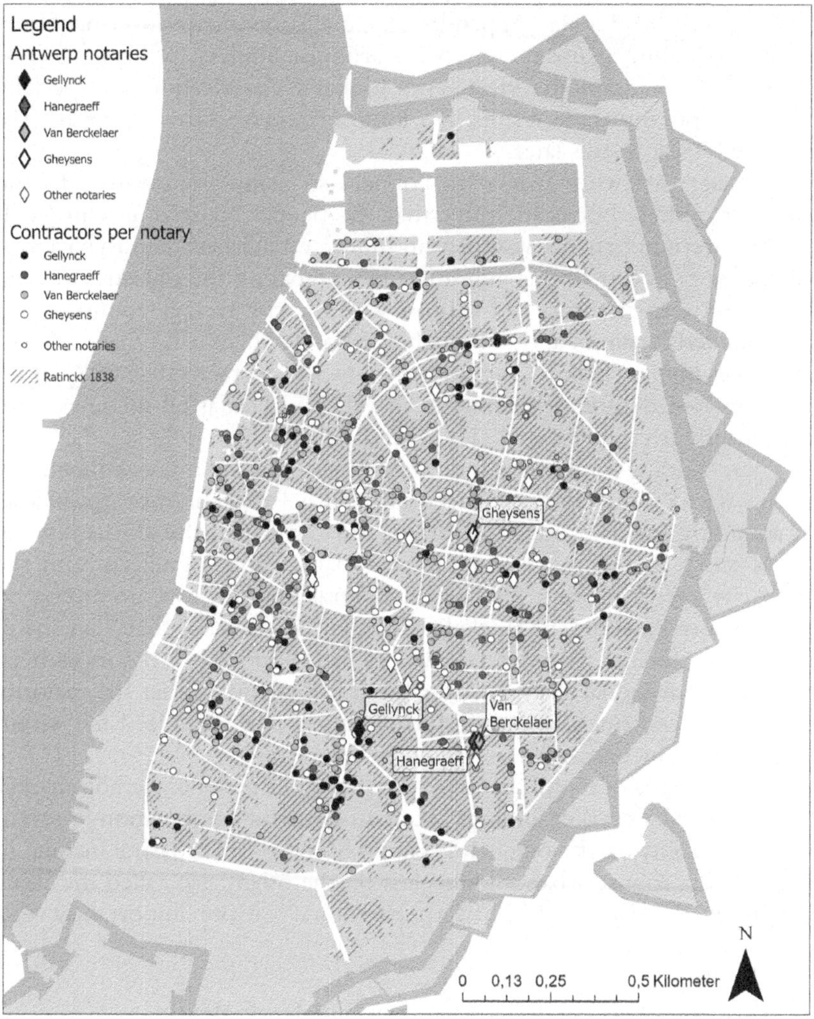

Fig. 6 Inner-city notarial credit contractors according to notary (1833–1837) (Source ANCRED/GIStorical Antwerp-1838)

underlines these results (Appendix A.3 compares merchants and bourgeoisie including many rentiers with artisans, masters, professions, and services).[28] Gelderblom, Hup, and Jonker's classification is especially helpful in placing these results in a long-term perspective (Table 3). We will come back to this later.

The fact that we managed to connect so many city dwellers to the Ratinckx address books indicates that the people registering loans with notaries were in general wealthier and more established than the average inhabitant.[29] A test of this indication by comparing the cadastral income of the Antwerp creditors and debtors with the city average confirms this: the matched creditors and debtors had cadastral income estimates almost two times higher (BEF 582) than the municipal average (BEF 298). Both creditors and debtors with middle to very high cadastral incomes were significantly overrepresented (Fig. 7 and Table 2).[30]

These findings are clear indications of the severe social inequality at the start of the nineteenth century, both between Antwerp and its surrounding municipalities and within Antwerp itself. But this is not the whole story. The Antwerp middle class participated significantly in the inner-city credit market: 29% of all contract parties can, according to their cadastral income, be labeled as middle class which is their 'fair share' considering their share in the overall city distribution (27%). A crosscheck with the professional sectors we analyzed earlier reveals that the majority of retailers, craftsmen, and food/hospitality specialists indeed fell within this cadastral income class.

The fair share of middle-class participation in the notarial credit market closely resembles earlier findings about an apparent combination of severe social inequality on the one hand (Gini 0.55 based on cadastral income in 1834) and a robust urban middle class on the other, also called the 'Low Countries Paradox' and 'Antwerp paradox'.[31] More importantly, this

[28] Gelderblom, Hup, and Jonker, 'Public Functions, Private Markets'.

[29] The Ratinckx address book lists inhabitants with their professional title. (Un)skilled laborers and unemployed are mostly absent.

[30] Unfortunately, we were not yet able to find cadastral or other fiscal sources to set up social class profiles for rural dwellers around 1830. The Popp cadaster only provides data from the late 1850 and early 1860's and not even for the city of Antwerp.

[31] Part of the paradox is that strong middling groups, while trying to maintain their distinctive social position, at the same time exclude lower social strata from entering their ranks and therefore contribute or even enhance existing social inequalities. See: Blondé,

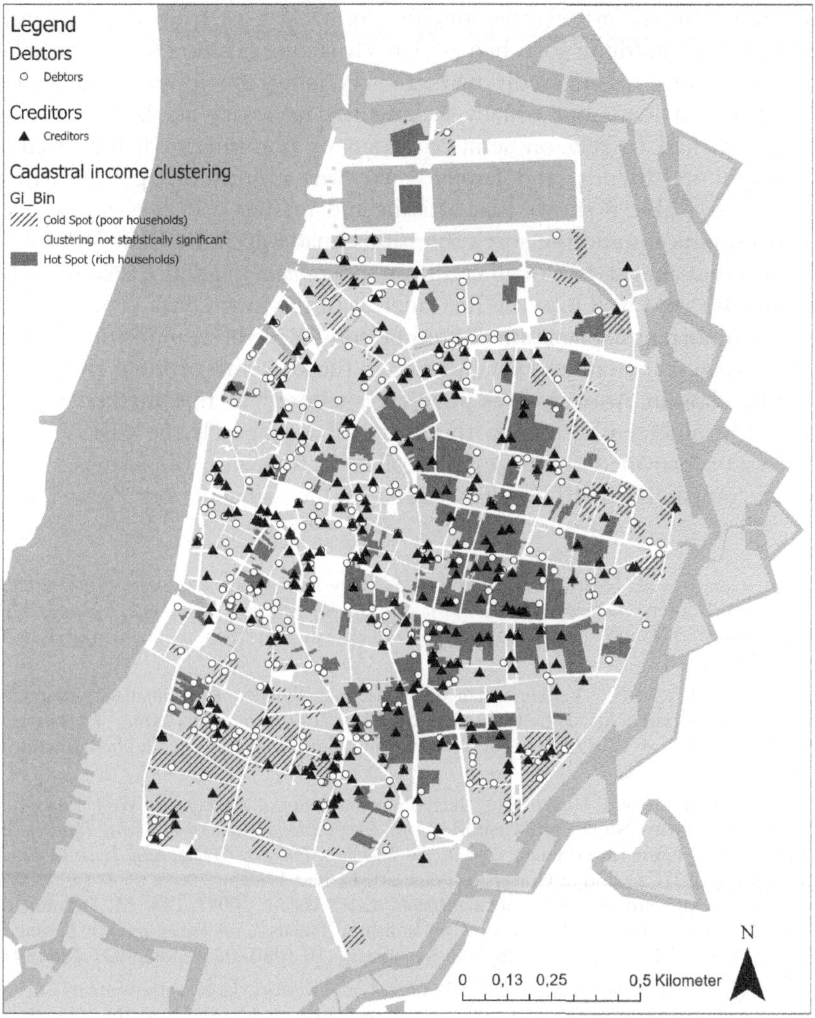

Fig. 7 Inner-city notarial credit contractors according to social class (1833–1837). Note: Hot spot analysis identifies statistically significant (with at least 90% confidence) spatial clusters of high values (hot spots) and low values (cold spots). In this case it indicates whether the observed spatial clustering of plots, based on their cadastral income estimation, is more pronounced than one would expect in a random distribution. More info: https://pro.arcgis.com/en/pro-app/latest/tool-reference/spatial-statistics/hot-spot-analysis.htm (Source ANCRED/GIStorical Antwerp-1830)

was not a nineteenth-century phenomenon. At least from the sixteenth century the 'middling sort' had a relatively strong position in the formally regulated intra-urban credit market.[32] People from lower social strata in need of a loan, but usually lacking the necessary assets to serve as collateral, had to rely on semi-regulated or non-intermediated circuits of neighbors, friends, and family.[33] We will address this point further in Sect. 5. Table 3 shows that artisans and masters and professions and services, typical middling sort professions, made up more than 50% of all debtors and almost 40% of all creditors *throughout* the entire seventeenth, eighteenth, and well into the first quarter of the nineteenth century.[34]

An important explanation should be sought in the composition of the intra-urban real estate market. Already in the sixteenth century, the urban middle class in Antwerp was strongly anchored in this market and in the early nineteenth century this was still very much the case.[35] This real estate provided the necessary collateral to secure the loans, a situation comparable with English towns in the same period.[36] As Hilde

Geens, Greefs et al. (eds.), *Inequality and the City in the Low Countries (1200–2020)*; Rogier van Kooten, *Antwerpen 1584: Oorlog en Ongelijkheid in de Stedelijke Ruimte*, PhD Thesis (Antwerp University, 2021), https://repository.uantwerpen.be/docman/irua/67071b/178741.pdf.

[32] Heidi Deneweth, 'A Fine Balance: Household Finance and Financial Strategies of Antwerp Households 17th-18th Century', in: *Tijdschrift Voor Sociaal Economische Geschiedenis*, no. 4 (2011), 15–43; Gelderblom, Hup, and Jonker, 'Public Functions, Private Markets'.

[33] Catharina Lis and Hugo Soly, 'Neighbourhood Social Change in West European Cities, Sixteenth to Nineteenth Centuries', in: *International Review of Social History* 38 (1993), 1–30; Laurence Fontaine, *The Moral Economy. Poverty, Credit, and Trust in Early Modern Europe*. (Cambridge University Press, 2014); Bart Willems, *Leven op de pof: krediet bij de Antwerpse middenstand in de achttiende eeuw* (Aksant, 2009); Elise M. Dermineur, 'The Evolution of Credit Networks in Pre-Industrial Finland', in: *Scandinavian Economic History Review* 70:1 (2022), 57–86, https://doi.org/10.1080/03585522.2021.1884594.

[34] It also shows that merchants and bourgeoisie (investors, large entrepreneurs) occupied a much stronger position on the formal regulated credit market in the nineteenth century than in the seventeenth and eighteenth century, a sign that Antwerp's resurrection as global port and trade hub was in full swing. The clergy was virtually absent in the nineteenth century.

[35] Van Kooten, *Antwerpen 1584*; Hilde Greefs, 'De Zakenelite en de Woningschaarste in Antwerpen tijdens de Eerste Helft van de Negentiende Eeuw: Een Terreinverkenning', in: *Bijdragen Tot de Geschiedenis* 87:1–2 (2004), 305–320.

[36] Geoffrey Crossick and Heinz-Gerhard Haupt, *The Petite Bourgeoisie in Europe, 1780–1914: Enterprise, Family and Independence*. (Routledge, 1998). The generalization of 'the'

Greefs found out, in early nineteenth-century Antwerp, large wholesalers, manufacturers, and rentiers were not interested in urban real estate but preferred, as had already been the case in the centuries before, to invest their surplus capital in rural properties and land. Urban housing only served as a sign of creditworthiness and status which could also be obtained by renting a representative property. This kept inhabitants flexible to relocate in case of economic hardship or better opportunities.[37] To the urban middle class on the other hand, this urban real estate provided the necessary collateral to keep access to (notarial) credit and maintain or expand their local businesses. Typically, 90% of the almost 4,500 private homeowners in 1834 owned four properties or less, a little more than 60% owned only one property. The professions of these homeowners revealed the relative importance of the middle-class property owner in the intra-urban real estate market.[38] These findings present an interesting starting point for further research into actors in nineteenth-century notarial credit markets, the interaction with real estate collateral and speculation behavior.

Apart from a divergent interest in the real estate market (compared to merchants and large entrepreneurs), urban middle-class professions in Antwerp provided all kinds of products and services to the urban elites and were therefore indispensable for the functioning of urban society. So, especially in large metropoles, where Hoffman, Postel-Vinay, and Rosenthal predominately point at the concentration of real estate property (and collateral) in the hands of a small group of urban landowners, we should not forget to look at the size, composition, and property ownership of the urban middle class and consequently their position on the notarial credit market. We have yet to find out to what extent the Antwerp middle class was able to maintain its position in the process of rapid urbanization that unfolded later in the century.

urban middle classes (petit bourgeoisie) as the main property owners has been nuanced by Michael Winstanley, pointing at differences between neighborhoods and between types of cities, e.g., cities with a strong mercantile background versus new industrial towns. See Michael J. Winstanley, 'Owners and Occupiers: Property, Politics and Middle - class Formation in Early Industrial Lancashire' in: Alan Kidd and David Nicholls (eds.), *The Making of the British Middle Class? Studies of Regional and Cultural Diversity since the Eighteenth Century* (Sutton Publishing, 1998), there 93–112.

[37] Greefs, 'De Zakenelite'.

[38] Greefs, 'De Zakenelite'; van Kooten, *Antwerpen 1584*.

5 Credit Flows Within and Between

In this section we have a closer look at the flows of credit within and between markets. How intertwined were Antwerp and rural circuits and why did people cross borders? At the start of the nineteenth century in France, Hoffman, Postel-Vinay, and Rosenthal found a clear positive relationship between the distance that borrowers or lenders had to travel and the size of the loan contracts.[39] This relationship held in small and large markets except in Paris and in the case of debtors also in some other large cities (>100,000 inhabitants). How did Antwerp and the surrounding municipalities fit in this picture? We compare both circuits, determine their interconnections, and address the possible impact of geographical distance on connectivity and loan sizes.

5.1 Within Antwerp

First we focus on the inner-city market of Antwerp. How important was distance within the walls of the city when it came to establishing credit relationships? From earlier research we know that in the case of non- or semi-regulated credit relations, social and spatial proximity played an important role in connecting parties and securing loans.[40] How important were these social and spatial ties in closing formal notarized loans within the city of Antwerp? Did distance play a role in the extent to which creditors and borrowers found each other within the urban walls? Was there, for example, a neighborhood effect similar to the semi-regulated or non-intermediated forms of credit such as consumer credit?[41]

The spatial integration of our Antwerp contractors with cadastral and Ratinckx data enabled us to look for spatial patterns and distance on the intra-urban level. Figures 6 and 7 in Sect. 4 already strongly suggested

[39] Hoffman, Postel-Vinay, and Rosenthal, *Dark Matter Credit*, there 91.

[40] Laurence Fontaine, 'Antonio and Shylock: Credit and Trust in France, c. 1680-c. 1780', in: *The Economic History Review* 54:1 (2001), 39–57; Willems, *Leven op de pof*. Bart Willems found that in eighteenth century Antwerp, based on estate inventories, two thirds of all credit relations were informal (semi-regulated or non-intermediated) and only one third of all loans was officially registered with a notary or alderman. Heidi Deneweth found, also based on inventories, an inverse relationship between wealth level and unregulated credit in seventeenth and eighteenth century Antwerp, see Deneweth, 'A Fine Balance'.

[41] Willems, *Leven op de pof*.

that the majority of the clients from our four sample notaries came from all parts of the city although there were, not surprisingly, concentrations of creditors in clusters of wealthy households close to the prestigious shopping streets and main thoroughfares (Fig. 8). Further analysis clearly exposed (the absence of) distinct spatial patterns. A proximity analysis revealed that in only in a minority of the credit relations the notary who drew up the contract was also the nearest to creditor(s) and/or debtor(s).[42] Neither did proximity matter much for the majority of debtors and creditors to find each other. More than half of all contractors lived more than half a kilometer apart.[43]

These findings confirm that *especially* in the case of formally regulated and notarized credit contracts, notaries were registering credit flows throughout the entire city. Because of residential segregation patterns, the

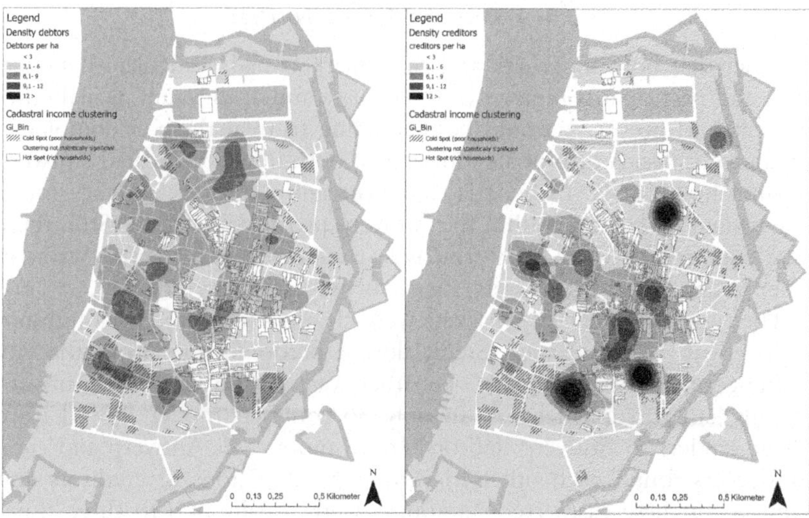

Fig. 8 Densities of creditors (left) and debtors (right) and residential segregation patterns (Source ANCRED/GIStorical Antwerp-1830/1838)

[42] ArcGIS Pro generated a Near Table for notaries and clients. More info: https://pro.arcgis.com/en/pro-app/2.9/tool-reference/analysis/generate-near-table.htm.

[43] ArcGIS Pro generated Origin–Destination Links between all contractors based on contract-id. More info: https://pro.arcgis.com/en/pro-app/latest/tool-reference/analysis/generate-origin-destination-links.htm.

predominantly wealthy Antwerp creditors and their mostly middle-class debtors did not necessarily live in the same neighborhood.[44] These findings supplement existing literature about informal non- or semi-regulated credit networks. As we saw earlier, especially in situations where the necessary collateral lacked and loan amounts were small, inner social (family, employers), and spatial (neighbors) circles could connect debtors and creditors.[45] But in other cases when real estate or financial assets served as collateral and loan amounts were usually large, neighbors, employers, or family members could not automatically fulfill these needs or did not want to without additional security. The same applied to creditors and debtors from larger social and spatial distances who stepped in. The Antwerp notaries positioned themselves in central and expensive locations to facilitate these credit flows throughout the entire city (and beyond).

5.2 *Between Municipalities*

The fact that both inner-city and rural markets had particular characteristics and participants hints at different uses and at different availabilities of capital. However, it would be misleading to treat them as completely separate entities. A fifth of all contracts in our sample connected Antwerp to rural households. In general, creditors and debtors were very much able to find each other within the Antwerp provincial borders. Still, there were contracts between Antwerpians or rural dwellers with contractors in other larger cities like Brussels, Liege, Bruges, and The Hague.

The rural and inner-city markets were clearly interrelated although not in an equal, balanced way. Credit flowed predominantly from the city to the countryside and hardly the other way: in 165 contracts Antwerp citizens lent to rural debtors. In only 36 contracts money flowed from village lenders to Antwerp debtors. In 25 more cases Antwerp and rural contractors found each other in various combinations of creditors and debtors. In these cases credit amounts were usually two to three times higher than usual in the countryside and much closer to the average and median Antwerp loan amounts (Table 4).

[44] Catharina Lis and Hugo Soly discussed rising residential segregation levels in the cause of the eighteenth and nineteenth century, fueled by a process of 'privatization'. The well-to-do distanced themselves both culturally and geographically from the lower classes (Lis and Soly, 'Neighbourhood and Social Change', there 18–19).

[45] Deneweth, 'A Fine Balance'.

Table 4 Geographic credit flows, 1833–1837

Credit flow	*# contracts*	*%*	*# persons*	*%*	*Median (BEF)*	*Average (BEF)*	*SD (BEF)*
Antwerp-Antwerp	312	30	963	31	4,300	10,640	1,156
Rural-Rural	458	44	1,303	42	1,270	1,735	83
City-City							
Antwerp-Other city[a]	7	1	23	1	7,000	9,431	4,030
Other city-Antwerp	7	1	20	1	4,233	7,806	3,552
Rural-City							
Antwerp-Rural	165	16	493	16	3,628	8,407	1,343
Rural-Antwerp	36	3	110	4	3,387	6,228	1,405
Other city-Rural	11	1	31	1	1,631	7,090	3,888
Rural-Other city	2	0	5	0	1,404	1,404	596
Mixed flows[b]							
Antwerp-Other city	8	1	36	1	20,000	67,798	31,396
Antwerp-Rural	25	2	118	4	1,200	3,598	978
Rural-Other city	0	0	0	0	0	0	0
Subtotal	*1,031*	*100*	*3,102*	*100*	*2,170*	*6,380*	
Missing[c]	90		158				
Total	1,121		3,260				

(Source ANCRED)

Note: Only contracts where creditors and debtors were clearly indicated are included. The share of Antwerp contracts compared to rural ones is relatively low because we included the contracts of only four (out of sixteen) Antwerp notaries in our data set. However, this should not severely impact average and median loan sizes

[a]Bergen op Zoom (NL), Bruges, Brussels, Calais (F), Dendermonde, Ghent, Leuven, Liège, Namen, Ostend, Paris (F), Lille (F), Roermond (NL), The Hague (NL), and Tilburg (NL)

[b]Mixed combinations of creditors and debtors for example: a creditor from Antwerp and one from Borgerhout lending to a debtor from Antwerp

[c]Location of creditor and/or debtor not mentioned in the contract

This suggests that the rural market was incapable of supplying the necessary sums and contracting parties found each other, sometimes in various combinations, on the Antwerp market. Still, although the city and countryside were strongly and unequally interrelated, the majority of the transactions and the bulk of the credit took place within separate city and rural circuits. The rural circuit exchanged relatively small credit amounts (compared to the inner-city circuit) among each other, although mostly over short distances and within the province of Antwerp.

The fact that just a small number of transactions was executed between persons in different municipalities or even countries (although borders were still very diffuse during the ongoing Belgian Revolution) suggests that creditors and debtors were able to find each other within a reasonable distance of a day trip. The average distance was about 8 kilometers for most loan sizes and even in villages, debtors, and creditors came from the same municipality in 40% of all credit contracts. In Antwerp, 60% of all credit contracts could be closed between local inhabitants, but for the largest loans (above 30,000 BEF). Antverpians had to travel much further to other cities to find a match (Fig. 9). Loan sizes mattered, but other things might have been at play as well. Jon Stobart argued that because of greater geographical mobility and external linkages of towns, urban-based social networks were substantially different from rural ones and much better equipped to facilitate geographically wider contacts.[46] In our case, if creditors could not fulfill the demand for credit, villagers usually went to Antwerp, but Antwerp residents went to other (larger) towns much further away.

To visualize the interconnectedness between municipalities and analyze whether village networks were different from the Antwerp network, we use Social Network Analysis (SNA). Figure 10 plots the network of the residences of contracting parties.[47] Per locality we counted the number

[46] Jon Stobart, 'Social and Geographical Contexts of Property Transmission in the Eighteenth Century', in: Jon Stobart and Alastair Owens (eds.), *Urban Fortunes: Property and Inheritance in the Town, 1700–1900* (Taylor & Francis, 2000), there 110.

[47] Most researchers interested in credit relations use SNA to visualize credit networks between actors (usually debtors and creditors) and identify clusters of stronger relationships (See: A. Gestrich and M. Stark (eds.), *Debtors, Creditors, and their Networks: Social Dimensions of Monetary Dependence form the Seventeenth to the Twentieth Century.* (German Historical Institute London, 2015); Dermineur, Elise. 'Peer - to - peer lending in pre - industrial France' in: *Financial History Review*, 26:3 (2019), 359–388; Francesca Odella and Cinzia Lorandini, 'Testing historical theories with SNA. Structure and evolution of a credit network' in: Giuseppe Giordano, Marialuisa Restaino and Andrea Salvini, *Methods and Applications in Social Network Analysis. Evidence from Collaborative, Governance, Historical and Mobility Networks* (Franco Angeli, 2021), there 181–200. In our case, such networks on the personal level would be sparse because we have few repeat debtors or creditors. Most people appear only once in our dataset (3,198 unique names). This is because notarized credit transactions are nearly exclusively mortgage transactions, which by their nature are large and infrequent in people's lives. Debtors needed to provide collateral in the form of real estate, which most people had very little of, while creditors' lending capacity was also limited with the exception of wealthy investors. Our dataset spans only five years, which is half the median maturity of ten years. The likelihood that people would take a mortgage straight after the previous one finished is small further limiting the possibility that people show up multiple times in our dataset.

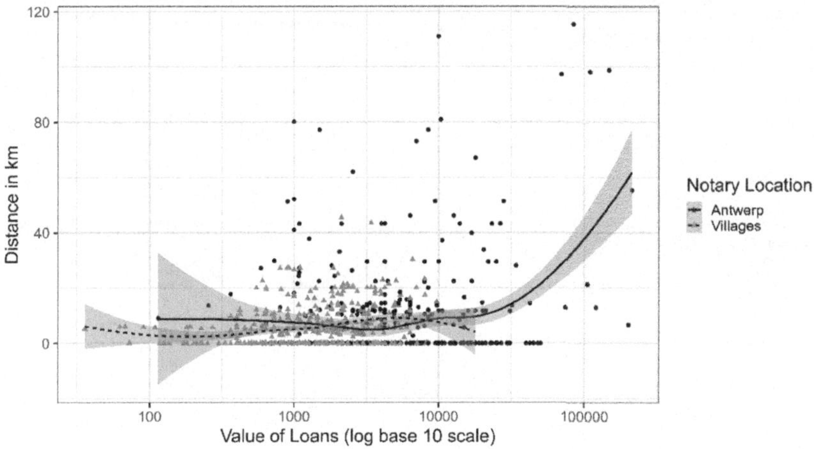

Fig. 9 The distance in kilometers between contracting parties against loan size, 1833–1837. Note: The distances are only calculated for contracts with information on the residences of both creditors and debtors, and with locations in Belgium (Source ANCRED)

of times a relation with another locality occurred in our dataset.[48] The graph is directed, with the arrows going from the residence of the lender to the one of the borrower. A loop indicates that the borrower and lender resided in the same place. The size of the nodes is determined by the degree centrality (how many different connections a place has) while the thickness of the edges is set by the number of times the connection appears in our dataset. Large nodes have many connections, while thick lines indicate strong connections. Only the nodes with a degree centrality larger than six are labeled, and all those nodes are municipalities in the province of Antwerp. The color of the node refers to the location of the municipality; Antwerp city, arrondissement in Antwerp province (Antwerp, Mechelen, Turnhout), Belgian region (Flanders, Wallony, Brussels), or abroad (Netherlands, France).[49]

[48] The data is unweighted.

[49] First, the city of Antwerp, then within the province of Antwerp villages are divided by administrative arrondissement (Antwerp, Mechelen or Turnhout), then within Belgium (Flanders, Brussels or Wallonia), and abroad (Netherlands, France).

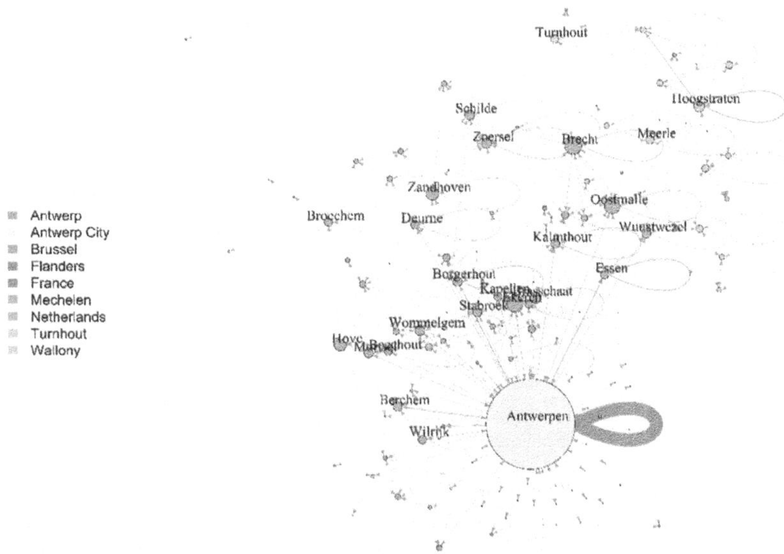

Fig. 10 Directed network of relations between places (Davidson-Harel layout), 1833–1837 (Source ANCRED)

Antwerp sits as a star in its own galaxy, with a degree centrality of 99. While being the most connected, it was mostly connected to itself. Antverpians contracted 312 times with another person residing in Antwerp, compared to 195 times with a borrower and 62 times with a lender from outside the city of Antwerp. Geographical proximity played a role, as the places closest to Antwerp in the network (Borgerhout, Ekeren, Berchem, Wilmarsdonk, Stabroek, etc.), are also geographically the closest to the city (all within the arrondissement of Antwerp). Localities such as Hoogstraten, Meer, Meerle, Wortel, and Rijkevorsel, located within the province of Antwerp but part of the further away arrondissement of Turnhout next to the Dutch border, are less connected to the center of the network and make up their own cluster. This cluster shows more relations to Turnhout, the medium-size city closest to them.[50]

[50] Because we do not observe notaries in Turnhout, we underestimate the density of this cluster. There are few relations with villages from the arrondissement Mechelen, but we also have no information on notaries active in that region.

Formal cluster analysis confirms these visual observations (Fig. 11). Using the fast greedy algorithm by Clauset, Newman, and Moore we identified clusters in the undirected version of the network shown in Fig. 10.[51] The clusters identified by the algorithm are similar to the geographical grouping used in Fig. 10. The clusters in pink (Noorderkempen) and red (Neteland) consist of nodes in the arrondissement Turnhout and across the Dutch border. The nodes located in the arrondissement Antwerp form three clusters, first the cluster South-East (light blue) comprising the southeastern villages including Boechout and Mortsel, second the cluster North-East/Voorkempen (light green), and third Current-Districts/Voorkempen (dark green) contains some villages which are part of the city of Antwerp today (Ekeren), and other municipalities directly east of the city (Brasschaat, Kapellen). The Antwerp cluster is the largest and consists of places that have strong connections to the city such as nearby Borgerhout and Deurne or large cities which only occur in relation to Antwerp in the network (Paris, Rotterdam, Gent, Brussels).

6 Notaries

The next question is how notaries fitted into this intermunicipal network and which connections ran through them. In Fig. 12, we think of the notaries as intermediaries between localities and place them as nodes between the municipalities they interacted with.[52] Even though notaries have contacts with people, these contacts are embedded in specific geographic locations and communities. Taking the connections between notaries and places, thus can proxy for the connectivity between different localities through the notary. The round nodes represent municipalities and the square ones notaries. The color of the node again indicates the location of the node. The width of the edges shows the number of times a notary drafted a contract for a resident of that municipality. Thicker edges indicate stronger ties between notaries and places.

[51] Aaron Clauset, M. E. J. Newman, and Cristopher Moore, 'Finding Community Structure in Very Large Networks', in: *Physical Review E* 70:6 (2004), 66–111, https://doi.org/10.1103/PhysRevE.70.066111.

[52] We chose an undirected network because we are interested in the times a notary interacted with people from a certain locality, regardless of their function in the contract.

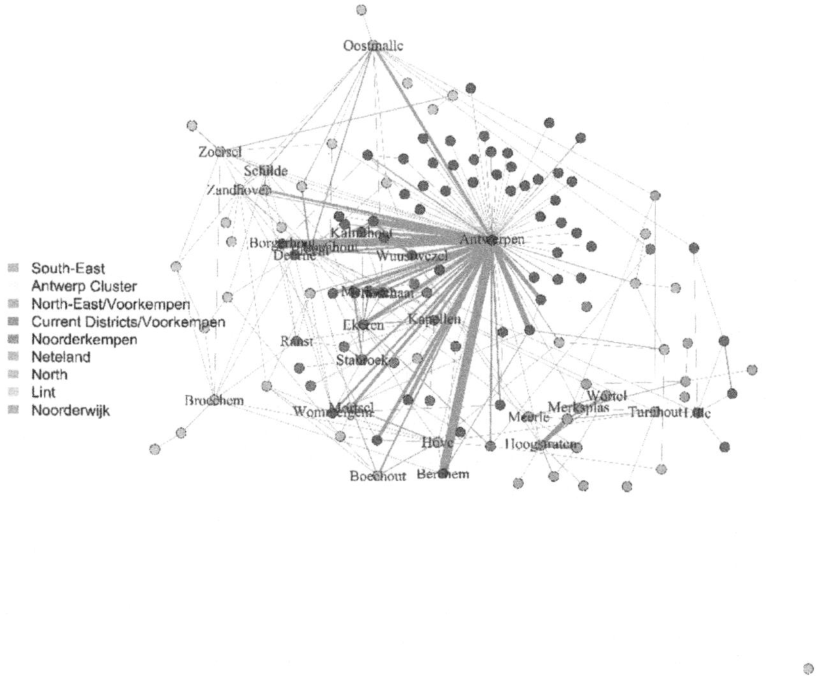

Fig. 11 Clustered Network (Davidson-Harel layout), 1833–1837 (Source ANCRED)

Antwerp again is clearly at the center of the network, with the four main Antwerp notaries in our set as its strongest links: Van Berckelaer (409 times), Hanegraeff (369) Gheijsens (275), and Gellynck (211).[53] The next notary with the thickest edges was De Boungne residing in Hoogstraten, a small town on the Belgian Dutch border, who interacted 93 times with residents from Hoogstraten and 54 times with ones from neighboring Rijkevorsel. This notary, together with De Chaffoy from Merksplas, was at the center of the Noorderkempen cluster around Turnhout, identified in Fig. 11. Those notaries drafted contracts between

[53] There is one more Antwerp notary in our dataset (Melchior Jozef Jan Colins), but he did not register any credit contract in this period.

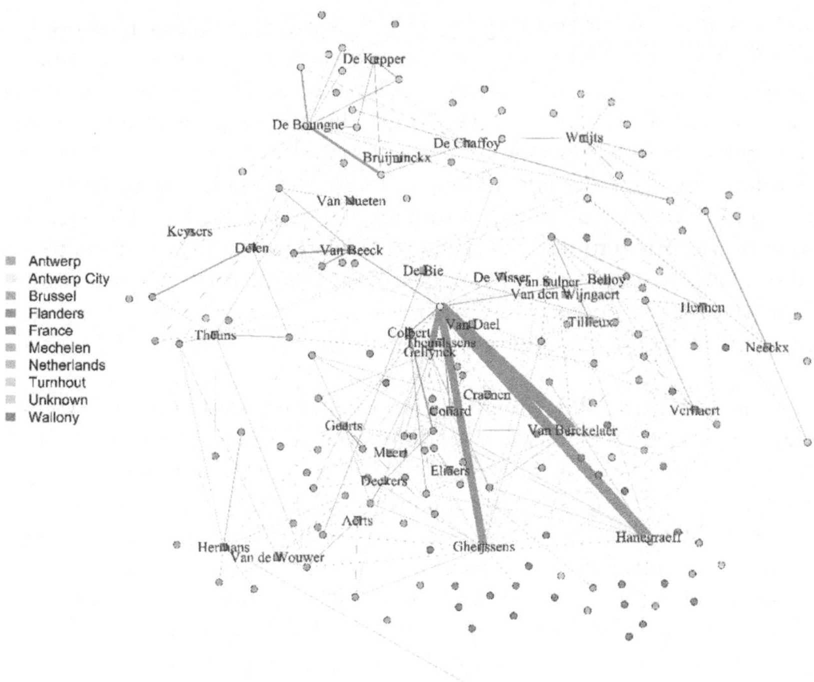

Fig. 12 Network of notaries and municipalities (Davidson-Harel layout), 1833–1837 (Source ANCRED)

residents from surrounding municipalities and nearby Dutch towns and villages, rather than interact with the further away city of Antwerp.

Antwerp notaries had the highest degree centrality (between 24 and 32), suggesting that they connected Antwerp to a variety of other places. This is visible in Figs. 10 and 12, as Antwerp city has a near monopoly on connections to places outside of the province or large cities abroad. The geographical variation appears to be an urban specificity and Antverpians found contracting counterparts in further away cities rather than nearby villages, much like Hoffman et al. and Stobart predicted. While Hoffman, Postel-Vinay, and Rosenthal argue that French notaries brought together lenders and borrowers across space, it is unclear if this was the case in Antwerp as well.[54] Antwerp notaries possibly had broader networks and more specialized knowledge because they drafted many more contracts and therefore interacted with residents from more places than village notaries. However, the urban population was also different with many more immigrants, foreign merchants, and elites with broader networks. Perhaps these groups simply made use of their own networks, rather than relying on notaries to make a match. The fact that none of the Antwerp notaries had a particularly strong connection to any other place, besides Antwerp, suggests that contracting parties presented themselves to the notary to draw up a contract, rather than the notary actively intermediating contracts by looking for counterparties in a specific market.

Other notaries with a high degree centrality were Van de Wouwer residing in Schilde, connecting 19 different places, and Hermans in Zandhoven linking residents of 18 municipalities. Both notaries connected many places, but mostly within the province of Antwerp, and even within the arrondissement Antwerp. They were thus much more active within their region, instead of connecting different regions. A quarter of the notaries had degree centralities of six or less, and those notaries also did a larger percentage of their business with residents from their home town. The only exceptions to this are the Antwerp notaries who did around 70% of their business with Antwerp residents while also connecting the most places. This paradox can be explained through the sheer number of contracts they drafted, with many smaller local contracts and fewer high value contracts with participants over larger distances.

The multitude of overlapping lines shows that it was possible for residents from most locations to interact with multiple notaries. And while the Antwerp notaries dominated the relations with Antwerp, many of the village notaries also still have lines going to Antwerp, indicating that they also interacted with urbanites (see also Sect. 4). The strongest connections to the city are through closeby notaries such as Belloy in Ekeren, Conard in Wilrijk, Colbert in Borgerhout, and Van Beeck in Essen.[55]

[54] Hoffman, Postel-Vinay, and Rosenthal, *Dark Matter Credit*.

[55] Ekeren, Borgerhout and Wilrijk are all boroughs of the city of Antwerp today. Essen is located about 30 km north of Antwerp, near the Dutch border.

7 Conclusion

As a starting point of a longer-term study, this chapter offered a first attempt to analyze the notarial credit market in the Antwerp region between 1833 and 1837. We estimated the size of the market in the province of Antwerp, and found the average stock of loans in the 1833–1837 period to be around 40% of provincial GDP and about 4% of Belgian GDP. This is a substantial sum, above the estimates by Hoffman et al. for France.[56] Notarial debt in Antwerp, despite it being large, was as important as bank debt. The Belgian banking system was already very developed in the 1830s and seemingly more important than in France in the same period. However, as in France, banks and notaries offered complementary types of credit. Banks specialized in short-term loans, while notaries mobilized long-term mortgage debt. The bulk of mortgage credit flowed through Antwerp notaries, who notarized many more and much larger credit contracts than their rural counterparts. The Antwerp market appears to have been thicker, but the per capita number of loans weas only slightly higher in the city, indicating also a vibrant (albeit smaller) notarial credit market in the countryside.

We also found large inequalities between Antwerp and rural credit networks: not so much in the number or type of transactions (mostly obligations; annuities, as in France, were scarce) but in credit sums, conditions, and direction of flows. Although both circuits flowed rather independently, there was also a significant flow from the city to the countryside, and not the other way. Some Antwerp and rural notaries, possibly capitalizing on their privileged information position, turned out to be real financiers by supplying credit to debtors. Because we only observe notarized contracts, it remains unclear whether they were also active outside the notarial credit network, for example, in private deeds or informal arrangements. The formal character of notarial credit is clearly reflected in the spatial form of inner-city credit relations: notaries sat as spiders in their web connecting debtors and creditors from all corners of the city, while bridging residential segregation patterns.

As expected, social groups' credit market participation differed greatly. Specifically in the Antwerp rural circuit we found a hesitant presence of Antwerp rentiers as creditors who traditionally, together with wholesale

[56] Hoffman, Postel-Vinay, and Rosenthal, 'Entry, Information, and Financial Development'.

merchants and manufacturers, were interested in land.[57] The inner-city notarial credit market was dominated by the upper classes of the Antwerp population with a distinct role for trade, industry, and rentiers as what might perhaps be seen as the cradle of a financial sector. At the same time, the Antwerp middle class still managed to hold on to their fair share of the market, a situation that had its roots at least as far back as the sixteenth century. As long as they kept their strong position in the intra-urban housing market, this provided them the necessary collateral to access mortgage credit. And continued access to credit might have reinforced their socio-economic position over time. Robust middle-class participation, especially as debtors, and significant urban–rural interactions went hand in hand with severe social and spatial inequalities. Lower social groups, those without or with limited real estate property, were mostly excluded from this market and had to rely on non-regulated, non-registered credit from nearby social and spatial circles (family, employers, and neighbors).

While most credit flowed within the Antwerp or rural villages, the city and its surroundings were firmly connected, with a fifth of all contracts linking the city to rural households. Social network analysis further revealed that the rural and urban networks were different. Rural networks were much more local in nature (including the occasional connection with a nearby municipality across the border), linking to Antwerp when larger sums were required. In such cases the contracts were mostly drawn up by Antwerp notaries. The urban network was, on the one hand connected to its surroundings, but also to places much further away. Antwerp notaries interacted with residents from all over Belgium and sometimes abroad. The patterns of travel and inter-urban connections resemble those of France, but we are unable to say yet whether notaries played an active role in bringing lenders and borrowers together.

Our findings underscore the importance and relevance of notarial credit markets in the Low Countries, even after decades of war and economic turmoil. We encountered a nuanced interplay between urban and rural economic networks, contributing valuable insights to the understanding of notarial credit markets beyond the scope of nineteenth-century France. We still have much to learn about the evolution of structure, functioning, and flows of notarial credit in nineteenth-century

[57] Greefs, 'De Zakenelite'.

Europe. One of the major questions is how urbanization and social inequality interacted with size, geography, and social structure of credit markets. How did these markets develop during a time of rapid urban growth, growing inequality, and a decrease in the value of farming land? We hope this contribution to be a renewed impulse for further investigation into the functioning of notarial credit markets in nineteenth-century Europe.

Appendix

A.1. Overview of types of actions registered by notaries in the Antwerp region, 1833–1837

Topic of Deed	*Rural*		*Antwerp*	
	n	*%*	*n*	*%*
Acceptance	0	0	2	0
Accounts	26	0	32	0
Agreement	**108**	**1**	**227**	**3**
Allocation Of Property	**919**	**8**	**124**	**2**
Annuity	**304**	**3**	**365**	**5**
Appointment	12	0	5	0
Approval	6	0	21	0
Cancelation Of Mortgage	**475**	**4**	**721**	**10**
Contract	37	0	24	0
Copy Of Deed	**92**	**1**	**651**	**9**
Credit	**650**	**6**	**535**	**8**
Declaration	**84**	**1**	**322**	**5**
Deposition Of Deed	23	0	159	2
Discharge	**360**	**3**	**597**	**8**
Partitions	**121**	**1**	**83**	**1**
Exchange	18	0	5	0
Extension	5	0	2	0
Gift	20	0	12	0
Ground Lease	30	0	16	0
Guarantee	33	0	62	1
Last Will	**1,114**	**10**	**434**	**6**
Liquidation	12	0	23	0
Marriage	**291**	**3**	**151**	**2**
Mortgage	7	0	19	0
Other	157	1	187	3
Ownership Transfer	113	1	24	0

(continued)

(continued)

Topic of Deed	*Rural*		*Antwerp*	
	n	%	*n*	%
Power Of Attorney	**397**	**4**	**922**	**13**
Probate	**248**	**2**	**213**	**3**
Public Auction	**289**	**3**	**303**	**4**
Ratification	14	0	28	0
Rental Contract	**309**	**3**	**254**	**4**
Renunciation	27	0	9	0
Replacement (in Militia)	39	0	48	1
Sale Movables	**3,440**	**32**	**24**	**0**
Sale Real Estate	**1,085**	**10**	**462**	**6**
Statutes	5	0	21	0
Unspecified Deed	35	0	30	0
Total	10,905	97%	7,117	96%

(Source NOTANT)
Note: Column percentages do not add up to 100% due to rounding error

A.2. Occupational structure of Antwerp credit contractors compared to the overall professional composition of the city based on Ratinckx 1838

	Antwerp		*Credit contractors*			
	N	%	N *Debtor*	%	N *Creditor*	%
Wholesaler	1,583	14.8_a	79	16.4_a	78	14.3_a
Retailer	1,381	12.9_a	62	12.9_a	40	7.3_b
Clothing / shoes	1,090	10.2_a	20	4.2_b	6	1.1_c
Luxury industry	288	2.7_a	8	1.7_a	9	1.6_a
Furniture	636	5.9_a	36	7.5_a	7	1.3_b
Building	638	6.0_a	37	7.7_a	8	1.5_b
Textiles	242	2.3_a	4	0.8_a	6	1.1_a
Food / Hospitality	1,167	10.9_a	73	15.2_b	40	7.3_c
Transport	445	4.2_a	13	2.7_a	3	0.5_b
Healthcare	268	2.5_a	5	1.0_a	29	5.3_b
Education	135	1.3_a	5	1.0_a	1	0.2_a
Finance / law	169	1.6_a	26	5.4_b	68	12.5_c
Public services	245	2.3_a	11	2.3_a	8	1.5_a
Military	84	0.8_a	1	0.2_a	0	0.0[1]

(continued)

(continued)

	Antwerp		Credit contractors			
	N	*%*	*N* *Debtor*	*%*	*N* *Creditor*	*%*
Agriculture	34	0.3_a	6	1.2_b	0	0.0^1
Nobility	1	0.0_a	0	0.0^1	4	0.7_b
Clergy	121	$1.1_{a,b}$	1	0.2_a	10	1.8_b
Skins / leather	16	0.1_a	1	0.2_a	1	0.2_a
Rentiers	972	9.1_a	73	15.2_b	212	38.8_c
Service personal	778	7.3_a	13	2.7_b	13	2.4_b
Workers	426	4.0_a	7	1.5_b	3	0.5_b
Total	10,719	100.0	481	100.0	546	100.0

(Source ANCRED / GIStorical Antwerp-1830/1838)
Note: The professional classification is based on M. Boone,M. Dumon en B. Reusens, *Immobiliënmarkt, fiscaliteit en sociale ongelijkheid te Gent 1483–1503*, Standen en Landen, dl. 78, (U.A.G., 1981). This classification has been slightly extended in the GIStorical Antwerp data. Note: Values in the same row and sub table not sharing the same subscript are significantly different at $p < 0.05$ in the two-sided test of equality for column proportions. Cells with no subscript are not included in the test. Based on the first mentioned occupation

A.3. Occupational structure of Antwerp credit contractors according to Gelderblom et.al. compared to the overall occupational structure of the city based on Ratinckx 1838

	Antwerp		Credit contractors			
			Debtor		*Creditor*	
	N	*%*	*N*	*%*	*N*	*%*
Nobles and Officers	85	1_a	1	0_a	4	1_a
Clergy	121	1_b	1	0_a	10	2_b
Merchants and Bourgeois	3,936	38_a	214	45_a	330	60_b
Artisans and Masters	3,405	32_a	159	33_a	63	12_b
Professions and Services	2,712	25_b	93	19_a	136	25_b
Rural	34	0_b	6	1_a	0	0^1
Laborers	426	4_b	7	2_a	3	1_a

(continued)

(continued)

	Antwerp		Credit contractors			
			Debtor		*Creditor*	
	N	*%*	*N*	*%*	*N*	*%*
Total	10,719	100.0	481	100.0	546	100.0

(Source ANCRED / EURY/VIDI database / GIStorical Antwerp-1830/1838)
Note: Values in the same row and sub table not sharing the same subscript are significantly different at $p < 0.05$ in the two-sided test of equality for column proportions. Cells with no subscript are not included in the test. Based on first mentioned occupation. Professional groups according to Gelderblom et al., 'Public Functions, Private Markets'

References

Primary Sources

ANCRED database

NOTANT dataset, see https://search.arch.be/nl/zoeken-naar-personen/projecten/10-notant-nl

Printed Primary Material

Royer, E. *Des institutions de Crédit foncier en Allemagne et en Belgique* (Paris, 1845).

Tarlier, H., *Liste alphabétique des notaires de Belgique depuis l'origine du notariat jusqu'en juillet 1864: supplém. jusqu'au 31 Décembre 1865* (Tarlier H., 1865).

Secondary Material

Blondé, Bruno. 2010. At the Cradle of the Transport Revolution? Paved Roads, Traffic Flows and Economic Development in Eighteenth-Century Brabant. *The Journal of Transport History* 31 (1): 89–111.

Blondé, Bruno, Sam Geens, Hilde Greefs et al. (eds.). 2020. *Inequality and the City in the Low Countries (1200–2020)*. Turnhout: Brepols.

Boone, M., M. Dumon, and B. Reusens. 1981. *Immobiliënmarkt, fiscaliteit en sociale ongelijkheid te Gent 1483–1503*, Standen en Landen, dl. 78. Kortrijk – Heule: U.A.G..

Briggs, Chris, and Jaco Zuijderduijn, (eds.). 2018. *Land and Credit*. Cham: Springer International Publishing

Chlepner, B.S. 1943. *Belgian Banking and Banking Theory*. Washington D.C.: Brookings Institute.

Clauset, Aaron, M.E.J. Newman, and Cristopher Moore. 2004. Finding Community Structure in Very Large Networks. *Physical Review E* 70 (6): 066111.

Crossick, Geoffrey, and Heinz-Gerhard Haupt. 1998. *The Petite Bourgeoisie in Europe, 1780-1914: Enterprise, Family and Independence*. London: Routledge.

Dambruyne, Johan. 2002. *Corporatieve middengroepen. Aspiraties, relaties en transformaties in de 16de–eeuwse Gentse ambachtswereld*, Verhandelingen der Maatschappij voor Geschiedenis en Oudheidkunde te Gent, dl. 28. Gent: Academia Press.

De Reu, Pieter. 2012. *Kopen en verkopen van vastgoed (1795 tot heden). Zoekwijzers*. Vol. 37. Algemeen. http://hdl.handle.net/1854/LU-3071901.

Deneweth, Heidi. 2011. A Fine Balance: Household Finance and Financial Strategies of Antwerp Households 17th-18th Century. *Tijdschrift voor Sociaal Economische Geschiedenis* 4: 15–43.

Dermineur, Elise. 2019. Peer - to - peer lending in pre-industrial France. *Financial History Review* 26 (3): 359–388.

Dermineur, Elise M. 2022. The Evolution of Credit Networks in Pre-Industrial Finland. *Scandinavian Economic History Review* 70 (1): 57–86.

Fontaine, Laurence. 2001. Antonio and Shylock: Credit and Trust in France, c. 1680-c. 1780. *The Economic History Review* 54 (1): 39–57.

Fontaine, Laurence. 2014. *The Moral Economy. Poverty, Credit, and Trust in Early Modern Europe*. Cambridge: Cambridge University Press.

Gelderblom, Oscar, Mark Hup, and Joost Jonker. 2018. Public Functions, Private Markets: Credit Registration by Aldermen and Notaries in the Low Countries, 1500–1800. In *Financing in Europe*, edited by Marcella Lorenzini, Cinzia Lorandini, and D'Maris Coffman, 163–194. Cham: Palgrave Macmillan.

Gelderblom, Oscar, Joost Jonker, Ruben Peeters, and Amaury de Vicq. 2023. Exploring Modern Bank Penetration: Evidence from the Early 20th-Century Netherlands. *Economic History Review* 76: 892–916.

Gestrich, A., & Stark, M. (eds.). 2015. *Debtors, Creditors, and their Networks: Social Dimensions of Monetary Dependence form the Seventeenth to the Twentieth Century*. London: German Historical Institute.

Greefs, Hilde. 2004. De Zakenelite En de Woningschaarste in Antwerpen Tijdens de Eerste Helft van de Negentiende Eeuw: Een Terreinverkenning. *Bijdragen tot de Geschiedenis* 87 (1–2): 305–320.

Hoffman, Philip T., Gilles Postel-Vinay, and Jean Laurent Rosenthal. 2015. Entry, Information, and Financial Development: A Century of Competition between French Banks and Notaries. *Explorations in Economic History* 55 (1): 39–57.

Hoffman, Philip T, Gilles Postel-Vinay and Jean-Laurent Rosenthal. 2019. *Dark Matter Credit: The Development of Peer-to-Peer Lending and Banking in France*. Princeton: Princeton University Press.

Hoffman, Philip T., Gilles Postel-Vinay and Jean-Laurent Rosenthal. 2001. *Priceless Markets: The Political Economy of Credit in Paris, 1660–1870*. Chicago: The University of Chicago Press.

van Kooten, Rogier. 2020. Levelling Through Space? The Redistributive Capacity of Demographic Decline in Antwerp's Darkest Hour (1584–1586). In *Inequality and the City in the Low Countries (1200–2020)*, edited by Bruno Blondé, Sam Geen, Hilde Greefs et al. Brepols.

van Kooten, Rogier. 2021. *Antwerpen 1584 : Oorlog en Ongelijkheid in de Stedelijke Ruimte*. PhD Thesis, University of Antwerp.

Lemercier, Claire, and Francesca Trivellato. 2022. 1751 and Thereabout: A Quantitative and Comparative Approach to Notarial Records. *Social Science History* 46 (3): 555–583.

Levy, Juliette. 2012. *The Making of a Market: Credit, Henequen, and Notaries in Yucatán, 1850–1900*. University Park: Penn State University Press.

Lis, Catharina. 1986. *Social Change and the Laboring Poor: Antwerp, 1770–1860*. New Haven & London: Yale University Pres.

Lis, Catharina, and Hugo Soly. 1993. Neighbourhood Social Change in West European Cities, Sixteenth to Nineteenth Centuries. *International Review of Social History* 38: 1–30.

Odella, Francesca and Cinzia Lorandini. 2021. Testing historical theories with SNA. Structure and evolution of a credit network. In *Methods and Applications in Social Network Analysis. Evidence from Collaborative, Governance, Historical and Mobility Networks*, edited by Giuseppe Giordano, Marialuisa Restaino and Andrea Salvini, 181–200. Milano: Franco Angeli.

Pringels, P. 2001. Le Franc Belge 1832–2001 Histoire et évolution des monnaies Taux de change des valeurs européennes en 1832. *Annales du Cercle archéologique d'Enghien* 35: 143–182.

Segers, Yves. 2003. *Economische groei en levensstandaard. Particuliere consumptie en voedselgebruik in België, 1800–1913*. Leuven: Leuven University Press

Stevens, Fred. 1994. *Revolutie en notariaat: Antwerpen 1794–1814*. Leuven: Koninklijke Van Gorcum Bv.

Stobart, Jon. 2000. Social and Geographical Contexts of Property Transmission in the Eighteenth Century. In *Urban Fortunes: Property and Inheritance in the Town,* edited by Jon Stobart and Alastair Owens, *1700–1900*. London: Taylor & Francis.

Têcheur, Pierre. 1957. Le crédit immobilier en Belgique de 1802 à 1954. *Bulletin de l'Institut de recherches économiques et sociales* 23 (2): 95–138.

Veraghtert, Karel. 1980. De Antwerpse Bankwereld En de Expansie van de Haven, 1820–1850. *Bank- en Financiewezen* 8: 9.

Willems, Bart. 2009. *Leven op de pof: krediet bij de Antwerpse middenstand in de achttiende eeuw*. Amsterdam: Aksant.

Winstanley, M. J. 1998. Owners and Occupiers: Property, Politics and Middle-class Formation in Early Industrial Lancashire. In *The Making of the British Middle Class? Studies of Regional and Cultural Diversity since the Eighteenth Century*, edited by Alan Kidd and David Nicholls, 93–112. Stroud: Sutton Publishing.

Winter, Anne. 2009. *Migrants and Urban Change: Newcomers to Antwerp, 1760–1860*. London: Pickering & Chatto.

Zegarra, Luis. 2018. Information Asymmetries, Personal Connections and Private Credit. Evidence from Lima, Peru, 1825–1865. In *Economic History Society Working Papers*.

Index

E. M. Dermineur and M. Pompermaier (eds.), *Credit Networks in The Preindustrial World*, Palgrave Studies in the History of Finance,
https://doi.org/10.1007/978-3-031-67117-3

SPRINGER NATURE

GPSR Compliance

The European Union's (EU) General Product Safety Regulation (GPSR) is a set of rules that requires consumer products to be safe and our obligations to ensure this.

If you have any concerns about our products, you can contact us on ProductSafety@springernature.com

In case Publisher is established outside the EU, the EU authorized representative is:

Springer Nature Customer Service Center GmbH
Europaplatz 3
69115 Heidelberg, Germany

The manufacturer's authorised representative in the EU is Springer Nature Customer Service Centre GmbH, Europaplatz 3, 69115 Heidelberg, Germany. If you have any concerns regarding our products, please contact ProductSafety@springernature.com

Printed and bound by CPI Group (UK) Ltd, Croydon, CR0 4YY

28/09/2026

02224060-0005